THE

"Aimed at educated, experienced travellers, the [Berlitz Travellers] Guides capture the flavor of foreign lands."
—*Entrepreneur*

"Filling a needed niche in guidebooks ... designed to eliminate the cumbersome lists of virtually every hotel and restaurant.... Special out-of-the-way places are detailed.... The books capture the personality and excitement of each destination."
—*Los Angeles Times*

"There's a different tone to these books, and certainly a different approach ... information is aimed at independent and clearly sophisticated travellers.... Strong opinions give these books a different personality from most guides, and make them fun to read."
—*Travel & Leisure*

"Aimed at experienced, independent travellers who want information beyond the nuts-and-bolts material available in many familiar sources. Although each volume gives necessary basics, the series sends travellers not just to 'sights,' but to places and events that convey the personality of each locale."
—*The Denver Post*

"Just the right amount of information about where to stay and play."
—*Detroit Free Press*

"The strength of the [Berlitz Travellers Guides] lies in remarks and recommendations by writers with a depth of knowledge about their subject."
—*Washington Times*

"The most readable of the current paperback lot."
—*New York Post*

"Highly recommended."
—*Library Journal*

"Very strong on atmosphere and insights into local culture for curious travellers."
—*Boston Herald*

"The [Berlitz Travellers Guides] eliminate cumbersome lists and provide reliable information about what is truly exciting and significant about a destination.... [They] also emphasize the spirit and underlying 'vibrations' of a region—historical, cultural, and social—that enhance a trip."
—*Retirement Life*

"Information without boredom.... Good clear maps and index."
—*The Sunday Sun* (Toronto)

CONTRIBUTORS

JOHN HECKATHORN, a former professor of English at the University of Hawaii and a resident of Honolulu for 18 years, is the editor of *Honolulu* magazine, for which he also writes a monthly dining column. In 1992 he received the White Award from the City and Regional Magazine Association for his food and restaurant writing. He is the editorial consultant for this guidebook.

RICK CARROLL, an author, journalist, and photographer, lives on Oahu and has written for the *Honolulu Advertiser* and the *San Francisco Chronicle*. He is United Press International's special Hawaii-Pacific correspondent and is the author of *From Mauka to Makai* and *Great Outdoor Adventures of Hawaii*.

THELMA CHANG is a Honolulu-based writer specializing in travel and human-interest stories. She is the author of *"I Can Never Forget": Men of the 100th/442nd*, a history of the much-decorated Japanese-American regimental combat team of World War II. Her articles have appeared in such publications as *Westways, Essence,* and the Smithsonian's *Air and Space* magazine.

BETTY FULLARD-LEO, formerly an editor at *Pacific Art & Travel,* has been writing about Hawaii and its art, culture, and visitor attractions for a decade and has lived on Oahu since 1962.

GEORGE FULLER, the managing editor of *Western Links,* is the author of *Hawaii Golf—The Complete Guide* and a contributor to many publications. He is based in Hilton Head, South Carolina, but still calls Hawaii home.

BILL HARBY is associate editor at *Island Scene* magazine and a contributing editor at *Honolulu* magazine. Besides various Hawaii publications, he has written for *Details, Modern Bride,* and *Guitar Player* magazines. He has lived in Honolulu for 17 years and travels often among the six main islands.

TOM AND KAREN HORTON are former residents of Hawaii now living in San Francisco. They are the authors of three Dolphin travel guides and write frequently about the Islands.

JOHN W. PERRY, a longtime resident of the Pacific area, is a contributor to several North American and Asia-Pacific magazines. He lives in Honolulu and travels often in the South Seas on magazine assignments.

THE BERLITZ TRAVELLERS GUIDES

THE AMERICAN SOUTHWEST

AUSTRALIA

BERLIN

CANADA

THE CARIBBEAN

COSTA RICA

ENGLAND & WALES

FRANCE

GERMANY

GREECE

HAWAII

IRELAND

LONDON

MEXICO

NEW ENGLAND

NEW YORK CITY

NORTHERN ITALY AND ROME

PORTUGAL

SAN FRANCISCO &
NORTHERN CALIFORNIA

SOUTHERN ITALY AND ROME

SPAIN

TURKEY

THE BERLITZ TRAVELLERS GUIDE TO HAWAII

Fifth Edition

ALAN TUCKER
General Editor

BERLITZ PUBLISHING COMPANY, INC.
New York, New York

BERLITZ PUBLISHING COMPANY LTD.
Oxford, England

THE BERLITZ TRAVELLERS GUIDE TO HAWAII
Fifth Edition

Berlitz Trademark Reg U.S. Patent and Trademark Office
and other countries—Marca Registrada

Copyright © Root Publishing Company,
1989, 1990, 1992, 1994

All rights reserved.

*No part of this book may be reproduced or transmitted in any form
or by any means, electronic or mechanical, including
photocopying, recording or by any information storage and
retrieval system without written permission from the publisher.*

Published by Berlitz Publishing Company, Inc.
257 Park Avenue South, New York, New York 10010, U.S.A.

Distributed in the United States by
the Macmillan Publishing Group

Distributed elsewhere by Berlitz Publishing Company Ltd.
Berlitz House, Peterley Road, Horspath, Oxford OX4 2TX, England

ISBN 2-8315-1701-X
ISSN 1057-4700

Designed by Beth Tondreau Design
Cover design by Dan Miller Design
Cover photograph by © Douglas Peebles
Maps by David Lindroth
Illustrations by Bill Russell
Fact-checked in Hawaii by Robert Mon
Edited by Amy K. Hughes

Printed in the United States of America
1 3 5 7 9 10 8 6 4 2

THIS GUIDEBOOK

The Berlitz Travellers Guides are designed for experienced travellers in search of exceptional information that will enhance the enjoyment of the trips they take.

Where, for example, are the interesting, out-of-the-way, fun, charming, or romantic places to stay? The hotels and resorts described by our expert writers are some of the special places, in all price ranges except for the very lowest—not just the run-of-the-mill, heavily marketed places in advertised airline and travel-wholesaler packages.

We are *highly* selective in our choices of accommodations, concentrating on what our insider contributors think are the most interesting or rewarding places, and why. Readers who want to review exhaustive lists of hotel and resort choices as well, and who feel they need detailed descriptions of each property, can supplement the *Berlitz Travellers Guide* with tourism industry publications or one of the many directory-type guidebooks on the market.

We indicate the approximate price level of each accommodation in our description of it (no indication means it is moderate in local, relative terms), and at the end of every chapter we supply more detailed hotel rates as well as contact information so that you can get precise, up-to-the-minute rates and make reservations.

The Berlitz Travellers Guide to Hawaii highlights the more rewarding parts of Hawaii so that you can quickly and efficiently home in on a good itinerary.

Of course, this guidebook does far more than just help you choose a hotel and plan your trip. *The Berlitz Travellers Guide to Hawaii* is designed for use *in* Hawaii. Our writers, each of whom is an experienced travel journalist who lives on or regularly tours the island or islands of Hawaii he or she covers, tell you what you really need to know, what you can't find out so easily on your own. They identify and describe the truly out-of-the-ordinary resorts, restaurants, shops, activities, and sights, and tell you the best way to "do" your destination.

Our writers are highly selective. They bring out the significance of the places they *do* cover, capturing the personality and the underlying cultural and historical resonances of each—making clear its special appeal.

The Berlitz Travellers Guide to Hawaii is full of reliable information. We would like to know if you think we've left out some very special place. Although we make every effort to provide the most current information available about every destination described in this book, it is possible too that changes have occurred before you arrive. If you do have an experience that is contrary to what you were led to expect by our description, we would like to hear from you about it.

A guidebook is no substitute for common sense when you are travelling. Always pack the clothing, footwear, and other items appropriate for the destination and for the things you expect to do there, and make the necessary accommodation for such variables as altitude, weather, and local rules and customs. Of course, once on the scene you should avoid situations that are in your own judgment potentially hazardous, even if they have to do with something mentioned in a guidebook. Half the fun of travelling is exploring, but explore with care.

ALAN TUCKER
General Editor
Berlitz Travellers Guides

Root Publishing Company
350 West Hubbard Street
Suite 440
Chicago, Illinois 60610

CONTENTS

This Guidebook	vii
Overview	5
Useful Facts	16
Bibliography	20
Honolulu and Waikiki	27
Getting Around	69
Accommodations	70
Nightlife and Entertainment	80
Shops and Shopping	92
Dining in the Islands	111
Oahu Outside Honolulu	153
The Big Island (Hawaii)	190
Maui	234
Molokai	279
Lanai	293
Kauai	301
Niihau	341
Historical Chronology	344
Index	353

MAPS

Hawaii	2
Honolulu Environs	29

ix

Honolulu: Downtown and Central	34
Honolulu: Downtown, Chinatown, and the Capitol District	38
Honolulu: Kakaako and Ala Moana	51
Waikiki	56
Honolulu: Diamond Head and Waikiki	66
Oahu	156
The Big Island (Hawaii)	192
Maui	236
Molokai	280
Lanai	294
Kauai	304

THE BERLITZ TRAVELLERS GUIDE TO HAWAII

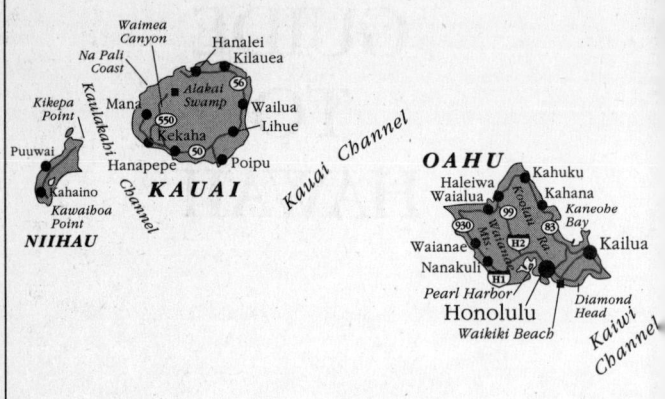

State of Hawaii
(main islands)
0 miles 50
0 km 50
MOLOKAI
Kualapuu
Kalaupapa
Kepuhi Beach
Mt. Kamakou
Halawa Valley
460
450
Pailolo Channel
MAUI
Kaanapali
Kalohi Channel
Keanapapa Point
Lanai City
Kaumalapau Harbor
Lanaihale
LANAI
Auau Channel
340
Lahaina
Kahului
Waipio Bay
36
Wailua
Wailuku
30
Kihei
Hana
Maalaea Bay
37
Hanakauhi
Makena
31
Haleakala Crater
Kealaikahiki Channel
Alalakeiki Channel
KAHOOLAWE
Alenuihaha Channel
Upolu Point
Honokaa
HAWAII
270
Kohala Mts
250
Kawaihae
19
Waimea (Kamuela)
Kohala Coast
19
Mauna Kea
Hilo
190
200
Keaau
Kailua Kona
130
Kona Coast
HAWAII VOLCANOES NATIONAL PARK
Mauna Loa
Captain Cook
Kilauea Crater
Kalapana
Honaunau Harbor
11
Punaluu
11
OCEAN
South Point (Ka Lae)

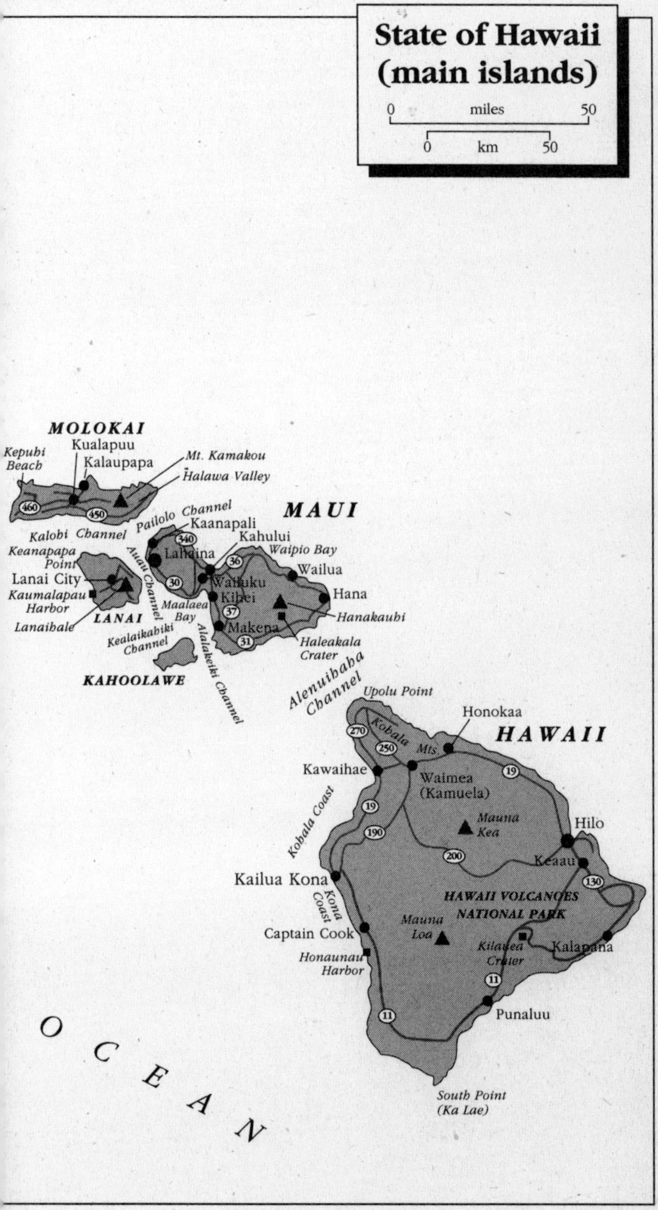

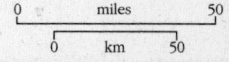

OVERVIEW

By John Heckathorn and Tom and Karen Horton

John Heckathorn, a former professor of English at the University of Hawaii, is the editor of Honolulu *magazine, for which he also writes a monthly dining column. He has lived in Honolulu for 18 years. He is the editorial consultant for this guidebook.*

Tom and Karen Horton are the authors of three Dolphin travel guides and write frequently about the Islands for other publications.

There is little need to parade evidence here in support of Hawaii as an estimable destination for a break from the world of the ordinary. Despite everything that Western civilization has done to them in 200 years, the Hawaiian Islands remain among the most naturally beautiful places on earth. There is, however, a need to help the traveller who is destined for Hawaii without knowing *which* Hawaii he or she wants. There are, as connoisseurs of the Islands have learned, many Hawaiis from which to choose. Disappointment sets in when visitors arrive in Hawaii for the right reasons, then head off in all the wrong directions. The beauty of Hawaii is clearly visible and reasonably accessible—it is the true Hawaii *experience* that can be elusive.

It is not hidden, however, and it is not a well-kept secret, and it is not something available only to the highest bidder. Hawaii is too small, and the tourists too great in number, for anything even remotely appealing to be kept out of the public grasp. The best way to experience Hawaii is simply to understand in advance the choices that must be made, so you can improve the odds of making the right choice.

Selecting an Island

The process begins with deciding which island—or how many islands—you are going to visit. There are six choices: **Oahu, Maui, Molokai, Lanai, Kauai,** and the island of **Hawaii** (commonly referred to as the **Big Island**). The two other full-size islands in the chain—Niihau and Kahoolawe— offer little to visitors.

For years **Niihau**, off the coast of Kauai, was known as the "Forbidden Island." The only people permitted on the island, which is privately owned by a Kauai family, were a small community of Hawaiians who worked the island as a ranch and lived in a kind of time warp, an environment more reminiscent of the 19th century than the 20th. But in order to afford the 20th-century luxury of regular helicopter service between Niihua and Kauai, the powers-that-be on Niihau decided two years ago to subsidize the helicopter by allowing visitors to come to the island—though not to stay there—for a steep sum. At first the flights went only to uninhabited areas of the island. Although visitors still may not visit the major settlements, contact with residents is now allowed, if not guaranteed. Unless you wish to buy one of the famous Niihau-shell leis at the source, there's little reason to go to the expense of visiting Niihau. Its main attraction all these years has been that you couldn't go there. Now that you can, the fascination of the forbidden has waned rapidly.

Kahoolawe, a small island southwest of Maui, is inhabited only by a small rotating group of U.S. Navy Seabees who live in a camp at Smugglers Cove. For years, the navy and other services used Kahoolawe as a target range, but for the moment, the bombing has been halted. Last year a presidential commission recommended a permanent halt, but the U.S. Congress has yet to make a final decision. In addition to being subjected to live fire, the island suffered tremendously from erosion, having lost most of its vegetation to a population of feral goats. Prompted by a group of native Hawaiian activists, the navy has begun to take better care of Kahoolawe in the last decade, preserving archaeological sites, reseeding several areas, and eliminating the goats. Access has been granted to many Hawaiians to conduct religious ceremonies on the island. Most of the state's residents would like to see the island transformed into a kind of native Hawaiian cultural refuge. But even if that were to occur, there would be little impetus for the average traveller to visit Kahoolawe. There is no fresh water there, no food, and the ground, though clearer than it has been in decades, is littered with ordnance, some of it no doubt still dangerous.

In truth, the average visitor narrows the choice to four islands. Molokai is usually bypassed because it offers so little except peace and quiet to the visitor. And most visitors also overlook Lanai, which for years was used by Dole almost exclusively as a pineapple plantation. But in the face of growing foreign competition, Dole shut down pineapple operations in 1993 (a few acres remain for local consumption). That means the island is moving rapidly into tourism. It has two new luxury resorts, for those who really want to get away from it all—and for whom expense is no object.

The most popular islands are, in order: Oahu, Maui, Kauai, and the Big Island of Hawaii. These are where you will find most of the 7 million people who visit Hawaii during the year. It follows that these four islands are also where you will find the greatest concentration of hotels, condominiums, restaurants, tourist shops, tour buses, rental cars, and traffic jams. So if you want to go to a Hawaiian island completely removed from all that, go to Molokai or Lanai. Or you could go to the east side of Maui, or the north side of Kauai, or.... And now we begin to get a glimpse of all those different Hawaiis.

Waikiki and Oahu versus the Neighbor Islands

If you are going to be in Hawaii for only one week, it is a mistake to book accommodations on more than two islands. At least two weeks are needed to extend your visit to three or four islands and leave with anything more than a cursory view of what each of those islands is all about. Don't be misled by the flying time between islands. You can hop from Oahu to Maui in 25 minutes by jet, and the longest interisland flight—from Kauai to the Big Island—takes less than two hours, including a stop along the way. But even with these abbreviated flights you'll find that the journeys are time-consuming. Island airports are crowded, baggage service is slow, and renting cars is a tedious procedure. Then you may have to drive for a half-hour or longer to reach your hotel or condominium, unless you take a shuttle van, which will move even more slowly. Add the inevitable delays of checking in and checking out of hotels and condominiums, returning rental cars, and packing and unpacking and you will find yourself exhausted if you try island-hopping without allowing three or more nights on each island. More important, you are sure to form an incomplete opinion, or a completely unfair one, of an island based on a hurried visit—and you simply won't have as good a time as you should.

A wise choice for the first-time visitor is to spend one part of the vacation on Oahu in **Waikiki**, Honolulu's tourist district, and the rest on a Neighbor Island, as the islands beyond Oahu are collectively known. Maui is the favored Neighbor Island by a wide margin, and was the first island to begin drawing its own exclusive clientele—visitors who chose to skip Waikiki entirely and go directly to Maui. Before Maui became a magical name, *all* tourists went to Waikiki, and then some went on to the Neighbor Islands. Now there are direct flights from the West Coast of the United States to Kauai and to the Big Island as well as to Maui.

Still, you are shortchanging yourself if, on an inaugural visit, you listen to the travel snobs who tell you to skip Oahu because Waikiki is an overcrowded, overbuilt, overly commercialized, concrete, high-rise mess. It *is* all that. It is also one square mile of around-the-clock, international-flavored energy, fun, and excitement that is worth the price of congestion. And nowhere else in the Islands is there such a wide range of prices. Waikiki has a more extensive choice of hotel rooms, dining, shopping, and entertainment than all the other islands combined. You can also just turn your back on high-rise Waikiki and, with your feet in the sand and your face in the sun, contemplate the balmy view from Waikiki Beach, a beach that may be elbow-to-elbow in people but is still a clean, safe beach massaged by cool-but-never-cold surf rolling out of an unpolluted sea and breaking in mild-mannered waves over coral reefs.

Beyond Waikiki are historic palaces and tombs containing the fascinating history of the kings and queens of 19th-century Hawaii; the military history of Pearl Harbor; and the less-than-flattering history of American merchants who stole the Islands from the Hawaiian monarchy so they could harvest fortunes in sugar and pineapple. Beyond the pineapple fields that still cover much of the central Oahu plain there are the beaches of the **North Shore**, where the only high rises are the monstrous waves of Waimea, Sunset, and Pipeline beaches, which provide a stage for some of the most spectacular surfing on earth.

The quality of life in Waikiki, it should be noted, *has*

improved lately, although the tiny area is unquestionably congested—but then this is true of the whole island of Oahu and its resident population of approximately one million. Public funds have been spent in the millions on a Waikiki face-lift that widened the sidewalks and generally improved the appearance of the two main thoroughfares, Kalakaua and Kuhio avenues, which have carried traffic through the heart of Hawaii's tourism ever since streetcars were hauling people from Honolulu to Waikiki Beach's first luxury hotel, the Moana, in 1901. Even more millions in private dollars have been spent upgrading the look and the quality of some of Waikiki's most venerable hostelries, including the vintage Moana. The result has not provided Waikiki with anything close to a country-club atmosphere, but it has improved the look of Waikiki and made its disfigurements seem just a little less obtrusive.

So unless you are a stress victim from an inner city who truly needs to escape any semblance of urbanization, include Waikiki in your introduction to Hawaii.

Maui

There is no secret to Maui's magic. It has the state's best combination of weather, beaches, mountain greenery, luxury resorts, budget-oriented condominiums, indoor, outdoor, and in-the-ocean activities, wide-open spaces where you can drink in the view, and plenty of places where you can eat and drink with a view. Maui has some of Hawaii's best golf courses, the absolute best windsurfing, the most prolific choices in sailing, scuba diving, and snorkeling, and the only dining and nightlife scene of any real substance and variety beyond Oahu. Even the migrating humpback whales choose the waters off Maui for mating and birthing, making whale-watching cruises a major tourist activity here from January to April. Maui has **Lahaina**, a bawdy old whaling port reborn as the most colorful little two-story, wooden-sidewalk, waterfront town ever to tempt a tourist with endless rows of souvenir tee-shirts, overpriced jewelry, and food and grog priced to pay for the view. Of the big four, only on Maui does the view include other islands clearly: From a Lahaina restaurant deck or a Kaanapali Resort beach you can gaze across glassy waters on which the sun is dancing and study the sloping profiles of Lanai and Molokai.

Maui has Haleakala, a 10,023-foot-high volcano you can drive to the top of, hike down into, or coast all the way down the side of on bicycles. Maui also has **Hana**, a heavenly place close to the sea but protected by no-growth gods who keep it almost out of reach on the other side of Haleakala at the end of a long, crooked road. If you are dead serious about getting away from it all, get yourself to Hana, where you have to fall in love with the raw beauty of the land because there is nothing else to do but look at the scenery.

Maui may seem to have it all, but be forewarned that the island also has traffic problems, high prices, and two of Hawaii's worst strips of concrete pollution, the condominium corridors of Kahana and Kihei. None of this has deterred the trendy traveller, who knows it's nothing special to explain a winter tan with, "I went to Hawaii," and so much more chic to say, "I just came back from Maui."

The Big Island versus Kauai

This brings us to Kauai and to the Big Island of Hawaii. They could not be more opposite in every sense. Kauai is at the northwestern end of the gentle curve of islands, 72 miles from the shores of Oahu; the Big Island holds the southeastern end of the chain, putting its northwestern coastline a scant 26 miles across the water from the east side of Maui. Kauai is small (553 square miles), easygoing, and as green as an Irish spring—a condition created by very wet weather. The Big Island is, by comparison, enormous (4,038 square miles, three times the size of Rhode Island), rough around the edges, full of fire in the belly, drenched with rain on one side and bone-dry on the other. Here is a perfect example of the need to choose between the different Hawaiis. At the risk of oversimplifying to make the point, it's reasonable to suggest that anyone who loves Kauai would not be attracted by the Big Island, and vice versa. Each has ardent admirers, although neither island draws visitors in numbers anywhere near those pulled in by Oahu and Maui.

That, in fact, is one attraction Kauai and the Big Island share: Repeat visitors who long ago gave up Oahu and now find Maui too crowded are beginning to choose the Big Island or Kauai. The two islands have responded with a burst of impressive new resort hotels and attendant amenities such as golf courses.

KAUAI
Kauai has bounced back from hurricane Iniki, which swept the island with 180 mile-per-hour winds in Septem-

ber 1992. Many of the island's facilities were shut down for six months—a few for longer—but the island once again offers a full range of accommodations and amenities and is eager for visitors.

Kauai's tourist facilities were always low-profile, even before hurricane Iniki. By law nothing on the island can be built higher than four stories. (A grandiose exception is the Westin Kauai, whose original ten-story structure predated the height limitations. Severely damaged in the hurricane, it may not reopen at all.) The personal style of the so-called Garden Isle is also low-profile. This island has a way of making you slow down, cool out, stay put. True, there aren't a lot of choices on Kauai, where the road only goes part of the way around the island and the bulk of the land mass is inaccessible except to helicopters and hikers. And maybe you have to slow down because traffic on Kauai's limited roadways is often bumper-to-bumper. A line heard often on Oahu is, "Kauai is beautiful, but what do you do the second day?" Actually, many choose Kauai precisely because they don't want to do much of anything even on the first day.

Visitors to Kauai who want the sun and safe swimming beaches choose the **Poipu Beach Resort** hotels and condominiums in the south. Serious golfers stay at the North Shore **Princeville Resort**, along with the nongolfers who enjoy the cooler, greener (because wetter) wide-open spaces and the accessibility to the bucolic Hanalei Valley and the awesome Na Pali Coast. In between the moist North Shore and the sunny South Shore is the east shore, where a woman in a gift shop once stripped Kauai to its basics by asking the clerk as she faced west, "Have I got this straight? If I want sunshine I go to the left and if I don't I go to the right?"

Kauai is also known for the most adventurous hiking in Hawaii, mainly into ancient Kalalau Valley; some of the most gorgeous, uncrowded beaches anywhere; thrilling Zodiac boat tours along the rugged **Na Pali Coast**; breathtaking "flight-seeing" helicopter tours of the little island's remarkably large natural wonders, such as Waimea Canyon, the Na Pali sea cliffs, and the 5,148-foot peak of Mount Waialeale, the mountain the Kauai Visitors Bureau hates because tour guides always point it out as the wettest spot on earth. Kauai is also known for Hawaii's only navigable rivers and for the almost nothing that goes on after dark.

THE BIG ISLAND

Of all the islands, the Big Island of Hawaii is the most difficult for the casual visitor to understand, appreciate, and enjoy. It's more than that the Big Island has very few good beaches of the white-sand quality found on the other islands. It's a problem of size, time, and diversity: The Big Island is so large, and its qualities so diverse, that there is not enough time to see and experience it all in one visit.

Maui and Kauai can be love at first sight. The Big Island often evokes fright at first sight. Visitors landing on the dry western side of the island leave the airport and travel through a flat, black, treeless, lifeless landscape composed of mile after mile of hard, mean-looking lava, and the same unspoken question is on every nervous mind: "My God, this is Hawaii?"

Nothing could be more Hawaii. This is the way all the islands began, smoldering volcanoes forcing themselves out of the earth's crust and exploding above the ocean in showers of fire that spilled over like burning rivers, cooled, and hardened into lava, a process repeated over and over through hundreds of years until permanent land masses were formed as islands in the sea. That process can still be seen on the Big Island, where Hawaii's only active volcanoes are found—and which happen to be some of the most active volcanoes in the world.

The volcanoes, however, have brought more discredit than credit to the Big Island's reputation among the world of discriminating travellers. Many shun the island on the assumption it is nothing but one large lava field. They never see the rain forests, the waterfalls, the lineup of nice beaches along the western shoreline, the high country where white-faced cattle graze in the tall grass, the snow-capped mountains, the verdant valleys, the calm seas teeming with giant marlin, the famous Kona sunsets. But it takes time to see all that. It takes much more time before you begin to *feel* the power of the Big Island, the island of Kamehameha the Great, who unified the Islands in the early 19th century, and a place where the physical evidence of ancient Hawaii is better preserved and the haunting memory of the Hawaiians who lived and died here is more strongly felt than on any other island.

But it is also an island full of *fun*. The volcanoes, even while erupting—and Kilauea is almost always erupting in one form or another—can be fun (they can also be tragic, so approach with respect). Only on the Big Island are volcanic eruptions a spectator sport—and a safe one, because the lava flows slowly out of shield volcanoes, which do not explode with the dangerous violence of a cone-type volcano. **Hawaii Volcanoes National Park** is one of the natural wonders of the world, as well as a dramatic place for long hikes through dense forests, across lava deserts, around crater rims, and even onto the floor of the lunarlike craters.

Unfortunately, the volcanoes are on one side of the island and the vast majority of the tourist facilities, and nearly every other attraction except the volcanoes, are on the opposite, or western, side of the island. This has added to the confusion over the Big Island. Simply put, the west side is where the **Kona Coast**, the village of **Kailua-Kona**, and the **Kohala Coast** are located, and this is where the sun shines and the resorts and hotels, condominiums, and golf courses bask in its persistent rays. The east side, a two- to three-hour drive from West Hawaii, has the Hawaii Volcanoes National Park, the island's largest town and seat of island government, **Hilo**, and a lot of rain. Additionally, the Big Island has sprawling cattle ranches (Parker Ranch is the largest privately owned ranch in the United States), macadamia-nut orchards, America's only commercial coffee farms, papaya farms, enough orchid growers to qualify the Big Island as the Orchid Isle, and even a few hidden marijuana fields, although both local and national park authorities have done much to discourage the illegal crop, which a decade ago looked as if it might compete with tourism as the dominant economy.

There is more to the Big Island—but that's the island's blessing and its burden: There's always more here than you can get to, which is why those who have found the time to recognize it keep coming back to what they feel is not just the biggest but the best of the Islands.

Hotels versus Condominiums versus Condominium-Hotels versus the Mega-Resorts

Hawaii's choice in accommodations, once limited to the traditional hotel or the up-and-coming condominium, has now been complicated by a third choice: the up-and-coming condominium-hotel. While the resort hotels have become larger and more spectacular, the condominiums have become more like small hotels.

Billing themselves as all-suite hotels or full-service condominium-hotels, these are usually high rises divided into studios and one- and two-bedroom apartments, all with kitchens. They appeal to the budget-minded couple or family that prefers the space and the privacy of a condominium, where they can prepare snacks or full meals, to the expense of a hotel where all meals are taken in restaurants or through room service and the tipping can kill you. The new configuration, the condo-hotel, offers many of the same services as a traditional hotel—front desk, restaurant, daily maid service, guest activities—combined with rooms larger than hotel rooms that include kitchens and are reasonably priced by Hawaii standards.

While there are choices of hotels and condominiums at various levels of luxury and price on every island, some basic differences characterize each island. Oahu, of course, has the greatest variety of accommodations, packed into Waikiki, where the average room rate is still about $100 a night. The Neighbor Islands, on the other hand, have been setting their sights more and more on the upscale traveller, meaning $200 and up for a hotel room.

Maui is generally considered the most expensive, especially West Maui where the popular Kaanapali Beach Resort and the silk-purse Kapalua Bay Resort are located. Wailea Resort, a half-hour away on the sunny southwestern shoreline, is a quieter alternative to West Maui. The beaches are even better, and in recent years the number of luxury resorts there has increased dramatically. Maui has far more choices in condominiums than all the other islands, including even Oahu, where the Waikiki hotels are still dominant. There are first-rate—and high-priced—condominiums at Kaanapali Beach Resort and Wailea Resort and some luxury villas at Kapalua Bay Resort. Careful research can yield some comfortable, reasonably priced condos in the Napili area north of Kaanapali—but beware the condo ghettos of Kahana and Kihei, where you might save a buck but wreck your vacation.

You may already have heard of a new kind of resort taking hold in Hawaii: the mega-resort. This is the sprawling, super-spectacular, action-oriented, deep-pockets kind of resort hotel introduced by flamboyant Honolulu developer Chris Hemmeter. His first entry in this category was something of a mini mega-resort, the highly successful Hyatt Regency Maui at Kaanapali. Since then he has dwarfed that project with the massive Kauai Lagoons, site of the opulent Westin Kauai, and the stunning Hyatt Regency Waikoloa, on the South Kohala Coast of the Big Island. These are not hotels by any ordinary definition of the word. Although all his Neighbor Island hotels are oceanfront, Hemmeter has an incredible fascination for filling his properties with water. At Westin Maui, Westin Kauai, and Hyatt Regency Waikoloa there are multiple swimming pools the size of football fields and water everywhere you turn: shooting upward from fountains, cascading as waterfalls, gushing out of the mouths of stone animals, and forming lagoons for dolphins, swans, and exotic fish. Hemmeter has departed the islands and was last sighted developing gambling resorts in Louisiana, but his legacy continues in Neighbor Island resort design. Before long, no doubt, someone will have a humpback whale swimming in a hotel lobby.

These hotels, often described as Disneylands for adults, are not for everyone. But they are exciting; kids love them, adults who want to act like kids love them, and people who like to spend a whole vacation just hanging out around the pool absolutely adore them. They are actually an extension of the ongoing trend on the Neighbor Islands toward "complete destination resort hotels," meaning hotels that provide such an attractive variety of activities, shopping, dining, and entertainment within the confines of the resort that there is no need ever to go anywhere else.

Indeed, this is where Hawaii is becoming divided into two kinds of visitors: the type who come to experience the Islands in all their beauty, history, culture, and available outdoor activity; and the type who come to stay at the very best hotel with the best amenities, and rarely leave it. There are sufficient accommodations in Hawaii to satisfy both desires.

The Other Hawaii

People searching for the real Hawaii should look in the heart of Waikiki and along every sunny, easily accessible western coastline of every Neighbor Island, where the luxury resorts and the manicured golf courses cover the shorelines. *This* is the real Hawaii of today, a state completely and totally dominated by tourism as the number-one industry, with no viable alternative in sight. Sugar is nearly dead, pineapple is soon to follow, other crops are minimal in importance, and there has been no industry to come along to replace King Cane, as sugar was once known, except tourism. Mass tourism anchors and propels the economy of the state of Hawaii.

Do not despair, however. There are still sides to Hawaii that have nothing to do with resorts and guided tours and all the other facilities and attractions designed specifically for the transient visitor. You can easily experience the other Hawaii, the one beyond the tourist track, if you are interested enough to search for it and energetic enough to pursue it. No guidebook can tell you exactly where to look, and certainly can't guarantee you'll find it, but you have to start by backing away from the centers of tourism and the well-marked destinations and let serendipity be your guide.

There is open space in Hawaii—barely 5 percent of the land is in urban use. The pristine Hawaii of old is still there, although its lush rain forests and the native plants and birds who inhabit them have declined alarmingly, ravaged by alien species as well as by development. Hawaii now ranks as the endangered species capital of the United States, with conservation efforts accelerating to protect the fragile tapestry of the state's outdoors. Fortunately, on every island there is a wealth of natural splendor to be respectfully explored, from ancient valleys that once held large communities of Hawaiians to mountain trails that are as silent now as when precontact Hawaiians hurried along them. On every island there are still golden beaches that are hard to reach, and if you go to the trouble to get there, your footprints may be the only ones made in the sand all day. Travel slowly through the Islands, taking the time to follow different roads, stopping in the country stores, talking to the people who work and live far from the shadow of construction cranes, and you will be surprised at how easy it is to find the kind of Hawaii experiences that can't be packaged and sold.

USEFUL FACTS

When to Go

The standard weather forecast in Hawaii is, "Another beautiful day in paradise." Most of the time it's true. Because climatic variations are so slight throughout the year, with sunshine and mild temperatures the norm, Hawaii is always a vacation destination, no matter the season. There are some subtleties to consider, however, if you want maximum sunshine. Summer in the Islands runs from May to mid-October, with plenty of sunshine and gusty trade winds. Winter, from late October through

April, is when the weather is cooler and there is more likely to be rain. August and September are usually the hottest and most humid months, with temperatures in the high 80s Fahrenheit and sometimes above 90. The coolest and often the wettest months are February and March, when evening temperatures can dip into the low 70s.

Hawaii's peak tourist traffic is launched with the Christmas season and runs through April, neatly coinciding with the worst elements of winter in the Northern Hemisphere. Some hotels raise their room rates during these months, but others don't. Another busy period is July and August, when children are out of school in North America. Good times to visit Hawaii are just before these two saturation periods begin. Rooms, rental cars, flights, and even restaurant reservations are easier to come by then.

Entry Requirements

Non–U.S. citizens must have a passport and visitor's or long-term visa to enter Hawaii. For Canadians, a document proving citizenship is required, such as a passport or birth certificate. There are no vaccination requirements.

Flying to Hawaii

There are daily direct nonstop flights to Honolulu from several major U.S. cities, most of them on or close to the West Coast. United Airlines offers the greatest number of flights from the most cities. Other U.S. carriers serving the Islands include Alaska, American, America West, Continental, Delta, Northwest, TWA, and Hawaiian Airlines.

It is possible to bypass Honolulu completely with direct flights to three Neighbor Islands. United, American, and Delta have direct flights to Maui. United also has direct flights to Kauai and to the Big Island of Hawaii.

Foreign carriers landing in Honolulu include Canadian Airlines International, China Airlines, Qantas, All Nippon Airways, Singapore Airlines, Air New Zealand, Japan Airlines, Korean Air, and Philippine Airlines.

Flying from Island to Island

Jet aircraft and smaller planes offer regular interisland service. Aloha Airlines and Hawaiian Airlines are the jet carriers serving the major airports on Oahu, Maui, Kauai, and the Big Island. IslandAir, a subsidiary of Aloha Airgroup, flies 18-passenger propeller-driven planes to the Princeville Resort on the North Shore of Kauai, to the Kapalua–West Maui Airport, to Hana on the far eastern side of Maui, to Lanai City on Lanai, and to Kalaupapa and Hoolehua on Molokai. Hawaiian Air flies 50-passenger De Havilland DASH-7 turboprops to Lanai, Molokai, and Kapalua–West Maui. Niihau Helicopter (Tel: 335-3500) departs from Kauai's Port Allen Airport Monday through Friday at 9:00 A.M., noon, and 3:00 P.M. for a flight with two stops on Niihau, for $200 per person (four to seven passengers).

Cruising Hawaii

An attractive alternative to negotiating air terminals in order to see the Neighbor Islands is to take a seven-day cruise aboard a 900-passenger ocean liner. American Hawaii Cruises' SS *Constitution* and SS *Independence* depart Honolulu Harbor from Piers 9 and 10 each Saturday for a week-long swing through the Islands, each following an itinerary the reverse of the other's. They visit four ports on three islands (Hilo and Kailua-Kona on the Big Island, Kahului on Maui, and Nawiliwili, near Lihue, on Kauai), with optional shore excursions available at each stop. The two transatlantic veterans, built in the 1950s, were refurbished for the cruise line's Hawaii program, which was launched in 1980. While their comfort and convenience are generally lauded, food and service aboard these vessels have been subject to criticism over the years. Tel: (800) 765-7000.

Renting a Car

Before arriving on any island, it is best to make a rental-car reservation in advance, especially during peak seasons. There are dozens of car-rental companies in the Islands, and the competition is very aggressive, with most firms offering flat per-day rates with unlimited mileage. When shopping for the best price, however, confirm that the rate is for unlimited mileage, and use caution on quotes for low daily rates: Some are linked to a three-day minimum rental (if you want the car that long, fine). A valid driver's license is required to rent a car. Use a major credit card to avoid paying a cash deposit. Because shuttle service is generally the rule between rental offices and their car lots, allow sufficient time for returning a car in order to make a flight.

What to Wear

This is easy: Light sportswear, bathing suits, sandals, sunglasses, and a hat are the daytime rule in Hawaii. So is sunscreen. Better restaurants expect the female clientele to be in dressier attire at night. Men can leave their ties at home. A jacket is advisable, however, since a few of Hawaii's premier restaurants do require a jacket for dinner (it is preferable to be wearing one's own under these circumstances, rather than an ill-fitting loaner provided by the restaurant). Retail clothing options in the Islands have improved dramatically in recent years; if you need more Chanel or Armani suits during the trip, there will be opportunities to buy them.

Local Time
Hawaii is 5 hours behind New York and the non-Maritime east coast of Canada, and 2 hours behind California and western Canada. It is 10 hours behind the United Kingdom. And when it is 10:00 A.M. in Honolulu, it is 8:00 A.M. the next day in Sydney, Australia, for a time difference of 22 hours. When daylight saving time is in effect elsewhere, add one hour to the time difference (Hawaii does not practice daylight saving time).

Telephoning
The area code for all of the state of Hawaii is 808. Each island has its own telephone directory. The information operator will ask you for which island you are requesting a number. Most of the major hotels in Hawaii, as well as many of the condominium chains, have toll-free 800 numbers for making reservations.

Electric Current
The state of Hawaii uses standard North American current: 110 volts, 60 cycles.

Business Hours and Holidays
The business day starts early in Hawaii. Offices open at 7:00 A.M. or 8:00 A.M. and close at 4:30 P.M. or 5:00 P.M. Banks are open from 8:30 A.M. to 3:00 P.M., later on Fridays. Big retail locations at shopping malls are open from 9:30 A.M. until 9:00 P.M., with reduced hours on Sundays. Hawaii's major holidays are similar to those on the U.S. Mainland, with two important additions: Prince Kuhio Day on March 26 and Kamehameha Day on June 11. Aloha Week is an annual statewide event that is celebrated island by island from mid-September through mid-October.

Cautions
Don't swim at untended beaches, especially during winter months, without first checking with knowledgeable

local people; undertows and other strong currents can surprise and drown even the strongest swimmers.

Also, avoid trekking on unmarked trails, or alone into wilderness areas anywhere. The dangers here can come from nature or from human beings with bad intent.

For Further Information
The main office of the Hawaii Visitors Bureau (HVB) is at 2270 Kalakaua Avenue, Honolulu, HI 96815; Tel: (808) 923-1811. There are branch offices in Kahului, Maui; Lihue, Kauai; and in Hilo and Kailua-Kona on the Big Island of Hawaii. HVB also maintains offices in New York, Chicago, Los Angeles, and San Francisco. Their addresses are: 441 Lexington Avenue, Suite 1003, New York, NY 10017; 180 North Michigan Avenue, Suite 1031, Chicago, IL 60601; 3440 Wilshire Boulevard, Suite 502, Los Angeles, CA 90010; 50 California Street, Suite 450, San Francisco, CA 94111.

—*John Heckathorn*

BIBLIOGRAPHY

Some of the volumes listed below are available only in Hawaii. Check with bookshops in Honolulu and on the islands you visit for titles about individual islands and their culture and history.

LAURIE BACHRAN, *Mrs. Hawaii's New Cookbook* (1988). Local recipes for *pupu* (appetizers), salads, entrées, and breads, with a health-recipe section, compiled by a former Mrs. Hawaii (1963). Two delightful recipes are Michel's mahimahi— prepared by the chef at Michel's at the Colony Surf Hotel in Waikiki—and Godmother Santos' Portuguese sweet bread.

MARTHA WARREN BECKWITH, *Hawaiian Mythology* (1940; reprinted, 1982). Classic work of Hawaiiana based on oral and written narratives. Beckwith focuses on gods, chiefs, heroes, and lovers to highlight a culture in which religion and mythology are interwoven.

ISABELLA L. BIRD (BISHOP), *Six Months in the Sandwich Islands* (1890; reprinted, 1985). In letters to her sister, this Victorian lady traveller records her tomboyish escapades in 1873 Hawaii, including a descent into Kilauea volcano and an excursion around Hilo on a horse.

OSWALD BUSHNELL, *Ka`a`awa: A Novel about Hawaii in the 1850's* (1972; reprinted, 1980). Historical fiction depicting social conflict in 19th-century Hawaii, by a writer with a strong knowledge of Hawaiian culture and history. Other Bushnell fiction includes *The Return of Lono* (1971), about Captain Cook's ill-fated visit to Hawaii, and *The Stone of Kannon* (1979), a saga of the first Japanese to work on Hawaii's sugar plantations.

SHERWIN JOHN CARLQUIST, *Hawaii: A Natural History* (1970). A comprehensive study of Hawaii's fascinating animal and plant life, useful as an aid in understanding and identifying hundreds of species.

THELMA CHANG, *"I Can Never Forget": Men of the 100th/442nd* (1991). An intriguing account of the highly decorated 100th Infantry Battalion and 442nd Regimental Combat Team of World War II, made up of Japanese-American soldiers, many of whom were volunteers from Hawaii. These units, fighting both racial prejudice and German soldiers, rescued prisoners of the Dachau concentration camp.

JOHN CHARLOT, *Chanting the Universe: Hawaiian Religious Culture* (1983). This slim volume offers a personal insight into the Hawaiian perception of life through place chants and songs.

CRAIG CHISHOLM, *Hawaiian Hiking Trails* (1985; reprinted, 1986). The best trails of all the Islands for the trekker at heart. Includes a short description and a tiny topographical map of each trail.

JOHN R. K. CLARK, *The Beaches of O`ahu* (1977; reprinted, 1982). A must read for beach-goers interested in the cultural history of Oahu sand. Clark has written companion beach volumes for Maui, Kauai, and the Big Island of Hawaii.

VIRGINIA COWAN-SMITH AND BONNIE DOMROSE STONE, *Aloha Cowboy* (1988). A short, entertaining glimpse of horsemanship in Hawaii, from the introduction of the horse in 1803 to modern-day parades, rodeos, and polo matches.

GLORIA L. CRONIN, *Tales of Molokai* (1992). Collected by Cronin, a folklorist, these legends and myths add welcome reading to Molokai's meager canon of published literature. The storyteller, Harriet Ne, was appointed cultural historian of Molokai by the governor of Hawaii.

JOHN L. CULLINEY, *Islands in a Far Sea: Nature and Man in Hawaii* (1988). This readable overview of nature's uneasy relationship with *Homo sapiens* explores the environmental impact of human settlement on Hawaii's wildlife and evolution. The author is a marine biologist.

GAVAN DAWS, *Shoal of Time: A History of the Hawaiian Islands* (1968, reprinted, 1974). Written by a former University of Hawaii professor of history, this reliable and entertaining book traces the Islands' history from Western contact and the missionary and whaling periods to annexation and statehood.

———, *Holy Man: Father Damien of Molokai* (1973; reprinted, 1984). A popular yet scholarly biography of the famous leper-priest martyred on Molokai's Kalaupapa Peninsula.

A. GROVE DAY, *Books about Hawaii: Fifty Basic Authors* (1977). An annotated guide to the writers and books that have contributed to Hawaii's literary history.

A. GROVE DAY AND CARL STROVEN, EDS., *A Hawaiian Reader* (1959; reprinted, 1984). A selection of writings from the last hundred years, featuring both obscure and big-name writers (Mark Twain, Robert Louis Stevenson, James Jones). A companion volume is *The Spell of Hawaii* (1968; reprinted, 1985), compiled by the same editors.

LOVE DEAN, *The Lighthouses of Hawaii* (1991). A history of Hawaii's navigational aids with descriptions of lighthouse sites, island by island, and short sketches of the lighthouses' hardworking keepers.

DAVID FORBES, *Encounters with Paradise: Views of Hawaii and Its People, 1778–1941* (1992). A comprehensive look at artistic visions of Hawaii. The creators of these paintings and drawings, which span 163 years of Hawaiian history, include artists onboard exploring voyages, artists affiliated with missionaries, and Hawaiian Modernists. The artwork is from collections in Hawaii and worldwide.

PAMELA FRIERSON, *The Burning Island* (1991). An insightful glimpse into the history and mythology of the Big Island's volcano country. This enchanting landscape—the region of Mauna Loa and Kilauea volcanoes—is considered harsh and desolate by many Westerners but sacred and spiritual to those Hawaiians who still revere Pele, goddess of volcanoes. The author contrasts these native and Western views, adding personal tales of adventure, including an ascent of Mauna Loa.

STEVEN GOLDSBERRY, *Maui the Demigod* (1989). A skillful modern retelling of the Maui story that captures the violent, bawdy, larger-than-life world of legendary Polynesia.

MARNIE HAGMANN, *Hawaii Parklands* (1988). Thumbnail sketches of the Islands' national, state, and county parks illustrated with fine photography. Includes a parklands directory for each island.

HAWAII AUDUBON SOCIETY, *Hawaii's Birds* (1967; reprinted, 1988). This easy-to-use, pocket-size guide for novice bird watchers covers the common birds seen in Waikiki as well as such rarer birds as the Kauai *oo,* a native of the high country.

JERRY HOPKINS, HANS HOEFER, LEONARD LUERAS, AND REBECCA CROCKETT-HOPKINS, *The Hula* (1982). A well-written introduction to Hawaii's traditional dance, complete with historical illustrations and a hall of fame of hula greats.

IRVING JENKINS, *The Hawaiian Calabash* (1989). Old-time and modern-day Hawaiian craftsmen have long excelled in making the wooden bowls known as calabashes. This is the complete story, with color illustrations, of the spirit of Hawaii expressed in wood.

EDWARD JOESTING, *Kauai: The Separate Kingdom* (1984; reprinted, 1988). A history of the Garden Isle from precontact to the close of the 19th century by a past president of the Hawaiian Historical Society and author of *Hawaii: An Uncommon History* (1972; reprinted, 1978).

JAMES JONES, *From Here to Eternity* (1951; reprinted, 1980). Wartime fiction about army life in Hawaii before and during the 1941 Japanese attack on Pearl Harbor. Jones, a soldier stationed on Oahu during the war, dedicated the novel to the U.S. Army.

PATRICK V. KIRCH, *Feathered Gods and Fishhooks* (1985). This richly illustrated introduction to Hawaiian archaeology and prehistory, from the Polynesian discovery of Hawaii to European contact, is the best book available about the settlement sites and cultural developments that shaped ancient Hawaiian culture.

RITA KNIPE, *The Water of Life: A Jungian Journey through Hawaiian Myth* (1989). The underlying themes and symbolism in selected myths are explored, with woodblock prints by Hawaii artist Dietrich Varez complementing the text.

RALPH S. KUYKENDALL, *The Hawaiian Kingdom, 1778–1893*. A detailed trilogy—*Foundation and Transformation* (1938), *Twenty Critical Years* (1953), *The Kalakaua Dynasty* (1967)—dryly written but considered a definitive history of 19th-century Hawaii.

JACK LONDON, *Stories of Hawaii* (1965). Reprinted short stories by a master of the genre, who visited the islands in 1907. The American people, said London about Hawaii, "don't know what they've got! Just watch this land in the future, when Americans wake up!"

GORDON A. MACDONALD, AGATIN T. ABBOTT, AND FRANK L. PETERSON, *Volcanoes in the Sea: The Geology of Hawaii* (1970; reprinted, 1983). Millions of years in the making, the Hawaiian Islands are geological masterpieces created and shaped by volcanoes and erosion. This is the most detailed book available on the processes that have formed the Islands.

JAMES A. MICHENER, *Hawaii* (1959; reprinted, 1982). The "big book" of Hawaii fiction by a Pulitzer Prize–winning author, this novel ranges from the Islands' geological birth to modern times. The film version was shot on Oahu's Waianae Coast.

CAREY D. MILLER, KATHERINE BAZORE, AND MARY BARTOW, *Fruits of Hawaii* (1965; reprinted, 1991). Description, nutritive value, and recipes for 36 Hawaiian fruits, from the banana to the exotic *ohelo* berry, once sacred to Pele, Hawaii's goddess of volcanoes. Of special interest is a short history of each fruit.

LINDA PAIK MORIARTY, *Niihau Shell Leis* (1986). An illustrated introduction to the Forbidden Island's shell leis—history, shell species, lei making—written by a shell enthusiast of Hawaiian ancestry.

THE NATURE CONSERVANCY OF HAWAII AND GAVAN DAWS, *Hawaii: The Islands of Life* (1988). Strong on photographs, with a short text by Gavan Daws, this book showcases Hawaii's fascinating, yet fragile, environment. The sponsor is an organization dedicated to protecting Hawaii's endangered ecosystems.

VICTORIA NELSON, *My Time in Hawaii* (1989). A personal memoir of an urban American woman who arrived in

Hawaii in 1969 and spent time at Honolulu's Bishop Museum, Oahu's Hanauma Bay, and on the outer islands.

GORDON W. PRANGE, DONALD M. GOLDSTEIN, AND KATHERINE DILLON, *At Dawn We Slept: The Untold Story of Pearl Harbor* (1981; reprinted, 1982). A massive account (873 pages) of that famous Sunday in December 1941, examined from both the American and Japanese sides. Prange spent 37 years preparing this book.

MARY K. PUKUI, SAMUEL H. ELBERT, AND ESTHER T. MOOKINI, *Place Names of Hawaii* (1974). A scholarly guide to the meanings of the Islands' curious place-names. A question frequently asked at Hawaii's public libraries is "What book will tell me the meaning of a Hawaiian name?" This is it.

RONN RONCK, *Ronck's Hawaii Almanac* (1984). Hawaii in a nutshell, packaged in a pocket-size fact book; dated, but still useful.

MICHAEL SLACKMAN, *Remembering Pearl Harbor: The Story of the USS* Arizona *Memorial* (1984). Short chapters highlight the ship; the attack; the fund raising for (Elvis Presley helped) and construction of the memorial; and the ship's underwater archaeology. Sponsored by the *Arizona* Memorial Museum Association.

JOHN J. STEPHAN, *Hawaii under the Rising Sun* (1984). Subtitled *Japan's Plans for Conquest after Pearl Harbor,* this is a fascinating account of the Imperial Navy's schemes to invade and occupy Hawaii prior to the disastrous defeat at Midway.

AUDREY SUTHERLAND, *Paddling My Own Canoe* (1978). Adventures of a woman and her inflatable canoe on Molokai's northern seacoast, one of Hawaii's most isolated areas.

RUTH M. TABRAH, *Ni`ihau: The Last Hawaiian Island* (1987). Homely history of Hawaii's privately owned island, which was purchased by a Scottish family in 1864.

ARMINE VON TEMPSKI, *Born in Paradise* (1940; reprinted, 1988). A popular autobiography by a Maui-born woman of Polish ancestry whom Jack London encouraged to become a writer. Daughter of a rancher, she grew up on the slopes of Haleakala on Maui.

GRADY TIMMONS, *Waikiki Beachboy* (1989). Masters of surfing and outrigger canoeing, local beachboys have built a lifestyle centered around Waikiki sand. This book, with a fine collection of photographs, offers an intriguing glimpse of a uniquely Hawaiian phenomenon.

RICHARD WILLIAM TREGASKIS, *The Warrior King: Hawaii's Kamehameha the Great* (1973; reprinted, 1984). Fictional biography of the Islands' best-known historical personage, who united and ruled all Hawaii. Kamehameha and Tregaskis shared common characteristics: One was a warrior-king, the other a war correspondent (*Guadalcanal Diary*), and both stood six foot six.

MARK TWAIN, *Mark Twain's Letters from Hawaii* (1966; reprinted, 1975). For four months in 1866 Twain roamed the Islands as a reporter for a California newspaper. These reprinted letters, first published in the Sacramento *Union*, helped launch his literary career. In one of his travel books, *Roughing It* (1872), Twain recounts another excursion to the Islands.

UNIVERSITY OF HAWAII, *Atlas of Hawaii* (1973; reprinted, 1983). A godsend for the cartographic-minded traveller, this collection of easy-to-interpret maps and data is presented in a colorful format, with special emphasis on Hawaii's ecology.

—*John W. Perry*

HONOLULU AND WAIKIKI

By Rick Carroll

Rick Carroll, an author, journalist, and photographer, lives on Oahu and has written for the Honolulu Advertiser *and the* San Francisco Chronicle. *He is United Press International's special Hawaii-Pacific correspondent and is the author of* From Mauka to Makai *and* Great Outdoor Adventures of Hawaii.

With its polyglot population, Honolulu, on the island of Oahu, is America's first true multinational city and its only metropolis to be declared a city by a king. Not even old Kamehameha III, however, could have guessed that his mud-and-thatch seaport on a tiny volcanic island in the middle of the sea would become one of the prime destinations of sun lovers everywhere.

MAJOR INTEREST

Tropical scenery in an urban setting
East-West cultural and historical mix
The waterfront
Views from Aloha Tower
Iolani Palace and the Capitol District
Chinatown
The Bishop Museum (Hawaiiana)
Nuuanu Pali Lookout
National Memorial Cemetery of the Pacific (Punchbowl)
Surfing and people-watching at Waikiki Beach
The Moana and other luxury hotels
Diamond Head volcano

Splendid oceanside scenery east of Diamond Head
Restaurants and nightlife
Cruises and boat charters
Shopping

Honolulu is more than just a port of entry to a vacation; it is also a major urban center of the Pacific, the westernmost American state capital, and the nation's 11th largest—and most exotic—city. Most visitors to Honolulu head to Waikiki and never veer off the path into the rest of this splendid city. Honolulu's population of 836,231 is more Asian than Caucasian, and none of a score of ethnic groups is a majority. The people here are as varied as their many points of origin, and each nationality contributes to the Amerasian mosaic that is modern Honolulu. "Half the world's races seem to be represented and interbred here," Jan Morris wrote in the London *Sunday Times,* "and between them they have created an improbable microcosm of human society as a whole."

Honolulu is a beautiful, cosmopolitan city, blessed by temperatures that seldom achieve more than 90 or less than 70 degrees Fahrenheit, with nearly 300 days of sunshine a year. The island of Oahu enjoys nearly the same climate as Acapulco and Havana and is just high enough in the tropic band to dodge the steaminess of her southern Polynesian sisters. Trade winds refresh the city and keep it from simmering in tropical heat. There are only two seasons—wet and dry—and when it rains, it's considered a blessing.

HONOLULU'S HISTORY
Honolulu has undergone a great deal since it was "discovered" in the late 1700s by the British, who introduced, among other things, venereal disease. Stern New England missionaries, who banned hula and dressed women in long, loose dresses called muumuu, came next. Eventually the native Hawaiian population was to lose land, language, and the monarchy at the hands of an oligarchy of prospering traders, merchants, and missionaries, who seized the kingdom and made sugar and pineapple profits king.

In 1800 Honolulu was a collection of "a thousand or more thatched huts, looking like geometrical haystacks, most of them low and filthy in the extreme, scattered higgledy-piggledy over a plain," according to James J. Jarves, editor of *The Polynesian* newspaper. "Here and

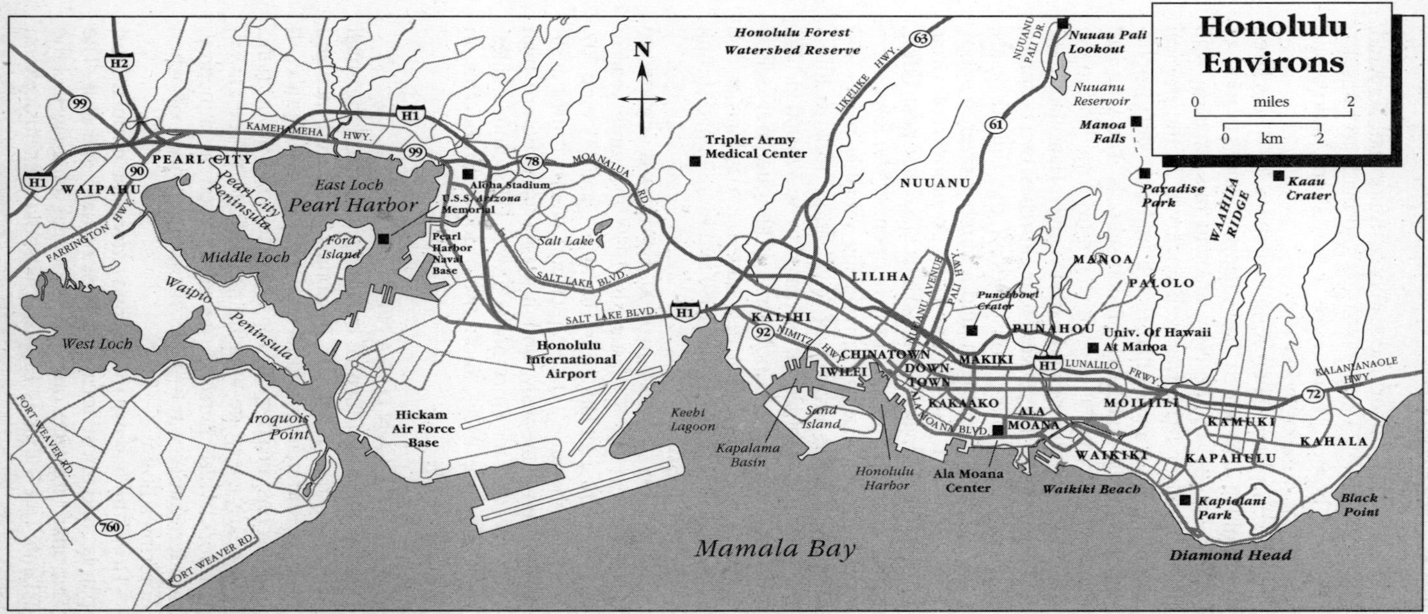
Honolulu Environs
0 miles 2
0 km 2
N
Honolulu Forest Watershed Reserve
Tripler Army Medical Center
Nuuau Pali Lookout
Nuuanu Reservoir
Manoa Falls
Paradise Park
Kaau Crater
WAAHILA RIDGE
NUUANU
LILIHA
MANOA
PALOLO
Punchbowl Crater
PUNAHOU
Univ. Of Hawaii At Manoa
KALIHI
CHINATOWN
IWILEI
DOWNTOWN
MAKIKI
KAKAAKO
ALA MOANA
MOILIILI
KAMUKI
KAHALA
KAPAHULU
WAIKIKI
Waikiki Beach
Kapiolani Park
Black Point
Diamond Head
Ala Moana Center
Honolulu Harbor
Sand Island
Kapalama Basin
Keehi Lagoon
Mamala Bay
Honolulu International Airport
Hickam Air Force Base
Pearl Harbor Naval Base
U.S.S. Arizona Memorial
Aloha Stadium
Salt Lake
SALT LAKE BLVD.
MOANALUA RD.
Pearl Harbor
East Loch
Middle Loch
West Loch
Ford Island
Pearl City Peninsula
Waipio Peninsula
Iroquois Point
PEARL CITY
WAIPAHU
KAMEHAMEHA HWY.
FARRINGTON HWY.
FORT WEAVER RD.
LIKELIKE HWY.
NUUANU PALI DR.
PALI HWY.
NUUANU AVENUE
NIMITZ HWY.
ALA MOANA BLVD.
LUNALILO FRWY.
KALANIANAOLE HWY.
H1
H2
99
90
78
63
61
92
72
760

there, a white trader, mechanic, or sailor had squatted, taken to himself a tawny mistress and made to himself a mongrel home. There were a few shops, stores and houses, of stone or wood."

Fifty years later, when King Kamehameha III declared Honolulu a city, much had changed. The salvation of "pagan babies" by the New England missionaries, who first arrived in 1820, was well underway in the tropical kingdom. Missionaries had established a Hawaiian alphabet, a printed Bible, and mission schools. The king had signed the Great Mahele, which put his royal land in the hands of commoners, and had also given Hawaiians their first legal rights. There were four churches, two hospitals, a library, two hotels, consulates of the United States, France, and Great Britain, and a number of grog shops. The first steam vessel, the HMS *Cormorant* of Great Britain, had arrived in the Islands. The first post office, courthouse, and fire department opened. The Royal Agricultural Society began introducing valuable plants and animals. But the advance of "civilization" took its toll—the Hawaiian population, estimated to be 300,000 in 1778 when Captain James Cook arrived (although new scholarly research suggests it may have been as high as one million), stood at 84,165 in 1850 and by 1872 had shrunk to 56,897 persons.

Made a U.S. territory in 1900, Hawaii was admitted to the Union as the 50th state in 1959, the same year in which the first jet landed in Hawaii, a Qantas Boeing 707. Honolulu became a state capital and a major tourist destination simultaneously, and it wasn't long before high rises dwarfed ten-story Aloha Tower (Honolulu's tallest building since 1926), and a five-o'clock rush became an evening ritual.

CULTURE AND LANGUAGE

Despite the rapid turn of events that changed the small port town into a big city, Honolulu has stayed nice and friendly and maintained its own peculiar social graces. It is still considered rude, for example, to honk in traffic. And nearly everyone—including *haole* (HOW-lee; Hawaiian for "white person," generally used in a neutral, nonderogatory way)—takes his or her shoes off when entering a house.

Honolulu has also maintained *pidgin,* the popular local patois, and most locals understand and speak it. The Hawaiian language, one of two "official" languages of the Islands (the other is English), is spoken exclusively on

Niihau and elsewhere throughout the Islands in circles of Hawaiian culture. The 12-letter Hawaiian alphabet, created by missionaries, consists of the five vowels and the consonants *h, k, l, m, n, p,* and *w.*

While many aspects of the old kingdom still run through life in Honolulu, the city has nonetheless become one of the most progressive in the Pacific Basin. Honolulu remains just far enough from the continent to possess its own smug, provincial style. Even at its urban heart the city manages to conjure up Conradian images and South Seas fantasies, but the truth is greater than all the fiction. Honolulu is like a hardware store: Whatever you're looking for is probably there.

Exploring Honolulu

Honolulu, the state capital, occupies the southern shore of the island of Oahu. The city rises from the waterfront and stretches inland to the base of the Koolau mountains. The downtown area, built first as a seaport, is that part of the city directly inland of Honolulu Harbor. Waikiki, the tourist quarter, where all the hotels are, is to the east, toward Diamond Head volcano. While you are exploring Honolulu and Waikiki you'll need to make use of the local directionals based on geographical landmarks that residents use in place of north, south, east, and west. *Makai* means "toward the sea" and in Honolulu is used to mean "south." *Mauka,* "toward the mountains," is north. *Diamond Head* is to the east, in the direction of that famous landmark; and *Ewa* is toward the westerly suburb of that name.

Politically, the city and county of Honolulu extend over the entire island of Oahu. The city proper is a diverse collection of neighborhoods and people, with oddly juxtaposed architectural styles, from plantation shacks and New England bungalows to hard-edged International high rises, scattered over hills and clefts between mountains and sea. The 22-mile-long residential corridor from the man-made lagoons of Hawaii Kai in the east to the "new town" sprawl of Mililani above Pearl Harbor in the west is divided lengthwise by H-1, an east–west, eight-lane freeway that goes island-wide. Along the corridor are areas and neighborhoods outside of downtown Honolulu and Waikiki that often go unexplored. These areas hold myriad attractions for visitors, ranging from rain forests and mountain-top views to museums, restaurants, nightclubs, and a pineapple-canning factory.

VENTURING BEYOND WAIKIKI

The Ala Wai Canal separates Waikiki from the rest of Honolulu but can be traversed at its western (Ewa) end by the Ala Moana Boulevard, Kalakaua Avenue, and McCully Street bridges. It's easy to get in and out of Waikiki, but many visitors are reluctant to venture out and explore the city at large. We strongly urge you to give it a try and spend a day or two mingling with real Hawaii urbanites beyond Waikiki's manufactured paradise. Downtown Honolulu is more cosmopolitan than Waikiki and has a nautical flair. Other neighborhoods have all sorts of offerings for the determined traveller. So get out beyond Waikiki and see the real city and the real people that live in it. McCully Street, mauka off Ala Wai Boulevard, is the easiest driving route out of Waikiki, but local public transportation, via TheBus, is the preferred method of travel in the Waikiki-downtown area.

Our coverage of Honolulu starts in the downtown area at Honolulu Harbor. We then explore the Capitol District and Chinatown, before heading into outlying areas: first west (Ewa) of downtown, then up toward the mountains (mauka), and finally to the east (Diamond Head), starting with the neighborhoods between downtown and Waikiki, then Waikiki itself, and finally the area beyond it, all the way to the island's southeastern tip.

DOWNTOWN HONOLULU

The jagged skyline set at the foot of mountains gives downtown Honolulu a look of tropical urbanity, with mynah birds, palm trees, and tropical fruit dangling from roadside trees to contrast with the high-rise buildings. The bustling downtown is graced by parks, fountains, and public sculpture. Most people who arrive on Oahu, however, never see any of this as they roll into Waikiki from Honolulu International Airport.

The best way to see Honolulu is on foot, starting on the waterfront downtown, where it all began with European "contact" in the 18th century when liberty sailors swaggered ashore to swap nails (which could be bent into fishhooks) for sex, a rite that continues with a different commodity now when ships are in port. The 17-acre Honolulu waterfront is soon to be transformed from a 1940s-era warehouse district to a modern, people-oriented arcade of seaside shops and restaurants by developer James Rouse, creator of Boston's Faneuil Hall and Baltimore's Harborplace. Take the number 19 or 20 bus from Waikiki, get off at the corner of Ala Moana Boulevard and Alakea Street, and walk two blocks Ewa to get to the waterfront.

ALOHA TOWER

Perched at the water's edge is the landmark Aloha Tower, built in 1926 as a lighthouse and the city's tallest structure until 1959. After the December 7, 1941, raid on Pearl Harbor, the 184-foot clock tower was painted regulation GI camouflage color in hopes of disguising it in the event of further enemy attack. Though now humbled by skyscraper office buildings, it still offers a grand view up **Fort Street Mall** to the cloud-wreathed, emerald-green volcanic peaks of the 3,000-foot-high Koolau Range to the northeast.

Ride the tower's poky elevator to the tenth-floor lookout for the best free view in town. The observation deck, posted with the official Schedule of Passenger Cruise Vessels, is decorated with 18 sun-faded color photos of famous ships entering Honolulu Harbor, from the world-cruising *QE2* to the outrigger *Hokulea*, which reenacted the ancient Polynesian canoe voyages between Hawaii and Tahiti in 1976. You can see some of this action yourself if you ascend the tower before sundown on any Saturday night when the interisland cruise ships SS *Independence* and SS *Constitution* are berthed at Piers 9 and 10. You'll see the shoreside lei sellers, in a pale imitation of the old "Boat Days" when *everyone* came by ship. The 360-degree view also takes in all the ships at sea; Honolulu Harbor, the largest of seven harbors in Hawaii; the distant Waianae Mountains; the two-mile-long reef runway at Honolulu Airport, which doubles as a Space Shuttle emergency-landing strip; the cherry-blossom-pink Tripler Army Medical Center Hospital on the hill; downtown Honolulu; and a peek at Diamond Head and Waikiki through the skyscrapers. Each side of the open-air observation tower features a new, bilingual viewing chart (in English and Japanese) that helps you identify what you are seeing. The "View Towards the Harbor" chart notes that Captain William Brown, a British merchant captain who sailed into the harbor in 1784 on the fur-trade route between Alaska and Canton, christened it "Fair Haven," a fair translation of Honolulu, which means "sheltered bay."

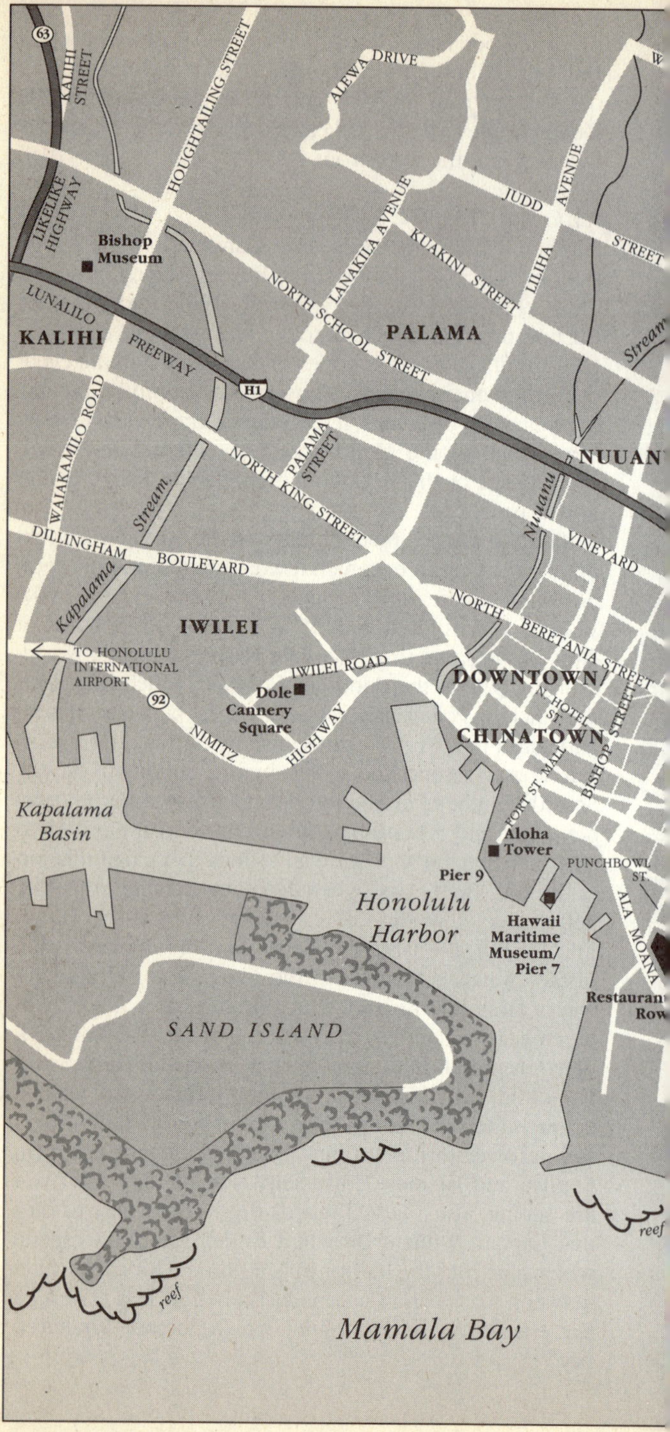

63
KALIHI STREET
LIKELIKE HIGHWAY
HOUGHTAILING STREET
ALEWA DRIVE
JUDD STREET
LILIHA AVENUE
LANAKILA AVENUE
KUAKINI STREET
Bishop Museum
LUNALILO FREEWAY
KALIHI
NORTH SCHOOL STREET
PALAMA
Stream
H1
WAIAKAMILO ROAD
PALAMA STREET
NORTH KING STREET
NUUAN
Stream
Nuuanu
VINEYARD
DILLINGHAM BOULEVARD
Kapalama
IWILEI
NORTH BERETANIA STREET
TO HONOLULU INTERNATIONAL AIRPORT
IWILEI ROAD
DOWNTOWN/
CHINATOWN
N. HOTEL ST.
BISHOP STREET
92
Dole Cannery Square
NIMITZ HIGHWAY
FORT ST. MALL
Kapalama Basin
Aloha Tower
PUNCHBOWL ST.
Pier 9
Honolulu Harbor
ALA MOANA
Hawaii Maritime Museum/ Pier 7
Restauran Row
SAND ISLAND
reef
reef
Mamala Bay

Honolulu: Downtown and Central

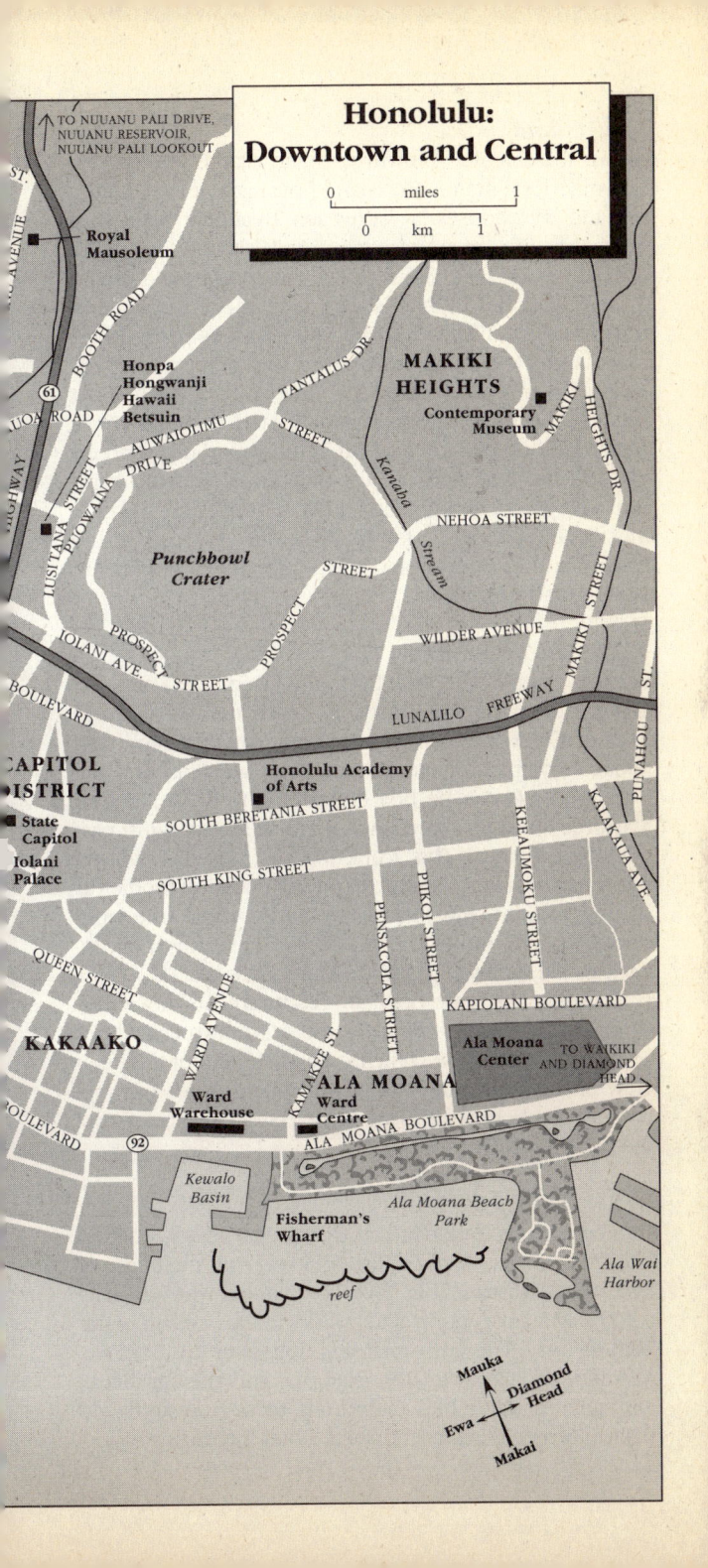

Sand Island

Across the channel you will see Sand Island, a one-and-a-half-mile-long man-made island housing Matson containers and warehouses, a wastewater treatment plant, and junkyards. (To drive there take Sand Island Access Road over the Kapalama Basin drawbridge.) On Sand Island Access Road the landmarks are a scrap-metal mountain of old rental cars, Kilgo's, a 300,000-square-foot hardware store, and a jetty inhabited by stray cats, feline and otherwise. If you're not sailing for Tahiti out of Keehi Boat Harbor, the only action on Sand Island is **LaMariana**, a raffish sailors' bar-and-grill on an unnamed dirt road off Sand Island Access Road just past the McKesson warehouse. If you're looking for a quiet respite, there's a large, mostly undiscovered state park at the very end of the road, with lots of grass and wind, a small beach, pleasant views—and no crowds.

THE WATERFRONT

Back on street level, walk Diamond Head (east) of Aloha Tower along the waterfront, to reach the 100-year-old **Falls of Clyde**, the only four-masted, square-rigged ship afloat. Now part of the **Hawaii Maritime Museum**, the *Falls of Clyde* can be boarded and toured. The Hawaii Maritime Museum's new Kalakaua Boat House is just past the ship on Pier 7. This artifact-packed museum right on the waterfront has 30 exhibits on such nautical themes as surfing, Matson ships, seaplanes, and whaling (the wonderful whaling mural is by Calley O'Neill), plus a humpback whale skeleton found on Kahoolawe island.

Coasters, the only open-air restaurant on the waterfront, is a lunchtime choice of the downtown crowd not so much for the food, which is passing fair, but the keen view of tugboats, sampans, Toyota-laden barges from Japan, sloops bound for Bora Bora, Hawaiian canoes, and the occasional cruise ship.

BISHOP STREET

To gain a sense of downtown Honolulu's center, walk up either Fort Street Mall or Bishop Street, still the home of two of the historic Big Five companies, who virtually ruled Hawaii's economy and politics in the first half of the 20th century. The last remaining houses of the Big Five, Alexander & Baldwin, for example, and the Big Sixth, Dillingham, stand like memorials to the oligarchy on Bishop Street. Bishop intersects Hotel Street five blocks mauka (toward the mountains), from which point you can continue on to the Capitol District to the right or Chinatown to the left.

The Capitol District

Head Diamond Head on Hotel Street to reach the Capitol District. You'll pass by Benny Bufano's irresistibly tactile bronze sculpture of a cuddly mother bear and her two cubs near the corner of Hotel and Alakea streets.

IOLANI PALACE

Continue Diamond Head one more block to reach the jewel of the Capitol District, Iolani Palace, a stone Italian Renaissance remnant of the monarchy, built in 1882 by King David Kalakaua, known as the Merrie Monarch, who filled the royal house with European period furniture shipped round the Horn. The king, who earned his nickname by reviving the hula, which had been banned, lived and entertained here, in America's only palace, until his death in 1891. His sister and successor, Queen Liliuokalani, lived in the palace until the end of her reign, which came about after 160 gun-toting U.S. Marines overthrew Hawaii's constitutional monarchy on January 17, 1893, deposed Queen Liliuokalani, and claimed the islands as an American territory. Queen Liliuokalani, who was strongly opposed to the annexation of Hawaii by the United States, was later imprisoned in the palace. People leave flowers every day at the base of the queen's statue mauka of the palace. The Friends of Iolani Palace, which supervised a restoration of the palace, conducts tours Wednesdays through Saturdays by reservation only (Tel: 522-0832).

The king's **Coronation Pavilion**, the green-domed, gazebo-like octagon on the palace grounds, is now used for the governor's inauguration and for free public concerts of Hawaiian, pop, and classical music by the Royal Hawaiian Band at 12:15 P.M. every Friday.

ALIIOLANI HALE

Across South King Street from Iolani Palace stands the State Judiciary Building, known as Aliiolani Hale (House of the Heavenly Chief). More grandiose than Iolani Palace, it was built in 1872 for Kamehameha V, but he died before it was completed. Step inside and take a quick look at the new **judiciary museum**, with its restored

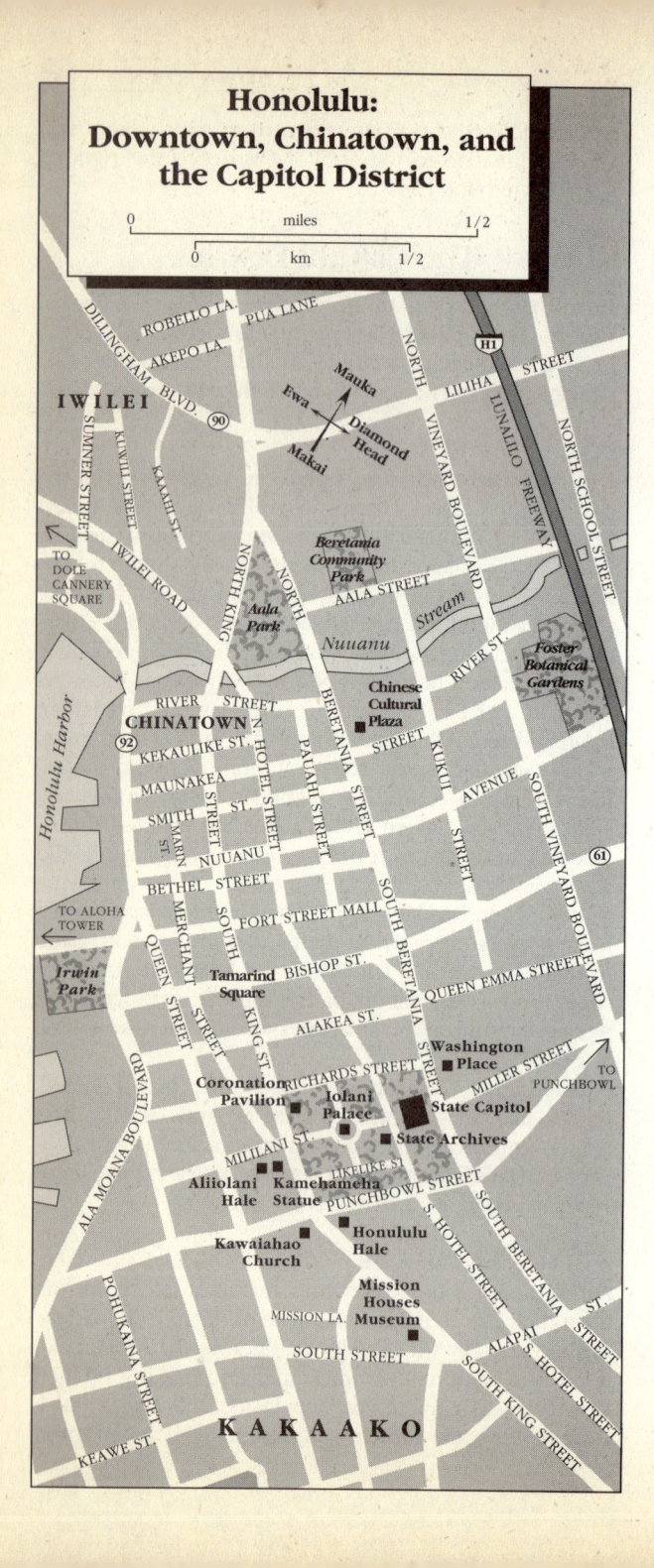

Honolulu: Downtown, Chinatown, and the Capitol District

historic courtroom, before continuing down South King Street.

The **statue of King Kamehameha the Great**, standing in front of Aliiolani Hale, the most photographed statue in Hawaii, is actually a replica. The original, crafted by American sculptor Thomas Gould in Italy in 1878, sank in a shipwreck off the Falkland Islands. Gould made another, which was erected here in 1883. Some weeks later an English sea captain arrived in Honolulu with the salvaged nine-ton original and sold it to King Kalakaua for $850. It now stands in front of the Kapaau courthouse on the Big Island. (A third version of the statue stands in Washington, D.C., 4,829 miles and five time zones from Honolulu.) None of this artful dodge bothers the busloads of tourists who disembark to photograph and all but worship the life-size, nearly seven-foot-tall, black-and-gold statue, which is draped with 18-foot-long leis on King Kamehameha Day, June 11, a state holiday.

SOUTH KING STREET
On the corner of Punchbowl and South King streets stands the coral-block **Kawaiahao Church**, which has been called the "Westminster Abbey of the Pacific." Dedicated in 1842 by the missionary Hiram Bingham, Kawaiahao Church was a five-year effort involving hundreds of workers who quarried 1,000-pound blocks from the reef and cut massive timbers to erect the church. Nowadays, Christmas services are held here in the Hawaiian language.

Early Hawaiians worshiped the sun and the gods Lono and Maui, among others. Today the Islands embrace 35 Christian denominations, 22 Buddhist denominations, 2 Jewish, 1 Muslim, 5 Shinto, 7 new religious movements, and 4 other movements, including Scientologists and Moonies. Some deeds of the first among these post-contact arrivals, the fire-and-brimstone New England missionaries, who arrived in 1820 on the brigantine *Thaddeus,* are told at **Mission Houses Museum** (Diamond Head of Kawaiahao Church, at 553 South King Street), a tract of their "proper" clapboard houses shipped around the Horn. Across King Street from the museum, in **Civic Center** (the area bounded by South King, Alapai, South Beretania, and Richards streets), Isamu Noguchi's sculpture *Skygate* looks like a giant black-steel pretzel on a tripod. Sit or lie on the grass under it and look up to get the full effect. Concerts take place here in summer.

Honolulu City and County stretches 1,500 miles west beyond **Honolulu Hale** (City Hall), the California Mission–

style building with a red-tile roof on the mauka corner of South King and Punchbowl streets (across South King from Kawaiahao Church), and encompasses all the northwestern Hawaiian Islands except Midway. Some of the Honolulu County islets, such as French Frigate Shoals and Pearl and Hermes atolls, are populated only by seabirds and monk seals, while others are underwater, emerging only at low tide.

THE STATE CAPITOL AREA

Hawaii's **State Capitol**, reached from Honolulu Hale by walking mauka on Punchbowl Street, then Ewa on the Hotel Street pedestrian mall, mimics the elements of air, land, and sea in its volcano-shaped chambers, which are surrounded by carp ponds and supported by graceful palm-tree-like columns. A bronze Marisol Escobar statue of Father Damien de Veuster, the "leper priest" of Molokai, greets mauka-side visitors. Inside the Senate Chamber, 620 pearlized nautilus shells from the Philippines filled with lights form the elaborate shellcraft chandelier, devised by German artist Otto Piene. Also of interest are giant tapestries by Ruthadell Anderson and a mosaic by Tadashi Sato in the center of the courtyard.

Under Queen Kapiolani's giant banyan (she planted the seedling) on the Iolani Palace grounds between the palace and the state capitol is a drab, modern government building that contains one of Hawaii's best-kept secrets. The **State Archives** has 40,000 historic prints by such photographers as James Williams, A. Montano, Menzie Dickson, and Rice and Perkins. The Hawaiian category, featuring hula girls, beachboys, and lei sellers, is the most popular. You can order blowup photos of early Hawaii here at bargain prices.

The governor of Hawaii lives across South Beretania Street from the capitol in **Washington Place**, a New England Colonial designed by Isaac Hart for John Dominis, a New England sea captain who was lost at sea and never took occupancy. The deposed Queen Liliuokalani took refuge here until her death in 1917. The house has served as the governor's mansion since 1921 and is the oldest continuously occupied dwelling in Honolulu.

HONOLULU ACADEMY OF ARTS

A short walk south of the State Capitol, at 900 South Beretania Street, is the Honolulu Academy of Arts, a small but important institution founded in 1929, housing a highly distinguished collection of objects, including van Gogh's *Wheatfield,* Tang dynasty porcelain, the James Michener collection of *ukiyo-e* prints, an unrivaled Korean cup collection, a rare Hubert Vos painting of an early Hawaiian fisherman's catch of the day, and a statue of Kwan Yin, the Chinese Buddhist goddess of mercy, circa 1025. Admission to the academy is free. There is a delightful garden café on the grounds.

TAMARIND SQUARE AREA
Tamarind Square, a grassy green mall with trees, benches, and a waterfall, is up South King Street from the State Capitol–Iolani Palace area at the Bishop Street intersection. The wistful vertical bronze that looks something like an Easter Island statue is Henry Moore's *Bronze Figure.* Downtown office workers eat brown-bag lunches in the sunshine here (Subway or Heidi's Sandwich Shop), especially on Fridays, when there are free concerts at noon. Otherwise, they head into **Café Che Pasta** (1001 Bishop Street), an art-filled, San Francisco–style bar and grill serving fresh clams and pasta with California Chardonnay by the glass, or eat dim sum at **Yong Sing**, around the corner on Alakea Street.

Chinatown

In Honolulu's Chinatown, a 130-year-old hangout of immigrant Asians, the barber at Sunday Barber Shop catnaps in her chair while yawning transvestites stroll on Hotel Street. But this mostly Vietnamese and Filipino neighborhood, also home to Japanese, Koreans, Laotians, Pacific Islanders, and only 5 percent of Hawaii's Chinese, is becoming gentrified: High rises now loom over old coralblock buildings with tin roofs; Hotel Street these days is wide and handsome (but still a tricky place to visit at night). Aphrodisiacs such as deer antlers and ginseng root still appear in herbalists' windows, but lately artists' lofts, bistros, boutiques, even a shopping mall (Maunakea Marketplace), have begun to pop up amid the lei stands. Nonetheless, Chinatown remains a vibrant, colorful neighborhood, despite the encroaching gentility. The best time to visit, to get the full experience of the place, is during the Chinese New Year (January or February, depending on the lunar calendar), when lions and dragons dance in the street, firecrackers explode, and thousands celebrate at the Maunakea Street party, eating *jai* and *jong,* good luck foods.

Chinatown is a 15-square-block ramshackle neighborhood bordered by River Street (Nuuanu Stream) on the Ewa side, Queen Street on the makai side, Bethel Street on the Diamond Head side, and Beretania Street on the mauka side. On your first visit, you might start your exploration with the **Hawaii Heritage Center**'s two-and-a-half-hour guided walking tour. This informative tour begins at Ramsay Galleries & Café, 1128 Smith Street, at 9:30 A.M. every Friday. Call the Hawaii Heritage Center for reservations; Tel: 521-2749.

NORTH KING STREET

If you wish to cover Chinatown on your own, simply continue Ewa on South King Street from the Capitol District or business area. Ewa of Nuuanu Avenue, South King Street becomes North King Street. There's a good Chinese restaurant, **Sea Fortune**, at 111 North King Street. Farther up the street, at number 145, is the open-air **Oahu Market**, which was saved from the wrecker's ball by 17 stall keepers who pooled their money to buy it, then kept it just the way it was: a thriving native market full of catch-of-the-day fish stands and other stalls that attract hundreds of Saturday-morning shoppers. Fresh flaky croissants and French coffee can be found just across the street at **Ba-Le**, a coffee shop run by refugees from Saigon. Just Ewa of the market at North King and River streets, you can visit the studio of Hong Kong artist **Ka Ning Fong**, who can be found painting moody oils of Honolulu at dusk in his second floor loft (941 River Street). Try him in the evenings; he's usually not there during the day.

HOTEL STREET

Head mauka on River Street one block to reach Hotel Street. Newly widened and lined with malls, Hotel Street now serves as a major transit artery for local buses and hardly resembles its former sleazy self when World War II GIs stood on line outside the hotels reading comic books while they waited for girls. But the old pagoda of **Wo Fat**, the oldest chop suey house in Honolulu, founded in 1882 by the baker Wat Ging, remains at 115 North Hotel Street. This showplace has a long history, but the menu needs rejuvenation. Another old standby is **Smith's Union Bar**, 19 North Hotel Street, an early-day watering hole for sailors, so named because the sailor's union used to be upstairs.

MAUNAKEA STREET

At Hotel and Maunakea streets is the **Maunakea Marketplace**, a mall of shops and restaurants (covered in our

Shops and Shopping section, below), yet another sign of the growing respectability of Hotel Street.

If you head mauka on Maunakea Street to Beretania Street, you'll come to the **Chinese Cultural Plaza**, a retail arcade housing primarily Chinese shops and restaurants. The **Tak Wah Tong Chinese Herb Shop**, across from the plaza's Moon Gate (a round wooden gate), is the largest of 17 such herb shops in Chinatown. Alan Lau, a direct descendant of a Ching dynasty emperor's very own herbal doctor, sells a concoction of 14 herbs that is, he claims, the Chinese cure for the common cold. In the mauka/Ewa corner of the plaza, at Phil Lau's **Royal Kitchen**, you'll find Honolulu's best baked *manapua*—baked dim sum stuffed with fresh *char siu* pork—for only 65 cents each. **Doong Kong Lau Hakka** is a good Chinese restaurant on the Ewa side of the plaza.

If you need a respite at this point in your Chinatown tour, head two blocks mauka of the Chinese Cultural Plaza on Maunakea Street, until you reach Vineyard Boulevard. **Foster Botanical Garden** is the last green space on the street, named for the grape vines that once flourished here. A five-acre public garden containing orchids, palms, native Hawaiian plants, and such unusual trees as baobab, kapok, and spice trees, this is a lovely oasis from the downtown hustle and bustle.

SMITH STREET

You can get another glimpse of the Chinatown of old on Smith Street, which runs one block Diamond Head of Maunakea Street. At **Ramsay Galleries & Café**, 1128 Smith Street, you can see the work of pen-and-ink artist Ramsay, a local patron of the arts who sketches historical Hawaiian buildings in her gallery in the 1923 Tan Sing Building. Head one block makai to see the work of Michael Malone, a pen-and-ink artist of a different type, at the **China Sea Tattoo Parlor**, 1033 Smith Street, founded in 1952. Malone still decorates sailors' arms, but the tattoo "Remember Pearl Harbor" is seldom requested now.

NUUANU AVENUE

Nuuanu Avenue, one block Diamond Head of Smith Street, has several art galleries as well. Walking mauka up Nuuanu from the corner of Hotel Street, you'll come to **Kramer and Associates**, 1128 Nuuanu Avenue, Suite DC-3. Aviation buffs will want to step in to see the firm's lobby, which is the fuselage of a 1944 Air Molokai DC-3 plane, complete with piped-in Frank Sinatra music and issues of 1944 *Life* magazines. At 1164 Nuuanu is the studio of **Pegge Hopper**, who paints colorful Polynesian women in the tradition of Madge Tennent. Other galleries along the avenue offer crafts and gifts (see Shops and Shopping, below).

You might end your tour of Chinatown at **O'Toole's Pub**, a matchbox-size Irish pub at 902 Nuuanu Avenue (makai of the galleries) that is often full of Australians. Just across Nuuanu Avenue from O'Toole's, at 2 Merchant Street, is **Murphy's Bar & Grill**, a sociable, glass-and-brass San Francisco–style bar that evolved out of the old Royal Saloon. Murphy's is especially popular in football season, because it shows Monday Night Football live (via satellite dish) on Monday afternoon, beating out the local television affiliate, which delays the telecast until evening.

WEST (EWA) OF DOWNTOWN

The neighborhoods of Iwilei and Kalihi lie to the west and northwest of downtown Honolulu, toward the airport and Pearl Harbor (covered in our Oahu Outside Honolulu chapter). While you wouldn't spend an afternoon wandering about these neighborhoods on foot, they have several attractions that could easily fill a day off the beach.

Iwilei

DOLE CANNERY SQUARE

In the old red-light district of Iwilei, Ewa of Chinatown, under the landmark Dole pineapple tower (slated to be dismantled in the near future) is Dole Cannery Square, an attraction that venerates the Hawaiian pineapple, which, now on the decline, was long the second-largest cash crop in the Islands. A 35-minute tour through the cannery, founded by James Dole in 1903, takes visitors to see the Ginaca device core and peel 98 pineapples a minute, then reduce the fruit to bite-sized pieces. The first marketable pineapple, the Smooth Cayenne, was imported to Hawaii from Jamaica in 1886 by Captain John Kidwell, an Englishman. The Spanish called it *piña* because of its resemblance to a pinecone, and the English name, pineapple, resulted. Take the Dole Pineapple Transit minibus from one of its dozen stops in Waikiki or head Ewa on North Hotel Street/Iwilei Road to reach the square.

GENTRY PACIFIC CENTER

Just across the street, at 560 North Nimitz Highway, the many-paned Gentry Pacific Center, the old pineapple-can factory, has been restored and converted by world-champion speedboat racer Tom Gentry into an assemblage of shops. A Continental restaurant, **Angelica's**, serves good, affordable food in a garden-like setting; Tel: 537-6619. Around the corner, at 322 Sumner Street, is the **Salvation Army Thrift Shop**, a likely source of old aloha shirts.

Kalihi

There are only two reasons to go to Kalihi (north of Iwilei): One is a fish market, the other is the Bishop Museum (officially called the Bernice Pauahi Bishop Museum). Take H-1 Ewa to exit 20A (the Likelike offramp) or ride the number 2 bus from Waikiki to the museum. If you are driving from Dole Cannery Square, go west on the Nimitz Highway, then north (mauka) on Waiakamilo Road, which becomes Houghtailing Street. The museum is on the left; look for the signs when you pass under H-1.

THE BISHOP MUSEUM

The forbidding, four-story cut-stone structure, which looks like something out of a Charles Addams cartoon, houses the premier collection of things Hawaiian and things Pacific. The Bishop is stuffed with 20 million acquisitions (there are 12 million insect specimens alone), from ceremonial spears to calabashes to old photos of hula dancers. A bas-relief sea map of the Islands makes keen visual sense of the 1,500-mile-long archipelago that points like a crooked finger across the Pacific at Japan.

The Bishop Museum owes its existence to real-life Hawaiian princess Bernice Pauahi, who once owned 12 percent of Hawaii and collected Hawaiian artifacts now considered priceless. Her will instructed her husband, Charles Reed Bishop, to establish a Hawaiian museum "to enrich and delight," which it has done for nearly a century. A world-renowned center for South Pacific studies, the Bishop Museum is the home base of such legendary South Pacific archaeologists as Dr. Yosihiko Sinoto and the late Dr. Kenneth Emory, who explored more Oceanic real estate than Captain Cook; excavated the remains of "lost" civilizations in Huahine, one of the Society Islands; traced the history of Hawaii through its fishhooks; and helped restore Easter Island's fallen statues.

The museum has a comprehensive collection of Polynesian artifacts, including seashells, historic photos, and such relics as koa-wood bowls, nose flutes, and war clubs. (The Easter Island statue in the front yard is a replica.) A 50-foot sperm whale with a papier-mâché skin, mounted in 1901, soars overhead in the Great Hawaiian Hall, where the last little grass shack in Hawaii still stands. The *pili hale* (grass house) was built in the museum in 1902 using rafters and posts from a pili hale built before 1800 in Milolii Valley on Kauai. Local fire and safety codes now prohibit anyone in Hawaii from actually residing in a grass shack, although a number of popular tourist attractions, such as the Tahitian Lanai restaurant in Waikiki and the Waioli Tea Room in Manoa Valley, have thatched-grass decor.

A four-story exhibit hall called the Castle Memorial Building, which opened in 1990 on the makai side of the Great Hawaiian Hall, features travelling exhibitions designed to broaden Islanders' horizons. Recent exhibitions have featured wolves, dinosaurs, and outer space. Tel: 847-3511 for current offerings. The museum's copper-roofed, 100-seat planetarium and observatory offers a look at the Pacific skies at 11:00 A.M. and 2:00 P.M. daily and 7:00 P.M. Fridays and Saturdays. **Shop Pacifica**, in the museum's lobby, has souvenirs and a good selection of books on Hawaii.

BUYING SEAFOOD IN KALIHI

Also in the Kalihi neighborhood is **Tamashiro's Fish Market**, on the corner of North King and Palama streets. From the Bishop, drive makai on Kalihi Street to North King Street, then Diamond Head through Kalihi until you spot on the left a two-story, New Orleans–style building with a giant orange crab out front. Inside are more than 100 varieties of fresh local seafood—some still kicking—including such varieties of fish as *ahi, aku, mahimahi, au, ono, opakapaka;* shellfish such as live abalone from the Big Island's Keahole aquaculture farm, *opihi,* and geoducks; and live Kahuku prawns, eels, and even live Maine lobster flown from the Mainland. If you don't have facilities to cook, take out some *poke,* Hawaii's version of Tahiti's *poisson cru*—marinated fish, usually *ahi* (tuna), with *ugu* (seaweed) and sesame-seed oil. It's the perfect Hawaiian *pupu* (hors d'oeuvre) with a cold beer, sold singly at Tamashiro's.

NORTH (MAUKA) OF DOWNTOWN

Spend a day or two exploring the area north (mauka) of downtown Honolulu to see how well the state's largest city melds with its tropical surroundings. You can drive through a tropical rain forest, stand atop 1,000-foot-high cliffs, stop by the burial grounds of war heroes and island kings, visit a museum of contemporary art as well as the renowned East-West Center, and end with a hike through lush forest to a waterfall.

Nuuanu

Nuuanu is the area roughly mauka of downtown and the H-1 freeway between Punchbowl crater and Nuuanu Stream. The Pali Highway (Highway 61) will take you directly to the scenic Nuuanu Pali Lookout, but we suggest you stop at a couple of cultural attractions along the way.

UP THE PALI HIGHWAY

The whitewashed minarets of the **Honpa Hongwanji Hawaii Betsuin** rise up Diamond Head of the Pali Highway like something out of an Eastern fairy tale. Built in 1918 to commemorate the 700th anniversary of the Shin sect of Buddhism, this temple, combining Japanese and Indian architectural elements, is the sect's island headquarters.

Farther up the hill (take the Pali to the Wyllie Street exit and go left on Nuuanu Avenue), high on sacred ground above Honolulu stands the **Royal Mausoleum**, where six Hawaiian rulers are interred. The Gothic Revival mausoleum, built in 1863 in the shape of a Greek cross, was designed by Theodore Heuck, Honolulu's first architect. The Royal Mausoleum is one of the few places open on Kuhio Day, March 26; Kamehameha Day, June 11; and Memorial Day. Only the Kalakaua crypt is open to visitors. The royal remains are guarded by curator Lydia Namahana Maioho, a descendant of Kamehameha I who lives in a small house nearby.

THE PALI LOOKOUT

From the mausoleum get right back on Nuuanu Avenue and head for the Pali Highway. **Nuuanu Pali Drive**, off the Pali Highway, is a refreshing detour through tropical rain forest, under many-trunked banyan trees and giant bamboo. The drive takes you past old *kamaaina* (longtime residents') estates and the catfish-filled Nuuanu Reservoir and back again to the Pali Highway. The **Nuuanu Pali Lookout** is the next—and well-marked—exit. Many scenic lookouts don't live up to expectations, but the Nuuanu Pali Lookout (Nuuanu means "cool height," Pali means "cliff") really does—especially on windy days, when updrafts strike the Pali, those corrugated volcanic peaks separating Honolulu from Oahu's Windward side, and make waterfalls spray uphill. This is where Kamehameha the Great is said to have vanquished his enemies by driving them off the cliff in 1795. (See the Oahu Outside Honolulu chapter for more on the Pali Lookout.)

The Punchbowl Area

PUNCHBOWL
Overlooking (and mauka of) downtown Honolulu—and often confused with Diamond Head by first-time visitors—is the ironically named Punchbowl, a graveyard in a now-extinct volcano that was once used for human sacrifices. To get to the crater, take the Pali Highway exit off H-1, drive mauka to the first exit (less than half a mile), which brings you to the intersection of Booth and Pauoa roads, and follow signs to the National Memorial Cemetery. If you are coming from the Pali Lookout, take the Pali Highway makai to the Pauoa Road exit, continue to Booth Road, and follow the signs.

The graveyard in the crater's bowl, the **National Memorial Cemetery of the Pacific**, attracts more than six million visitors a year who come to pay respects to America's fallen war heroes. Almost 35,000, many of them casualties of three American wars in Asia and the Pacific, are buried here, as are such other heroes as World War II correspondent Ernie Pyle and Hawaiian astronaut Ellison Onizuka, a victim of the *Challenger* explosion. The 112-acre Punchbowl is an almost perfect bowl-shaped crater that has, after all these years, been used nearly to capacity.

MAKIKI HEIGHTS AND MOUNT TANTALUS
In the Makiki Heights neighborhood above Punchbowl crater—and just down the street from the late Philippine dictator Ferdinand Marcos's mansion-in-exile—stands the **Contemporary Museum**, 2411 Makiki Heights Drive, which houses a collection of art from the last 40 years, including works by Andy Warhol, David Hockney, George

Rickey, Tony Berlant, and Robert Graham. The museum is on a three-acre hillside estate with landscaped gardens and a panoramic view of Honolulu. It has a small café that serves tea and sandwiches.

To get to the Contemporary Museum from Waikiki, exit the H-1 freeway at Punahou Street, go mauka to Wilder Avenue, turn left, proceed to Makiki Street, turn right and follow it one block past Nehoa Street, then turn left on Makiki Heights Drive; the museum is about a mile farther, on the right. If you are driving from Punchbowl, turn right upon leaving the crater onto Puowaini Drive, which then becomes Tantalus Drive. After about three-quarters of a mile, turn right on Makiki Heights Drive; the museum will be on the left.

The Contemporary Museum puts you in a fine position for a drive up to **Mount Tantalus**: The drive skirts the Tantalus rain forest in the city's backyard and winds along ridge tops past multi-million-dollar estates and scenic outlooks with lovely views—especially at sunset and later, when the city lights come on. From the museum, go mauka on Makiki Heights Drive, then go right on Tantalus Drive, and head up the mountain. Once you've reached the top and started down the eastern (Diamond Head) side of Mount Tantalus, Tantalus Drive becomes Round Top Drive and eventually leads back to Makiki Street.

Manoa

Manoa, a neighborhood of early *haole* houses, sits in the misty, canyonlike valley of the same name, Diamond Head of Makiki Heights, about 2 miles (3 km) from Waikiki and about 5 miles (8 km) from downtown Honolulu by way of University Avenue (also an H-1 freeway exit).

UNIVERSITY OF HAWAII

You probably didn't come to Hawaii to go to college, and the odd lot of architecture on the campus of the University of Hawaii, at Dole Street and University Avenue, is hardly worth seeing ("A lot of bad architecture by a lot of good architects," one Honolulu architect has said), but the campus itself, set in the misty Manoa Valley, often streaked by rainbows, *is* worth visiting. The view of Waikiki and Diamond Head from the parking garage (or "structure," as it's known here) alone is almost worth the trip.

The renowned **East-West Center**, founded in 1960 to promote transpacific understanding, adjoins the campus on East-West Road, on the Diamond Head side of the campus. Architecturally it surpasses the university; it was designed by I. M. Pei. The East-West Center's public reading room has exhibits of Pacific Rim artwork as well as Asian newspapers and magazines. The center also hosts public events; recent highlights have included the Art of Bali, India's Anjani Ambegaokar Kathak dance troupe, and koto recitals by Tadao and Kazue Sawai of the Sawai koto school in Tokyo. Ask at the front desk for the schedule; Tel: 944-7111.

PARADISE PARK AND MANOA FALLS

On up University Avenue and Manoa Road, past bungalows built by early *haole* settlers, the road ends at **Paradise Park**, a lovely botanical garden and park featuring such kid stuff as an exhibit of life-like mechanical dinosaurs. Just beyond Paradise Park, at 3680 Manoa Road, is the more grown-up **Lyon Arboretum**, 124 acres of rain forest with some 4,100 species of tropical plants, more than half of which are native to Hawaii. Past Lyon Arboretum you'll find the trail head to **Manoa Falls**, a popular hike. It's about an hour's walk 800 feet up a muddy trail past wild guava and natural pools to the falls in their lush green setting. Go on a weekday to avoid crowds—and be sure to bring along mosquito repellent.

EAST (DIAMOND HEAD) OF DOWNTOWN

East of downtown Honolulu a number of the neighborhoods surrounding Waikiki have become virtual extensions of that quarter, and are thus heavily visited. Other areas in this part of the city are relatively untrod. Kakaako and Ala Moana, the neighborhoods wedged between Waikiki and downtown, are cases in point. Ala Moana, within easy access of Waikiki, has a gigantic shopping mall and a beach park that draw hordes of people. Kakaako, an old waterfront district, is the last low-rent district of Honolulu and, although rapidly gentrifying, stubbornly retains its salty character.

Kakaako

As tin-roof shanties topple in Honolulu's new wave of urban redevelopment to make way for a thicket of

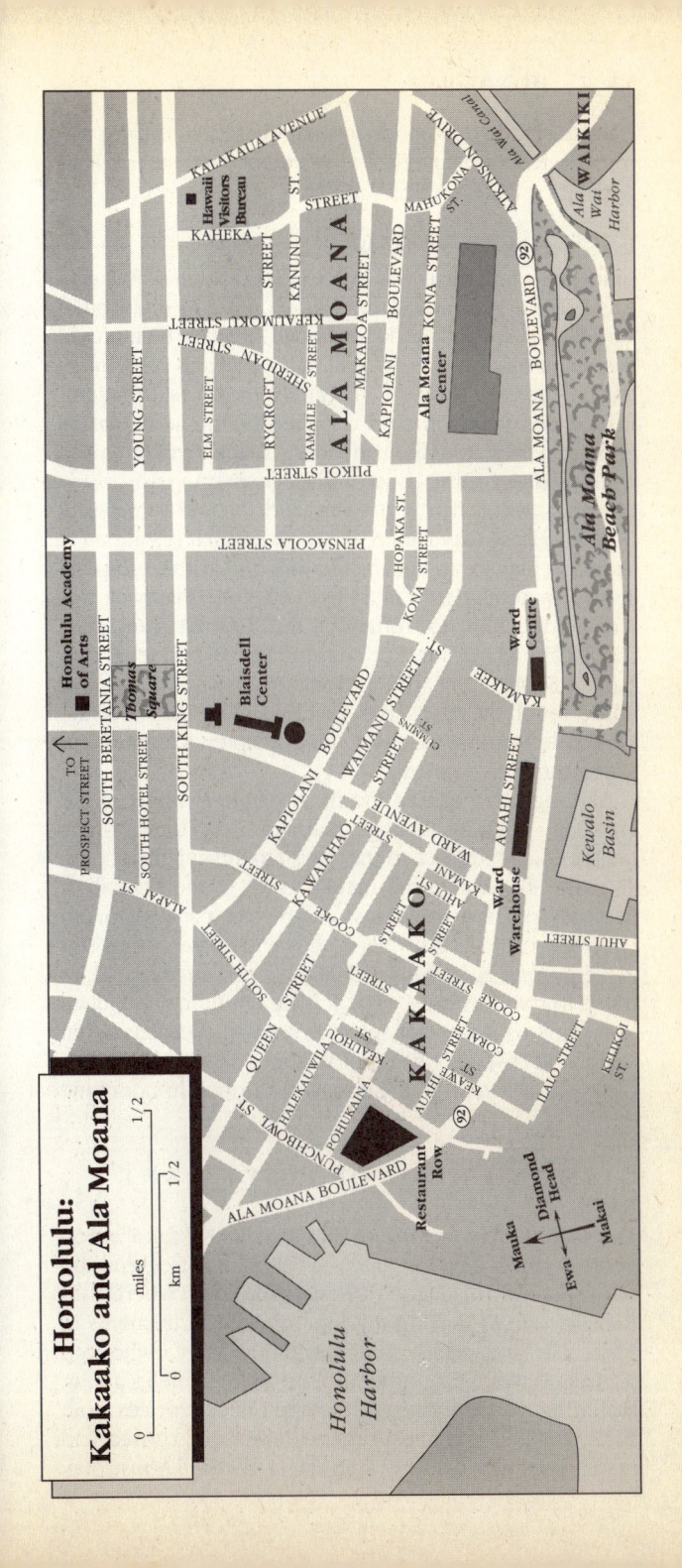

Honolulu: Kakaako and Ala Moana

multistoried luxury condo towers, the old waterfront district of Kakaako, the last undeveloped chunk of land between downtown and Waikiki, is fast disappearing.

RESTAURANT ROW

Among the first casualties of the gentrification of Kakaako was the old Honolulu Iron Works on Ala Moana Boulevard between South and Punchbowl streets, which reconstituted itself as a vertical mall of 13 bars and restaurants and 11 specialty shops in a complex known as Restaurant Row. Here you will find a collection of moderate to expensive restaurants, from **Rex's Black Orchid** to the smoky **Sunset Grill**, a see-and-be-seen L.A.–style bistro offering grilled fish and meat, and the 1950s-inspired, doo-wop **Rose City Diner**. The most popular restaurant is **Trattoria Manzo**, an Italian sidewalk café, with fresh pasta served by black-tied waiters who offer the snappiest service on the Row. Customers at the **Row Bar** can order food from any of the Row restaurants by phone. A taco bar, **La Salsa**, is big with aficionados of *tacos al carbón*, while **Touch the East** serves sushi at a glossy bar. (See the Honolulu section of our Dining chapter for more on Restaurant Row's offerings.)

Although it is one of the most visible symbols of the changes sweeping through Kakaako, Restaurant Row is probably a good place to start a visit to the neighborhood. Take the elevator in the mauka tower to the skymall (a favorite spot for weddings and private parties) for an overview of Kakaako, where body-and-fender shops still jostle Korean girlie bars and take-out restaurants, such as those in the decrepit Caesar J. Lopez Building, at Queen and Cooke streets, that serve teriyaki chicken, macaroni salad, and "two scoops rice," wrapped in foil on a paper plate, for less than four bucks—*the* Honolulu noontime treat.

DIAMOND HEAD OF RESTAURANT ROW

The last ukulele factory in Hawaii is in Kakaako at 550 South Street, mauka of Queen Street (South Street runs up the Diamond Head side of Restaurant Row), where Sam Kamaka started making the four-stringed instruments in 1916. His sons, Sam Junior and Frederick, who run **Kamaka Hawaii, Inc.**, now turn out 5,000 ukuleles a year, including the rare pineapple-shaped uke, at prices from $150 to $500. Their instruments have been owned and played by Arthur Godfrey, Hilo Hattie, and Neil Armstrong, who placed his order from outer space and picked it up in person after splashing down in the Pacific and coming ashore from the pick-up ship in 1969. Brought to Hawaii in the late 1800s from the island of Madeira by Portuguese, the ukulele caught the ear of King Kalakaua, the Merrie Monarch, and became an Island favorite. The word *ukulele* is Hawaiian for "jumping flea," as in nimble fingers on the strings.

A few blocks Diamond Head, at 831 Queen Street, stop by the **Lion's Coffee** roasting house for a cappuccino made with fresh-roasted Kona coffee and take home a sampler of Hawaii's own at the lowest prices in the Islands. You might want to head makai a couple of blocks (down Cooke Street) to 753B Halekauwila Street, a historic spot on which former New Yorker Stephen Gelson baked the first bagel in the Pacific and opened the **Hawaiian Bagel, Inc.** Gelson, who imported the bagel maker from the Big Apple, still sells his bagels—the onion are to die for—at 40 cents each. (Now there's even a bagel shop on Maui—that's progress.)

At 1112 Auahi Street, toward the waterfront, is a clothing shop for those weary of mundane mall offerings, the **Ultimate You**, the self-proclaimed "Bergdorf Goodman of consignment shops." This is one of those discount stores that sells designer castoffs of the rich and famous for ten cents on the dollar, so the inventory changes constantly but is always worth a look.

THE WATERFRONT AREA

Kakaako's waterfront still bustles with life as fishing boats head out to sea here, returning later with their catch. Savvy anglers seek out **K. Kida Fishing Supplies**, 212 Kamani Street (near Auahi Street), where trophy-winning *ono* and *ahi* hang on the wall and exotic lures like eels, frogs, and hula-skirted psychedelics are snapped up by resident and visitor fishermen alike. Pick up K. Kida's annual Hawaiian Tide Calendar and the latest issue of *Hawaiian Fishing News,* and head across the street to Fisherman's Wharf at **Kewalo Basin**, from which depart some two dozen different fishing excursions. **Captain Dudley Worthy** goes out daily on his 50-foot luxury trawler, the *Kahuna Kai,* to catch marlin, mahimahi, ahi, ono, and aku in the Molokai Channel, a 26-mile stretch of ocean separating Oahu's south shore from Molokai's north shore. This popular captain lets you keep your catch of the day (other captains sell your catch), and there's nothing finer than a freshly caught mahimahi grilled in butter, garlic, and wine by your hotel chef. Reservations with Captain Worthy recommended; Tel: 235-6236. Rates are $400 for a half day, $500 for a full day (if you can gather half a dozen people it's quite affordable).

Ewa of Kewalo Basin, at the end of Ahui Street, is **Kakaako Waterfront Park**, which opened in 1993. A large, rolling, grassy expanse right on the water, it's a lovely spot for a picnic at sunset.

WARD CENTRE AND WARD WAREHOUSE

On Ala Moana Boulevard, makai of Auahi Street, the two barn-sized structures that look like the packing crates the Ala Moana Center (see below) came in are **Ward Centre** and **Ward Warehouse**, informal specialty-shopping and restaurant clusters. At Ward Centre, Sandee Garcia's **Mocha Java** is a European-style coffee bar that everyone in Honolulu seems to walk past or drop into—for a cup of Hawaii's own Maui Mocha Java with a fresh pastry and the morning paper. Ward Centre also distinguishes itself with the nouvelle California–cuisine restaurant **Fresco** and **Andrew's Italian Restaurant**, which spotlights Mahi Beàmer singing real Hawaiian songs in the pitch-black piano bar while waiters in black tie serve a nice, garlicky Caesar salad and good, cheesy cannellone. At Ward Warehouse, **Dynasty II** is a very good Chinese restaurant (but Dynasty I, in the Dynasty Hotel in Waikiki, is also very good and is cheaper).

Ala Moana

ALA MOANA CENTER

A favorite pastime in Hawaii is people-watching, and one of the best places to do it is the Ala Moana Center, a 180-shop, tri-level mall at the gateway to Waikiki near the eastern end of Ala Moana Boulevard, Diamond Head of Kakaako and Ward Centre. Ala Moana Center claims to attract 56 million people a year (more than Disneyland) and has become a shopper's paradise—not the typical Waikiki tee-shirts and tiki gods mall. New shops include Charles Jourdan, Waterford/Wedgwood, Christian Dior, Jaeger, Adrienne Vittadini, Georg Jensen, Royal Copenhagen, Chanel, Gucci, and Bruno Magli. The first Emporio Armani in the United States outside New York City opened here a couple of years ago.

Everybody's favorite attraction at the center is **Makai**

Market Food Court, an assemblage of 20 fast-food restaurants under one roof, on the center's makai side. Don't look for the Kentucky colonel here; this is fast food Hawaii style: inexpensive ethnic foods such as *manapua, kim chee, poke, lumpia,* Japanese *soba* noodles, Thai *sateh,* and Hawaii's own shave ice.

Saimin, a restorative, uniquely Hawaiian soup of uncertain ethnic derivation, made with noodles, sliced green onion, and usually Spam in a clear broth, can be readily found in Ala Moana. The saimin at **Chicken Alice's,** on Kapiolani Boulevard near Keeaumoku Street (mauka of Ala Moana Center), is *ono*—delicious—and an excellent hangover cure.

ALA MOANA BEACH PARK

Directly across the boulevard from Ala Moana Center is Ala Moana Beach Park, a 118-acre beach park popular with Island families and visitors alike. The beach isn't the sole attraction here; there are ten tennis courts, three softball fields, a bowling green, facilities for kayak and canoe paddling, walking and jogging paths, picnic areas with barbecue grills, and a large peninsula called Magic Island—good fun in the busy city, away from the Waikiki hotel zone.

SHOPS AND BARS IN ALA MOANA

A couple of other worthwhile stops in the Ala Moana neighborhood include **Jelly's Comics and Books,** at 835 Keeaumoku Street, a used-books and -records shop, and **Asian Food Trading Co.,** between Keeaumoku and Piikoi streets on South Beretania Street, Honolulu's only complete Asian grocery, with Thai, Malay, Singaporean, and Indonesian spices and unidentified dried objects, including crack seed, a local Chinese treat (it's really dried fruit).

Avoid the string of sleazy nightclubs on Keeaumoku Street, between Ala/Moana Center and H-1. These so-called Korean bars, with names like Crystal Palace and Butterfly Lounge, offer "free pupus and exotic dancers" to entice the unwary, who are soon parted from their cash by skilled hustlers.

WAIKIKI

The Oahu coast covers 112 miles, elbowroom enough to surf, snorkel, and sunbathe, but it is Waikiki's thin cres-

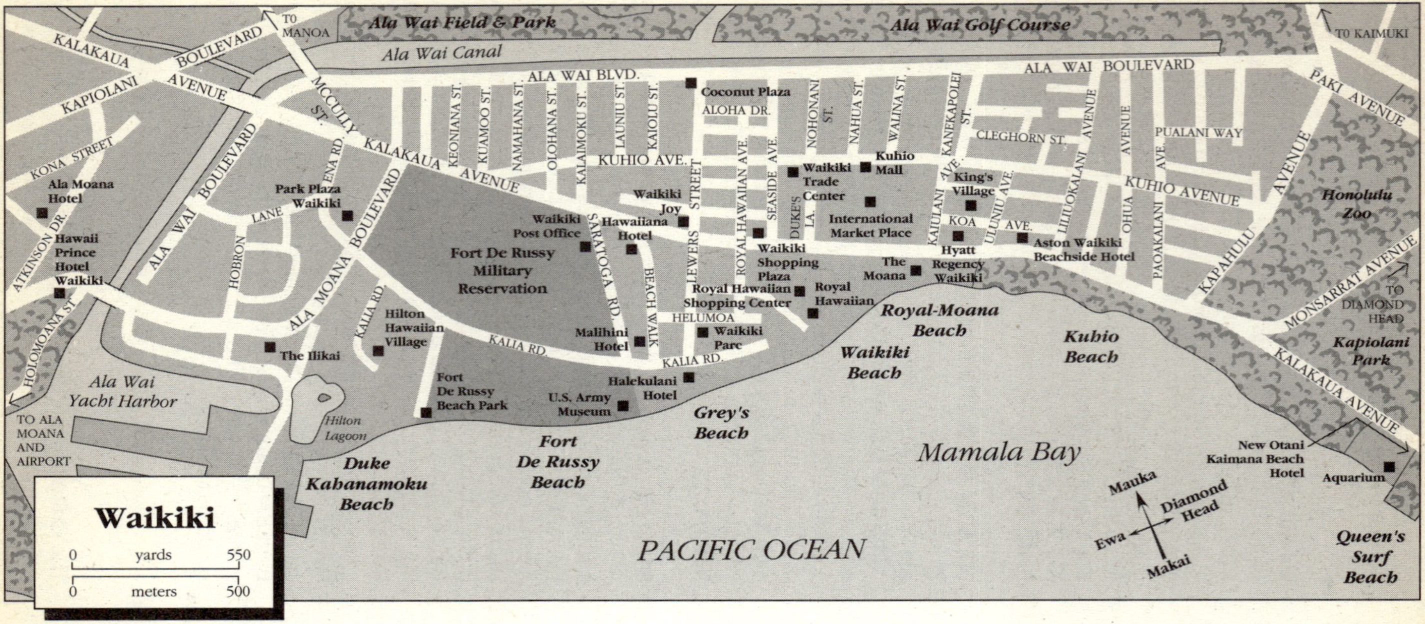

Waikiki
0 yards 550
0 meters 500
Ala Wai Field & Park
Ala Wai Golf Course
Ala Wai Canal
TO MANOA
TO KAIMUKI
KALAKAUA BOULEVARD
KAPIOLANI AVENUE
ALA WAI BLVD.
ALA WAI BOULEVARD
MCCULLY ST.
KALAKAUA AVENUE
PAKI AVENUE
KONA STREET
ATKINSON DR.
HOLOMOANA ST.
ALA WAI BOULEVARD
ENA RD.
LANE
HOBRON
ALA MOANA BOULEVARD
KALIA RD.
KEONIANA ST.
KUAMOO ST.
NAMAHANA ST.
OLOHANA ST.
KALAIMOKU ST.
LAUNIU ST.
KAIOLU ST.
KUHIO AVE.
SARATOGA RD.
BEACH WALK
LEWERS STREET
HELUMOA
ROYAL HAWAIIAN AVE.
SEASIDE AVE.
DUKE'S LA.
ALOHA DR.
NOHONANI ST.
NAHUA ST.
WALINA ST.
KANEKAPOLEI ST.
KAIULANI AVE.
KOA AVE.
ULUNIU AVE.
CLEGHORN ST.
LILIUOKALANI AVENUE
OHUA AVENUE
PAOAKALANI AVE.
PUALANI WAY
KUHIO AVENUE
KAPAHULU AVENUE
MONSARRAT AVENUE
KALAKAUA AVENUE
TO DIAMOND HEAD
Coconut Plaza
Ala Moana Hotel
Hawaii Prince Hotel Waikiki
Park Plaza Waikiki
The Ilikai
Hilton Hawaiian Village
Fort De Russy Beach Park
Fort De Russy Military Reservation
Waikiki Post Office
Hawaiiana Hotel
Waikiki Joy
Malihini Hotel
Waikiki Parc
Halekulani Hotel
U.S. Army Museum
Waikiki Trade Center
Kuhio Mall
International Market Place
Waikiki Shopping Plaza
Royal Hawaiian Shopping Center
Royal Hawaiian
The Moana
King's Village
Hyatt Regency Waikiki
Aston Waikiki Beachside Hotel
Honolulu Zoo
Kapiolani Park
New Otani Kaimana Beach Hotel
Aquarium
Ala Wai Yacht Harbor
TO ALA MOANA AND AIRPORT
Hilton Lagoon
Duke Kahanamoku Beach
Fort De Russy Beach
Grey's Beach
Waikiki Beach
Royal-Moana Beach
Kubio Beach
Mamala Bay
PACIFIC OCEAN
Queen's Surf Beach
Mauka
Diamond Head
Ewa
Makai

cent of white sand, right on the Pacific doorstep of scores of high-rise hotels, that attracts the masses.

This two-mile-long urban beach is the magnet for nearly seven million annual sun-absorbing guests, who come to attend the never-ending beach party that begins each sunrise when surfers catch the day's first wave and doesn't end until just before sunset, when "beach bums" sweep the beach with metal detectors in search of lost coins and jewelry, followed by raking machines that comb out all the litter.

Waikiki is a peninsula bordered on the north and west by the Ala Wai Canal, which doglegs makai (seaward) and runs out to sea at the Ala Wai Yacht Harbor. Downtown Honolulu lies to the west and Diamond Head volcano, perhaps Hawaii's best-known landmark, rises to the east. Waikiki Beach and the neighboring Queen Kapiolani Beach Park provide Waikiki with splendid outdoor space, while the hotels, restaurants, and shops inland—many found along the main drag, Kalakaua Avenue—offer plenty of indoor entertainment.

At Waikiki, ancient kings worshiped the sun, played in the surf, and generally set the tone for what would go on here for years to come: having a good time, all the time. The seat of power for King Kahuhihewa in the 1500s, Waikiki was sparsely inhabited swampland before the hotels began to go up around the turn of the 20th century. By the 1920s Waikiki's potential as a resort was foreseen, and development began in earnest. The original planners wanted to make Waikiki into an island but they ran out of money and the district remains tied to land. Although it seems to be wall to wall hotels, Waikiki is not strictly a tourist quarter and is home to some 20,000 permanent residents.

Waikiki's fun zone may never develop the "fashionable urban resort" image those Honolulu burghers yearned for in the 1920s, but Waikiki is what it is: a dynamic cross section of the world at the beach. While some may grumble about the good old days, Waikiki's hip gaudiness only contributes to its festive airs.

ARRIVING IN WAIKIKI

Hire a taxi at Honolulu International Airport and head for Waikiki (about $18). (You'll need a car only for day trips on the island of Oahu, and parking in Waikiki is a hassle even if your hotel validates. You can rent a car from one of the agencies near your hotel when you are ready to venture out.) When you first arrive, tell the cab driver to cruise Kalakaua Avenue, which goes one-way Diamond Head (east). You will wonder what all the fuss is about as you traverse this canyon of high-rises that blocks all beach views—until you clear the newly restored Moana hotel and the last surfboard racks. Then look right and catch that first dazzling view of the sunlit Pacific with its bright shades of jade green, deep blue, and turquoise. The sweet scent is coconut oil wafting off the basting bodies on Kuhio Beach, that great open strand on the Diamond Head side of the Moana.

Check into your hotel, hit the beach, and take the plunge. Go anytime day or night and the water will be warm (average: 77 degrees Fahrenheit) and wonderful, the best cure for jet lag. In the morning, go early to stake out a spot; on any day there are about 16,000 people on the beach at Waikiki, according to lifeguards' head counts.

Waikiki Beach

Waikiki Beach consists largely of a splendid collection of prone, semi-naked bodies that covers nearly every square inch of sand until sundown, then vanishes. When it rains, it's hell: traffic piles up; people get cabin fever; and tempers get short. Some big hotels, the Halekulani, for example, give out rain checks good for free drinks to keep guests mellow at such times. Not to worry, almost every day is perfect year round—temperatures in the low 80s, light and variable trade winds, average relative humidity 66 percent, and water temperatures in the mid-70s, except on August afternoons, when they can hit 82 degrees.

THE BEACHES

Waikiki Beach is actually a string of beaches on Oahu's Mamala Bay, which extends from Diamond Head west to Barbers Point, on the other side of Pearl Harbor. **Royal-Moana Beach** is "action central" on Waikiki Beach, where the beautiful bodies go to see and be seen—no elbow-room here. Inside the rope are Royal Hawaiian hotel guests, outside are not, but the sun strikes all with equanimity. This beach, stretching from the Royal Hawaiian hotel to the Moana, is perfectly sited for viewing the graceful seacoast curve to Diamond Head and all the beach action. The late afternoon sun is better here than at other beaches to the east.

Diamond Head of Royal-Moana Beach is **Kuhio Beach**.

Hawaii's most famous beachboy, Duke Paoa Kahanamoku, cast in bronze, appears to have just come out of the water here, carrying his long, old-fashioned surf board. Sculpted by Jan Fisher and erected in 1990, the statue celebrates the local hero and Olympic swimmer who travelled the world. The four huge stones implanted in the sand near Duke's statue are known as the "**wizard stones**" (also as the Kapaemahu stones). They are said to have been brought here in the 14th century by Tahitian priests, and were believed to have healing powers. Now they are irreverently used for drying wet beach towels, although more sensitive souls who trust in the *mana* (power) of the wizards still place bright flower leis on the stones in respect.

If all the men look too good to be true and they're lounging around in Band-Aid-size *cache-sexe,* you've probably just found **Queen's Surf Beach**, east of Kuhio. It is so called because royal ladies used to take the waters here. Now it's a gay hangout—though you'll be perfectly comfortable here if you're not gay.

Away from the crowd, **Sans Souci**, a quiet strip of fine sand on gentle water, is also known as "Dig Me Beach" because of all the young things in skimpy suits. The beach is out near the eastern end of Kalakaua Avenue, past Queen's Surf, in the front yard of the New Otani Kaimana Beach Hotel and near the Natatorium War Memorial (once the biggest saltwater pool in the United States, now a ruin).

SURFING AT WAIKIKI

Waikiki is, first and last, a great surfing beach. The perfect surf that rolls ashore has been ridden since at least the 1500s, when, according to Hawaiian chants, chiefs held *hee nalu* (wave sliding) contests and bet on the outcome. Surfing is how Waikiki really got its start; it was happening when Captain Cook first cruised around Diamond Head, and it seemed to be even more popular 100 years later when the straitlaced missionaries arrived—and tried to stop it as a frivolous pastime involving seminudity and having a sexual connotation.

"The appearance of destitution, degradation, and barbarism, among the chattering and almost naked savages, whose heads and feet and much of their sunburnt skins were bare, was appalling," wrote the missionary leader Hiram Bingham in 1820, upon seeing Hawaiians on surfboards. "Some of our number, with gushing tears, turned away from the spectacle. Others, with firmer nerve, continued their gaze, but were ready to exclaim, 'Can these be human beings?'"

Ancient Hawaiians regarded surfing as vital to their social and spiritual life, in fact, something of a courtship ritual, and they carved that message in stone above Kaunolu Bay on Lanai, where the petroglyph of a tandem surfer may still be seen.

Old-time beachboys such as Duke Kahanamoku, Splash Lyons, Fat Kala, and Panama Dave are gone, and the legendary "golden man," Kelly Kanakoa, existed only in James Michener's best seller *Hawaii,* but the tradition continues. Rabbit Kekai and his brother Jammer, Uncle Gabby, Cowboy, and Mr. Ah Choy still give surfing lessons to *malahini.* They work out of the **Star Beachboys** kiosk on Kuhio Beach. The oldest and best of the beach kiosks, Star Beachboys is also the place to book a ride on an outrigger canoe.

Once you're up on a long board, veteran surf photographer Bobby Achoy, who shoots while surfing, will snap the classic shot of you surfing the "beeg wahns" at Waikiki with your choice of Diamond Head or the Royal Hawaiian in the background. It's eight dollars for two shots. He's on Kuhio Beach between 8:00 A.M. and 11:00 A.M. daily.

Offshore, the surfing lanes all bear colorful, self-explanatory names, according to use, coastal landmarks, or what's underwater. There are Canoes, the Wall, and Rock Pile (there's also Shark's Hole, near Point Panic at Kewalo Basin on the Honolulu side of Ala Moana Park). Good for beginners are Paradise or Canoes, just off the Pink Lady (the Royal Hawaiian Hotel).

It's always perfect surf at Waikiki in the summertime, when the south swells run and the trades blow offshore against the waves to lift their faces and send spindrift trailing behind the crest. Of Oahu's 594 surfing sites, all things considered, Waikiki is the ideal place to experience what devotees call "the ultimate pleasure."

Shopping for Surfboards

The best surfboard shop in Hawaii is like the perfect aloha shirt—always being sought—but **Wave Rider Hawaii**, at 214 Sand Island Access Road, Bay G, is where locals go for new and used boards and to "talk story" about their rides. You can rent surfboards at Kuhio Beach or at **Seaction Surfco**, 1735 Kalakaua Avenue (just outside of Waikiki), which buys, sells, and rents boards; **Titou's Surf City**, 419 Nahua Street, north of Kuhio Avenue in central Waikiki, the

Waikiki specialist in used boards; or at **Local Motion**, the tin-roofed shop with the teeny bikinis in the window at 1714 Kapiolani Boulevard (outside of Waikiki, just one block Ewa of Kalakaua Avenue).

QUEEN KAPIOLANI BEACH PARK

On the Diamond Head side of Kapahulu Avenue, stretching southeast from the edge of Waikiki, is **Kapiolani Park**, donated by King Kalakaua to the people of Hawaii in 1877. This green open space is 200 acres of high-energy, seaside fun, where there's always something going on—a luau, soccer matches, stunt kite-flying, juggling, and running races (the finish line of the Honolulu Marathon, held in December, is in the park), while flocks of pigeons wheel above it all. The eastern stretch of Waikiki Beach—including Queen's Surf and Sans Souci—is right across the street.

A great grassy plain, the park is ideal for those who love the beach but don't like sand. There are lovely gardens, as well as the charming habitat-type **Honolulu Zoo** with free-roaming animals and birds and the **Waikiki Aquarium**, which houses more than 250 marine species, most of which are native to Hawaii, including two rare Hawaiian monk seals and a chambered nautilus.

The park's **Waikiki Shell** (covered in Nightlife and Entertainment, below) is an outdoor concert stage that also hosts the **Kodak Hula Show**, Hawaii's longest-running song-and-dance act, now celebrating its 55th year. The free show, at 10:00 A.M. every Tuesday, Wednesday, and Thursday, features family-style entertainment by ukulele-playing hula dancers of the Royal Hawaiian Girls Glee Club.

Waikiki off the Beach

There's almost too much to see and do in this tourist quarter, cut off from the rest of Honolulu by the **Ala Wai Canal**. Ala Wai means "freshwater way," and that's what the three-mile-long canal is, built in the 1920s to drain Waikiki's swamp. The canal, which once harbored Honolulu's fishing fleet, is now used for training by outrigger canoe clubs—and serves as a sort of moat for Waikiki. On the mauka banks, the 18-hole municipal **Ala Wai Golf Course** is the nation's busiest, with more than 600 players daily. Make reservations a week in advance by calling at 6:30 A.M.; Tel: 296-4653. Good luck. (See the Golf Courses section at the end of the Oahu Outside of Honolulu chapter for more on golfing on the island.)

Ala Wai Boulevard runs along the Waikiki side of the canal. Parallel to it is **Kuhio Avenue**, the mid-Waikiki thoroughfare. Kuhio Avenue is home to many less-than-posh accommodations and restaurants. And more or less parallel to Kuhio to the south is the center of it all, the main drag, Kalakaua Avenue.

KALAKAUA AVENUE

Named for Hawaii's Merrie Monarch, who ruled like a party host from 1874 to 1891, Kalakaua Avenue is by day an eastbound, one-way traffic jam intersected by beach-bound pedestrians in various stages of undress, with rolled-up straw mats under their arms, seeking their place in the sun. It's a street of shops, where fast-food joints and tacky souvenir shops stand chockablock with French designer boutiques and parfumeries.

Not everyone likes Waikiki. Some locals brag that they haven't been on Kalakaua Avenue in years, but they are due for another look. The Kalakaua neighborhood sports a new international face today, the result of an extensive face-lift that introduced wide brick sidewalks, manicured palms, and Italianate streetlights. Pedicabs, daytime delivery vans, skateboards, and roller skates have been banned from the avenue.

The big, open space makai of Kalakaua Avenue between Ala Moana Boulevard and Saratoga Road is **Fort DeRussy**, a 70-acre armed forces recreation center. The chief attraction for civilians, besides a nice beach park, is the free **U.S. Army Museum**, which traces Hawaii's military history from sticks and stones to the nuclear age.

Peer in the windows of the **First Hawaiian Bank** at 2181 Kalakaua Avenue (at the corner of Lewers Street) to see the magnificent Jean Charlot murals that trace the lives of Hawaiians from precontact (i.e., before Captain Cook arrived in 1778) to the arrival of Boston missionaries in 1820. Paris-born Charlot painted in Mexico and California before coming to Hawaii in 1949; his murals grace many Honolulu buildings.

Two blocks Diamond Head on the mauka side of Kalakaua Avenue is the Art Deco **Waikiki Theater**, built in 1936 and site of the world premiere of the Bing Crosby movie *Waikiki Wedding*. If you go to the movies here, check out the theater's interior before the house lights dim: The arches of the stage feature life-size replicas of banana and palm trees, and the ceiling has movable clouds.

You don't have to leave Waikiki to see Hawaii's Neighbor Islands anymore. The **Hawaii IMAX Theater Waikiki**, 325 Seaside Avenue, just around the corner from the Waikiki Theater, has a 35-minute film called *Hawaii: Born in Paradise* that brings them alive on the five-story, 70-foot-wide IMAX screen. You'll "dive" 4,000 feet into the Pacific to Loihi, the submarine volcano bubbling to the surface, and "climb" Molokai's sea cliffs to save a rare plant, and experience other Island adventures. There are shows on the hour from 11:00 A.M. to 9:00 P.M. daily.

The **Hawaii Visitors Bureau** is located at 2270 Kalakaua Avenue (corner of Seaside). Stop by the seventh-floor information desks for pamphlets and guide booklets. The **International Market Place**, under a grove of banyan trees across Kalakaua Avenue from the Royal Hawaiian (one block Diamond Head of the Waikiki Theater), is a cluster of 50 shops run mostly by Koreans and Pacific Islanders who sell everything from wood carvings to pearls. A tree house in one old banyan served as the first home of KCCN radio, Honolulu's all-Hawaiian-music station, now celebrating its 25th anniversary.

EAST (DIAMOND HEAD) OF WAIKIKI

On the eastern side of Waikiki are the Kapahulu (funky shopping quarter) and Kaimuki (restaurants, covered in our Dining chapter) neighborhoods, to which locals and visitors alike find reason to go. Along the coast are Diamond Head volcano, the suburbs of eastern Honolulu, and finally the volcano in the sea, Hanauma Bay, and its neighbor, Koko Head.

Kapahulu and Kaimuki

KAPAHULU AVENUE
On the Diamond Head border of Waikiki, Kapahulu Avenue is a funky adjunct to Waikiki's neon glitz, a district of shops, restaurants, and bars that is fun to explore. A variety of retail merchandise displays itself here in typical, mile-long strip zoning, anchored by Hale Niu Formal Wear on one end and **Hee Hing**, where the lemon chicken isn't

what it used to be, on the other (at number 449). In between there's a bunch of good restaurants, such as **Irifune** (number 563), a serene Japanese restaurant with *joto miso;* and **Keo's Thai Cuisine** (number 625), an orchid-filled celebrity hangout where everyone from Elton John to Michael J. Fox has chopsticked through the *mee krob*. Of all the restaurants, only **Harpo's Pizza** (number 477), which delivers free to Waikiki, stays open after 10:00 P.M.

After dinner go to **Dave's Ice Cream** (819 Kapahulu Avenue) for two scoops of home-style mango, *lilikoi,* or *poha* ice cream, voted Hawaii's best in *Honolulu* magazine reader surveys. Along this avenue you may find one of those threadbare swimsuits you've seen on Waikiki Beach, or you can continue the search for the perfect aloha shirt at **Bailey's Antique and Thrift Shop** (758 Kapahulu Avenue), which claims to have the largest collection in town—imported mostly from California now that local closets have been depleted. Vintage silkies go for as much as $1,000 apiece.

KAIMUKI

Mauka of Kapahulu is Kaimuki, which has a restaurant district on Waialae Avenue between 11th and 12th avenues. In this one area are a chic pasta café, **Iroha Jaya**, which is the best Japanese *kaiseki* restaurant in Honolulu (across from the Kaimuki Public Library on Koko Head Avenue), a Mexican restaurant, a Chinese restaurant called Red Rooster Chop Sui, a nine-seat sushi bar, and a Vietnamese restaurant, as well as Thai, Italian, and Korean. Many Kaimuki restaurants are covered in the Honolulu section of our Dining chapter.

Diamond Head

Hawaii's most famous landmark calls to those who want the big view of Honolulu. Thousands have climbed to the crater's summit, a rite of passage like climbing Japan's Mount Fuji.

To get to the crater, drive east along Monsarrat Avenue and follow the signs, or take the number 8 bus from Waikiki to the entrance. A narrow, 90-year-old tunnel penetrates the crater wall, and across the wide flat valley the first set of 99 steps awaits you on the three-quarter-mile hike to the summit of the rim. Bring a flashlight for the tunnels.

This dormant (don't say extinct, you never know) volcano is twice named. Early Hawaiians called it Leahi (which means "brow of tuna"), because it resembles the tuna's profile, and British sailors, who thought they saw crystals sparkling on its steep flanks, called it Diamond Head. Because it is only 760 feet high at the south rim, this hike is for everyone; it takes less than an hour to reach the summit. The 360-degree view takes in all of Waikiki, downtown Honolulu in the middle distance, and the Waianae Mountains beyond, the jagged Koolau Range, its ridges and valleys dotted with houses, as well as miles and miles of the deep-blue Pacific.

East of Diamond Head

East of Kapiolani Park a real-people neighborhood appears as Kalakaua Avenue becomes Diamond Head Road and winds along the coast past **Diamond Head Beach Park** and the Diamond Head Lighthouse. A wide scenic turnoff on the high bluff here opens up a Pacific view and a real close-up of Diamond Head. You may also watch the windsurfers here smash waves head-on and go airborne.

Nearby is a bronze plaque honoring Amelia Earhart, the first woman to fly solo from Hawaii to the U.S. Mainland. Her 1935 flight from Honolulu to Oakland, California, took 12 hours and 50 minutes.

The panorama to the east takes in **Maunalua Bay** and Black Point, a small peninsula where rich people and celebrities have homes behind guarded gates. Koko Head, the remains of an ancient volcano, curves into the bay in the distance.

KAHALA

Just down Diamond Head's eastern slope lies the "gold coast" of Kahala, where Japanese speculators have luxed up an already ritzy neighborhood of multi-million-dollar seaside estates. This ultra-rich enclave (homes here sell for $20 million and up) has included such neighbors as Saudi Arabian arms dealer Adnan Khashoggi and the late Clare Boothe Luce.

On Kahala Avenue look for sand alleys between the mansions to gain access to the beach, but be prepared for disappointment—the beaches are thin and gnarly, the water shallow, and there are no waves. The beach at the end of Hunakai Street is as good as it gets in Kahala.

At the end of Kahala Avenue stands the **Kahala Hilton**

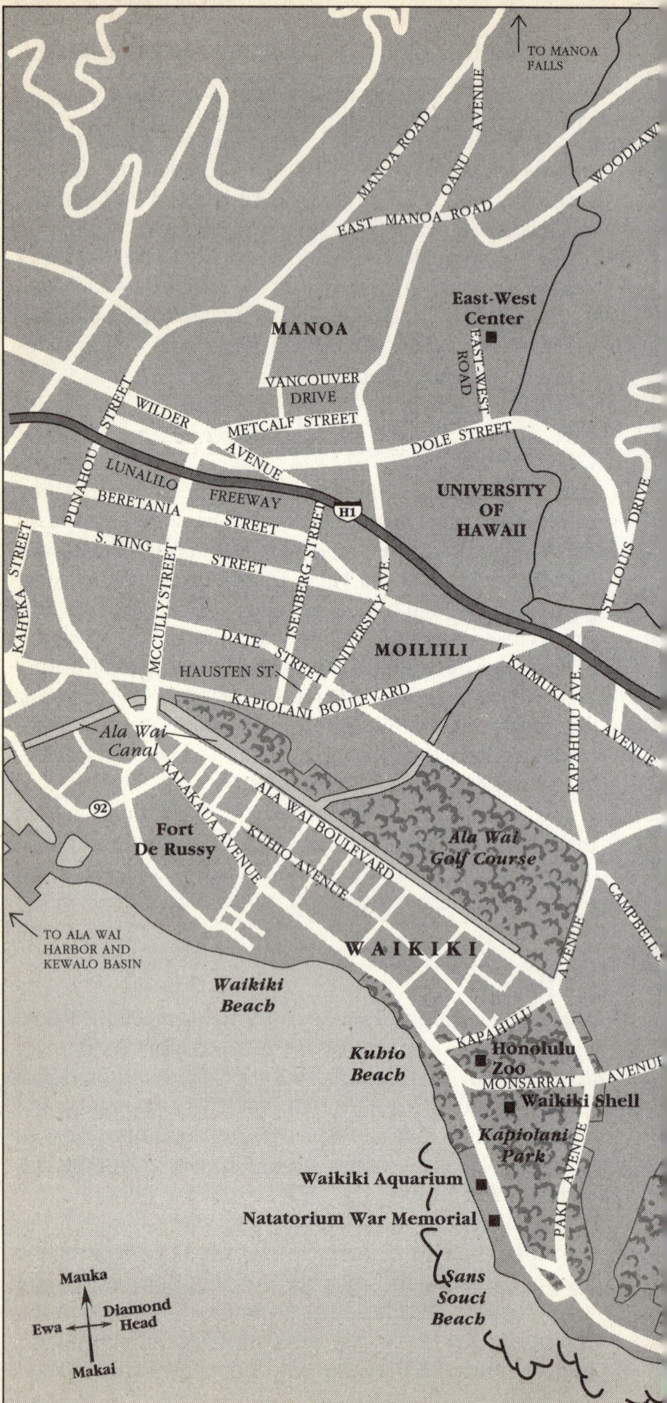
TO MANOA FALLS
MANOA ROAD
OAHU AVENUE
WOODLAWN
EAST MANOA ROAD
East-West Center
EAST-WEST ROAD
MANOA
VANCOUVER DRIVE
WILDER AVENUE
METCALF STREET
DOLE STREET
PUNAHOU STREET
LUNALILO FREEWAY
H1
BERETANIA STREET
UNIVERSITY OF HAWAII
S. KING STREET
KAHEKA STREET
MCCULLY STREET
ISENBERG STREET
UNIVERSITY AVE.
ST. LOUIS DRIVE
DATE STREET
MOILIILI
HAUSTEN ST.
KAIMUKI AVENUE
KAPIOLANI BOULEVARD
Ala Wai Canal
KAPAHULU AVE.
92
KALAKAUA AVENUE
ALA WAI BOULEVARD
Fort De Russy
KUHIO AVENUE
Ala Wai Golf Course
CAMPBELL
TO ALA WAI HARBOR AND KEWALO BASIN
WAIKIKI
Waikiki Beach
KAPAHULU
AVENUE
Kuhio Beach
Honolulu Zoo
MONSARRAT AVENUE
Waikiki Shell
Kapiolani Park
PAKI AVENUE
Waikiki Aquarium
Natatorium War Memorial
Sans Souci Beach
Mauka
Ewa
Diamond Head
Makai

Honolulu: Diamond Head and Waikiki

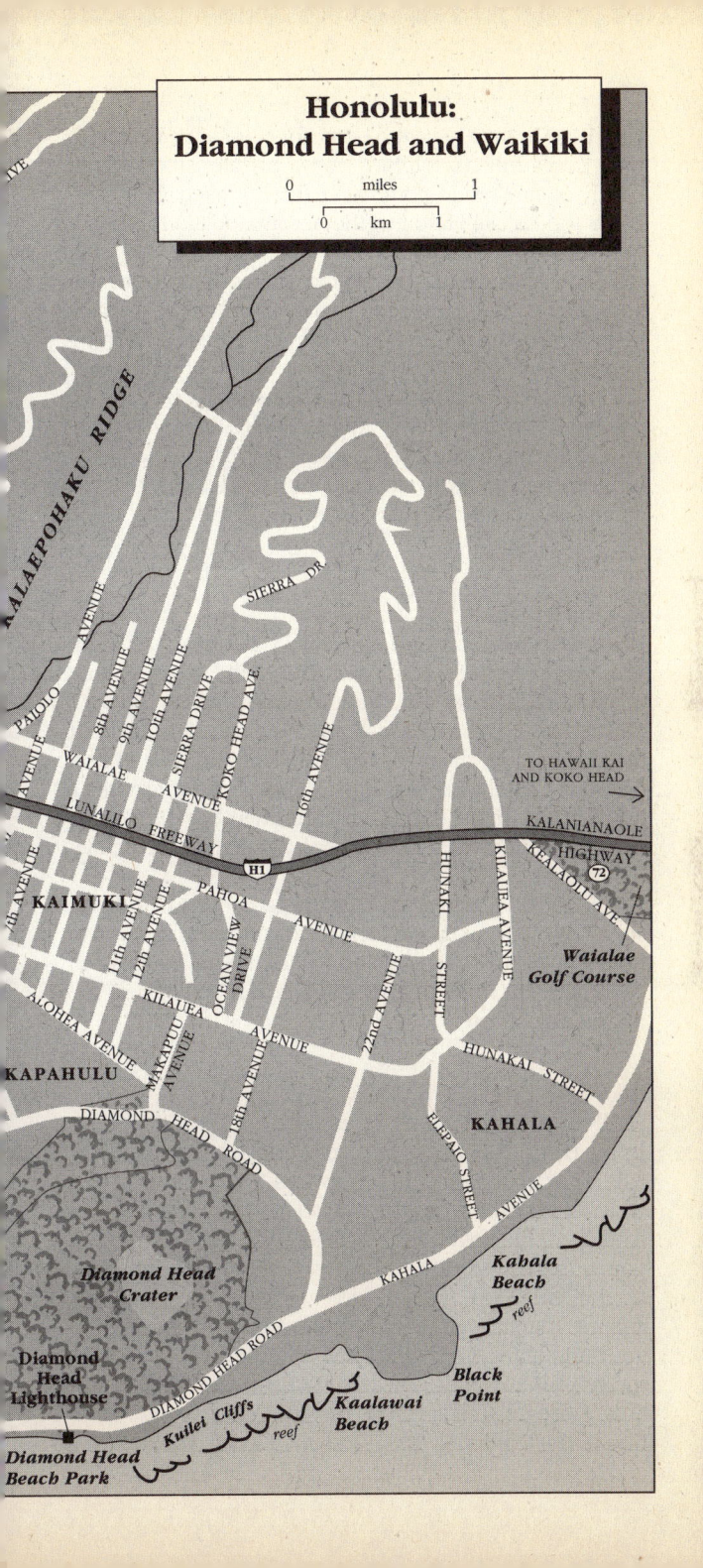

Hotel, the home away from home for presidents and kings, with pools full of dolphins and a private, silky-smooth beach of fine-grade coral sand that is raked daily. (We cover the Kahala Hilton in the Accommodations section, below.)

Inland from Kahala Avenue the homes diminish in size and value until they more resemble a suburban California neighborhood clustered around the Kahala Shopping Center, which offers valet parking at peak shopping times. This enclosed mall contains all the usual shops and two restaurants worth a visit: the **California Pizza Kitchen,** started by two former Los Angeles lawyers who concoct innovative pizzas with such toppings as Thai chicken and ginger, and **Yen King,** considered one of Honolulu's best Chinese restaurants.

HAWAII KAI

If you continue eastward on trafficky Kalanianaole Highway (Highway 72), you'll reach Honolulu's first commuter suburb, Hawaii Kai, built by industrialist Henry J. Kaiser. Kaiser came to Hawaii in 1954, at age 72, and built the 20-acre Hawaiian Village in Waikiki (now a Hilton property), ostensibly because he hadn't been able to get a hotel room on an earlier visit. He then developed this 6,000-acre subdivision on former swampland near Maunalua Bay.

Hawaii Kai's biggest draw is a restaurant named **Roy's,** after Roy Yamaguchi, the former Los Angeles chef whose nouvelle French-Asian cuisine has foodies raving coast to coast (Roy's is located in Hawaii Kai Corporate Plaza; see our Dining chapter).

EAST TO HANAUMA BAY

Past Hawaii Kai, Highway 72 leads up the slope of ancient **Koko Head,** and the suburban world of east Honolulu falls away as the land becomes arid and barren, spiked with an occasional cactus. Ahead, in the caldera of an extinct volcano whose side facing the sea has broken down, is one of Oahu's major attractions, **Hanauma Bay.** In this fishpond like no other, Hawaii's tropical fish abound but are outnumbered seven-to-one by visitors to the beach park and underwater park here. To help ease the crowds the park now bans tour buses from the bay. (For more on this area, see the Southeastern Coast section of the Oahu Outside Honolulu chapter, below.)

GETTING AROUND

Honolulu Airport

Honolulu International is one of the busiest jetports in the nation, yet one of the easiest to get around—big, clear, international graphics are the secret, and everyone here has "plenny aloha" for visitors. Arriving travellers may catch the free WikiWiki van to the baggage carousels on the street level, where taxis are available. Taxi is the best and fastest way to Waikiki and costs about $18 for the nearly 8-mile (13-km) trip. All the major car-rental agencies are on the airport's street level.

Driving in Honolulu

Honolulu is congested like any big city, but island drivers are different. They don't honk (because it is rude), they signal religiously with blinkers and hand signals, and most even let you merge without *huhu* (Hawaiian for fuss). Commuters crawl along bumper-to-bumper twice a day during rush hour, and traffic is always heavy in Waikiki.

Around in Waikiki

The ideal way to get around Waikiki is on foot. The popular pedicabs (and skateboards) are now restricted to the side streets of Waikiki, and traffic is too intense for bicycling with any comfort. There are more than a dozen moped rental agencies in Waikiki, all with competitive rates. The best deal can be found at Aloha Funway Rentals, at two locations in Waikiki: 2025 Kalakaua Avenue, and 408 Lewers Street, where you can rent one for half a day—which is plenty long enough for most people to scoot around in Waikiki's traffic.

Buses and Trolleys

Exploring Honolulu and Oahu is easy on **TheBus**, Honolulu's excellent municipal transit system, which will take you almost anywhere on the island for 60 cents, exact change. The most popular route is the number 8, which shuttles between Waikiki and Ala Moana and back about every ten minutes. TheBus goes to all the fun places, including Sea Life Park (number 57 and 58; see the Oahu Outside Honolulu chapter) and the Bishop Museum (number 2). There's also the daily Beach Bus (number 22) from Waikiki to Hanauma Bay, east near Koko Head. Every day of the week the Circle Island buses, number 52 (which goes clockwise) and number 55 (counterclockwise), go around the island, from Ala Moana Center and back; they take almost all day. The number 57 and 58 swing around the southeastern loop of Oahu via Kailua, Waimanalo, Sea Life Park, and Hawaii Kai. You can also catch TheBus (number 8) to Diamond Head crater.

The **Dole Pineapple Transit** minibus shuttles visitors to and from Dole Cannery Square. It leaves every five minutes from 12 Waikiki locations between 8:30 A.M. and 3:30 P.M., for 50 cents, and travels through downtown and Chinatown and on to Cannery Square.

Another way to get around Honolulu is the **Waikiki Trolley**, a motorized replica of a San Francisco cable car that loops out of Waikiki to a variety of destinations. The 34-passenger, open-air trolley goes on a 90-minute tour of historic sites, hotels, parks, and beaches. It runs from about 8:00 A.M. to 5:45 P.M. and follows part of the original route of Hawaii's turn-of-the-century streetcars. The route originates at the Royal Hawaiian Shopping Center and goes to the Hilton Hawaiian Village, then downtown along Bishop Street to Honolulu Harbor, on to Hilo Hattie's garment factory, and then Dole Pineapple's Cannery Square before returning to Waikiki via Chinatown and Ward Centre. Passengers may get on and off all day along the route to explore, eat lunch, shop, or go to the beach. The all-day fare is $15 for adults, $5 for children under 11. Tel: 526-0112.

—*Rick Carroll*

ACCOMMODATIONS

Oahu has 175 hotels and condos with 37,270 rooms—nearly all in Waikiki. Waikiki's landmark luxury hotels are on the beach, while the others are back between the sand and the Ala Wai Canal. Room rates vary in direct proportion to distance from the beach. The range of choices is vast. The one-bedroom Royal Suite at the Halekulani tops out at $3,500 a night. At the opposite end of the scale you might expect a room equipped with a can of Raid and directions to the beach. As you will see, our list below is *highly* selective.

Accommodations in Waikiki are changing, becoming luxurious and expensive. Many Waikiki hoteliers have upgraded their establishments, then bumped up rates, but new, small "boutique" hotels, such as the Waikiki Joy and the Waikiki Parc, offer affordable alternatives. And special little "finds" still exist on side streets. Nonetheless, the average daily room rate is about $100, plus Hawaii's 5 percent hotel tax and 4 percent sales tax. (We consider anything under $75 to be "inexpensive.")

Hoteliers used to define "high" season as that time between the first snowfall in New England and the first day of spring, but now that Japan, Canada, Australia, Great Britain, Germany, and the rest of Europe have discovered Waikiki there is really no such thing as "high" or "low" season; it's always busy here.

The rate ranges given here are projections for winter 1993-1994. Rates are always subject to change, however; we recommend that you check the price before reserving. Unless otherwise indicated, rates are for double room, double occupancy.

Hawaii's telephone area code is 808. For all the following accommodations, unless otherwise indicated, the city and zip code are: Honolulu, HI 96815.

LUXURY

The ▶ **Moana.** The name has been corporately revised (it's officially the "Sheraton Moana Surfrider" now), but she'll always be the Moana to her fans. And they're going to love her new "old" look. This grand old beach hotel, on the Diamond Head end of the hotel row at Kuhio Beach, is all dressed up for the new century with a multi-million-dollar make-over that once again makes her the First Lady of Waikiki. The open, airy, triple-wing Victorian beach resort has been restored to its original simple elegance with an Ionic-columned lobby facing onto the Pacific, a grand staircase, and a three-story porte cochere.

The first major hotel in Waikiki, designed by architect Oliver G. Traphagen in the Beaux Arts style, and built for $150,000, the Moana opened March 11, 1901, "the costliest, most elaborate hotel building in the Hawaiian Islands," according to a journalist of the day. Now she's the fairest of them all and once again a first-class luxury hotel, right down to the royal palms. Newly air-conditioned rooms are furnished in period pieces, with armoires and bedside computer command centers. The Victorian treasure is wedded to the Sheraton Surfrider's bland concrete tower on the Ewa side.

The hotel's famous banyan tree still stands in the beachside courtyard (the best ocean-view rooms are in the old Banyan Wing), and in place of the late, unlamented Polynesian show a variety of local talent now performs Hawaiian and classical melodies on the verandah—so you may drink under the spreading tree at sunset in relative peace. A period-piece restaurant, **W. C. Peacock & Co., Ltd.** (named after the original developer), is an alfresco bistro on the beach featuring fresh Hawaiian seafood and produce. The Lady's back in town and, as before, she's still "a sight to behold."

2365 Kalakaua Avenue. Tel: 922-3111; Fax: 922-5049; elsewhere in U.S., Tel: (800) 325-3535. $195–$315; suites $590.

▶ **Halekulani.** A marbled oasis in Waikiki, this contemporary seafront hotel is the first to meet Asian standards (it's in league with Hong Kong's Regent, Singapore's Raffles, and the Manila Hotel), even though it has more seawall than beach. The hotel is sited just so, to catch the perfect postcard view of Diamond Head. Established in 1917 but completely rebuilt as a high rise in 1983, the Halekulani has a high-pitched roof and an indoor-outdoor design that exemplify modern Hawaiian architecture. The hotel's lanai, the **House Without a Key**, became famous for its part in Earl Derr Biggers's 1925 Charlie Chan detective classic of the same name. The lanai is still unrivaled at sundown when Alan Akaka, Sonny Kamahele, and Benny Kalama, who appear as the Islanders, play and sing *hapa-haole* steel-guitar favorites such as "Farewell Malihini" and "Sweet Leilani." The open, airy, expensive **La Mer**, one of Honolulu's finest restaurants, is redefining Honolulu's *nouvelle tropicale* cuisine, while **Orchids**, the lower-priced version downstairs, makes an unforgettable seaside lunch. And for a clubby bar (with no view), drop into **Lewers Lounge**, which features light jazz and contemporary songs by vocalist Loretta Ables.

2199 Kalia Road. Tel: 923-2311; Fax: 926-8044; elsewhere in U.S., Tel: (800) 367-2343. $245–$425; suites $580–$3,500.

▶ **Kahala Hilton.** The guest register reads like a who's who in the world at this genteel retreat east of Diamond Head. The starkly elegant hotel heads an avenue of multi-million-dollar beachfront estates wedged between the blue Pacific and the manicured greens of Waialae Golf Course, a private course that hosts the Hawaiian Open. There are dolphins, penguins, and turtles in its waterfall pools; white-sand beaches and a palm-fringed island offshore; nearby tennis courts that are lit at night; tropical gardens; and Honolulu's best oceanfront Sunday brunch at the **Hala Terrace**. The menu at the **Maile Restaurant** includes veal fillet with lobster ravioli and chanterelles and, in a nod to New Orleans, blackened *opakapaka* fillets on fresh tomato *coulis* with linguine *al pesto*.

Singer Danny Kaleikini, beginning his 26th anniversary at the hotel, offers his vintage Polynesian revue at the Hala Terrace, while Kit Samson and orchestra play old favorites for dancing in the **Maile Lounge**. May some good things never change.

5000 Kahala Avenue, Honolulu, HI 96816. Tel: 734-2211; Fax: 737-2478; elsewhere in U.S., Tel: (800) 367-2525. $175–$495; suites $495–$2,195.

▶ **Royal Hawaiian.** Dwarfed by high rises, this pink, Spanish Baroque palace with Alice-in-Wonderland gardens and colonnaded walkways right on the middle of the main beach in Waikiki is worth a visit if only for nostalgia's sake. Now owned by Japanese tycoon Kenji Osano, the Royal has received a fresh coat of paint, but needs to improve service. The **Surf Room** is still a dramatic beachside setting for lunch, with the blue-green water a vivid contrast to the pink paint, but the food is unimpressive. The **Surf Bar** is one of the few on-the-beach, open-air bars on Waikiki. The romantic **Mai Tai Bar** offers free Hawaiian song and dance by Keith and Carmen Haugen; the 3,000-seat Monarch Room showcases the Brothers Cazimero (see Waikiki Nightlife and Entertainment, below).

Opened in 1927, the "Pink Palace" was the choice of all who came by steamship to stay in luxury's lap. Eclipsed now by newer, fancier hotels, the Royal lives on its laurels, but nostalgia buffs, old-hotel freaks, and honeymooners check in year after year. Stay in the old wing or the $2,400-a-day Kamehameha suite if you want the full Royal experience.

2259 Kalakaua Avenue. Tel: 923-7311; Fax: 924-7098; elsewhere in U.S., Tel: (800) 325-3535. $235–$425; suites $350–$2,400.

EXPENSIVE

▶ **Hawaii Prince Hotel Waikiki.** When Yoshiaki Tsutsumi, one of the world's richest men, builds a hotel, it's a prince. The new $150-million Hawaii Prince, a twin-towered structure, is the most "uptown" hotel on the Islands.

Built with pink limestone and rose-tinted glass, it rises on the waterfront of Ala Wai Yacht Harbor; its stone, marble, and bronze are European in origin and Southern Californian by design. The Bauhaus-inspired glass towers are separated by a 60-foot-wide Italian-marble lobby that frames a mast-high view of bobbing yachts. The Hawaii Prince is an elegant, understated urban hotel that will appeal more to the blue-blazer and Gucci-loafer set than to the *zori*-shod couples in matching aloha shirts, although the see-through lobby is an irresistible invitation to passersby.

All 521 rooms, including 57 suites, have an ocean view through windows that actually open so guests can enjoy Hawaii's trade winds. The Prince has no beach, and it's a block-long hike to the sands of Ala Moana Beach Park, but a pocket-sized swimming pool on a stepped rooftop lanai offers a spectacular sunset view.

The Prince's executive chef Gary Strehl, who trained under Chinese, French, and Swiss chefs, synthesizes American regional cuisine with delicacies of Hawaii and Asia. The main dining room, the 186-seat **Prince Court**, overlooks the Ala Wai Yacht Harbor and offers Oahu's premier restaurant view, especially at sunset. The Prince has two of Honolulu's best Japanese restaurants, **Takanawa** for sushi and **Hakone** for *kaiseki ryori* (ask for the *tatami* room at Hakone). The Prince now has a fitness center on the fifth floor and an executive center with Macintosh and IBM computers, laser printers, copiers, modem, fax, and 24-hour secretarial service. Other Prince touches, such as full-menu, 24-hour room service, and daily high tea with fresh-baked scones and Devonshire cream, add to the pleasures here.

The well-appointed rooms are small and lack lanais, and the six high-speed elevators (700 feet per second) are a bit of a rush, but the overall elegance, attention to detail, and special siting make Waikiki's new harborfront hotel the jewel in the crown.

100 Holomoana Street, Honolulu, HI 96814. Tel: 956-1111; Fax: 946-0811; elsewhere in U.S., Tel: (800) 321-OAHU. $200–$330; suites $450–$2,500.

▶ **Hilton Hawaiian Village**. A mega-resort in Waikiki, this 20-acre beachfront park between Fort DeRussy and the Ala Wai Yacht Harbor is a destination all its own, a vacation resort that includes the exclusive ▶ **Alii Tower**, right on the beautiful beach, which has a $2,455-a-night two-bedroom suite. A three-year remodeling has transformed Waikiki's biggest resort (2,523 rooms) into a showplace full of gardens, pools, exotic birds, and works of art, with ten restaurants (including the **Golden Dragon**, one of Honolulu's few Chinese restaurants with an ocean view, and the award-winning **Bali-by-the-Sea**); the **Paradise Lounge** jazz club, featuring Jimmy Borges; curio shops on Hong Kong Alley; designer shops such as Esprit, Benetton, and Giorgio Armani; Waikiki's biggest swimming pool, a 10,000-square-foot plunge; and a 5,000-seat ballroom.

The Hilton Hawaiian Village boasts two beaches: the one that encircles the man-made lagoon, and Duke Kahanamoku Beach, which honors Hawaii's Olympic gold medalist beachboy-surfer-swimmer. A 150-passenger twin-hulled catamaran and the submarine **Atlantis** offer scenic cruises on (and in) Oahu's Mamala Bay.

2005 Kalia Road. Tel: 949-4321; Fax: 955-3027; elsewhere in U.S., Tel: (800) HILTONS. $185–$355; suites $335–$2,455.

▶ **Hyatt Regency Waikiki.** This 40-story, twin-towered hotel on Kalakaua Avenue across the street from Waikiki Beach—but on a part of the avenue where there are no buildings blocking out the beach—has views, both beachy and urban, and a village of shops and restaurants at its feet. The hotel has completed a renovation of its 1,230 rooms, now done in soft pastels with Oriental rattan and whitewashed oak furniture. A three-ton sculpture dangles over **Harry's Bar & Café**, at the foot of a man-made waterfall, while Japanophiles converge on **Musashi**, one of the Islands' best Japanese restaurants. (Bagwells 2424, the hotel's chic supper club, has closed; in its place is a new restaurant called **Ciao Mein**—that's right—serving Chinese and Italian food.)

2424 Kalakaua Avenue. Tel: 923-1234; Fax: 923-7839; elsewhere in U.S., Tel: (800) 233-1234. $180–$380; suites $475–$2,500.

▶ **Aston Waikiki Beachside Hotel.** With only 79 tiny rooms, this former Motel 6 has had a face-lift and is now Waikiki's newest boutique hotel. The Aston's location—on Kalakaua Avenue directly across from Duke Kahanamoku's statue on Kuhio Beach—is excellent. The hotel is full of wonderful antiques and paved with Italian marble, with touches of black lacquer and polished brass everywhere, even in the bathrooms. The drawbacks are: There's no restaurant or room service, and 24 rooms have no windows, because of an insoluble architectural problem (the rooms themselves are lovely nonetheless). All rooms have two telephones, a mini-refrigerator, a videocassette recorder, and an in-room safe. Service is personal and the setting is perfect—but by all means ask for a room with a view.

2452 Kalakaua Avenue. Tel: 931-2100; Fax: 931-2129; elsewhere in U.S., Tel: (800) 92-ASTON. $160–$290.

▶ **Waikiki Park Plaza.** You can see the sparkling Pacific from the 38 suites and many of the 313 rooms in this hotel near the outer limits of Waikiki, but you'll have to hike around Fort DeRussy's parade ground to reach the beach. Nevertheless, a discriminating business tycoon looking to swing a big international deal at the crossroads of the Pacific could hardly ask for a better setting, between Bishop Street, the center of Honolulu's business district, and the beach. The hotel's facilities were done by one of Honolulu's better known interior designers, Mark Masuoka, and the food—breakfast, lunch, dinner, room service, and banquet catering—is the work of Hawaii's celebrated chef Roy Yamaguchi, whose staff runs the new **Roy's ParkBistro** restaurant in the hotel. (Yamaguchi continues to serve *nouvelle tropicale* cuisine in his original Hawaii Kai restaurant). The hotel's five penthouse suites are huge and lavishly decorated. The $2,000-a-night Royal Amethyst Suite, with a spotlighted amethyst geode on a pedestal in the landing, has a spacious outdoor lanai wrapping three sides of the 19th floor. In the Heliconia Bar there is a collection of 24 Picasso ceramics showcased under glass. In addition to the usual corporate travel features—executive center, fitness center, meeting rooms—and the commissioned modern artworks in the lobby and other public areas, the upscaling of the old mid-priced Waikiki Marina Hotel includes a gallery for local art exhibits and openings.

1956 Ala Moana Boulevard. Tel: 941-7275, Fax: 949-0996; elsewhere in U.S., Tel: (800) 367-6070. $120–$160; suites $240–$2,000.

MODERATE TO INEXPENSIVE

▶ **Ala Moana Hotel.** Just across the Ala Wai Canal in Honolulu, next door to Ala Moana Center, is Honolulu's Ala Moana Hotel. The best location in town for business people, the Ala Moana sits at Waikiki's gateway, minutes to downtown Bishop Street banks and offices and only a 5-mile (8-km) taxi ride to the airport. The top choice of Asia-Pacific flight crews, this Japanese-owned hotel has undergone an extensive make-over that created a lobby the size of a football field, improved all rooms, and rewired the disco, **Rumours**, into a high-tech lounge with flashing lights and walls of video panels. The **Royal Garden**, a Chinese restaurant on the third floor, escaped renovation and still serves the city's best Hong Kong dim sum from 11:00 A.M. **Nicholas Nickolas**, the skyroom restaurant on the 36th floor, provides a glittering nightscape along with dining and dancing.

410 Atkinson Drive, Honolulu, HI 96814. Tel: 955-4811;

Fax: 944-2974; elsewhere in U.S., Tel: (800) 367-6025. $110–$175; suites $215–$2,000.

▶ **New Otani Kaimana Beach Hotel**. It's small, private, and wonderful, just enough east of Waikiki's center stage to be sophisticated, yet not too far away to miss the carnival. The choice of writers, artists, and jazz musicians, the Kaimana, as it's called, is right on Sans Souci Beach opposite Kapiolani Park, with the high rises of central Waikiki in walking distance. The **Hau Tree Lanai**, on the site where Robert Louis Stevenson wrote poems, is a romantic beachside restaurant, one of the very few in Waikiki. Upstairs, **Miyako** is a *kaiseki*-style restaurant in a Tokyo teahouse setting, with a Pacific view from the white-pine *tatami* rooms. There's an easy, personal feeling at the low-rise Kaimana, generated by hotelier Steve Boyle, who runs this small hotel on a first-name basis as if a few hundred close friends were popping over for a glass of Chardonnay, a little fish dinner, and a good night's sleep at his house.

2863 Kalakaua Avenue. Tel: 923-1555; Fax: 922-9404; elsewhere in U.S. and in Canada, Tel: (800) 421-8795 or (800) 733-7949. $99–$220; suites $170–$475.

▶ **Waikiki Parc Hotel**. It's got the right address—just across the street from the Halekulani (see above)—at the right price, albeit in one of the most built-up, congested areas of Waikiki. The Waikiki Parc Hotel's rooms even seem identical to those of its neighbor, except for the price—starting at a mere $135 a night compared to the Halekulani's $245. Owned, built, and operated by its ritzy neighbor, the Parc isn't on the beach, but it's nearby. It features well-appointed rooms, upscale amenities, a free *Wall Street Journal* daily for business guests, and remote-control cable television. Each room has a lanai with either ocean, mountain, or city view. Eight rooms are wheelchair accessible. There are two excellent restaurants that cater to both Japanese and *haole* visitors: **Kacho**, a 40-seat sushi bar serving bento (braised vegetables, pickled vegetables, soup, rice, and fruit in a box) and California rolls, and the **Parc Café**, a garden-terrace Continental restaurant offering Island specialties, with an outstanding wine list.

2233 Helumoa Road. Tel: 921-7272; Fax: 923-1336; elsewhere in U.S., Tel: (800) 422-0450. $140–$225.

▶ **Waikiki Joy Hotel**. Its airy, bright lobby and marble floors give this new, small boutique hotel an uptown look. On a quiet Waikiki side street at the edge of the gay district, the Joy only looks expensive. It has unusual amenities, like Jacuzzi baths and Bose stereo systems in the rooms, and a courtyard pool. This is the best of the new boutique hotels popping up on Waikiki's side streets between Kuhio Avenue and the Ala Wai Canal. The trade-off here is the three-block hike to Waikiki Beach. The Waikiki Joy also offers business guests a handy corporate suite, with free local phone calls, secretarial services, fax, photocopiers, and conference room. The Joy has a tiny restaurant, **Cappuccino's**, serving seafood dinners for less than $20 per person.

320 Lewers Street. Tel: 923-2300; Fax: 924-4010; elsewhere in U.S., Tel: (800) 733-5569. $120; suites $150–$250.

▶ **Coconut Plaza.** A small hotel full of Old World charm, the 90-room, ten-story Coconut Plaza overlooks the 14th hole of the Ala Wai Golf Course and offers an island view of rainbows, volcanic peaks, and night lights (only the King Kalakaua Penthouse catches the ocean view). The beach is three blocks makai, but a kidney-shaped pool fills a sun-washed lanai. A shady courtyard is perfect for afternoon lounging with a book from the lobby shelf.

With a gazebo in the garden and revolving door at the entry, the hotel is Euro-troppo eclectic, with pastel Spanish terra-cotta tile and antique lobby furniture amid palm trees and framed portraits of early Hawaiians. All rooms are decorated in soft pastels and feature microwave oven, refrigerator, color television, two phones (one in the john), privately controlled air conditioner, private lanai, and mirrored walls. Complimentary breakfast is served in a patio garden. The affordability, ambience, and hospitality make Coconut Plaza one of Waikiki's best boutique hotels.

450 Lewers Street. Tel: 923-8828; Fax: 923-3473; elsewhere in U.S., Tel: (800) 882-9696. $80–$150; suites $150.

▶ **Hawaiiana Hotel.** Nestled in lush tropical gardens a half block from the beach between Kalakaua Avenue and the Halekulani, this charming, three-story hotel is a relic from Waikiki's past, a comfortable lodge with an all-Hawaiian staff that embraces its loyal guests like family. Everyone gets a flower lei upon arrival, and fresh pineapple juice and Kona coffee are served poolside every morning. The modern rooms have kitchenettes and are air-conditioned, but windows open to catch the trade winds. The tranquil surroundings and warm hospitality really will take you back in time.

260 Beach Walk. Tel: 923-3811; Fax: 926-5728; else-

where in U.S. and in Canada, Tel: (800) 367-5122. $85–$165; suites $135–$165.

▶ **Malihini Hotel**. There's no television, no air conditioning, no restaurant (but Buzz's Steak House is next door), not even a Coke machine—and legions of Malihini Hotel loyalists like it that way. If this cozy little 39-year-old hotel, owned by a Stanford University lawyer, changed a thing, there would probably be an uproar. It's nothing fancy, just a small, cheap, tidy hotel near the beach, facing Fort DeRussy, with the lowest rates in Waikiki.

217 Saratoga Road. Tel: 923-9644. $45–$75.

SPECIAL

The ▶ **Manoa Valley Inn**. Out of the way, on a hill in the misty Manoa Valley, about three miles back from Waikiki Beach, this charming, antiques-filled, plantation-style mansion built in 1915 has seven bedrooms and a common lanai with an unobstructed view of Diamond Head, which seems to change by morning light. Mornings here bring a free full breakfast, not just a muffin and coffee; evening begins at five o'clock with wine and cheese on the lanai. The former John Guild Inn, the mansion was restored to Old World opulence in 1984 and attracts those who like to be surrounded by wonderful old curiosity pieces. A separate cottage is also available at $150 a night.

2001 Vancouver Drive, Honolulu, HI 96822. Tel: 947-6019; Fax: 946-6168; elsewhere in U.S., Tel: (800) 634-5115. $95–$175.

The ▶ **Honolulu Airport Mini Hotel**. Airport seats are never big enough to stretch out on between flights, but Honolulu International has something better—eight hours' sleep and a shower in a private room for $32.70 a person. One of Hawaii's most popular hotels, it is located at the airport's center lobby, across from the cocktail lounge. Rooms also rent for $17.50 and up for two hours and a shower from 9:00 A.M. to 9:00 P.M.; showers are $7.50, including towels, soap, shampoo, all toilet articles, and use of a hair drier. Call ahead; beds are limited.

Honolulu International Airport Center Lobby, Terminal Box 42, Honolulu, HI 96819. Tel: 836-3044; Fax: 834-8985. $32.70.

BED AND BREAKFASTS

The bed-and-breakfast boom has hit Hawaii. The Islands now offer a wide range of accommodations (more than 200 in private homes on Oahu alone), in areas ranging from Honolulu to the big surf town of Haleiwa to Lanikai Beach and its two offshore islets (often seen on travel and surf magazine covers). These privately operated B and Bs offer visitors an inside look at the local lifestyle and are a reasonable alternative to Waikiki's hotels. Some hosts serve tree-ripened tropical fruit from their yards and Kona coffee; others provide facilities only. Rates start at about $45 a night.

Several operators now provide listings to special island places: Mahina Maxey lists the best bed and breakfasts on Oahu's Windward Coast. Her own popular garden studio on Lanikai Beach is available from $55 a night. ▶ **Lanikai Bed & Breakfast**, 1277 Mokulua Drive, Kailua, HI 96734; Tel: 261-1059; elsewhere in U.S., (800) 258-7895. Barbara Campbell offers her hand-picked selection of bed and breakfasts in Hawaii from Hilo to Hanalei at prices from $60 to $120 a night. ▶ **Hawaii's Best Bed & Breakfasts**, P.O. Box 563 Kamuela, HI 96743; Tel: 885-4550; Fax: 885-0550; elsewhere in U.S., (800) BNB-9912.

Other agents include: ▶ **Pacific Hawaii Bed & Breakfast**, 19 Kai Nani Place, Kailua, HI 96734; Tel: 262-6026; elsewhere in U.S., (800) 999-6026. ▶ **Bed & Breakfast Honolulu**, 3242 Kaohinani Drive, Honolulu, HI 96817; Tel: 595-7533; elsewhere in U.S., (800) 288-4666. ▶ **Bed and Breakfast Hawaii**, P.O. Box 449, Kapaa, Kauai, HI 96746; Tel: 536-8421; on Kauai, 822-7771; elsewhere in U.S., (800) 733-1632.

—*Rick Carroll*

NIGHTLIFE AND ENTERTAINMENT

After sunset, in the sudden tropical darkness highlighted by neon, Honolulu takes on a new look, as afternoon card players fold their hands and pocket their penny-ante pots, and teenage "boom cruisers" in garishly painted Volkswagen Bugs start to cruise the avenues. The greater Honolulu nightlife scene is diverse, traditional, spontaneous, corny, sophisticated, sometimes illegal—and always fun.

Out on Waikiki's Kalakaua Avenue, jet-lagged people from all over the world sleepwalk in neon brightness, pushing past handbill distributors, street musicians, and local kids selling honey-dipped oregano as *pakalolo* (marijuana). Then come the miniskirted streetwalkers, motor-scooter cops, sidewalk Bible thumpers, and bad saxophone players. The Waikiki night is in gear.

Nightlife in Honolulu and Waikiki is like an aloha shirt:

full on, gaudy, and hanging out everywhere. It's celebrated in sky-room restaurants, offshore on "booze-cruise" boats, over sundown mai tais under banyan trees, at Hawaii-style *pau hana* (which means "work over") street parties, on teak-railed fantails of sloops in Ala Wai Yacht Harbor, in dimly lighted bamboo-and-thatch bars such as Tahitian Lanai, at rowdy Chinese restaurants, over tropical cocktails at the Moana (home of the original mai tai), in Japanese *karaoke* (singalong) bars, by waterfalls at Harry's Bar & Café at the Hyatt Regency, inside Hula's Bar & Lei Stand, on top of the marble dance floor at the glitzy Maharaja disco, with caviar and Dom Perignon at black-tie Hawaii Prince penthouse parties, and on luxury cruise ships gliding by Diamond Head.

The pursuit of earthly pleasure goes on nearly around the clock every night of the year. It commences about 3:00 every afternoon when luau vans pull away from hotel curbs and ends shortly after 4:00 A.M. the next day when the last disco closes. In that 13-hour span the Hawaiian night belongs to anyone with courage and cash enough to enjoy all the fine dining, good music, and live entertainment available here 365 days a year.

The Honolulu Weekly, a free weekly publication, lists and reviews what's happening, and the free *Waikiki Beach Press* regularly highlights current shows, activities, and attractions. Entertainment listings also appear in Honolulu's morning *Advertiser,* while the evening *Star-Bulletin* reviews restaurants and nightlife.

In the listings below we discuss the nightlife options in Waikiki, by category, followed by those in the rest of the Honolulu area.

WAIKIKI

Hawaiian Music

The amount of square footage dedicated to nightlife in Waikiki is incalculable. Sadly, little of that is devoted to Hawaiian music, the steel-guitar, slack-key, and falsetto-voiced sound that originally attracted hundreds of thousands to Waikiki via Webley Edwards's "Hawaii Calls," a popular radio show of the 1940s broadcast "live" from the banyan tree court of the Moana hotel on beautiful Waikiki Beach.

Hapa-haole music (those old pseudo-Hawaiian songs such as "Cockeyed Mayor of Kaunakakai") of that era may still be heard in Waikiki, but engagements by Hawaiian performers are limited, and anyone in search of the local sound must work to find it. Such great Hawaiian entertainers as Eddie Kamae and the Sons of Hawaii, the Makaha Sons of Niihau, Tony Conjugacion, Cyril Pahinui and Bernard Kalua, Sonny Chillingworth, Moe Keale, Palani Vaughan, Jimmy Kaina, Mahi Beamer, Haunani Apoliona, and steel-guitar virtuoso Jerry Byrd, and such groups as Olomana and the Peter Moon Band seldom appear in Waikiki, although they often can be sought out elsewhere in the city.

The lack of contemporary Hawaiian music in Waikiki is offset slightly by two Hawaiians, the Brothers Cazimero, who sing and play at the Royal Hawaiian Hotel's **Monarch Room**. The current darlings of Waikiki, Roland and Robert are accomplished musicians who write and compose their own versions of Hawaii-inspired songs. They are real brothers, too, sons of Bill Cazimero, a Big Island orchestra leader in the 1930s. The Cazimero brothers got their start as two-thirds of a trio called Sunday Manoa, with slack-key guitarist Peter Moon (more on him later), and in the summer of 1982 followed Hilo Hattie and Alfred Apaka to become Monarch Room headliners. The Caz, as they are affectionately known, have even played Carnegie Hall and have recorded 13 albums, including *Waikiki, My Castle by the Sea,* with the Ray Jerome Baker cover photo of Waikiki in the 1930s, when only the Royal Hawaiian and Moana hotels dominated the beachscape. For reservations, Tel: 924-5194.

Some of the best shows in Waikiki are free or come with the price of a tropical cocktail. Under the *kiawe* tree of the Halekulani's **House Without a Key** lanai/lounge on certain nights at sundown, Sonny Kamahele, joined by Alan Akaka on steel guitar and Benny Kalama on ukulele, sings old Hawaiian favorites. This nostalgic trio, which calls itself the Islanders, usually features hula dancer Kanoe Kaumeheiwa Miller, a former Miss Hawaii, and if the music and hula don't give you goose bumps then maybe you should have gone to Jamaica after all.

Waikiki Shell, the open-air Kapiolani Park bandstand (2805 Monsarrat Avenue), attracts the rock and jazz stars of the day—but, unfortunately, they must hang it up at 10:00 P.M., just as they start getting it on. Curfew aside, the 3,257-seat bandstand is Waikiki's best outdoor club on warm tropical nights, and after the performance you can still go out for a late show somewhere else.

But rock and jazz may not be the best reason to go to the Shell: "Does the moon still dance to music at the Shell?" goes the local pop hit "Hello Honolulu." Yes, especially when slack-key guitar virtuoso Peter Moon hosts one of his "Blue Hawaiian Moonlight" shows, featuring the Islands' best Hawaiian music, including rare appearances by Niihau church choirs. (Bring an umbrella to any outdoor concert in case of a sudden shower.)

Performances are held at the Waikiki Shell almost every week year-round; admission prices vary. Tickets are available at the Waikiki Shell Box Office during concerts (Tel: 924-8934), or may be purchased in advance at the Neal Blaisdell Center Box Office, at Ward Avenue and South King Street (Tel: 521-2911).

Hula

Tourist luaus should be avoided if you have any sensitivity to Hawaii's cultural past. Even at the best commercial luau the dinner is a thin imitation of a real Hawaiian meal (overcooked chunks of roast pig, a cup of salty salmon, no-fish entrée, a slice of macadamia-nut pie), served on paper plates while the announcer makes lewd remarks about "hula girls" (who look Filipino and dance a Tahitian *tamure*, not a hula at all).

Like Hawaiian music, the real hula takes some effort to see, for despite a comeback of sorts, the ancient, sensuous dance banned by missionaries is still almost an underground event, forbidden even at the Kamehameha Schools until the 1960s. The faux hula is show biz; it meets expectations and keeps thousands off the streets.

Those who want to see authentic hula should go to the **Kodak Hula Show** in Waikiki's Kapiolani Park (Tuesdays, Wednesdays, and Thursdays at 10:00 A.M.), or to **Waimea Falls Park** at Waimea Bay on the North Shore (where the dance is a daily feature). Mid-July visitors looking for a day-long feast of authentic hula in a stunning outdoor setting shouldn't miss the **Prince Lot Hula Festival**, at Moanalua Gardens, off Highway 78, Ewa of downtown Honolulu (Tel: 839-5334 for the specific date). If you are heading to the Big Island, dont' miss the **Merrie Monarch Festival**, held in Hilo each spring (Tel: 936-9168). You may also look for a special appearance by a *hula halau* (hula school) such as Mapuana De Silva's Halau Mohala Ilima, one of Hawaii's best. See Honolulu Nightlife and Entertainment, below, for information on the King Kamehameha Hula Competition in June.

Dinner Shows and Clubs

The dinner-show circuit in Waikiki is overshadowed by hokey acts in vast hotel clubs, and while these old fixtures are a big part of the local scene, other musicians provide the quarter with a dose of sophistication. Honolulu's three resident jazz singers—Jimmy Borges, Andrea Young, and Sonia Mendez—are among this latter group.

Borges, the velvet-voiced crooner, sings the standards in front of his jazz quartet at the Hilton Hawaiian Village's **Paradise Lounge**, a big, airy, casual, palm-filled room that is packed on weekends; Tel: 949-4321. Singer Andrea Young, daughter of the late trombonist Trummy Young, appears weekends at the Ala Moana Hotel's **Mahina Lounge** (410 Atkinson Drive, Tel: 955-4811), while Sonia Mendez packs **Nick's Fishmarket**, at 2070 Kalakaua Avenue, in the Waikiki Gateway Hotel (Tel: 955-6333).

The undisputed king of Waikiki hokiness is **Don Ho**, a laid-back, Dean Martin–like singer who has camped his way through a 25-year show-biz career on the strength of his 1967 hit "Tiny Bubbles" and the old "Hawaii Calls" favorite, "Pearly Shells." Can you name any other Don Ho songs? It doesn't matter. His fans stand on line like teenagers for hours to see this Waikiki legend, who continues to showcase young talent and hug grandmas onstage. After ten years at the Hilton Hawaiian Village Dome, which is scheduled for demolition, Ho now appears at the **Outrigger Polynesian Palace**, 227 Lewers Street, with another act, the Krush, a glitzy, Vegas-style revue board.

The Ho show costs $45 for dinner or $27 for cocktails and goes on every night except Friday and Saturday. Reservations required; Tel: 923-7469.

In the **Tropics Surf Club** at the Hilton Hawaiian Village, Charo, the aging Las Vegas "cuchi-cuchi girl," who now lives on Kauai, enters her fifth season as headliner in the 250-seat showroom. Tel: 949-4321, ext. 74000.

The Waikiki pop club scene is dominated by **Wave Waikiki**, at 1877 Kalakaua Avenue, which has booked Grace Jones, George Thorogood and the Destroyers, Dave Valentin, the Boomtown Rats, Fleetwood Zoo (the garage band of Mick Fleetwood, with Stevie Nicks), Cinderella Rockefella, Bronski Beat, and Bow Wow Wow. Most nights, however, you'll find rock bands from Hawaii and the West Coast. Tel: 941-0424.

Pink Cadillac, a two-minute walk away at 478 Ena Road, is a strobe-blitzed dance club that caters to young trendies. The Euro-pop play list keeps the dance floor jammed. If you're looking for a scene that's more down-to-earth, drink in the atmosphere at **Malia's Cantina**: raw wood, Mexican food, largely local crowds, and "Jawaiian"

(Jamaican-Hawaiian) music. It's laid-back and cozy, located at 311 Lewers Street.

The **Honolulu Comedy Club** is still going strong at Waikiki's Ilikai Hotel (1777 Ala Moana Boulevard), where owners Eddie and Charlotte Saxe book the nation's best stand-up comedians from the David Letterman, Arsenio Hall, and Tonight shows, as well as local comics who offer ethnic humor about Island life. Tel: 922-5998 or 943-9623.

No one gets more laughs in town than Waikiki's Frank DeLima, however, the freewheeling funnyman with the devilish mind who is Hawaii's reigning comic genius. A master of impression, DeLima makes good fun of everyone, from Japanese tourists to his own Portuguese folks. He voices the unspoken and gets away with it at the **Polynesian Palace**, 227 Lewers Street, Tuesdays through Saturdays. His Imelda Marcos is better than the original. Tel: 923-9861.

Gay Hangouts

Some of the most fun after dark occurs in the Tivoli-lighted gay quarter of Kuhio, named for Hawaii's last prince. The Kuhio district, a two-block area between Kuhio and Kalakaua avenues and Lewers and Kalaimoku streets, is Honolulu's Castro Street, a collection of gay men's shops, such as 80 Percent Straight and Down There, as well as restaurants and bars. **Hula's Bar & Lei Stand**, on the corner of Kuhio Avenue and Kalaimoku Street, across from the Kuhio Theater, is a predominately gay disco where non-gay patrons feel comfortable, too. Hula's plays videos and infrequently features Hawaiian singers in an open-air courtyard.

Hamburger Mary's Organic Grill, just around the corner on Kuhio Avenue, features what many believe are Hawaii's best hamburgers. The bar in back, **Dirty Mary's**, draws a clientele that favors leather, studs, and tight muscles. The nearby ► **Honolulu Hotel**, 376 Kaiolu Street, is a small hotel that caters to gays (Tel: 926-2766).

Disco

The disco never died in Waikiki and probably won't until the last person under 35 in North America and Japan has been to **Bobby McGee's Conglomeration**, a holdout of late-1970s disco fever. At 2885 Kalakaua Avenue, near the entrance to the New Otani Kaimana Beach Hotel, Bobby McGee's is a dance hall inside a restaurant, where you can eat, drink, and boogie all in one place.

And just when you thought disco was history, the Japanese have reinvented the genre in Waikiki with **Maharaja**, a pull-out-all-the-stops multi-million-dollar dance hall. This 13,000-square-foot showplace on the ground floor of the Waikiki Trade Center at Kuhio and Seaside avenues combines Tokyo's latest high-tech sound and light wizardry with a glitzy European style, around a marble dance floor. This architectural bazaar of sound and light includes five bars, three restaurants, and an 80-seat glass-encased VIP lounge where the high-rev sound is reduced to a whisper. Maharaja is the first U.S. venture by Japan's Nova 21 group, which has more than 100 clubs from Hokkaido to Okinawa and hopes to have the same from Honolulu to New York.

Cafés and Bars

Two popular bar-restaurants in Waikiki offer a loud and/or rowdy atmosphere. The **Hard Rock**, on the edge of Waikiki (corner of Kalakaua Avenue and Kapiolani Boulevard), offers food, music, and self-serving tee-shirts. The **Shore Bird Beach Broiler**, 2169 Kalia Road, in the Outrigger Reef Hotel, is a popular perch at sunset and every Sunday at 4:00 P.M., when the weekly bikini contest begins.

Come evening everyone in Waikiki finds a favorite spot from which to watch the sunset. The two best vantage points are outdoors, on two special hotel lanais: **House Without a Key**, at the Halekulani Hotel (2199 Kalia Road), where the Islanders sing *hapa-haole* songs (those pseudo-Hawaiian classics like "Yacka Hula Hickey Dula" cranked out by Tin Pan Alley from 1915 to 1925), and **Hau Tree Lanai**, at the New Otani Kaimana Beach Hotel (2863 Kalakaua Avenue), on the spot where Robert Louis Stevenson wrote poems to Kaiulani, a real Hawaiian princess. (Other bars with a sunset vantage point are at the Moana, Royal Hawaiian, and Hawaii Prince hotels.)

Waikiki's last neighborhood bar is long gone (try Smith's Union Bar, at 19 North Hotel Street, in Chinatown), but three special bars are worth a visit. **Lewers Lounge** at the Halekulani, a leather-lined, Manhattan-style tavern with big comfortable chairs, gracious stewards, but no ocean view, is the perfect place to relax over a Bombay up. Wednesday through Saturday evenings the lounge features live jazz. Tel: 923-2311. The **Tahitian Lanai**, a nostalgic South Seas–style bamboo-and-thatch bar and restaurant on the beachfront of the Waikikian Hotel (1811 Ala Moana, between the Ilikai and the Hilton), is an old favorite for sipping mai tais and staring out to sea. A Tongan roofing crew has just re-thatched the bungalow, a sure sign that this 1950s landmark will endure. Up on the third floor of the Royal Hawaiian Shopping Center, a block-long merchandise mart on Kalakaua Avenue, **Naniwa-ya** is an oasis in the midst of retail that makes you feel as if you're in Tokyo, especially late in the evening when the customers start singing *karaoke*.

Evening Cruises

The best way to see any island is by sea, and if surfboards or outrigger canoes seem too small a craft, ships come in all different sizes and shapes at Waikiki. There are booze cruises, glass-bottom cruises, Pearl Harbor cruises, sportfishing cruises, snorkeling cruises, sunset cruises, dinner cruises, all-day cruises, and seven-day, around-the-Islands cruises on the SS *Independence* and SS *Constitution*, which call on ports of the Big Island of Hawaii, Maui, and Kauai. Ask at your hotel's front desk for details on cruises and excursions; for the *Independence* and *Constitution* call American Hawaii Cruises, Tel: 521-0384 in Honolulu, or (800) 765-7000 from elsewhere in the United States.

The best sunset cocktail cruise is also one of the least expensive, aboard the 45-foot racing catamaran **Leahi**, a sleek, green-sailed craft that departs from Waikiki Beach five times daily. The last cruise of the day is the best, a 90-minute sail on Mamala Bay at just the right time in the evening. Tel: 922-5665; elsewhere in U.S., (800) 462-7975.

If you suffer *mal de mer*, go to sea on the sleek-looking 140-foot **Navatek I**, the smoothest (and most expensive, $140 for adults) cruise on Honolulu's Mamala Bay. Its torpedo-like hull is designed to slash through the waves so there's very little motion. A two-and-a-half-hour sunset cruise departs Pier 6 seven nights a week at 5:30 P.M.; for information contact Royal Hawaiian Cruises Ltd., Tel: 848-6360; elsewhere in U.S., (800) 852-4183.

The newest, most luxurious vessel in Honolulu's sunset fleet is the **Star of Honolulu**, a 232-foot cruise ship. The ship has a deep V-bottom hull for smooth, steady sailing. A chauffeured Rolls-Royce delivers you to Kewalo Basin for dinner served by white-gloved waiters in tuxedos on the ship's Super Nova deck in an intimate 80-seat Art Deco restaurant where strolling minstrels play. If you have to ask what it costs, you may consider dinner on the Main Deck, which seats 550 and forgoes the amenities but observes the same Hawaiian sunset. Reservations, Tel: 536-3641; elsewhere in U.S., (800) 334-6191.

The biggest vessel in the sunset fleet is the Windjammer cruise line's **Rella Mae**, a 282-foot triple-decked square-rigger that once plied Washington's Potomac River. It offers limousines from Waikiki hotels, first-class service, and white-tablecloth dinners of steak and lobster. The ship also serves as a "laugh boat" when the **Honolulu Comedy Club** show goes to sea. Tel: 922-1200; elsewhere in U.S., (800) 367-5000.

Late-Night Eats

After the fun, night owls, the post-disco crowd, and other insomniacs hurry to the all-night eatery **Eggs 'n' Things**, at 1911B Kalakaua Avenue, which opens at 11:00 P.M. Other red-eyed patrons wolf down all-you-can-eat pancakes, bacon, and eggs for $3.99 at the 24-hour **Wailana Coffee House** (open since 1941), at 1860 Ala Moana Boulevard.

HONOLULU OUTSIDE WAIKIKI

Dinner Shows and Clubs

Beyond the traditional dinner-show scene, Honolulu supports a lively range of musical styles: rock, pop, Caribbean, fusion, and jazz. Around the island, look for such local players as pianists Ed Moody and Rich Crandall, the Bob Klem Jazz Quartet, or Rolando Sanchez & Friends at various clubs. Pick up a copy of *Honolulu Weekly, Waikiki Beach Press,* the morning *Advertiser,* or the evening *Star-Bulletin* for entertainment listings and reviews.

One old standby in Honolulu is the tourist show at the **Kahala Hilton** (east of Diamond Head on Kahala Avenue), where Danny Kaleikini holds the endurance record as Hawaii's longest-running act in show business, second nationally only to New York's Bobby Short, who never played the *ohe hano ihu* (Hawaiian nose flute) or the ukulele or the slack-key guitar and doesn't sing in 12 languages. The Kahala star, who makes Kyoto honeymooners giggle as easily as their Kansas counterparts, has logged 25 years as the hotel's **Hala Terrace** headliner and has sung the *haole* version of "The Hawaiian Wedding Song" more than 10,000 times in the two and a half decades that he has performed his 75-minute, Hawaiian-Polynesian variety show. He sings in Spanish, Italian, Chinese, Korean, and Japanese, and cracks jokes in pidgin. Tel: 734-2211.

For something completely different, downhill from the University of Hawaii and across from Moiliili baseball field at 2440 South Beretania Street there is a classic college hangout, **Anna Bannanas**, weekend home of the Pagan Babies, one of Honolulu's most creative bands, with musical roots in Third World rhythms of reggae, *soca,* Antillean *zouk,* and African *soukous.* Not just another boogie band, the Pagan Babies is an Afro-Caribbean band of Asian, Portuguese, and American musicians that often seems far ahead of its usually beery audience until the itchy rhythms kick in and everybody starts dancing. This is the Afro-Asian split Duke Ellington first discovered, crossed with Hawaii's own ethnomusical undercurrents—and great fun to dance to. The band's name refers to those poster waifs for which Christian charities used to solicit money. Their black tee-shirt bears the painted red-and-yellow face of a Papua New Guinea highlander from Malcolm Kirk's book *Man as Art in New Guinea.* Other down-and-dirty bands playing blues and reggae take the stage Sunday through Thursday. Tel: 946-5190.

The Garage, 955 Waimanu Street (in the Ala Moana area), is Honolulu's best venue for live progressive and regressive imported rock (Pearl Jam, L-7, Bo Diddley, Los Lobos). The post-industrial blackness fills with a twenty-ish crowd that rubs thighs at the "smart bar," which besides the usual well drinks and brew serves non-alcoholic vitamin-packed concoctions that keep the kids shaking and kicking into the wee hours. Tel: 537-1555.

The velvet-voiced Hawaiian sound is captured by Mahi Beamer, who accompanies himself on piano in the inky-black lounge at **Andrew's Italian Restaurant**, a popular *hula halau* (hula school) hangout at Ward Centre, 1200 Ala Moana Boulevard. Occasionally, jazz notes emanate from the ivories of the white baby grand at the friendly **Ramsay Galleries & Café**, on the site of Honolulu's first Chinese-language newspaper office. The club is the latest venture of artist–jazz patron Ramsay, who also has a gallery on the premises, at 1128 Smith Street, between Pauahi and North Hotel streets, in Chinatown.

Out in Pearl City (about 10 miles/16 km Ewa on H-1 past Aiea), at 98-713 Kuahao Place, **Reni's Back Room**, founded by Roger Mosley (he flew the helicopter on the TV show "Magnum, P. I."), features Island fusion favorite Nueva Vida and various other rock and jazz groups on a regular basis.

Performance Venues

Highbrow entertainment may be found in Chinatown at the Neoclassical-style **Hawaii Theater** (1130 Bethel Street, between Hotel and Beretania streets), the first movie palace in the Islands, which opened in September 1922.

The only remaining theater in downtown Honolulu, the Hawaii Theater is currently undergoing renovation but is open in a limited way for special local events, such as the Chinese Opera of Canton, the Hawaii State Ballet, and the International East-West Film Festival. Tel: 522-5666.

Neal Blaisdell Center, named for a former mayor of Honolulu, is the spiky building that looks like a fallen star on Ward Avenue at Kapiolani Boulevard. It serves as the city's star arena for main events and road shows—from the San Francisco Ballet to the latest pop sensations. The touring entertainers, like all visitors, appear briefly, but nevertheless do keep Honolulu from becoming "Racine, Wisconsin, Saturday night," as Joan Didion once called it, perhaps too harshly. The best thing about any Honolulu concert is the proximity to the performer that spectators enjoy; the aloha spirit seems to relax even security goons. Tel: 521-2911.

In the nearby **Neal Blaisdell Center Concert Hall** (Ward Avenue at South King Street), the spirited **Honolulu Symphony** performs a 127-concert season. The symphony often features such guest artists as Vladimir Ashkenazy, Peter Nero, and Seiji Ozawa. Tel: 537-6191 for the symphony; Tel: 521-2911 for other events in the hall.

See also the Waikiki Shell in the Waikiki Nightlife section, above.

Hawaiian Music

At 1007 Dillingham Boulevard, across from Honolulu Community College in Lower Kalihi (Ewa of Iwilei), the **Jubilation** is the last true bastion of live Hawaiian music, where every weekend aficionados of slack key, steel guitar, and falsetto may find the Peter Moon Band, the Makaha Sons of Niihau, Ledward Kalapana, Olomana with Jerry Santos, Wally Suenaga, Haunani Apoliona and Willy Paikuli IV, the Kamalamalama Brothers, Kipapa Rush, the Nuuanu Brothers, Kalani Okalani, and Island Magic. Host Richard Kashimoto is "holding on," keeping the endangered Hawaiian music alive in Honolulu at this small, intimate nightclub that stays open until 4:00 A.M. on weekends (closed Mondays). So there's no excuse to go to the Islands and not see or hear *real* Hawaiian music. Tel: 845-1568.

Hula

Looking for authentic Hawaiian hula? Hawaii's best *hula halau* (hula schools) compete in modern and ancient hula categories at the **King Kamehameha Hula Competi-**

tion, held for two nights on the third weekend in June at Neal Blaisdell Center, 777 Ward Avenue (tickets go on sale at the center box office on June 10). This big international competition, sponsored by the State Council of Hawaiian Heritage, attracts dancers from New Zealand to Texas. A five-dollar ticket in the balcony is the best way to see and hear hula the way it's supposed to be. To reserve tickets for the competition, write to the State Council of Hawaiian Heritage, 355 North King Street, Honolulu, HI 96817; or call the Blaisdell Center box office, Tel: 521-2911.

See the Hula section in Waikiki Nightlife and Entertainment, above, for more on hula on the island.

Pau Hana Parties

A favorite expression in Hawaii is *pau hana* (work finished). The end of the work day is celebrated with impromptu, local-style affairs, a few friends getting together after work with some *tako poke* (marinated bits of octopus) and a six-pack of Budweiser. But canny barkeeps now offer more organized pau hana parties, with food, drink, and live entertainment, usually after work on **Aloha Friday**. (Observed every Friday in Honolulu, Aloha Friday is TGIF Hawaii style. Nearly everyone who works downtown, from company presidents to office clerks, celebrates the end of the work week by wearing bright aloha shirts, tentlike muumuu, and beach togs. To visitors, every day in Honolulu must look like Aloha Friday since almost everyone dresses in the colorful tropical style. Only lawyers, morticians, some ministers, and jewelry salespeople regularly wear suits and ties. Nearly all women eschew pantyhose in the tropical heat, and cotton, linen, and silk are *de rigueur*.)

Some of the best barroom pau hana parties are at **Rumours**, at the Ala Moana Hotel, near Ala Moana Center, and **Studebaker's**, at Restaurant Row (see below), in Kakaako between downtown Honolulu and Waikiki.

Restaurant Row

Restaurant Row, a bar and restaurant mall occupying a square block at 500 Ala Moana Boulevard (bordered by Punchbowl, South, and Pohukaina streets), contains many sociable if sterile bars. The open-air **Row Bar** offers free, live entertainment by local bands such as Nueva Vida and Rolando Sanchez & Friends. The classy restaurant **Rex's Black Orchid** (formerly owned by Tom Selleck), whose new owners have improved the menu *and* lowered the prices, features live jazz in the bar on weekends. Other trendy bars and restaurants in the complex, such as **Studebaker's**, whose pau hana party is a wall-to-wall jumble of bodies, attract great crowds of local folks out on the town on the weekends, but there's nothing in this sterile food condo that says Hawaii, not even a Trader Vic's.

Korean Hostess Bars
There are 400 Korean "hostess" bars in Honolulu, with such names as Crystal Palace and Saigon Passion, featuring "naked Penthouse dancers" and free *pupu*—usually fried chicken wings. Inside, young, attractive Asian women hover like flies to hustle $20 drinks with promises of sexual favors. These clip joints, periodically raided by Honolulu Vice, are designed to empty your wallet and should be entered only at your own risk.

They are called Korean bars because Korean refugees started them in the 1950s; now most are owned by Vietnamese refugees, who hire blue-eyed, blonde California girls to dance totally naked to the delight of Japanese tourists, men and women.

If you must attend a nudity night spot, these are more or less safe: the Classic Cat on Sheridan Street and Club Rock-Za on Kapiolani Boulevard.

—*Rick Carroll and Bill Harby*

SHOPS AND SHOPPING

In the days before the Matson container ships changed Island consumerism, well-heeled Honolulu matrons sojourned in San Francisco and Los Angeles to replenish their fall wardrobes, or in Tokyo and Hong Kong for silks, jewelry, and furniture. Today, it seems, Rodeo Drive has come to Waikiki. Treasures from the Orient are to be found in any number of shopping plazas, and fine collectibles from the past are abundant in downtown Honolulu antiques shops. As a matter of fact, the problem with shopping in Hawaii is ferreting out the worthwhile from the schlock before your eyes glaze over and you quit looking because there's just too much stuff that all looks the same.

Here we cover the enormous shopping bounty of the city in two separate sections: shops and shopping in Waikiki, followed by shops and shopping in Honolulu beyond the Waikiki tourist quarter.

WAIKIKI

Shopping is as much a part of the Waikiki scene as lying on the beach. As you might expect, you'll find everything under the sun in Waikiki's shops and markets. In tee-shirts alone, the variety in Waikiki ranges from souvenir cotton tees for $4.50 (which might make you feel like a shrink-wrapped sausage after the first washing) to one-of-a-kind $40 Chinese tees hand-painted with lavender orchids. Waikiki's open-air International Marketplace is like some overcrowded Asian emporium, with merchants hawking wares made in Taiwan, the Philippines, China, Japan, and maybe even Hawaii. Fine arts, crafts, jewelry, and resort wear *are* produced in the Islands; they're just not easily found among the jumble of plastic flower leis and aloha-stamped key chains, coffee mugs, and ashtrays sold from sidewalk stalls in Waikiki. On the other hand, the Royal Hawaiian Shopping Center on Waikiki's main street, Kalakaua Avenue, is home to the first Chanel boutique ever opened in the United States. Such prestigious and internationally known shops as Louis Vuitton, Hermès Paris, Cartier, Benetton, and Lancel also have opened in Waikiki.

Waikiki's department stores include Liberty House and McInerney's. There are also 48 ABC Discount Stores, where you can find macadamia-nut products, Hawaiian perfumes, beach mats, tanning lotions, liquor, whatever. The best deals on postcards, beach mats, suntan lotion, and such may be found at the Woolworth on Kalakaua Avenue, the only variety store in America that sells sushi, *saimin* (noodle soup), and macadamia-nut brittle. Their aisle of zori is especially worth perusing, because it has a full range of sizes and classic styles.

In our coverage below, however, we skip over these prosaic offerings and concentrate on three types of shopping areas, each progressively more expensive: stalls, malls, and hotels.

In general, stores and shopping centers open at 9:00 or 9:30 A.M., and many of those in Waikiki stay open until 9:00 P.M. or later.

Stalls

You can buy gold chains by the inch from a street stall; the salesperson will tell you it's 14-karat gold mixed with silver and your satisfaction is guaranteed for a lifetime. Beware; by the time the golden glow is gone, most travellers have lost the receipt and the address for making any exchange.

Buy it for fun, for the spur of the moment, and try not to pay full price.

In stalls along **Duke's Lane** (a side street off Kalakaua Avenue just Diamond Head of Seaside Avenue) and in the adjacent **International Market Place** (2330 Kalakaua Avenue), the gold-chain sellers—many of them advertising 50 percent off—often drop their prices as soon as you hesitate to buy. In the Market Place you don't even have to bargain. Merchants, many of them fairly recent Asian immigrants, face stiff competition, and, particularly on semiprecious jewelry such as coral and even costume bracelets, necklaces, and earrings, their final price will be a third off the original when you declare, "I'm just looking." Other good buys in the Market Place are brightly colored beach towels and the ever-popular tee-shirt. Since its inception more than 30 years ago, the International Market Place has grown from a laid-back little place where you could hear the birds chatter in the branches of the giant banyan tree to a crowded maze of stalls and kiosks. Yellow lines are painted on the cobbled and paved ground beneath your feet to lead you through.

Behind and adjacent to the Market Place is **Kuhio Mall** (2301 Kuhio Avenue), a two-story cluster of stalls selling tee-shirts, beach towels, and costume jewelry.

Malls

Excluding the International Market Place, Kuhio Mall, and the Rainbow Bazaar at the Hilton Hawaiian Village, there are three shopping malls of some size in Waikiki—King's Village, the Royal Hawaiian Shopping Center, and Waikiki Shopping Plaza. There is also a walkway through the **Waikiki Trade Center** (2255 Kuhio Avenue) that houses **C. June Shoes**, one of the best (and most expensive) shoe stores in the area, **Town and Country Surf Shop**, for bathing suits, wet suits, surf wallets, and tank tops in the brands that are cool with honest-to-goodness local surfers, and **Bebe's Galleria**, which has a wide selection of leather clothing.

When perusing Waikiki's three multilevel malls, be sure to investigate the upper reaches, as often the most interesting little specialty shops are found on the upper-level, lower-overhead floors.

The **Royal Hawaiian Shopping Center** (2201 Kalakaua Avenue, in front of the Royal Hawaiian Hotel) is a three-story, three-building mall—the buildings are known as Hibiscus Court, Orchid Court, and Ilima Court—with a ten-story parking lot attached (many merchants validate parking with purchases; otherwise, paying $2 every 20 minutes can put a serious dent in your shopping budget). On the ground level in Hibiscus Court, a laser-disc information system called Info-Vision provides shoppers with detailed information on stores, restaurants, and activities at the touch of a button. Free hula, ukulele, Hawaiian quilting, and coconut-frond-weaving lessons are regularly offered at various locations throughout the center, as is a minishow sponsored by the Polynesian Cultural Center, featuring music and dances of the South Pacific.

In **Hibiscus Court** you'll find **Swimsuit Warehouse** on the third level, featuring truly discounted prices on brand-name swim wear.

Then return to ground level and wander past the kiosks full of flowers and perfumes, kites and suntan lotion, to **Orchid Court**. Check out the **Hawaiian Heirloom Jewelry** kiosk, where beautiful 14-karat gold engraved bracelets can be ordered in various widths, styles, and designs. Engraved plumeria flowers or maile vines are two popular designs that form the background for the wearer's name, usually engraved in Hawaiian ("Peke" for Betty, for example) in black enamel.

If you are in need of a coffee break, ride the glass-enclosed elevator next to Chanel up to the second level for a cup of cappuccino at **The Coffee Connection**. Continuing to the third level, you'll find the **Little Hawaiian Craft Shop**. Fifty or more local craftspeople are represented in this shop, and all the items are made by craftspeople in Hawaii or the South Pacific. A lady on Maui contributes sandalwood necklaces, but if you prefer to string your own, you can buy sandalwood or coconut-shell beads and other polished nuts separately. This is a good place to purchase all those small gifts for people back home—maybe handmade bookmarks with pressed flowers for $2.50, or Christmas tree ornaments of tiny Hawaiian angels or miniature *ipu* (musical gourds) for $5 to $12.50. At the other end of the price range, deftly stitched hatbands in brilliant red and yellow feathers or shimmering peacock feathers ($88 to $450) can add a rakish touch to a man's or woman's hat. The ultimate indulgence, rare Niihau-shell leis, will cost you from $40 to $7,000. The tiny shells are found primarily around the privately owned island of Niihau, and the creation of these delicate necklaces is becoming a dying art. Every true *kamaaina* (longtime resident) has a Niihau necklace tucked away for safekeeping or else has aspirations of owning one. If Kauai is a scheduled stop on your itinerary, save this ultimate splurge for that island, which has the closest ties and location to Niihau (see Shops and Shopping in the Kauai chapter). If you do buy a Niihau necklace on Oahu (either at the Little Hawaiian Craft Shop or in Honolulu at Hildgund), be sure to ask where you can have repairs made, and safeguard the address in case you ever break a shell.

Ilima Court houses such upscale boutiques as **Loewe** (fine leathers from Madrid), **Lancel** (leather goods), **Hermès** (scarves and other accessories), and **McInerny Galleria**, featuring fine designer wear and name brands such as Coach leather, Ferragamo, and Mark Cross. On the third floor, **Boutique Marlo** features hand-painted and tie-dyed originals: Artful Wear painted tee-shirts, raw-silk outfits, and handwoven skirts from Bali—all in natural fibers.

Across the street is the five-story **Waikiki Shopping Plaza** (2250 Kalakaua Avenue; you can't miss it, it's got a fountain spraying in the trade winds just inside the entrance). Perhaps the hottest stores for fashionable day and evening wear for women at the Waikiki Shopping Plaza are **Chocolates for Breakfast** and, for the sportier set, its sister shop, **Villa Roma**, together on the first floor. On the second floor, you might browse through **Waldenbooks** or stop by the **Cloisonné Factory**, **Nagai, USA**, to see modern interpretations in brooches and bracelets of this ancient Chinese art of enameling. You'll find **Leather of the Sea** on the mall's fourth floor, the best place to buy eel-skin wallets, key chains, purses, and shoes. (Buy wallets and purses that are cloth-lined to prolong the life of credit cards; contact with the eel skin supposedly voids the information carried on the cards' magnetic strips.) Most of the fifth floor is occupied by jewelry retailers and wholesalers, but the bargains and the fantastic variety of necklaces, earrings, and bracelets at **Betty's Import and Export** make this a great place for inexpensive gift shopping. Betty's carries the biggest selection (at the cheapest prices) of capiz-shell items such as place mats, dishes, and boxes.

Amble toward Diamond Head along Kalakaua Avenue and turn left at Kaiulani Avenue to enter **King's Village** (131 Kaiulani Avenue). This charming low-rise mall has a cobblestone lane that wends its way past a surf shop (Hawaiian Island Creations), a Burger King, the **Rose and Crown** bar and restaurant, and a noodle restaurant called **Itoguruma** on the ground level. The lane continues upward to the second level past **Harriett's**, which carries bolts of Hawaiian fabric amid its line of sportswear (clothing, hats, and purses), **Hime Woods**, with elegant wood and crystal creations, and the **Royal Peddler** with nautical-themed scrimshaw, Coca Cola memorabilia, and fine Italian music boxes. Small plaques along the lane in King's Village describe incidents in Hawaiian history during the reign of the monarchy, and a changing-of-the-guard ceremony is staged at the entrance every evening at 6:15 (King's Village is open until 11:00 P.M.).

Many of the malls in Honolulu outside Waikiki—especially those along Ala Moana Boulevard, such as Ala Moana Center, Ward Centre, Ward Warehouse, and Restaurant Row—are easily accessible from Waikiki via TheBus (see the Honolulu Outside Waikiki shopping section, below).

Hotel Shopping

The cream-of-the-crop shops in hotels are generally for the shopper with discriminating taste—and money to spare—but no one should hesitate to walk through any of the finest hotels. (You will find addresses of the hotels in our Accommodations section, above.) With Waikiki's casual dress code, clerks in even the most expensive jewelry stores and boutiques won't look down their noses; any prospective customer might turn out to be Bruce Springsteen or Bette Midler.

Clothing and Accessories. As a matter of fact, **Bebe**, in the Hawaiian Regent (2552 Kalakaua Avenue), Hyatt Regency Waikiki, and Hilton Hawaiian Village hotels (and also at the Waikiki Trade Center), carries sparkle-studded leather bustiers that only someone with Bette Midler's chutzpah could get away with wearing. Bebe also has great leather skirts and jackets. If you're seeking more conventional garb, the Kahala Hilton and other upscale hotels offer designer wear at **Collections**, an elite branch of Liberty House.

Several hotels have branches of shops that you won't find elsewhere in Hawaii, but that you can find somewhere else in the world, such as the **Mitsukoshi Department Store** at the Hyatt Regency Waikiki. Many hotel shops carry merchandise that is of an especially fine quality or that is rarely found in the average shopping center. At the Royal Hawaiian hotel, **Kula Bay** carries what it claims are "the world's finest Panama hats," Montecristi Fino, which take two to six months to make in Ecuador. At **Poi**, another fine men's store at the Royal Hawaiian and other leading hotels, are silk shirts, blazers, polo shirts in

Hawaiian designs, as well as authentic-looking reproductions of antique silkies, the original rayon aloha shirts that now sometimes sell for hundreds—occasionally even thousands—of dollars.

Jewelry. The shopper who's got the urge to splurge on jewelry should stop at the Sheraton Waikiki Hotel's jewelry shop (2255 Kalakaua Avenue), called **Rachel's Chateau D'Or**. The designs of lapis lazuli, emerald, sapphire, and red and black coral rings, necklaces, and bracelets are from the shop's own factory. Nearby, the Halekulani hotel carries award-winning designs by Hawaii's Harry Haimoff at **Haimoff & Haimoff Creations in Gold**. **Bernard Hurtig** carries wonderful faux jewelry to fool the eye at his shop in the Alii Tower of the Hilton Hawaiian Village, while his shop in the Kahala Hilton offers the real stuff, too. But for a visual feast, stop by either of the two **Helen and Suzanne** jewelry boutiques at the Royal Hawaiian Hotel. These small shops are bursting at the seams with glittering baubles and outrageous faux jewels from around the world. You'll find everything from $15 earrings to Judith Leiber handbags at $3,500. Of course, if it's a simple little diamond Madam needs to go with basic black, **Tiffany's**, at the Moana, is the only place to go, while **Alfred Dunhill**, across the hall, is sure to have the perfect cufflinks, wallet, belt, or shirt for Monsieur.

Gifts. The **Rainbow Bazaar** at the Hilton Hawaiian Village (2005 Kalia Road) is a self-contained shopping mall strung out in three separate theme villages. A large, round red gate marks the entrance to the Bazaar and Hong Kong Alley; Imperial Japan has a Japanese farmhouse; and the South Pacific shops suggest a sugar plantation theme. Check out **Elephant Walk** for interesting silkscreened prints that resemble earth-toned *kapa* (pounded bark the ancient Hawaiians used as cloth). Here you'll also find such treasures as blown-glass unicorns and dolphins mounted on crystal rocks, for $80 and up, and, for the conservation-minded, a custom-designed line of tee-shirts featuring endangered species.

Other elegant, upscale shops are clustered at the Alii Tower at the Hilton Hawaiian Village, where the plush hotel rooms even have miniature televisions in the bathrooms. In the Diamond Head tower, **Lamonts Gift and Sundry Shop** carries framed scrimshaw pictures for $33 and little refrigerator magnets decorated with starfish and other colorful tropical friends for $4.50. In all, Hilton Hawaiian Village houses more than 100 shops and services.

Art connoisseurs will find galleries in hotels and at Ala Moana Center (see Honolulu Shopping, below) stocked with delightful paintings by Maui's Guy Buffet, picture-perfect scenes by Gary Reed, and the surreal undersea world depicted by Robert Lyn Nelson. More than one of these leading painters, however, began his climb to fame by selling at the **Zoo Fence**, on Monsarrat Avenue at the Diamond Head end of Waikiki. You just might discover an unknown talent among the many artists who display their work there every Friday and Saturday. You can find small original works for $25 and large oil paintings of oceans and mountains for $400.

If you've gone as far as the zoo, you might as well stop, on your return walk, at the **Zoo Gift Shop**, which carries original little remembrances with animal themes suitable for young nieces and nephews.

HONOLULU OUTSIDE WAIKIKI

Central Honolulu is small compared to other major cities, but what it lacks in size it makes up for in character. Certain streets have their own distinct flavor. Along the western end of King Street between River Street and Fort Street Mall, for example, are little Vietnamese and Thai restaurants, Asian markets, and inexpensive shops with made-in-Taiwan clothing, while just around the corner, Maunakea Street in Chinatown harbors herb shops, lei stands, Oriental bakeries, noodle factories, and jewelry and variety stores. Bishop Street is the financial center of the city, while a block away, **Fort Street Mall** is considered the walk-and-shop center of the business district. The major streets that run mauka to makai (mountains to sea) are Bishop Street, Fort Street Mall, Nuuanu Avenue, and Maunakea Street in Chinatown, the area that furnishes the most interesting shopping diversions.

Ala Moana Boulevard separates the downtown area from Honolulu Harbor. Fort Street Mall runs perpendicular to Ala Moana, directly inland from Aloha Tower (the spire with the big clock on the waterfront). The shops along Fort Street Mall, for the most part, carry the same merchandise as Anytown, USA. There's a branch of Longs Drugs, a Woolworth variety store, a few dress shops, and shoe stores, all anchored by one of the Liberty House department stores. Bargain-hunting office workers head for the **Penthouse** on King Street and Nuuanu Avenue, where merchandise is 50 percent off the price originally charged in the Liberty House stores and on the first Monday of every month is marked down another 30 percent. In addition to discounted clothing and shoes, attractive gift items, silver-plated bowls, wine glasses, and fine china can often be found here.

Downtown shopping hours are quite different from those in Waikiki or Ala Moana Center, because the city stores cater to working residents. Many city shops are open Monday through Saturday from 7:00 A.M. to 5:00 P.M. and Sunday from 9:00 A.M. to 3:00 P.M. Small, independently owned stores may open later in the morning, but in general Honolulu "rolls up" its shopping sidewalks to coincide with the closing of business offices. (A short section of Hotel Street is the only downtown area where there is any after-dark action, but it seems to appeal mostly to curious sailors and single men—most definitely not to shoppers.)

Antiques and Art
In the last few years the lower (waterfront) end of Chinatown's **Maunakea Street** has become a collectors' haven frequented by antiques buffs and gallery lovers. In talking to the proprietors of these interesting little shops you'll discover there's a bit of rivalry among Honolulu's antiques dealers. One will tell you that his neighbor doesn't carry authentic antiques; another will gossip about the outrageous prices of the dealer next door.

Robyn Buntin Galleries (900-A Maunakea Street) features contemporary artwork, Oriental art objects, a framing gallery, a jewelry boutique, and an indoor-outdoor café. All are housed in a historic building dating from 1911 that was originally used for smoking beef. Among the extensive offerings of contemporary Japanese art are watercolors, oils, wood-block prints, and lithographs. When artwork by early renowned artists of Hawaii such as David Hitchcock and Madge Tennent occasionally finds its way to the gallery, it seldom remains for long, but lithographs of fish and birds dating from the late 1800s are normally in stock. A connecting room carries Oriental antiques—a ladle from the Han dynasty dating back 2,000 years, a Tang dynasty camel, and fine pieces of Chinese jade, as well as Japanese lacquer pieces and carved netsuke. **Robyn Buntin's Jewelry Collection** features sterling, crystal, Art Nouveau, and Art Deco glass and jewelry.

Next door, at 926–930 Maunakea, **Aloha Antiques and Collectibles** has a marvelous jumble of "stuff." Perhaps not everything is quite so authentically antique, but a prowl through the overcrowded basement, main floor, and loft is intriguing. Amid the river jade from China, the cobalt glass, the amber pieces, and the figurines from occupied Japan are dusty pieces of Hawaiiana—old stone bowls, *ulu maika* (polished stones used in a Hawaiian game similar to bowling), poi pounders, pig boards, koa-wood ukuleles, and 1940s koa-wood furniture (the beautifully grained koa wood was also used by early Hawaiians for their canoes). The store is a thrift-shopper's paradise, though not exactly at thrift prices. But the proprietor has been known to deal, so don't hesitate to negotiate if you really want something.

Sword collectors can cut a wide swath through all the sword paraphernalia and head right for the basement of **Bushido**, at 936 Maunakea Street, where antique Japanese swords are priced from $500 to $150,000. Proprietor Robert Benson, who for years studied traditional sword polishing in Japan, is an expert in this field. At street level the shop displays more variety: old jade buttons for $5 each, antique Korean ceramics, and obis and kimonos. Finally, at 938 Maunakea Street, **Gallery Mikado** is a pleasant little shop featuring a vast array of vintage Japanese, Chinese, and Korean ceramics, plus a nice collection of modern and antique Japanese woodblock prints.

For those interested in truly exquisite gifts, a shop on Bishop Street is worth the five-block walk to the east (toward Diamond Head). **Martin & MacArthur** (841 Bishop Street) carries beautifully crafted koa-wood furniture (ready-made as well as made to your specifications), plus boxes, books with koa covers, games, and other specialty items, many of which are created by Hawaii artisans.

Chinatown

Back on Maunakea Street, turn left onto King Street to find the **Oahu Market**, where, if you trust your senses, you'll think you're in another country. Ducks hang on display hooks, and pigs' heads lie in butcher cases; the butcher will slice off a taste of red pork if you intend to buy. The chatter is in Japanese, Chinese, Vietnamese, and pidgin along the crowded aisle that leads past the fresh produce—mounds of Chinese cabbage, kale, lemon cress, and daikon.

In the last few years the end of King Street near Nuuanu Stream has become a dynamic, bustling stretch of small shops operated by recent Vietnamese immigrants. Stop for lunch at **Ba-Le**, an inexpensive Vietnamese sandwich shop where the fresh bread and flaky croissants rival those baked in a French *boulangerie*. Returning to Maunakea Street, you'll find the **Chinatown Mall** (formerly the Lee and Young Mall), a conglomeration of stalls under one roof where the freshwater-pearl necklaces are cheap enough that you can take home several for friends.

As you continue inland on Maunakea Street you pass through the heart of Chinatown. This historic district has prospered despite two fires, the first of which, in 1886, destroyed eight blocks. The second was set deliberately by the board of health in 1900 to halt the spread of bubonic plague, but it raged out of control when burning embers spread to nearby rooftops. The buildings standing in Chinatown today were built after 1900. Recently, private developers, with help from government agencies, have been restoring these turn-of-the century buildings. A shopping mall, **Maunakea Marketplace**, which opened in 1990 on Hotel and Maunakea streets, has 70 shops, restaurants, an open market, and a food court, where you can sample Thai, Japanese, Malaysian, and Filipino dishes. Check out the intriguing collectibles from the East (cloisonné boxes, eggs, vases, artwork, and jade and pearl jewelry) that fill every corner of the mall's small shops.

All along Maunakea Street are bakeries, lei stands, herb shops, noodle factories, and restaurants. Almond cookies, candied ginger, and salty *li hing mui* (preserved plum), which local children suck on like jawbreakers, are tasty treats to buy at **Shung Chong Yuein**. Incense burns at an altar in the **Fook Sau Tong** herb shop, where you can describe your ailment and receive a mixture of ginseng, herbs, powdered deer horn, and the like from tiny drawers that line the back wall. You can watch the ladies stringing fragrant *pikake,* crown flower, or ginger leis at **Cindy's Lei Shoppe** or **Sweetheart's Lei Shop**—both of which charge lower prices than do the airport lei stands. At Hawaii's oldest Chinese restaurant, Wo Fat, a pink building with a distinctive Oriental green-tile roof right around the corner on North Hotel Street, lunch in the upstairs dining room is about seven or eight dollars. At the top of Maunakea Street, across King Street and bordered by Nuuanu Stream, is the **Chinese Cultural Plaza**, with more shops and restaurants, which by now may be an anticlimax—except for the statue of Sun Yat-sen, which stands as a reminder of his years as a student in Hawaii.

The Chinese Chamber of Commerce (Tel: 533-3181), the Hawaii Heritage Center (Tel: 521-2749), and the Chinatown Historical Society (Tel: 521-3045), conduct inexpensive walking tours of Chinatown. The historical society tours offer lunch as an option. The area can be reached from Waikiki by catching TheBus (number 2) on Kuhio Avenue.

Galleries

Just a block or two away from Chinatown, artists' galleries and studios proliferate. At 1128 Smith Street, the artist Ramsay, best known for her detailed drawings of buildings, displays the works of many other Hawaii artists as well at **Ramsay Galleries & Café**. Here you can sip a cooling libation in the clean, modern gallery bar, enjoy lunch or dinner, or even reserve the private dining room free of charge if you buy your refreshments from the gallery. (While you're in the neighborhood, peek into **Young's Noodle Factory** across the street to see the bakers up to their arms in flour and dough making fresh chow mein noodles.)

A couple of blocks away, at 1164 Nuuanu Avenue, **Pegge Hopper** displays her ever-popular paintings of Hawaiian women in soft shades of rose, green, and beige. Calendars, notecards, and tote bags all carry her signature artwork.

At 1118 Nuuanu is **Lai Fong Department Store**, not a gallery, but a long-standing tradition anyway. The name is deceiving, as the store is a sort of glorified secondhand emporium of Chinese teak and rosewood furniture, ivory and jade jewelry, dishes, clothing, and other artifacts. You can even order a custom-made, figure-fitting, silk-brocade Chinese *cheong sam* with a high collar and frog fastenings. Lai Fong also carries Niihau-shell necklaces— one beauty was recently priced at $7,000.

Museum Shops

Hawaii's museum gift shops offer an exciting array of Pacific treasures that usually reflect the focus of the museum. The **Contemporary Museum**, at 2411 Makiki Heights Drive (above the Punchbowl area), specializes in fun and funky items, many one-of-a-kind, fashioned by artists. Dolls—a mermaid in a chair, a soft doll with a ceramic teapot for a head—and other original creations might be $60 to $100. Signed and numbered ceramic jewelry is in the $30 to $100 range. Everything in the shop is unusual and the selection changes often.

The **Academy Shop** at the Honolulu Academy of Arts, 900 South Beretania Street, garners goods from around the world: wonderful Indonesian textiles, silver and unusual costume jewelry, handblown glass, and art prints are available throughout the year. But the best time to visit the Academy Shop is during the annual Folk Art Bazaar, beginning the day after Thanksgiving and running for about ten days through the following Sunday, when a multitude of imported items is for sale.

At the Bishop Museum's **Shop Pacifica**, 1525 Bernice Street (exit 20A off H-1), the emphasis is on collectibles and artifacts from Hawaii and the Pacific. Koa-wood bowls and boxes, Niihau-shell leis, petroglyph items such as magnet sets, pitchers, and vases (from $5 to $130), and handmade Hawaiian crafts, including bone fish hooks and feather hat bands, are available. There is also a fine selection of Hawaiiana, South Pacific, and natural history books.

The **Hawaii Children's Museum** and its adjoining gift shop at Dole Cannery Square, 650 Iwilei Road, offer diversion for kids and parents alike. As with the museum itself, the shop's gifts are both educational and entertaining. Bubble blowers in odd shapes, wooden puzzles, pop-up books, science, history, and geography learning games, and other imaginative packable toys line the shelves.

Finally, military buffs will want to take in the gift shop at the **U.S. Army Museum** at Fort De Russy's Randolph Building on the beach in Waikiki. Patriots will find flags, reprints of newspapers published on December 7, 1941, books, badges, hats, and souvenirs with military emblems.

Special Hawaiiana

If you want an authentic made-in-Hawaii remembrance of your trip, you might consider watercolors, pastels, or oil paintings by local artists; 14-karat-gold engraved heirloom jewelry; Niihau-shell leis; resort wear (including bathing suits, muumuu, and aloha shirts); beautifully crafted and finished bowls, boxes, and hand mirrors of koa, milo, or monkeypod wood; perfumes with Island scents such as *pikake,* tuberose, and ginger; and grown-in-the-Islands food items: macadamia nuts and candies, Kona coffee, guava, passion fruit, *poha* (wild cape gooseberry) jams and jellies, and fresh pineapples and other fruit. (See the Plants and Produce section, below.)

Hawaii residents purchase made-in-the-Islands crafts from **Pacific Handcrafters Guild**. The guild sponsors four major sales a year—spring, summer, fall, and before Christmas—at either Thomas Square (a park bounded by South King and South Beretania streets and Ward Avenue near the Honolulu Academy of Arts and the Blaisdell Center) or Ala Moana Beach Park. Stringent requirements ensure the amount of handwork done on an item, the quality of the work, and so on. Call or write the main office of the guild for specific dates and locations: P.O. Box 90663, Honolulu, HI 96835; Tel: 254-6788.

Within walking distance of Ala Moana Shopping Center is a cluster of antiques dealers in one big shop at 1347 Kapiolani Boulevard called **Antique Alley**. In addition to the goods that most antiques shops carry, such as bone china cups, old jewelry, crystals, and antique buttons, two dealers specialize in Hawaiiana. **Pake Zane** stocks collectible hula dolls, spoons, surfer and military items, bottles, bowls, license plates, stamps, coins, and precontact stone, feather, and shell pieces. At an adjacent shop, **Steve Goodenow** displays authentic Hawaiian stone artifacts: poi pounders, adzes, mortars, and *ulu maika*—game stones from the past.

For a large selection of rare Niihau-shell necklaces as well as other Hawaiian jewelry, the place to go in Honolulu is **Hildgund**, at 119 Merchant Street, downtown. (For more about these necklaces, see the Kauai and Niihau chapters.)

Plants and Produce

The quintessential Hawaiian souvenir may be the coconut, which can be mailed anywhere in the world from any post office in Hawaii. If you aren't lucky enough to find one lying on the ground, pick out a coconut for about a buck at any grocery store—they're cheaper outside Waikiki. Coconuts weigh three or four pounds, and the flat rate, domestic, is $4.10 for three pounds and $4.65 for four pounds. Duke Gum of the U.S. Postal Service, which mails nearly 2,000 a year from here, says the coconut's own plain brown wrapper meets postal shipping requirements. Just ink on the address, add the stamps, and mail a coconut to someone anywhere on the Mainland.

If you wish to buy other produce or plants to bring home, it is wise to check with your customs office regarding import regulations before departing your homeland (although information can often be obtained locally from the airline offices). You cannot take fruit, plants, or other produce into the U.S. Mainland, Canada, or Britain unless it has been inspected and approved by the U.S. Department of Agriculture. Pre-inspected and packaged pineapples, papayas, and assorted plant cuttings are sold at Hawaiian airports. Cut flowers (except gardenias and long-stemmed roses) and leis (except jade leis, made from the unusual green jade flower, and purple woven orchid leis—called maunaloa leis—both of which can harbor some sneaky little bugs) can be transported to the U.S. Mainland. The USDA recently instituted a telephone service to answer questions about bringing agricultural products to the Mainland; Tel: 541-1991.

Hawaii Wear

If you're looking for the perfect muumuu or aloha shirt, you will want to strike out from Waikiki. To the uninitiated, the styles and incumbent status of these casual pieces of tropical fashion might be indistinguishable. To a resident, however, a muumuu can place its wearer precisely at a certain economic level, and it definitely reveals something about style and taste. No local couples, unless they are 80-year-old new arrivals, would walk arm-in-arm dressed alike in bold prints from **Hilo Hattie's Fashion Center** (700 North Nimitz Highway, the road to the airport); if your aim *is* to look like a tourist, however, the center's free bus will take you there from several hotels and other locations in Waikiki.

If you are status conscious, like many Island career women, you might choose a designer muumuu by Princess Kaiulani or Mamo. The **Princess Kaiulani** outlet is at 1222 Kaumualii Street (on the airport, or northwestern, side of Honolulu); **Mamo Howell, Inc.**, is at Ward Warehouse on Ala Moana Boulevard (see below); and many fine brands are carried by Liberty House. Designer muumuu range from $90 to $200.

Middle- and upper-income men, on the other hand, will undoubtedly buy their inside-out-print aloha shirt from **Reyn's**, at Ala Moana Center (see below), or **Andrade Sale Studio**, at the Royal Hawaiian Shopping Center in Waikiki, or perhaps they'll choose a Tori Richard shirt from Liberty House. Those whose tastes lean to Art Deco or who fondly remember their days as flower children will find their way to **Bailey's Antique and Thrift Shop** (758 Kapahulu Avenue, bordering the Diamond Head edge of Waikiki) to buy a "silkie," the wildly colorful early rayon shirts that now run from $75 to $2,000. These oldies but goodies never seem to fade—neither out nor away. When it comes to Hawaiian shirts, "more is more," according to Ellery Chun, who created them in 1931 to save his father's sagging garment business after coming home from Yale. Bailey's also carries all kinds of collectibles from the 1940s and 1950s—hula-girl figurines, barefoot ashtrays, scenic old Matson menu covers, ukuleles, and more.

Another good place to find aloha shirts and muumuu is

Linda's Vintage Isle (373 Olohana Street, south of Kuhio Avenue on the Ewa side of Waikiki), an antique haberdashery specializing in "silkies"; most are in the $250 to $350 range, but certain collectibles cost up to $2,000, such as a 1937 hand-printed and hand-screened crepe de chine tiger-print shirt. Cotton shirts range from $45 to $150. A collector for 15 years, owner Linda Sheehan has between 200 and 300 shirts, as well as Hawaiian quilts, muumuu, and other Hawaiiana.

In the Ala Moana neighborhood, behind Ward Centre (see below), is a boutique of another ilk. Kelsey Sears, a vibrant former flight attendant, opened the **Ultimate You** (1112 Auahi Street) in 1983 when she realized Hawaii had nothing like it. Honolulu's society folks bring in their designer clothing on consignment for resale. A $2,500 Chanel suit might be priced at $650. All merchandise—slacks, dresses, suits, muumuu and jewelry—must pass Kelsey's critical eye.

When you feel as if you've shopped till you're ready to drop, it's time to head for the beach. **Ann Tongg Swimwear** (Tel: 537-6255 for an appointment) will custom design a new suit from your favorite old one in any combination of prints or solids you choose from among her lycra swatches. She actually charges less than ready-made (from $35). She can whip up a two-piece suit to cover the female form with some degree of modesty—yet not make the wearer look like an old fossil—and on request she will even sneak a little fiberfill lining in the top. For visitors who want to wear their new suits when they get to Hawaii, Tongg works by mail order. Simply send her an old bathing suit and list your color preferences; she'll send you swatches and have the suit ready for a fitting when you arrive. Otherwise, it might take about ten days and two visits to have a custom suit completed.

Shopping Malls
Honolulu's major shopping mall, **Ala Moana Center** (from Waikiki catch TheBus, number 8, 19, or 20, for 60 cents exact change, on Kuhio Avenue and take it to 1450 Ala Moana Boulevard), located on the way into Waikiki from the airport, is open Monday through Saturday from 9:30 A.M. to 9:00 P.M. and Sunday from 10:00 A.M. to 5:00 P.M. It houses Honolulu's leading department store, Liberty House, as well as Mainland standbys JC Penney and Sears Roebuck.

The shops and restaurants on the lower level (near the

stage where Hawaiian entertainment is regularly featured) seem more interesting than the standard mall shops on the upper level. **Iida's** has Japanese goods: cups with covers to keep your tea steaming, elegant fans for a couple of dollars, lacquered trays, trinket boxes, and coasters; while on the opposite (makai) side, **Irene's Hawaiian Gifts** carries made-in-Hawaii everything, from key chains to etched glass. For lunch, stop in the **Makai Market Food Court**, a complex that dishes out every kind of fast food you can possibly crave—*saimin* (a noodle soup), pizza, plate lunches with rice and teriyaki beef, hamburgers—or make your way back upstairs to order something exotic from **Shirokiya's** sushi bar. All in all, the Ala Moana Center is well worth a stop if you have the time; it resembles a modern Mainland mall, but it has a definite Hawaiian flavor, with colorful *koi* (carp) in the center ponds, blue skies overhead, and local shoppers in shorts and thongs.

Palm Boulevard, a row of shops housing leading designers, opened in 1990 at Ala Moana. Names such as Gucci, Georg Jensen, Bruno Magli, Cartier, Waterford/Wedgwood, Lancel, and Adrienne Vittadini might intimidate all but the most well-heeled shopper, but the boutiques are wonderful for browsing. Located here are Christian Dior's first boutique in the United States, Chanel's first fine-jewelry boutique in the world, and the second and largest Emporio Armani in the United States. If you splurge on nothing else, treat yourself to tea served with breads or cookies in Island flavors—double-chocolate macadamia-nut bread, lemon lilikoi cookies—at the **Royal Copenhagen** shop.

Three other shopping malls along Ala Moana Boulevard rate acknowledgment: **Ward Centre** (1200 Ala Moana Boulevard), **Ward Warehouse** (1050 Ala Moana Boulevard), and, closer to downtown, **Restaurant Row** (500 Ala Moana Boulevard). Ride TheBus (number 19 or 20) from Kuhio Avenue, or catch the Waikiki Trolley—$15 for a daily pass—which will take you to all three shopping malls (10 to 20 minutes from Waikiki), as well as to Chinatown.

Much of the success of Ward Centre and the new Restaurant Row has come about because of the innumerable restaurants located in each. Both attract the upwardly mobile crowd. Ward Centre has a wonderful bakery, **Mary Catherine's**, and a **Lady Judith** for gorgeous and dear evening gowns and sweaters. The **Row Bar** in the center of the Restaurant Row complex is a popular after-work meeting place, and on Sunday afternoons live local entertainment is often featured there.

At Ward Warehouse, **Nohea Gallery** presents the most elegant of Hawaiian gifts. Works by 180 Hawaii artists include wattle baskets by Maui artist Mika McCann, painted silk scarves, and one-of-a-kind wall hangings appliquéd with Polynesian scenes. Look for translucent-thin wooden bowls by Ron Kent and other Hawaiian woodworkers but be prepared for the $300 to $5,000 price tag. Wood-block prints depicting Hawaiian legends by Big Island artist Dietrich Varez are more affordable, from $12 to $23, unframed.

Bargain Hunting

It's the excursions off the beaten track to outlying markets and sales that result in real finds in Honolulu. Be sure to wear comfortable walking shoes and cool clothing. Some shoppers even take umbrellas to shade themselves from the tropical sun at the year-round shopping phenomenon called the **Aloha Flea Market**, at which more than 1,500 merchants rim Aloha Stadium every Wednesday, Saturday, and Sunday from 7:30 A.M. to 3:00 P.M., selling new and used goods from every corner of the earth. In the last few years commercial sellers with new merchandise have come to predominate the "swap meet," but if you go during the cooler early-morning hours, especially on weekends, you might find a real deal among the few sellers who have cleaned their cupboards and closets of grandma and grandpa's heirlooms. But even if you don't find an English bone-china cup for 50 cents, or a Baccarat bowl for ten dollars, it's great fun to browse for an hour or two, and the entry fee is only 35 cents; parking is free. The inevitable tee-shirts are here in heaping piles, and the sweat shirts are actually a good buy. You'll find a wider variety of Hawaiian-print cotton material than in the fabric stores—and it will cost less, too. Eel-skin purses, wallets, and briefcases are also a deal here.

You can get to Aloha Stadium from Kuhio Avenue in Waikiki aboard TheBus (number 20). If you expect to make many purchases, Eastmark Enterprises, with large baggage compartments on its buses, will shuttle you to the stadium in air-conditioned comfort for six dollars round trip; Tel: 955-4050 for boarding schedules.

Maybe they're not uniquely Hawaiian, but **garage sales** in Hawaii are a marvelous Saturday-morning diversion. Though you might find a few Sunday sales, the best hunting is on Saturday mornings from eight to noon during

June, July, and August. To find the best locale, look through the ads in either of the two daily newspapers, the *Honolulu Advertiser* or the *Star-Bulletin,* or check out the *Penny Saver* (free at street dispensers) or the *Sun Press,* a weekly paper that covers various Oahu neighborhoods. Adventurous types who don't give in to disappointment might simply head for a well-populated suburb like Hawaii Kai, Enchanted Lake, or Lanikai, on the Windward side, and look for Garage Sale signs tacked on mailboxes and lampposts. Handymen are bound to find old monkeypod bowls sorely in need of rescuing and refinishing—but even if you find nothing of interest, it's a great way to get out and talk with some local people. They'll tell you about the high cost of living and the low rate of pay, and you won't feel so bad about going back to sub-freezing temperatures.

—*Betty Fullard-Leo*

DINING IN THE ISLANDS

By John Heckathorn

At an informal lunch during one of the recent yearly Kapalua wine festivals, California vintner Robert Mondavi recalled that when he first started travelling to the Islands 20 years ago the culinary offerings were less than inspiring. "You couldn't get fresh fish or fresh vegetables," he said. "It was hard to find a decent bottle of wine, and if you did, it hadn't been properly stored."

Fortunately, things have improved significantly in the intervening decades, and now, Mondavi says, "The ingredients are fresh, the wine is good, and the chefs here can hold their heads up with chefs from anywhere in the world."

It's hard to imagine that Hawaii, with its isolation and its relatively small resident population, could ever compete with the top-level restaurants of, say, Paris or New York. But compared to less-lofty culinary concentrations, Hawaii does extremely well. In fact, it has to: The food must be good here because Hawaii is in competition with the rest of the world's resorts for its 7 million yearly visitors, and people on vacation like to eat well—or at least as well as they do at home.

Hawaii's hospitality industry draws chefs from all over the world and patrons whose tastes have been developed in dozens of different cultures. The result is a remarkably dynamic and continually interesting Island cuisine: a collision of European tradition and flair, Asian refinement, and an emerging Hawaii regional cuisine based on fresh local ingredients. So, what is the food like in contemporary Hawaii? How about a soft taco filled with Beijing Duck? Or wok-charred fresh tuna heaped with Maui onion rings as thin as angel hair? Or *lumpia* (a Filipino variety of egg roll) filled with Chinese chicken salad made with *kiawe*-smoked (mesquite-smoked) chicken? The possibilities are endless, and all the permutations of cultures, cooking styles, and ingredients add up to a kind of culinary fun that can't be found elsewhere.

Of course, you can get the basics in Hawaii if you want them: There's always decent pasta or prime rib or an authentic Caesar salad. But there are also the basics of half a dozen Asian cultures (fish in black-bean sauce, miso soup, Vietnamese roll-ups) as well as the basics of Polynesia (*poi,* raw fish with seaweed, tropical fruits). It is sometimes difficult to decide what to eat in Hawaii because the choice is so overwhelming. But you can probably find whatever you crave in the Islands.

EATING SEAFOOD IN THE ISLANDS

Visitors to Hawaii often have difficulty finding what they think of as seafood restaurants, those large, relatively inexpensive fish houses that dot the coasts of the Mainland. Seafood is not hard to find here, it's just that the restaurants that serve it don't have a large neon lobster on the sign outside or fishing floats and nets as part of their decor. The demand for fresh fish in the Islands is so great that virtually every quality restaurant prepares it in some fashion or another. Much of the seafood finds its way into Asian restaurants: The choicest bits end up in high-priced sushi bars, but Japanese cuisine being what it is, virtually every Japanese restaurant is largely a seafood restaurant. In addition, a number of Chinese restaurants now bill themselves as Chinese seafood restaurants.

Local fish are usually served under their Hawaiian names. As these are unfamiliar to most visitors, here's a quick glossary of frequently served fishes. *Opakapaka, onaga,* and *uku* are all snappers—white-fleshed and delicate in flavor, a good bet for people who do not like their fish too fishy. The best grades of *ahi* (yellowfin tuna) are often served as *sashimi* (raw fish slices, Japanese style). *Aku,* another local favorite, is skipjack tuna, which is redder and has a more pronounced fishy taste than ahi. *Mahimahi* is dolphin*fish*—not the mammal. Unless it specifically says "fresh," the mahi on the menu probably arrived frozen from Taiwan. *Au* is marlin, similar in taste and texture to swordfish, best served as a fillet. *Ulua* is a deep ocean game fish, tasty if cooked right, tough if not. If you order a whole fish steamed in a Chinese restaurant, you will most likely get *ubu*—a brightly colored reef fish commonly called parrotfish for its beaklike mouth. Most local fish is well worth eating if served fresh—which is why the catch of the day is always so expensive, especially if it's a popular fish such as opakapaka or onaga.

CHOOSING A RESTAURANT

For the traveller, the issue often is not what to eat, but where. Is it worth the trouble of seeking out the restaurants where local residents eat—or is the restaurant in, or across the street from, your hotel just as good or better? If you want to eat well and to do some experimenting while you are in Hawaii you'll probably want to try both. The meal in your hotel will be more costly, and the one in the local joint will be less refined, but both will have their merits.

What follows is a highly selective guide to Hawaii's restaurants, beginning with Waikiki, where the vast majority of visitors spend at least part of their stay. Our culinary horizon then expands to include the rest of Honolulu, with its many interesting restaurants, followed by quick forays to the other parts of Oahu and to the Neighbor Islands.

The telephone area code for all of Hawaii is 808.

WAIKIKI

Waikiki has more wonderful restaurants than anyplace else in Hawaii—and more awful ones, plus a vast number that are stunningly mediocre. The key to dining well in Waikiki is to focus on top-of-the-line establishments.

With only a few exceptions, expensive Waikiki restaurants provide better value than those that are moderately priced. The basic reason is rent. Waikiki claims some of the most expensive real estate on the planet. Decent restaurant space can now run as high as $200 per square foot a year. So a restaurant with a mid-range menu probably has to combine some overpricing with skimping on food costs or service, or both, to pay the landlord.

In addition, few Honolulu residents are willing to venture into the congestion of Waikiki except for a special occasion or a memorable meal. For an average restaurant, they won't bother. And why should they? The city proper outside Waikiki has plenty of restaurants that are both cheaper and better. So an unexceptional Waikiki restaurant depends almost entirely on tourist business. And too great a reliance on transient rather than repeat customers is never good for a restaurant: It breeds cynicism and slackness in even a well-intentioned establishment.

If you wish to dine well at moderate cost while staying in Waikiki accommodations, your best bet is to rent a car or catch a cab. Travelling just a few blocks out of Waikiki can cut your dinner tab in half—and probably guarantee a more interesting evening, or at least more interesting food (see Dining in Honolulu Outside Waikiki, below).

Inside Waikiki, the best restaurants are top-rank hotel dining rooms where service is formal, the wine list extensive, and dinner costs $75 to $100 a person, not including wine. Most travellers are rightfully wary of hotel restaurants, but the best half-dozen Waikiki hotel restaurants all enjoy a wide local following and are too good to ignore. Despite their pricey menus, some of these establishments lose tens of thousands of dollars a month. They aren't there so much to make money as to satisfy guests who expect a high level of cuisine. The rest of a hotel's operations essentially subsidize both the talent in the kitchen and the trained staff on the floor. These restaurants are, at their own level, bargains—and can be counted on to provide among the best prepared and presented meals the Islands have to offer.

THE TOP OF THE LINE

When the Hilton Hawaiian Village (2005 Kalia Road) spent nearly $100 million remodeling its facilities in 1987–1988, it gave its star restaurant, **Bali-by-the-Sea**, a stellar setting, right on the ocean. When you make a reservation, you might ask for a table along the open outside wall, where you can hear the surf. The furnishings, including the fussy white chairs, are a bit overdone, but the moonlight on the water makes up for it all.

The restaurant was named Bali years ago when it was an Indonesian *rijsttafel* restaurant. The name stuck, but the cuisine, under the direction of chef Yves Menoret, is now Continental with a number of Italian touches. *Opihi,* a strongly flavored Island limpet, is served on ice with oysters, clams, and prawns as an appetizer. Kaiwi Channel opakapaka comes in fresh basil sauce. Other noteworthy dishes include a coquille of shrimp and scallops, a red snapper soup topped with puff pastry, and tenderloin of beef with black peppercorns. The Bali's soufflés—sweet, light, and steaming—can round off a meal nicely. Wine steward Stephen Fuller helpfully recommends good values from the wine list. Tel: 941-BALI.

Also at the Hilton is the **Golden Dragon**. With only a couple of exceptions, it's absurd to eat Chinese food in Waikiki. Outside Waikiki, Honolulu is dotted with inexpensive, good-to-great Chinese eateries, and the best-known Chinese restaurants inside Waikiki (House of Hong, Lau Yee Chai) have been resting on their laurels for decades. But the Golden Dragon is one of the exceptions (another is Dynasty, described below in the Moderate to Inexpensive category). The Golden Dragon is a first-string restaurant that happens to have a Chinese chef, Steven Chiang.

The black-and-red lacquered dining room, filled with Chinese antiques, is divided by pillars into small, intimate areas, most with a view of the Hilton's artificial lagoon. The menu here may sound familiar—almond duck, lobster with black-bean sauce, imperial beggar's chicken—but the food and the presentation are out of the ordinary. The stir-fried lobster with curry sauce, raisins, and *haupia* (a Hawaiian pudding) is not to be missed, and the grilled Szechwan beef starts as filet mignon. The service is unobtrusive, except for the tea lady, who after your meal brings a half dozen varieties of tea on an antique cart. She allows you to choose your own tea, brews it, and then tells your fortune. This is one of the few Chinese restaurants with an excellent wine list. Call 24 hours ahead if you would like to order Peking duck or beggar's chicken. Tel: 946-5336.

If the Golden Dragon is Waikiki's most elegant Chinese restaurant, its most elegant Japanese restaurant is **Kyo-ya** (2057 Kalakaua Avenue). For years, Kyo-ya was a landmark, a cute little red-and-white Japanese-style building near the McCully Street entrance to Waikiki. It is no longer so. A couple of years ago its owners spent millions of dollars to turn it into a multi-story, first-class Japanese restaurant with several dining rooms. The result is breathtakingly beautiful, though austere: gray-on-gray with stainless-steel accents.

For the real Kyo-ya experience, skip the downstairs dining room, which is disappointingly plain in the Japanese fashion, and book instead a private dining room upstairs. To do so, you have to promise to eat one of the relatively expensive top-of-the-line *kaiseki* dinners (ranging from about $50 to $90 per person). Kaiseki, which evolved out of the tea ceremony, comprises many small courses, served one after another on a succession of fancy plates. You can ask for a menu in advance, but all you get is general categories. For instance, you'll be told that *zensai* (appetizers) will be followed by *suimono* (clear soup), then by *sashimi* (raw fish). But you don't get details—it's up to the chef to do his best with what's fresh that night.

The food tends to be traditional Japanese with great attention to detail. Don't worry if you are not too crazy about one of the dishes: If you should hate the *chawan-mushi* (a custard cup with bits of chicken, shrimp, and mushroom), you'll probably love something else, the *yakimono* (perhaps grilled butterfish) or the tempura. All in all, a Kyo-ya dinner is likely to knock your socks off, even if they forget to sprinkle gold foil on the sashimi. Reservations are a must for a private room; Tel: 947-3911.

La Mer (at the Halekulani, 2199 Kalia Road) is the most formal restaurant in Hawaii. Men do not usually feel compelled to wear coat and tie to dinner in Hawaii, although the practice is not unknown. Still, La Mer positively requires jackets for gentlemen, but not—in deference to the climate—ties. La Mer is in an upstairs dining room, done in muted browns and tans, with a pleasant view of the ocean.

Service is designed to be impeccable, with elaborate tableside presentation of each dish. The water in your glass is Evian. The menu is contemporary French cuisine, modified somewhat to use locally available ingredients, by chef George Mavrothalassitis. (The name is Greek, but the man and his training are thoroughly French.) The Kahuku prawns au gratin in a zucchini shell and the salad of sautéed *moana* (a local fish), smoked bone marrow, and fried angel hair potatoes are the stars of the appetizer menu. Among the entrées, the stand-out is clearly the onaga baked in a thyme and rosemary rock-salt crust—a preparation both beautiful and practical, since it creates a perfectly tender and aromatic fish fillet. The sautéed Lanai venison in a black-pepper wine-vinegar sauce is another dish you won't find anywhere else.

The cheese course is served with an excellent walnut bread (but watch the prices on the vintage Port cart that accompanies the cheese). It's hard to stay hungry for dessert here, but if you are oriented toward sweets you might try a sampler of such desserts as dark and white chocolate pâté, warm pineapple tart, and passion-fruit soufflé. La Mer's wine list is heavily French, with California adequately represented. Tel: 923-2311.

Michel's at the Colony Surf Hotel (2895 Kalakaua Avenue) is the grande dame of Waikiki restaurants, aging perhaps, but still beautiful. Michel's is a well-appointed formal restaurant, saved from stuffiness because one wall opens directly on Sans Souci Beach, which is just east of Waikiki Beach, across Kapiolani Park near Diamond Head. At lunch you can sometimes smell the coconut oil of the beach-goers lying on the sand a few feet away. At sunset the view over the water is spectacular.

The problem with Michel's is that the menu literally had not changed since the restaurant opened in 1961. Last year the hotel hired a new chef, Michel Saragueta of the Beverly Hills Hotel, and instructed him to update Michel's cuisine. No sooner had word leaked to the local media than the arriving chef found his mail filled with letters telling him not to change a thing. So some classics are bound to remain. Michel's will probably always be a place where you can get onion soup, Caesar salad, chateaubriand, and the fresh opakapaka in velvety hollandaise that is deservedly a classic. But now you can get Saragueta's more adventurous cuisine here as well. His pasta dishes are nearly magical; the one with vegetables in curry sauce with grilled shrimp is supreme. The wine list has been slowly updated, but its specialty remains, alas, high prices.

Alone among Waikiki's glittering dining rooms, Michel's also does breakfast, lunch, and Sunday brunch. If you enjoy ambience but are not quite up to dinner, one of the earlier meals is less expensive and likely to be very good. The cool of the morning is a particularly pleasant time to be dining at the beach. For reservations (call well ahead for weekends and Sunday brunch), Tel: 923-6552.

There's a new entry among the top Waikiki dining rooms, the **Prince Court**, at the Hawaii Prince Hotel (which is just outside of Waikiki at 100 Holomoana Street). Austerely elegant, the large third-floor restaurant has a sweeping view of the Ala Wai Yacht Harbor and perhaps the greatest sunset view of any Waikiki restaurant. To give an indication of how well thought out the dining room is: A see-through bronze screen keeps the sun from overheating the window tables in the afternoon and early evening—but just as the sun begins to set the screen automatically rises to allow an unobstructed view.

Chef Gary Strehl's food is as carefully considered as the setting in which it is served. The stars of the menu are the sesame-grilled crab and shrimp hash—a fall-apart-in-the-mouth concoction with a crispy crust enlivened by three quite disparate sauces (black bean, tomato, and fennel cream)—and an extraordinary update of a salad Niçoise with fresh seared *ahi,* slices of white and blue potatoes, and a delicate herb dressing. The desserts include Kilauea's Revenge, a chocolate mousse volcano erupting with raspberry and apricot sauces.

In addition to these wonders at dinnertime, the Prince Court now sets the standard for Sunday brunches in Honolulu: acres and acres of seafood, salads, cheeses, and desserts. All entrées are cooked to order—no limp, steam-table fare here—and for a slight surcharge the Prince Court will pour all the Champagne and wine you can consume without drinking yourself silly on a Sunday morning. A plus for those who hate cigarette smoke: The entire restaurant is nonsmoking. The Prince Court is a good-size restaurant, but reservations are still recommended. Tel: 956-1111.

For years the **Secret** (Hawaiian Regent Hotel, 2552 Kalakaua Avenue) was known as the Third Floor. But then two Japanese corporations got into a very nasty, very public fight over control of the hotel, and the loser made the winner change the copyrighted restaurant name. The new name is not perhaps a happy choice, but the Secret is by far the most comfortable of Waikiki's haute cuisine dining rooms. It's a local favorite for sentimental occasions such as anniversaries. No view here, but there's a towering ceiling and a large tiled carp pond in the center of the restaurant. High-back rattan chairs provide a pleasing sense of privacy for each diner in the vast room.

Service is excellent, though a bit informal. Your waiter may very well introduce himself by saying, "Hi, my name is ———." Over the years, a dinner here has become heavily ritualized. It begins with warm East Indian *naan* bread and duck-liver pâté and ends with ice-cream bonbons served with a chip of dry ice underneath, giving off theatrical billows of steam. The printed menu is conventional stuff; it is better to order from the long list of daily specials. Frogs' legs Provençal or in garlic butter are usually available, as either an entrée or an appetizer. There are always a fresh fish or two and excellent veal dishes. You may be tempted by the vast appetizer bar buffet called Promising Start, but unless you're very hungry it's best skipped, because there's nothing *nouvelle* about the size of the portions served here.

The wine list is particularly strong in German whites and French reds. Sommelier Richard Dean is one of the best (and least pretentious) in Hawaii; his advice is worth taking. Reservations a must; Tel: 921-5161.

EXPENSIVE TO MODERATE

In addition to the top-of-the-line restaurants, Waikiki has a mixed bag of other restaurants that have distinguished themselves, most of which are also expensive. These are usually not hotel restaurants, although some are located in smaller hotels, from which they lease space. None has the extensive menus, the legions of sous chefs, or the deep wine lists of the hotel dining rooms, but they have found a niche in the market and fill it well.

By far the best moderately priced restaurant in Waikiki is **Bon Appetit**, which is located on the second floor of a towering condominium called Discovery Bay (1778 Ala Moana Boulevard). Under owner Guy Banal and chef Hervé Chabin, Bon Appetit has evolved into an unpretentious but comfortable eatery that specializes in French country cooking, especially from the south of France. Perhaps the signature dish here is *cassoulet au confit de canard,* rich with the taste of double-cooked duck, veal, and sausage. The food at Bon Appetit is rich: fresh goose liver with truffle sauce, baby chicken with morel mushrooms, and both steak and crab tartare. Each week there are three- or four-course dinner specials. The wine list includes about 50 wines, French with a sprinkling of California, ample enough for a small restaurant. Tel: 942-3837.

There seem to be steak houses on every corner in Waikiki, but **Hy's Steak House** (2440 Kuhio Avenue) is the reigning red-meat champion—steaks of all cuts and varieties, wonderful rack of lamb or lamb Wellington, with, as you would expect, Caesar salad and flaming cherries jubilee on the menu as well. In deference to emerging health trends, the menu also lists some lighter items, including vegetarian entrées. There are two dining rooms here: The Art Deco room is smaller and quieter than the large, wood-paneled "library" room, which tends to get smoky from the grill in the corner. There is good attention to detail, both in the kitchen and on the restaurant floor. The wine list, not surprisingly, is especially deep in red wines, and the house Cabernet from California's Ridge Vineyards is a bargain. Tel: 922-5555.

For years **Matteo's** (364 Seaside Avenue, across from the Waikiki theaters) enjoyed a large local following; it used to be the only good Italian restaurant in town. That following has diminished, ironically, at a time when the restaurant, under new ownership, has improved greatly. Gone are the red-vinyl booths and tacky decor; they have been replaced by French brocade and koa-wood wine cabinets outlined in tiny white Tivoli lights. The restaurant has branched out from its Italian roots and now includes such standard Continental items as rack of lamb. The wine list here puts many larger establishments to shame; if you are a devotee of Italian wine, no other place in Hawaii has a comparable cellar. Tel: 922-5551.

It's usually a good idea to stay out of restuarants whose major asset is the view from the top of a tall building, but **Nicholas Nickolas** (410 Atkinson Drive, near Ala Moana Center) is an exception. It's perched atop the 36-story Ala Moana Hotel, with a sweeping panoramic view of Waikiki, the Ala Wai Yacht Harbor, and the ocean. The room was designed so that the view is accessible from every seat— and, incidentally, so that it is easy to see and be seen by the other patrons. More a supper club than a dinner house, Nicholas Nickolas has a limited menu. But what it does, it does well, including an extraordinary grilled artichoke-heart salad and a double thick veal chop with Barolo-and-truffle sauce. And—a rarity among Honolulu restaurants—you can get a late-night supper here seven nights a week, with live music (usually jazz) and a dance floor. Tel: 955-4466.

The dining room is dark and intimate at **Nick's Fishmarket** (2070 Kalakaua Avenue; parking is on Kuhio Avenue), but the tempo of this dressy Waikiki night spot is set by the crowded cocktail lounge and dance floor. In his tiny kitchen chef Mariano Lalica accomplishes some good work with fresh local fish and imported seafood, including live Maine lobster and green-lipped New Zealand mussels. The young, well-dressed waiters strive for elegant service; occasionally they overdo it and become obtrusive. Tel: 955-6333.

Orchids is the second-string dining room at the Halekulani (2199 Kalia Road), which also boasts the more formal La Mer (see above). But there's nothing really second-string about Orchids' open-air, oceanfront dining room. Ask for a table on the terrace if you can get it; over a little stretch of grass and a low concrete wall is Waikiki Beach. The food is contemporary American with an Island accent—seared ahi with mustard-*shoyu* sauce, steamed onaga Oriental style, double breast of Oahu chicken in macadamia pesto. Orchids is less expensive than La Mer but is far from inexpensive. The table d'hôte lunches and dinners are usually the best deal. Service—surprisingly in this kind of establishment—has occasional lapses, perhaps because the dining room is so large. Orchids also serves breakfast and Sunday brunch. Tel: 923-2311.

Restaurant Suntory (Royal Hawaiian Shopping Center,

third floor, 2233 Kalakaua Avenue) is owned by the Japanese whiskey company. The restaurant has a nice, understated elegance and has been recently refurbished. Suntory is one of the few Japanese restaurants in Waikiki that hasn't aggressively raised prices in the last few years. Displayed on lighted glass shelves in the lounge are customers' individual bottles of Suntory. In the elegant *shabu shabu* rooms you cook at the table by dipping items into a pot of hot broth. The real star here, though, is the *teppanyaki* room. Teppan cooking is almost a cliché in the United States because of the success of the Benihana chain, but this is teppanyaki as the Japanese themselves do it. And you will find Japanese travellers dropping by to enjoy the steaks and seafood. Lovers of strong spicing should try the pepper steak. Good, unobtrusive service. Tel: 922-5511.

The star among Waikiki's new restaurants is **Roy's ParkBistro**, in the newly renovated Waikiki Park Plaza Hotel (1956 Ala Moana Boulevard). This is one of four restaurants in chef Roy Yamaguchi's Island empire (see Roy's in Honolulu Dining, below), but the restaurant really bears the stamp of Yamaguchi's chef/partner Gordon Hopkins. Hopkins has made a point to distinguish himself from the original Roy's, just 10 miles (16 km) down the road. The results include innovative Italian-influenced dishes such as shrimp and Japanese eggplant *crostini*; Asian-style half-moon pasta with ricotta, spinach, and mushrooms; and shrimp-and-prosciutto-mousse spring rolls. The cooking perhaps lacks the brilliance of the original Roy's, but it's certainly a step above the usual Waikiki fare. This is the quietest and smallest Roy's, and the only one open for lunch. Reservations necessary; Tel: 944-4624.

The Royal Hawaiian hotel, opened in 1927, was one of Hawaii's first luxury resorts. And the **Surf Room** at the Royal Hawaiian (2259 Kalakaua Avenue) still has something of the unhurried elegance that marked the grand pink hotel in the old days. You can be comfortable in this beachfront restaurant, with its pink-and-white awnings and pink tablecloths, whether you're wearing a suit or more casual clothes. The emphasis here is not so much on culinary innovation as on quality. The dinner menu is largely made up of classics—shrimp cocktail, onion and snapper soups, lobster tail and filet mignon, veal chops, and prawns in herb butter. But lunch, when the sun is glistening off the water and the beach is packed with bodies, may be the meal of choice here. A bountiful buffet is offered as well as lighter entrées such as tempura and a cold, poached chicken breast stuffed with herbs.

The mai tai reached the peak of perfection at the Royal Hawaiian, and this is still the best place to drink one, complete with orchid, pineapple slice, and sliver of sugarcane, plus, of course, a healthy dose of rum. Tel: 923-7311.

Italian food may the favorite cuisine on the planet. It has penetrated Japan, where even the smallest town is likely to have an Italian-style eatery. The newest of Waikiki's Italian eateries, **Villa Paradiso** (Royal Hawaiian Shopping Center, third floor, 2233 Kalakaua Avenue), is exactly that—an Italian-style Japanese restaurant. The cuisine has been lightened considerably but is still recognizably Italian. The presentation, however, is all Japanese. The antipasto plate, for instance, is not the usual mound of stuff; it's four or five small items (smoked marlin with melon, grilled eggplant, one butterflied shrimp, and so forth), all carefully selected and separately arranged on the plate. The most interesting entrée on the menu is the smoked chicken ravioli in tomato cream sauce with chopped macadamia nuts—a dish of wonderful taste and texture contrasts, all much less filling than your usual bowl of pasta. A well-selected wine list is reasonably priced. The decor is overly bright and cheerful, especially for those who like their Italian restaurants dark—but you can forgive much for the food. Reservations taken, though perhaps not necessary; Tel: 926-1717.

MODERATE TO INEXPENSIVE

Unfortunately, a good number of Waikiki restaurants that should be moderately priced are instead designed to turn travellers upside down and shake every last nickel out of their jeans, without providing a decent meal in return. But there are a few oases of sanity: restaurants that provide decent food at reasonable prices, often $25 or less per person.

Their restaurant in suburban Honolulu was such a hit that the owners of **California Pizza Kitchen** opened a new, larger restaurant in the heart of Waikiki (1910 Ala Moana Boulevard, second floor). The brainchild of two Beverly Hills lawyers, the California Pizza Kitchens are designed to bring California pizza to the masses. The pies come out of the wood-burning ovens topped with Peking duck; Thai chicken; bacon, lettuce, and tomato; even traditional sausage and pepperoni. There's a similarly irreverent attitude toward pastas: angel hair topped with black-bean sauce or fettucini with Cajun chicken and tequila sauce. But stick to the pizzas. They're not as strange as they sound. In fact, they tend to be as cheerful and accessible as the colorful black, yellow, and white decor. There's a small, reasonably priced selection of California wines, a few good desserts, and the promise of a good time at a reasonable price here. No reservations, and an occasional wait during rush periods. (If you're east of Diamond Head, the first California Pizza Kitchen, at the Kahala Mall on Waialae Avenue in Kahala, is still going strong.)

Okonomiyaki is a food fad in Japan, especially in Osaka and Kobe: It's a large pancake made of egg, flour, tempura batter, potato, and cabbage, grilled with a choice of meats, seafood, and vegetables. At **Chibo Okonomiyaki Restaurant** (Royal Hawaiian Shopping Center, 2201 Kalakaua Avenue), the house special comes with sirloin, prawns, squid, and scallops, plus sprouts, peppers, chopped cabbage, a sprinkling of *nori,* and bonito flakes. Chibo is fun. Customers huddle around long teppan grills. The cooks go for speed instead of presentation, and the whole atmosphere is casual, noisy, and bustling—a pleasant change from the endless subtleties of the more refined kinds of Japanese dining. In addition, the food is relatively inexpensive, fast, and out of the ordinary. This is a big place so you might get away without a reservation, but it is also a popular one, so call ahead if you can. Tel: 922-9722.

A real find in Waikiki is **Dynasty**, in the Discovery Bay Condominium (1778 Ala Moana Boulevard, near Bon Appetit), with the same owners as the upscale Dynasty II in Ward Warehouse (see the Honolulu dining section, below). While it is not as splendidly decorated as Dynasty II, the original Dynasty has moved recently into pleasant, harmoniously decorated quarters. But it remains essentially a modest, family-style restaurant, with excellent Chinese food. While the entire menu (mostly, but not exclusively, Cantonese) is fairly reliable, the Hong Kong sizzling platters, the roast duck, and the garlic prawns on *chow fun* noodles are stand-outs. The tapioca-honeydew dessert is a little soupy but an eye-opener for those who assume Chinese restaurants can't do sweets. Tel: 947-3771.

Perched on the edge of Waikiki (1837 Kapiolani Boulevard) is the ninth outpost of that trendy international chain, the **Hard Rock Café**. Rock 'n' roll is foreground rather than background music here, there's a classic woody station wagon hanging over the bar, and the walls are hung with gold records, guitars, and other rock 'n' roll and surfing memorabilia. People stand in long lines outside to purchase tee-shirts and other merchandise emblazoned with the brown and yellow Hard Rock logo. All this brouhaha obscures the fact that the Hard Rock is a pretty good place to eat, with simple food from a limited menu: lime-grilled chicken, Texas ribs with watermelon barbecue sauce, fresh fish, burgers, fries, shakes, and hot fudge sundaes. House wine only, but several brands of beer. If you must buy a Hard Rock tee-shirt, take note: If you eat in the restaurant, you don't have to stand in the long merchandise line outside. Just ask your waitress for what you want; she'll add it to your check.

At the **Hau Tree Lanai** (New Otani Kaimana Beach Hotel, 2863 Kalakaua Avenue, a few doors from Michel's) the main attraction is the location. The Hau Tree Lanai is an open courtyard that sits next to the stretch of Waikiki Beach called Sans Souci (the name comes from a 19th-century hotel that once occupied this spot). Robert Louis Stevenson, who spent hours sitting under the spreading *hau* tree that still graces the courtyard, wrote, "If anyone desires such old fashioned things as lovely scenery, quiet, pure air, clear sea water, good food and heavenly sunsets hung out before his eyes over the Pacific and the distant hills of Waianae, I recommend him cordially to the Sans Souci."

The Hau Tree Lanai is essentially the New Otani Kaimana Beach Hotel's coffee shop, and it does three meals a day. Over the past few years the food has risen considerably above its original coffee-shop standards. The most extraordinary offerings are the Hau Tree's "fitness" selections. The special fitness menu lists grams of fat and milligrams of sodium but also makes concessions to taste and texture. The vegetable curry on a brown rice ring or grilled fish with light garlic pasta would be worth eating even if they weren't so sensible. As the quality has risen here, so have the prices, but this is still a place to eat on the beach without spending a fortune. Tel: 923-1555.

If you are very hungry, there is probably no better place to eat dinner in Waikiki than the **Parc Café** in the Waikiki Parc Hotel (2233 Helumoa Road, across the street from the Halekulani). There are lots of dinner buffets in Waikiki—horrid steam-table stuff, most of them—but the food on the buffet tables at the Parc Café is better than that served in many cook-to-order Waikiki restaurants. The selection is not huge, just sufficient and interesting. There's an international assortment of salads (green papaya, caponata, celery remoulade, Chinese chicken salad, and so forth); a fresh fish dish, such as *ulua* in Champagne-basil sauce; and two carved entrées (one meat, perhaps leg of lamb or roast beef, the other fowl, maybe turkey or Peking duck). The desserts are usually fun: fresh fruit, real chocolate mousse, floating island, and so forth. And to top it all off, the Parc Café buffet is reasonably inexpensive, with a nice assortment of wines by the glass. Reservations recommended; Tel: 921-7272.

Most Waikiki restaurants are dressy casual, but you can wear shorts and a tee-shirt to the **Shore Bird Beach Broiler** (2169 Kalia Road, at the back of the Outrigger Reef Hotel). About half of this large beachfront restaurant is taken up by the bar, which at 9:00 P.M. turns into a disco with a ten-foot video screen and a laser light show. But this is no flashy, high-tech dance parlor. The floors are wood planks, the interior decoration consists mainly of painted signs, and there are overhead fans and two powerboats parked in alcoves. The waitress will bring your order—steaks, chicken, fish, or hamburgers—uncooked; you do the honors yourself at a massive barbecue grill at the far end of the dining room. In addition, there's an unfancy, but substantial salad bar where you can load up on chili, pasta, and rice, as well as greens. The food is far from dazzling, but it's certainly adequate. The whole atmosphere says you're allowed to have fun here. If you could love a restaurant that holds weekly bikini contests, this one's for you.

HONOLULU OUTSIDE WAIKIKI

The hotel rooms in Hawaii's state capital are in Waikiki, but many of the interesting restaurants are in Honolulu proper. It's often worth it—in terms of both food and money—to rent a car or grab a cab and get out of Waikiki to eat. The Hawaiian street names may seem disorienting at first, but a map or a helpful concierge should set you on the right path. It's difficult to get seriously lost; Honolulu is a compact city, squeezed between the mountains and the ocean. Even in heavy traffic there are plenty of restaurants within 15 minutes of most Waikiki hotels.

For the past 25 years it has been the custom here to put restaurants in shopping centers—freestanding locations are simply too expensive. Many of the major centers are dotted like loosely strung beads along Ala Moana Boulevard, one of the arteries leading out of Waikiki: Ala Moana Center, Ward Centre, Ward Warehouse, and Restaurant Row. All are easy to find and have ample parking.

For such a small city, Honolulu is singularly blessed with restaurants. Honolulu residents tend to eat out a great deal. They tend to be sophisticated in several cuisines and crave variety, and a promising new restaurant is likely to be flooded with curious diners in its first few weeks. The best of the Honolulu restaurants are also patronized by the more adventurous travellers who bring to these restaurants a level of prosperity they could not achieve just servicing the local market.

An inexpensive Honolulu restaurant—a real restaurant, not a coffee shop or a lunch counter—will probably provide dinner for two at less than $40, not counting wine. A moderately priced restaurant will serve dinner for two for about $50 to $80. There are a few expensive restaurants (triple-digit dinner checks for two) outside of Waikiki, but they tend to be rare.

A note on dining hours: Local residents eat early, visitors tend to eat later. Outside Waikiki, therefore, where there are fewer visitors, it's much easier to get an 8:30 or 9:00 P.M. dinner reservation than one at 7:30, especially on weekends.

FINE DINING

The hottest restaurant in Honolulu at the moment is, without a doubt, **3660 On the Rise** (Diamond Head of Waikiki in the large and very difficult to miss Waialae Building, 3660 Waialae Avenue, a few blocks from the Koko Head Avenue exit on the H-1). 3660 was created by two veterans of Honolulu's most prominent downtown private club, who moved their act to one of Honolulu's aging residential neighborhoods and managed to combine downtown flash with local flair. The food here is mainly upscale versions of Island favorites: steak pan-fried with red Hawaiian salt, roasted tomato stew with homemade sausage, and wonderful ahi *katsu* (fresh tuna wrapped in dried seaweed, coated with tempura batter, and quickly deep-fried so it remains raw in the middle). Save room for dessert: It would be regrettable to leave a bite of the burnt cream topped with a layer of chocolate mousse. The restaurant is bright and crowded, with a bustling display kitchen, adequate service, and an excellent by-the-glass wine selection. You will need a reservation at both lunch and dinner; Tel: 737-1177.

Byron II Steak House (Ala Moana Center, 1450 Ala Moana Boulevard) is a haven for those who long for old-fashioned restaurants. The menu is familiar, portions are ample, the veteran waiters are courteous, the tablecloths are white linen, and the whole atmosphere is calm. Byron II will do a chateaubriand for one, finishing it off tableside and serving it with a forest of fresh vegetables. Massive portions of French onion soup, avocado salads with jumbo shrimp, and fresh fish in a variety of preparations are some of the other things offered here—all at moderate prices. The wine selection is limited, but you can't have everything. Tel: 949-8855.

The **Maile Restaurant** (5000 Kahala Avenue) is the top-of-the-line dining room at the Kahala Hilton, which is not in Waikiki, but sits in splendid isolation between a swank residential district and the ocean, east of Waikiki, about 2 miles (3 km) past Diamond Head. The Maile has always maintained a high standard with its food, but in recent years prices have skyrocketed. Now the Maile is holding down prices by allowing its patrons to assemble a fixed-price dinner out of virtually any of the menu items: for example, seared scallops on mango and balsamic-vinegar coulis, Hawaiian sunfish fillet and lobster dumplings on black linguine, roast duckling cooked tableside with lychees, peaches, banana, and mandarin oranges. There's always beluga caviar and it's always extra. The wine list is excellent and expensive. Dancing is offered during dinner in the adjoining lounge. The Maile only does dinner, so those planning a daytime visit to see the Kahala Hilton's tame dolphins and penguins might try the open-air **Hala Terrace**, which offers extensive breakfast and lunch menus. Reservations for both restaurants; Tel: 734-2211.

Several good restaurants, most notably Roy's, are located in residential East Honolulu, past Diamond Head near Hanauma Bay. East Honolulu locations are easy to find: Follow the H-1 freeway until it ends and then keep driving on Kalanianaole Highway (Highway 72)—just don't try it until rush hour ends, about 7:00 P.M.

Hanatei (6650 Kalanianaole Highway) is worth the drive—if only to see the place. It is the last gasp of the Japanese investment boom, millions of dollars poured into a relatively small restaurant. There's a wooden bridge at the entry to take you over the rock-lined stream that wanders through the dining room. The modern chairs look as if they cost a small fortune, as does almost everything here: the service on the table tops, the artworks on the walls, and the giant origami sculpture hanging from the ceiling. If you can focus on the food, you will find it surprisingly innovative. You can have sushi—made not with fish or the usual Japanese pickles but with fresh Island produce served with raspberry vinaigrette—and then follow it with a bouillabaisse pared down to Japanese simplicity: the freshest possible seafood in a prodigiously aromatic saffron-herb broth. The desserts here resemble nothing so much as Postmodernist sculptures; try the banana split. The restaurant seems to have survived some rocky first months and now offers adequate service, but don't expect anything in a hurry. The good wine list has a surprisingly French turn of mind. Lunch offers a well-priced buffet and draws a large crowd. Reservations suggested; Tel: 396-0777.

Roy's (6600 Kalanianaole Highway, east of Diamond Head in the Hawaii Kai Corporate Plaza, the building with the golden shell logo) has a multi-million-dollar location with a sweeping second-story view of Maunalua Bay, but Roy's is more than just a good-looking suburban eatery. Young chef Roy Yamaguchi works alongside his crew in a large display kitchen, turning out food that combines his French training with his Asian heritage. The appetizers alone show off Yamaguchi's cuisine: perfect grilled shrimp with *wasabi* cocktail sauce, rich seafood pot stickers with sesame-seed butter sauce, and steamed pork *shu mai* with mustard-soy vinaigrette. Among the entrées the star is a slightly sweet, remarkably low-fat, mesquite-smoked crispy duck—a dish that owes its inspiration to both China and California. The duck arrives taken off the bone and beautifully arranged on top of a passion-fruit and ginger sauce. Another good choice is the seared scallops swimming in Cabernet butter. The food is memorable, and there's another reward for driving 20 minutes out of town: Prices here are about half what you would expect in Waikiki. Yamaguchi recently opened three new restaurants, one in Waikiki and two on Maui. You may want to sample his food while he still cooks every night in his original location. Tel: 396-ROYS.

The **Swiss Inn** (5730 Kalanianaole Highway, about a mile closer to town than Roy's, above), located in Niu Valley Shopping Center in East Honolulu, is one of Honolulu's best-kept secrets. Owner-chef Martin Wyss cooks every meal personally, and his wife, Jeanie, presides over the unpretentious little dining room as if it were her own home. A whole range of wonderful veal dishes tops the menu, including, when Wyss feels like making it, osso buco. There is good fresh fish, roasted chicken redolent of rosemary, heartwarming *rösti* potatoes (with bacon and onions), and fresh fruit tarts and coupes for dessert. The Swiss Inn is always packed—reservations are a must. Tel: 377-5447.

SEAFOOD

The closest thing Honolulu has to a large-scale Mainland fish house is **John Dominis** (43 Ahui Street, a block seaward from Ala Moana Boulevard, a few minutes out of Waikiki toward downtown). The large modern restaurant sits in a warehouse district near the wholesale fish auction and boasts a sweeping view of the ocean and Kewalo Basin. You enter the large dining room on a bridge overlooking an artificial pond full of live local lobsters. There's no question about the quality of seafood here—especially the tiger prawns and the wide variety of fresh local fish, prepared virtually any way you'd like it, including *en papillote*. But there are some who grumble that no matter how high the quality of the food, it's never as high as the check. Unpretentious but attentive service, adequate wine list. Reserve ahead, especially on weekends. Tel: 523-0955.

There's no such thing as an inexpensive seafood restaurant in Honolulu, but **Horatio's** (Ward Warehouse, 1050 Ala Moana Boulevard) does an excellent job at moderate prices. Although the interior is gray and dark, the atmosphere is actually relaxed and comfortable. The restaurant always has an assortment of fresh local fish, done in interesting preparations (Szechwan chile butter, for instance). There is a wider menu for those who aren't crazy about fish. The signature dessert here is burnt cream. Expect a lot of business talk at neighboring tables at lunch. Service is informal, but reasonably good. Tel: 521-5002.

CHINESE

With its art collection, vases, folding screens, and carved furniture, **Dynasty II** (Ward Warehouse, 1050 Ala Moana Boulevard) is as attractive and upscale a Chinese restaurant as you could hope to find anywhere. Stay away from the lunch buffet, but you can make a wonderful meal from the Cantonese menu: Peking duck, tofu pillows with broccoli, crystal shrimp on candied walnuts. Tel: 531-0208.

King Tsin (1110 McCully Street) was once a stylish small restaurant packed by devotees of Szechwan cuisine. It has since moved to larger, far less attractive quarters, but it now has parking and is located a few blocks from the McCully Street bridge, one of Waikiki's main gateways. The kitchen still turns out marvels, including beggar's chicken and steamed whole fish with ginger and onion. Call ahead for a whole fish; Tel: 946-3273.

Also close to Waikiki is **Maple Garden** (909 Isenberg Street, just off Kapiolani Boulevard near University Avenue). Maple Garden has a conventional, vinyl-booth interior that is far from dazzling, but this small restaurant has attracted the attention of a number of West Coast food writers. There is a good selection of Szechwan and Mandarin dishes, but the star here is the smoked tea duck, which is made on the premises and always available, served with small rice-flour buns. Supplement the duck with the braised spinach and the meal will be praiseworthy. Tel: 941-6641.

All things considered, Howard Co's **Yen King** (Kahala Mall, a major shopping center on Waialae Avenue, east of Diamond Head) may be Honolulu's best everyday Chinese restaurant. The decor is more comfortable than that of most shopping-center restaurants: wooden tables, nicely papered walls. The kitchen reliably cooks more than 100 Szechwan, Hong Kong, and vegetarian dishes, including excellent hot-and-sour soup, pot stickers, *kung pao* shrimp, and Mongolian beef, and now offers crab and lobster fresh from the tank. Sometimes the service at Yen King is wonderful; other times it's hard to figure which of the young staff bustling through the dining room is your waiter. Unpretentious and reasonably priced, Yen King is also the right place to arrange a ten-course banquet if you can raise a large party. Tel: 732-5505.

More than a century old, **Wo Fat** (115 North Hotel Street, Chinatown) was Hawaii's first restaurant. Originally a cooking shack set up by a group of Chinese immigrants, Wo Fat has prospered for generations, despite being burned down twice in Chinatown fires. Its present landmark building, which combines Chinese motifs with Western construction, was a sensation when it first opened in the 1930s. The high-ceilinged upstairs dining room is painted in a riot of red, green, and gold. The food is not the attraction here: It is pallid, cornstarchy Cantonese. This is a historic spot—thousands of visiting servicemen ate here during the war. If you ask the dining room hostess if she remembers you from the war years, she always says, "Yes, and you were a handsome young man then." She didn't work at the restaurant during the war; she was with the police department.

THAI

Celebrities ranging from Jimmy Carter to Tina Turner have eaten in the plant- and orchid-filled dining room of **Keo's Thai Cuisine** (625 Kapahulu Avenue, a few blocks up from the zoo). This reasonably priced restaurant is a big favorite when local residents take Waikiki guests to dinner. The food, while certainly adequate, is not as impressive as the restaurant's reputation. It's the atmosphere and not the Evil Jungle Prince (a Keo invention made with chicken, beef, shrimp, or fish in a sauce of coconut milk, fresh basil, and Thai spices) that keeps the tables full. Keo owns most of Honolulu's other Thai restaurants, so you may as well try the flagship. Tel: 737-8240.

VIETNAMESE

Vietnamese refugees make up the latest wave of immigrants to the Islands, and tiny Vietnamese restaurants are springing up all over town. Most might as well be in Saigon; they make few concessions to English-speaking clientele. But the freshness of the cuisine, the spicy sauces, and the profusion of fresh basil and mint are worth the trouble. By far the best of these restaurants, especially if you do not speak Vietnamese, is **A Little Bit of Saigon** (1160 Maunakea Street, in Chinatown). Duc Nguyen has put together a restaurant that is clean, air-conditioned, and stylishly decorated, the walls dotted with art for sale. The menu takes the time to explain the dishes in English. Try the *pho* (pronounced "fa," like the musical note), a ginger-spiced beef broth that is the national dish of Vietnam. Even more fun is *cuon ban trang*, a traditional dish that the menu lists as "do-it-yourself roll-ups"—rice-paper pancakes you fill with noodles, herbs, vegetables, and such delicacies as garlic pork, spring rolls, or *chao tom* (shrimp paste cooked on sugar cane). The restaurant does not take credit cards. Reservations for large groups only; Tel: 528-3663.

KOREAN

Highly spiced Korean food has become a permanent part of Island cuisine, but Honolulu still lacks an elegant Korean restaurant; most are fast-food or take-out places. In the absence of a more glittering establishment, the reigning champ is Henry Chun's **Kim Chee II** (3569 Waialae Avenue, along Kaimuki's main commercial strip; ample parking in the rear). Kim Chee II is the best of a small family chain. It's a red-vinyl-booth establishment, with some uninspired oil paintings on the walls. The specialty of the house is ample portions of beef, short ribs, and chicken marinated in sesame oil with green onion, garlic, ginger, and red pepper. Also excellent are the small pork pastries called *mandoo*. Prices are unbelievably low here. No liquor is served, but you can bring your own (beer is probably the beverage of choice with food of this fervor).

JAPANESE

You're likely to see three generations of the same family seated at the next table in **Kamigata** (Manoa Marketplace, 2756 Woodlawn Drive), located in a neighborhood shopping center mauka of the University of Hawaii. Although it looks attractively Japanese—full of fans, kimonos, masks, and shoji partitions—Kamigata, like much of Hawaii, is solidly Japanese-American. You keep your shoes on, and the seating is Western chairs and tables. Even the tatami rooms have wells under the low tables in which you can dangle your legs. The small sushi bar, with its tiny artificial stream, is often full, but sushi is also available in the dining room, as are excellent sashimi, tempura, *tonkatsu, udon,* and so forth, all moderately priced. The combination dinners, served in bento boxes, are often the best of the menu. The signature dessert here is an Island favorite, shave ice (flavored syrup poured over shaved ice, usually called a snow cone on the Mainland). The reservation policy is inconsistent; call ahead for a large party, at least. Tel: 988-2107.

Yanagi Sushi (762 Kapiolani Boulevard, in Kakaako) is so popular that the parking valet won't even take your car unless you assure him you have a reservation. This low-profile Japanese eatery (located about 2 miles/3 km west of Waikiki along a main artery) started as a storefront. Over the years it has expanded to fill its own little minimall and now draws a mixed crowd of Japanese tourists, local Japanese-Americans, and everyone else in town. Yanagi is also reputed to be a *yakuza* (Japanese gangster) hangout, but that rumor always attaches itself to a place where the sushi is exceptional. And the sushi certainly is exceptional here, including such house specialties as scallops mixed with crunchy little flying-fish eggs and beautifully translucent fresh *onaga*. It seems criminal not to eat sushi here, but there's a full menu for those sitting at the tables, including that Americanized favorite of the Japanese tourist, steak and lobster, served, of course, with miso soup and rice. As sushi bars can be ferociously expensive, Yanagi's moderate prices are, relatively speaking, a bargain, and there's no skimping on service: The young busboys in bow ties set an exemplary standard, making sure you have everything you could wish for. Reservations always needed; Tel: 537-1525.

HAWAIIAN

Hawaiian restaurants are surprisingly difficult to find in Hawaii, even though Hawaiian food is a staple at parties and catered affairs. The Hawaiian food offered to visitors at commercial luaus is often supplemented by pseudo-Hawaiian touches such as batter-dipped *mahimahi* (a white-fleshed fish nowadays often imported frozen from Taiwan) and "Polynesian" chicken. But if you want real Hawaiian food, short of finding a community luau, you have to go looking for little hole-in-the-wall restaurants. Of these, the best is **Ono Hawaiian Foods** (726 Kapahulu Avenue, a few blocks up from Keo's Thai Cuisine, above), which is run—in one of those twists typical of Hawaii—by a family of Okinawans. Ono is so small that on the sidewalk outside there is often a line of prospective patrons with six-packs of beer tucked under their arm (Ono does not serve liquor). Once inside, you find yourself jammed into a small wooden booth to eat excellent *kalua* pig (shreds of pork with the smoky taste of an underground barbecue), *lomilomi* salmon (rubbed salmon in tomatoes and green onion), *laulau* (pork or fish and taro leaves, steamed inside a green ti leaf), or *pipi kaula* (a local beef jerky). You have your choice of rice or poi, and all meals come with raw onions and coarse Hawaiian salt. Prices are commensurate with the decor, which features trophies, faded pictures, and baseball hats. Despite the crush, the atmosphere is friendly. Don't dress up.

It is not exclusively a Hawaiian restaurant, but the **Willows** (901 Hausten Street, a small street near University Avenue that runs between South King Street and Kapiolani Boulevard—once you find Hausten Street you can't miss the restaurant) does offer a Hawaiian plate as part of its extensive international menu, which includes wok cooking and curries as well as more conventional shrimp, steak, chicken, and veal dishes. But the food at the Willows pales beside the splendor of its setting: five and a half acres of landscaped grounds with a winding carp pond spanned by footbridges. Walking into the Willows is like turning the clock back 40 years, before the Islands discovered high rises and concrete. An ideal time to visit is during Thursday's Poi Luncheon, when there is an informal Hawaiian show, presided over by Irmgard Aluli, Hawaii's most prolific female composer since Queen Liliuokalani. Prompted by the musicians on stage, guests rise out of the audience to sing and dance hula. Some of the talent is amateur, but often the show includes some of the top performers in the Islands. Reserve well ahead for the Poi Luncheon; Tel: 946-4808.

MEXICAN

Honolulu is not rich in Mexican restaurants. The best of them, **Compadres** (Ward Centre, 1200 Ala Moana Boulevard), was designed to serve not Mexican food, but fresh California cuisine with a Mexican accent. Still, all the standard Mexican specialties are available in this bright, cheerful, bustling restaurant: rich *carnitas* and *fajitas* with plenty of fresh salsa, for example, and excellent grilled chicken and shrimp. The margaritas here are large and potent. The open lanai is a popular gathering spot for drinks after work or for whiling away a hot afternoon. The waiters and waitresses are largely young and enthusiastic. No reservations are taken, but the dining room is quite large and there's usually a table.

ITALIAN

A decade ago the only Italian food in Honolulu was in Waikiki. Suddenly, small Italian restaurants have sprung up all over town, offering creative Italian food at reasonable prices. One favorite is **Andrew's Italian Restaurant** (Ward Centre, 1200 Ala Moana Boulevard), which was deliberately designed to look like a San Francisco restaurant, to the point of bricking up one wall that would otherwise offer a pleasant view of the fishing-boat harbor. Whatever the wisdom of that, this is a dignified, hushed atmosphere in which to sample some excellent spaghetti alla carbonara made with real *pancetta,* or *linguine tutto mare* with shrimp, crab, scallops, and squid. There are veal and seafood dishes and daily specials; everything comes in large portions. Although not inexpensive, Andrew's is a bargain compared to the Waikiki places and provides much of the same kind of formal dining experience. Tel: 523-8677.

On the other end of the scale from the formal Andrew's are two of Honolulu's newest Italian eateries. The first, **Baci Due** (3196 Waialae Avenue, in Kaimuki), is located in an old house that has been scrubbed up and enameled until it shines. An offshoot of a Waikiki restaurant called Baci ("kisses"), Baci Due (*due* means "two") is more upscale—offering beautifully presented antipasti such as smoked mozzarella with sun-dried tomatoes, prosciutto, and roasted peppers. You could fill up on the appetizers here (the appetizer menu has daily specials). Two people may want to split one of the rich risottos or a pasta dish (the *bucatini alla matriciana,* macaroni in spicy tomato sauce, is good) to make a graceful transition to dessert. It's a tiny place, so make a reservation; Tel: 735-5899.

The second of Honolulu's new Italian restaurants is Sergio Mitrotti's vibrant new **Café Sistina** (First Interstate Bank Building, 1314 South King Street, located between Waikiki and downtown). Mitrotti is a graphic designer and artist; his copy of Michelangelo's Sistine Chapel ceiling is slowly taking shape behind Sistina's bar. Mitrotti's restaurants are always relentlessly trendy, from waiters in black to high-style modern Italian glassware. But his pastas, reasonably priced and generously portioned, really draw a crowd. The *linguine alla puttanesca* is a spicy marvel full of black olives, capers, and anchovies. There are always new concoctions here and they are invariably good: fettucine with chicken, fresh rosemary, and pine nuts; veal with wild mushrooms in wine sauce. The wines by the glass include such Italian imports as a crisp Frascati or a soft fruity Valpolicella Amarone. Late at night on weekends Café Sistina adds live jazz to its already considerable attractions as a restaurant. Tel: 526-0071.

In its first few years, the Black Orchid became one of the best-known restaurants in Honolulu, principally because Tom Selleck was one of the partners. Now Selleck is gone, but the restaurant, renamed **Rex's Black Orchid** (Restaurant Row, 500 Ala Moana Boulevard), has transformed itself into Honolulu's best contemporary Italian restaurant. The key to eating here is to order a variety of things, for instance, the lamb ravioli in sun-dried-tomato sauce and feta cheese, the gnocchi with rich rabbit *ragù,* and the remarkably fresh tasting risotto with shrimp and asparagus. Many of the dishes are available in appetizer sizes. Save room for the lemon tart. The wine list remains eccentric and over-priced, but it should improve as the old Black Orchid cellar gets drunk. The lounge does late-night dinners from a limited menu. Reservations necessary, especially at lunch; Tel: 521-3111.

FUN
You sit on the floor and eat with your fingers at **Hajjibaba's** (4614 Kilauea Avenue), a new Moroccan restaurant near the swanky residential district of Kahala, east of Diamond

Head. From the marinated vegetables and lentil soup that kick off the meal to the glass of mint tea and sprinkling of rosewater that conclude it, you feel you are in competent hands at Hajjibaba's. The food is bright with spices, delicately prepared, and delicious; the lamb couscous with baby vegetables is especially noteworthy. Don't order à la carte; order one of the reasonably priced prix fixe meals, called "feasts" here, and revel in the quantity of food while watching the belly dancers. The restaurant serves only two wines, neither of which goes particularly well with the food, so you'll want to bring your own. Tel: 735-5522.

Murphy's Bar & Grill (2 Merchant Street) is a favorite downtown watering hole and lunch spot in a historic building that once housed the Royal Tavern, frequented by King Kalakaua. The food here is surprisingly good. Look especially for fresh fish or lamb specials, as well as the entrée salads (the cobb is a classic here). Jammed at lunch, far less busy at dinner. Tel: 531-0422.

Rose City Diner (Restaurant Row, 500 Ala Moana Boulevard) is a re-creation of a 1950s diner, complete with a jukebox playing old-time rock 'n' roll in each gray-and-pink booth. Although a bit cluttered with memorabilia, the diner manages to avoid being precious. The atmosphere is invigorating, and the food remarkable for its genre: fresh vegetables with the entrées, lumpy homemade mashed potatoes with gravy, meat loaf, chicken-fried steak, burgers, chili, and shakes. And where else are you encouraged to blow toothpicks through straws and try to make them stick in the ceiling? Tel: 524-7673.

Ryan's Parkplace Bar & Grill (Ward Centre, 1200 Ala Moana Boulevard) draws a large bar crowd attracted by the open, airy seating, the huge back bar with its vast collection of single-malt scotches and imported beers, the free happy-hour *pupu* (Hawaiian for hors d'oeuvres or snacks), and the informal atmosphere. The dining room is large and the menu eclectic—everything from mesquite-grilled fish to Japanese noodles with shrimp. The appetizer choices are vast, and you are welcome to assemble a meal in any fashion you like. Tel: 523-9132.

OAHU OUTSIDE HONOLULU

The best advice we can give about dining on Oahu outside of Honolulu is: Don't waste a major meal. If hunger strikes, have a burger or a sandwich. It's a small island, and you'll be back in civilization soon.

THE WINDWARD COAST

That said, there are a couple of restaurants in **Kailua**, Oahu's second-biggest town (on the other side of the Koolau Range from Honolulu, on the Windward Coast), where you can get something decent to eat. The first is **Jaron's of Kailua** (201-A Hamakua Drive), which has an easy-to-spot location on one of the town's main commercial strips. The modern interior of this storefront restaurant is bland but pleasant, and the kitchen makes a real effort. The walnut-mint salad is full of fresh and jazzy tastes. The best of the entrée menu is the fresh fish, simply broiled and served with three sauces (teriyaki, lemon garlic butter, and basil cream). The fish is supplemented with a swirl of pasta dotted with red and green pesto (the red "pesto" is made with bell peppers). Jaron's is moderately priced, with moderately good service, and a moderately interesting wine selection. Reservations are a good idea on weekends; Tel: 262-6768.

The other Kailua restaurant of note is **Buzz's Original Steak House** (413 Kawailoa Road, just over the bridge near Kailua Beach Park). This is an old-fashioned steak house in a small old house. The menu is relatively simple (you're best off with a steak/salad-bar dinner), but the kitchen is competent, and the atmosphere is pleasant and casual. From the lanai you can see the water, and if you get cold out there, the restaurant will loan you a sweatshirt. Tel: 261-4661.

The traditional stop on a round-the-island drive is the **Crouching Lion Inn** (51-666 Kamehameha Highway), located under a lion-shaped rock formation right on the shore highway in Kaaawa, on the Windward Coast. The restaurant is under new management, and there has been a real attempt to upgrade the "Continental" cuisine, which has never been wonderful. It still isn't wonderful, honestly. Come for the friendly service, the rural location, and the blue-water ocean view from the stone terrace of this 1920s mansion. It's a nice stop if it's not full of tour groups. Reservations probably a good idea; Tel: 237-8511.

THE NORTH SHORE

The best place to eat on Oahu's North Shore is not a restaurant at all. It's a roadside shack called **Amorient Aquafarm**, which lists no address but is located right on Kamehameha Highway (Highway 83) in Kahuku, between two major landmarks, the Kahuku Sugar Mill—now a shopping center—and the Turtle Bay Hilton. For a nominal charge, Amorient serves up a "pupu combbo"—*pupu* is the Hawaiian word for "snack," *combbo* is just a misspelling. The plastic tray contains a bounty of crustaceans fresh out of the aquaculture pond: half a dozen shrimp tempura, two unshelled freshwater prawns, and two *dozen* large shrimp still in the shell. It's messy but satisfying fare. Amorient does not sell drinks—it's just a shack with a couple of picnic tables. Bring soft drinks or, better yet, a chilled California Sauvignon Blanc and a loaf of crusty French bread. Life offers few more satisfying meals.

THE BIG ISLAND (HAWAII)

Although Maui residents will no doubt dispute this, the Kona Coast of the Big Island (the western coast) is probably the best place to eat in the Islands outside Honolulu. The major resorts there are scrambling to get on the culinary map—not just the Island map, but the world map. And there's also been a happy bit of culinary fallout, as some chefs have left the resorts to start up small restaurants in the area. The wet, eastern side of the island, where most of the residents live, has not shared in these culinary riches, but nonetheless has a number of restaurants that serve a respectable meal to a mainly local clientele.

EAST HAWAII

Hilo, the principal town on the Big Island's eastern coast, has done wonders in the last few years in preserving and revitalizing its downtown. And with that revitalization has come a number of pretty good new restaurants. The best of these is **Pescatore** (235 Keawe Street, right in downtown). The small, square dining room has limited charm, but the charms of the restaurant's *carpaccio de pesce* are unbounded. Instead of the usual raw beef, this carpaccio uses ahi, the fish of choice in the islands for eating raw. The fish is so light and the lemon, olive oil, caper, and onion marinade so delicate that one guesses this is the kind of first course served in heaven to the angels. For a more substantial second course, try the tender calamari steak. Desserts aren't a strong point here, and the wine list is not much either. But this is Hilo: Be grateful for good food. Tel: 969-9090.

The most upscale and unexpected Hilo restaurant is **Roussel's** (60 Keawe Street, about two blocks north of Pescatore), a white-tablecloth dinner house in a converted bank building. (The wines are stored in the vault.) Roussel's is Hilo at its dressiest. The blackened fish here is first rate, if only because fresh fish tends to be wonderful in Hilo. Roussel's aims to be an authentic New Orleans eatery; if the gumbo and shrimp Creole are not quite authentic here, at least they add a bit of spice to Hawaii's quietest city. Reservations recommended; Tel: 935-5111.

WEST HAWAII

On the western side of the Big Island, things are a bit more lively. Good food seems to have penetrated everywhere, even a little pizza place like **Café Pesto** (Kawaihae Center) in the tiny **Kohala Coast** industrial port of Kawaihae (if you can find Kawaihae—it's on the map—you can find Café Pesto). Why should a pizza place in the middle of nowhere serve wonderful smoked salmon/Maui onion/spinach pizzas? Because a couple of young chefs from the nearby Mauna Lani resort liked the area and decided to go out on their own. Everything is great here: artichoke-heart and gorgonzola pizzas, Italian wines by the glass, gelato. Café Pesto also does takeout; Tel: 882-1071.

The outdoor terrace at the **Mauna Kea Beach Hotel** (1 Mauna Kea Beach Drive, Kohala Coast) serves a number of dining functions depending on the time of day. But the most famous meal here—legendary even in Honolulu—drawing local residents and crowds from other resorts, is the lunchtime buffet. This is essentially an elaborate Sunday brunch, available every day of the week. The contents of the six heavily laden buffet tables vary, of course, but there are always acres of salads, cold cuts, shrimp, sashimi, and crab claws, plus such local touches as *hoio* ferns, sliced octopus, and guava frappé. It's an invitation to gluttony, but who can resist the impulse to sit outdoors in luxurious surroundings and eat all the rare cold roast beef or out-of-season strawberries or chocolate mousse that one can hold—all at a reasonable price? Reservations recommended; Tel: 882-7222.

The little ranch town of **Waimea** (also called Kamuela), situated just inland above the Kohala Coast megaresorts, is rapidly becoming gentrified. Say what you will about gentrification, it often results in new and interesting restaurants. Of these, **Merriman's** (Opelo Plaza, Highway 19, right in town) is clearly the star. Young chef Peter Merriman makes sure to buy local produce—bright red tomatoes, wonderful sweet crisp corn, bright green watercress—and locally supplied meats, such as Palani Ranch beef. The resulting products from his noisy display kitchen—that's Merriman in the baseball cap—are often inventive and always interesting. Fish will pop out of the wok and be garnished with black Thai rice, fresh seaweed, and pickled ginger. Local lamb will become wonderful soup with watercress. The service is uneven and the wine overpriced, but the food is worth the trip. Reservations necessary; Tel: 885-6822.

Also of note in Waimea is **Hartwell's at Hale Kea** (Kawaihae Road, Waimea, about half a mile west of Merriman's). Hale Kea is a refurbished 1890s ranch house, complete with gardens and upscale arty shops. The restaurant's dining rooms fill the original house; you might end up eating in a bedroom decorated with period hats or the library with a vintage typewriter. Fish salads, with plenty of local greens and flowers, are a standout amid the usual steak and seafood offerings. Sunday brunch is a particularly pleasant meal here. Reservations recommended; Tel: 885-6094.

Kailua-Kona, the principal small town on the **Kona Coast** (the stretch south of the Kohala Coast), has suddenly given birth to a number of good restaurants. A young couple from Honolulu has breathed new life into **La Bourgogne** (77-6400 Nalani Street, on the road south out of Kailua toward Captain Cook). La Bourgogne seats a maximum of three dozen, and the new proprietor-chef, Ron Gallaher, personally delivers every entrée. Gallaher is slowly revamping the old-style menu, but the escargot and Caesar salad remain classics, and Gallaher's fresh fish in saffron sauce is likely to become one. If Gallaher has made his updated version of baked Alaska for dessert, order it. There is a very limited but well-priced wine list; ask for a recommendation. Make sure to call ahead; Tel: 329-6711.

On a bigger, more modern scale is the **Palm Café** (75-5819 Alii Drive, on the main drive in Kailua). Located on the second-floor verandah of an old lava-rock commercial building, Palm Café has a sweeping harbor view and an innovative East-West menu that is especially strong in seafood and vegetarian items. It's a great place to watch the sunset and eat such unusual, full-flavored items as Chinese ravioli in ginger *beurre blanc;* five-spice tiger prawns with Hoshi *udon* noodles and fresh papaya-mango chutney; and a timbale of locally grown vegetables with a fiery Hawaiian chile curry sauce. The wine list runs to big California wines. The decor is soothing and attractive, the whole operation is professional and warm, and the Palm Café is destined to become Kona town's premier dining room. Tel: 329-7765.

Sam Choy's Restaurant is hard to explain to anyone outside Hawaii. Choy is a well-known Big Island chef, but his restaurant is located among construction supply firms in Kailua's Kaloko Industrial Park (73-5576 Kauhola Street). At night Choy throws tablecloths on the tables and serves such entrées as Oriental lamb chops with shiitake and vegetable pasta, and macadamia-nut chicken with papaya-pineapple compote. But to get the full flavor of the place, you should really arrive at lunch. During the day, Choy's is essentially an unpretentious "plate lunch" eatery (see the Plate Lunch section at the end of this chapter). The Formica-topped tables are jammed with a wide cross-section of local residents, the din is incredible, and the food is much better than you'd expect. Among the choices are a green salad topped with mahimahi marinated in Thai spices, chow mein noodles with fresh vegetables in a crispy wonton bowl, and teriyaki steak with grilled local onions—all at entirely reasonable prices. This restaurant exactly fits its location, and it would be a good idea to visit before Choy gets the money to go upscale. No credit cards accepted, no alcohol served. Reservations taken for dinner only; Tel: 326-1545.

MAUI

Restaurants should reflect a sense of place. Maui restaurants seem to reflect both the strengths and weaknesses of their home island. At their best, they have a laid-back exotic glamour; at their worst, a kind of lackadaisical trendiness. Although Maui dining has improved incredibly in the last decade or so, it still lacks, for better or worse, the businesslike atmosphere of the Honolulu restaurant scene. Maui service tends to be more friendly than professional, and wine lists are too expensive, even by Hawaii standards. What Maui restaurants do best is create a sense of fun.

WEST MAUI

The most fun restaurants on Maui are the small ones that have sprung up in the old whaling town of **Lahaina**. **Avalon Restaurant** (844 Front Street, Lahaina) is perhaps the archetypal Maui restaurant. Half inside, half out, in the middle of an open-air shopping mall, the restaurant is packed nightly by patrons whose tropical-chic clothes are almost as bright as the art on the walls. Avalon does Pacific Rim cuisine, which means you can have at the same meal a Thai chicken salad, Vietnamese spring rolls, steamed fish in black-bean sauce, and sugar snap peas with Szechwan spices. There are some that grumble that you could get better Thai food in a Thai restaurant, better Chinese in a Chinese place... but few of those restaurants would have the élan of Avalon—or the wit to name a fresh fruit and brown sugar dessert Caramel Miranda. Reservations necessary; Tel: 667-5559.

Also noteworthy in Lahaina is **La Bretagne** (562-C Front Street), a dressed-up old house of a place right off Maui's main street. The key to La Bretagne is to order what the restaurant does well (which is not fish). The confit of duckling served on a reduction of Port is perhaps the star of the menu, although the appetizer portion of mushrooms in red wine comes quite close. Order both, plus the multi-chocolate house dessert: chocolate mousse cake, flourless chocolate cake, and white chocolate mousse, all three atop a berry coulis. The wine list is limited and too expensive, but you have to expect as much on Maui. Reservations necessary; Tel: 661-8966.

A landmark among the Lahaina restaurants is **Longhi's** (888 Front Street). Longhi's main idiosyncrasy is that it has no printed menus. Your waiter is likely to plop himself down at your tiny table (the restaurant is big, just the tables are small) and recite not just the list of specials, but every single item on the bill of fare. The cooking is Northern Italian, which means here, as it often does elsewhere, plenty of butter and pretty expensive. Even the asparagus and artichokes, which are always miraculously fresh whatever the season, come drenched in butter. The star of the pastas is the angel hair with clams and fresh tomato sauce, but what's available changes daily. People love Longhi's. All the windows are open, patrons wear their best tee-shirts to dinner, and everyone in the place always seems to have a tan. Reservations a good idea; Tel: 667-2288.

Perhaps the most fun of all the Lahaina eateries is **Tasca's** (608 Front Street). Tasca stretches, almost as thin as a string, from its street entrance to the Mediterranean-style garden around the bar in the back. The food here is *tapas*. This is a great place to drink wine and sample the oysters, the medallions of beef in green-pepper sauce, the garlicky scallops, and, especially, the rabbit in fig sauce, a dish of surpassing sweet meaty richness. Tel: 661-8001.

On the well-established **Kaanapali** resort strip, just north of Lahaina, the most reliable dining choice is the **Swan Court** at the Hyatt Regency Maui (200 Nohea Kai Drive, Lahaina). The Hyatt Maui is a carefully constructed artificial wonderland—and the Swan Court is one of the best-engineered restaurants imaginable, an open amphitheater of tables descending to a lagoon filled with exotic waterfowl, including, of course, swans in several shades of black and white. Across the lagoon is a romantic-looking narrow footbridge across which from time to time you'll see couples strolling. The food, while not as innovative as that in some of the trendier Maui eateries, has its strong points: charred lamb on fiddlehead ferns, steaks buried in Maui onions, and fish "eichenholz"— baked and served on an oaken platter that imparts a subtle woody flavor to a delicate fish such as opakapaka. There are splendid soufflés for dessert. Reservations recommended; Tel: 661-1234.

Finally, located in a small harbor on the southern shore of the piece of land that connects West Maui to the rest of the island, well away from the major tourist centers, is perhaps Maui's best small dining room, the **Waterfront Restaurant** (Milowai Condominium, Hauoli Street, Maalaea Harbor). Surprisingly convenient for an out-of-the-way spot (ten minutes south of the airport at the confluence of several main roads), the Waterfront is a little family-run establishment at the bottom of an unprepossessing condo building. Ignore the corny decor, which includes red wallpaper and chandeliers. This is the best place on Maui to eat fresh fish (in a choice of nine preparations, including *en bastille*—in a cage of shoestring potatoes—covered with extraordinarily fresh tomatoes and mushrooms), and it's also the best place in the Islands to eat venison and other wild game (availability varies, of course, with the luck of the hunt). Also exceptional are the homemade gravlax and the seared ahi with tamarind sauce. To match the wild game, there's a separate wine list exclusively of wines with animals in their names—Stag's Leap, Rabbit Run, and so on. But the real story about the Waterfront's wine list is that it's well chosen, especially the California wines, and, miracle of miracles, it's reasonably priced. Somebody here likes wine, knows a bargain, and likes to pass it on to the customers. Reservations necessary; Tel: 244-9028

SOUTH MAUI

The explosion in resort development in South Maui has, fortunately, brought forth three or four noteworthy restaurants. Two of the best, Seasons and Pacific Grill belong to the **Four Seasons Resort** (3900 Wailea Alanui Drive, Wailea). Both are terrace restaurants with an ocean view. **Seasons**, the more upscale of the two (upstairs), features such extraordinary fare as pan-seared opakapaka with a Kula vegetable strudel, and rack of lamb with a hazelnut crust, served with a lasagna made from Japanese eggplant and feta cheese. Desserts include such splendors as a chocolate terrine with Molokai apple-bananas, served with an orange caramel sauce. An excellent, though pricey wine list is especially strong on California Chardonnays. Downstairs at **Pacific Grill**, the fare is lighter and, for a resort, moderately priced. Like Avalon in Lahaina, Pacific Grill allows you to eat your way around the Pacific Rim in a single dinner—shrimp tempura, charred Korean beef, wok-charred Pacific salmon, Hawaiian seafood stew—while seated on the pleasant open terrace. At lunch there's a refreshing salad buffet with plentiful local greens of all varieties, plus some substantial additions such as poached chicken breasts and smoked fish. The health benefits of eating salad are mitigated somewhat by the fact that the buffet also offers unlimited portions from the dessert tray, which contains a dazzling array of pastries made with local fruits. Reservations recommended; Tel: 874-8000.

The Grand Wailea, next door, also has two noteworthy restaurants. The best Japanese restaurant in Hawaii is **Kincha**, the Grand Wailea's multi-million-dollar re-creation of a Japanese country inn. A stream flows through Kincha, over rocks imported from Japan, and the restaurant actually seems to capture some of the tranquility and elegance of that country at its best. Although Kincha has both a sushi and a tempura bar, the best way to eat here, by far, is to eat a *kaiseki* dinner in one of the tatami rooms. The restaurant boasts that it is less expensive than comparable restaurants in Japan, but that's not saying much. Prices on the kaiseki dinners range from simply expensive (about $70) to the stratospheric ($500). Some advice: As all the kaiseki dinners consist mainly of what the chef has found that day to be fresh and seasonally appropriate, order the daily special. It's virtually the best the kitchen has to offer anyway and it is, comparatively speaking, moderate in price. Finding a good wine to go with kaiseki is a problem. Instead order from the sophisticated menu of regional sakes—and because Maui's climate is warm and these are wonderfully aromatic and fruity rice wines, order them chilled instead of heated. The restaurant will be happy to oblige.

The resort's **Grand Dining Room**, located on an ocean-view terrace, is quite pleasant, but like most hotel dining rooms suffers from trying to be all things to all people. The only time that's an advantage is during Sunday brunch, when the buffet is truly staggering in its extent and variety. In addition to the usual array of hot and cold dishes, there are a sushi chef, a pasta chef, an omelet chef, a chef turning out pancakes and waffles, another doing Japanese meats on a skewer, and yet another cooking brisket of beef and vegetables in the Japanese manner in a heavily spiced broth. There are also a fresh doughnut machine, desserts by the tableful, and even a candy display. If you're willing to sacrifice the rest of your Sunday to somnolence and digestion, there is no better brunch. Reservations a must for both Kincha and the Grand Dining Room brunch; Tel: 875-1234.

UPCOUNTRY

Far from Lahaina, but trendy nonetheless, is **Haliimaile General Store** (900 Haliimaile Road, off Highway 390 between Paia and Mokawao), a plantation store that's now an upscale tourist stop in lush, green Upcountry Maui. There are interesting items on the menu here: an ever-varying house lasagna, a vegetable torte, fish in various guises. The pastries that line the glass butcher's counter are always artistic, though sometimes they look somewhat better than they taste. Haliimaile's is not quite a top-of-the-line eatery, although its kitchen makes an effort, but the drive Upcountry is certainly a pleasure, and the restaurant is far better than any of the other alternatives in its setting. Reservations are a good idea since you can't just go down the street if it's full; Tel: 572-2666.

KAUAI

In culinary terms, it's still 1964 on Kauai. Two and a half out of every three Kauai restaurants turn out to be steak and seafood broilers. If you want a tropical drink and a surf-and-turf platter, you're in luck almost everywhere on the island.

THE EAST COAST

If you're after interesting wine and innovative Pacific cuisine, there's only one Kauai restaurant worth mentioning, Jean-Marie Josselin's **A Pacific Café** (Kauai Village, Kuhio Highway, Kapaa, on the eastern coast). No matter where you stay on the island, it's worth the drive to this Kapaa shopping center to check out such wonders as grilled Japanese eggplant in chile-pepper vinaigrette, sizzling squid salad, Beijing-duck soft tacos, wok-charred mahimahi with a sesame-seed and garlic crust. Josselin, the recipient of a number of national honors for his seafood recipes, has created a bright, noisy, low-keyed environment to show off his food, which tends to be colorful with fresh herbs and hot peppers. The wine list is eccentric (Chilean reds, Italian whites, German Rieslings), but reasonably priced, as is the menu. If you eat only one dinner on Kauai, eat it here. Reservations highly recommended; Tel: 822-0013.

Among the other bright spots on Kauai is **Gaylord's** (Kilohana Plantation Estate, Highway 50, Lihue). The food at Gaylord's is always reasonably good—scampi on linguine, fresh fish, steaks—and the setting is marvelous: a beautiful 1930s plantation house restored to splendor, with the restaurant tables lining the stone terrace along the main lawn. So felicitous is the outdoorsy setting that you might consider a daytime meal here, lunch or Sunday brunch. The service can be slow, but you wouldn't be here if you were in a hurry, would you? Reservations recommended, especially for brunch; Tel: 245-9593. (Damaged by the hurricane, Gaylord's has been closed, but is scheduled to reopen in August 1993.)

THE NORTH SHORE

The newly renovated and drop-dead-elegant Princeville Hotel (520 Kahaku Road, Princeville), on Kauai's North Shore, has put in an equally splendid Italian restaurant, **La Cascata**, named for the waterfalls you can see tumbling down the walls of Hanalei Valley during the rainy season. But any season is a good time for such items as La Cascata's carpaccio with its big tasty flakes of authentic parmesan from Parma, or its grilled vegetables and polenta, or even its simple spaghetti alla carbonara. Veal and seafood preparations also abound, and most items can be ordered in small sizes, so that you can sample more of them. The wine list has a number of out-of-the-ordinary selections, mainly French and Italian—ask the sommelier if he's serving anything special by the glass that evening. And for dessert it's hard to turn down a whole pear wrapped in phyllo dough thin as paper, baked, and served atop a red wine sauce dotted with apricot purée. Tel: 245-9593. (Closed for repairs after hurricane Iniki, La Cascata expects to reopen in November 1993.)

Princeville is a long drive from many of Kauai's tourist centers, and if you are up in the area, you may wonder whether it's worth the even longer drive to **Charo's Restaurant and Cuchi Cuchi Cantina**, due west of Princeville (along Kuhio Highway) in Haena. That's looking at the matter the wrong way around: The drive, which takes you virtually to the end of the road on Kauai's North Shore, is the real pleasure; it winds over half a dozen one-lane bridges and past some of the most beautiful beaches on the planet. The beach outside Charo's is a big sweep of white sand and aquamarine surf. You'll put up with the average Mexican fare—the tostada with fresh fish is perhaps the best item—as you enjoy just being in this quiet corner of Kauai. The restaurant pushes alcohol, but the drive back is difficult enough with a clear head. Tel: 826-6422. (Also damaged in the hurricane, Charo's plans to reopen in August 1993.)

MOLOKAI

Nobody goes to Molokai for the food. For the sightseeing, for the peace and quiet, the ancient Hawaiian spiritual charge that seems to hang over the island, yes—but for the food, never. The offerings are limited enough that anyone staying more than a night will no doubt exhaust them without advice. One nice place you might possibly miss on your own, however, is **Kanemitsu Bakery and Coffee Shop**, which is downtown Kaunakakai's last remaining restaurant now that the Mid Nite Inn has burned down and Hop Inn has shut its doors. The food at Kanemitsu is not the point—it's just breakfasts and plate lunches (see the following section on the Plate Lunch)—the down-home atmosphere is what counts here. If you want to assure yourself that you've gotten as far away from glitzy tourist-trodden Hawaii as possible, then waving the flies away as you eat your Molokai-bread french toast and Portuguese sausage from mismatched plastic plates should do the trick.

LANAI

There's nothing else to do on Lanai that's as much fun as eating. The first of the island's luxury resorts, the cool upcountry **Lodge at Koele** (Keomoku Highway, just north of Lanai City) immediately established a reputation as a place where you leave wishing you'd been hungry enough to try every single dish on the menu. And what a menu it is—pineapple-bran-smoked salmon with lentil salad, lilikoi-marinated venison with marjoram potato cake, guava-smoked duck breast with green beans and watermelon. Part of the reason everything tastes so good is that acres of former pineapple land were turned into an organic garden for the hotel, growing anything the chefs desired, from haricot vert to crinkly leaf basil, from yellow teardrop tomatoes to tiny white eggplants. It may be this fresh, organically grown produce that gives the Lodge's cooking its depth and clarity. Tel: 565-4580.

The organic garden is now shared by the newer of the island's resorts, the **Manele Bay Hotel** (Manele Beach Road), which after a slow culinary start lured talented chef Philippe Padovani from the Ritz-Carlton on the Big Island. Padovani has put together a simple, light, eclectic menu, everything from steamed dim sum appetizers to crisp-roasted squab breast with pan-fried mushrooms and sautéed salsify—all using the fresh Lanai ingredients. And dessert lovers can rejoice in the fact that he's pioneering the use of Hawaiian vintage chocolate, made from premium Island-grown cocoa beans. Although his menu is limited on any given night, it's hard to go wrong with Padovani's cooking, either the multi-course "degustations" at the hotel's Ihilani Dining Room or more casual meals at the Hulopoe Court. Reservations; Tel: 565-7700.

THE PLATE LUNCH

Nowhere does the confluence of cultures that make up contemporary Hawaii manifest itself more clearly than in "local" food—that is, in the food that people who live in the islands actually eat. There is a kind of "local" cuisine—cheap, plentiful, and generally available—that has kept Hawaii from succumbing entirely to pizza, burgers, and fried chicken. Hawaii does have all three members of the American fast-food trinity, mind you, but it also has the plate lunch.

The essential element of the plate lunch—its *sine qua non*—is two scoops rice. (That's not two scoops *of* rice; to include the preposition is to mark yourself a linguistic as well as culinary outsider.) A century and a half of Asian influence has made rice an indispensable part of the Island diet. But not just any rice will do: It has to be medium-grain white rice that sticks together when it's cooked. This sticky rice is picked up with an ice-cream scoop, and placed on the plate in two symmetrical mounds—two scoops rice.

In addition to the rice, there is usually a scoop of macaroni salad in the plate lunch. It's just standard mayo-and-pasta salad, and how it ever became a staple of Island chefs is a culinary mystery that has never been satisfactorily explained. Some plate lunch sellers will let you substitute tossed green salad for macaroni, but, oddly, you seldom get potato salad—although sometimes potatoes (or green peas or carrots or watercress) are added to the macaroni.

PLATE LUNCH CUISINE

If rice and macaroni salad are the unvarying elements of a plate lunch, the choice of entrée is wide open. It can be any dish or combination of dishes, from any of the many cultures that have made their way to the Islands. It doesn't matter whether the recipe originated in Boston or Bangkok, Tokyo, or Manila. It can be a plate lunch entrée as long as it's both tasty and filling.

Many plate lunches are Japanese in origin, in part because the whole plate lunch concept may well be a spin-off of the Japanese bento box. Any Island plate lunch emporium will offer most of the following: grilled teriyaki beef, chicken, or fish; *shoyu* chicken, marinated in soy sauce and slow-roasted; *tonkatusu* (pork dipped in batter and deep-fried and served with sweet-and-sour sauce); and shrimp tempura. In addition, when a plate lunch menu includes curry, it invariably means the mild golden curry that the Japanese favor, served over rice.

But plate lunches can also be Chinese, or at least Chinese-style, dishes, such as fried noodles, lemon chicken, beef with broccoli, and a dish known universally in Hawaii as "chop steak"—small slices of beefsteak stir-fried with vegetables and served, inevitably, over rice.

The hot and garlicky barbecued meats from Korea have had a strong impact on the Island plate lunch. On a Korean plate lunch menu, *kalbi* is marinated beef short-ribs and *bulgoggi* is Korean-style teriyaki beef. A Korean plate lunch often includes a choice of three or more side dishes from a wide array of prepared salads. Make sure to take some of the marinated bean sprouts and the watercress and shoyu salad, but watch out for the stuff that looks like, and is, cabbage covered with red pepper—it is of course *kim chee,* and it should be approached by the uninitiated with caution.

Most plate lunch counters serve a Hawaiian plate, some combination of kalua pig, laulau, lomilomi salmon, and *haupia* (a Hawaiian pudding), often with poi served on the side in a little plastic cup. (For a gloss on those dishes, see the Hawaiian section of Honolulu Dining, above). A number of popular Filipino dishes have also found their way onto the plate lunch menu, especially *lumpia* (a pork and vegetable spring roll) and *adobo* (meat slowly simmered in vinegar and spices).

In addition to all this Asian exotica, no plate lunch menu would be complete without a list of items straight from the heart of Middle America: roast pork, meat loaf, fried chicken, and beef stew (which, through the influence of the New England missionaries, became Hawaiian by adoption). Chili is also a favorite but it is always served over rice or noodles.

Even more startling than the variety are the combinations. Order if you can a "mix plate" (not "mixed"—the Island vernacular has little patience for English past participles). You could end up with laulau, *char siu* (Chinese roast pork), teriyaki fish, fried noodles, and meat loaf in brown gravy. Or Spam. (Perhaps from the days when much meat reached the Islands in cans, people in Hawaii eat three-and-a-half times as much Spam per capita as people on the Mainland: 10,270 cans a day.) Or curry. Or a hamburger steak with onions.

The permutations are endless, and there's bound to be a generous quantity of food: The joke is that plate lunch eaters don't stop eating when they're full, they stop when they're tired. And all this food should cost less than five dollars, certainly less than six. For the traveller who wants to say he or she has tasted the "real" Hawaii, at least one plate lunch is an indispensable experience.

FINDING A PLATE LUNCH

Where to find a plate lunch? Outside of Waikiki or any other tourist strip, plate lunches are ubiquitous. They are served in little drive-in fast-food places, in unassuming storefronts, and in catering trucks parked outside businesses or construction sites. The whole point of a plate lunch is that you shouldn't have to look too far to find one. If you want a recommendation, just ask the valet who brings your car or the clerk behind the store counter. Virtually everyone in Hawaii has his or her own favorite place to get a plate lunch. A few suggestions in **Honolulu** follow.

At **Grace's Inn** (1296 South Beretania Street, a few blocks Diamond Head of the Honolulu Academy of Arts), everything is served on a bed of *chow fun* noodles. The pork cutlet plate with gravy on the rice sings arias in your mouth, even if it probably conducts sit-down strikes in your arteries. If you're feeling adventurous—and happen to be in the blue-collar Kalihi district (northwest of Chinatown) at lunchtime—drop by **Gulick Delicatessen** (1512 Gulick Avenue, a few blocks west of Highway 63). Gulick is dark, dingy, and crowded, but it has more food crammed into its small space than any other eatery in Hawaii. You probably won't recognize all the Japanese and Filipino specialties, but just point to whatever looks interesting and the friendly women behind the counter will add it to your plate.

If you drive up Ward Avenue mauka (toward the mountains), you'll see a little red lunch truck on the Diamond Head side of the street called **Tsukenjo's**, which piles its mix plate about four inches high with food. The exact dishes change from day to day. Pick up a couple of plates and drive to Ala Moana Park. Eating a mix plate at a seaside picnic table is one of those experiences that reminds you that life is to be enjoyed, not endured.

Makai Market Food Court

Finally, the most convenient place for a traveller in Hawaii to pick up a plate lunch—or at least food served plate lunch style—is the Makai Market Food Court at Ala Moana Center. When the shopping center turned 40,000 square feet of the city's most desirable retail space into a food court, it made sure not to alienate the local population, which still makes up two-thirds of the center's customers. So among the 20 small restaurants operating here there's an interesting ethnic variety. The favorite among Honolulu residents is **Patti's Chinese Kitchen**. Its owner, Calvin Chun, perfected the Chinese-style plate lunch 20 years ago, long before there even was a food court. He's had people standing in line for his food ever since. Although its vast clientele doesn't seem to mind, Patti's food is a bit heavy on the soy, sugar, and MSG. Instead, you might try the Hawaiian plate at the **Poi Bowl**, which, in deference to its origins, is designed to look exactly like a shiny red lunch wagon. Or, even better, choose a range of barbecued meats and salads at **Yummy Korean B-B-Q**.

For the adventurous there is also a whole range of Filipino food at **Jo-Ni's**, whose proprietor, Nini Go, is serious about exposing Americans to the high points of Filipino cuisine. Little **Café Siam** aims to be the Baskin-Robbins of Thai food: You can taste anything first before ordering it. And, finally, you can seek out the little **Tsuruya** noodle shop hidden in one of the back corners. Its eight-stool counter is an oasis of calm in the often crowded food court. Tsuruya provides a good place to sample that staple of lunchtime Tokyo, buckwheat soba noodles in a light shoyu dressing. It's not hard to order here; all the dishes are modeled in plastic so you can simply order by number.

The Makai Market is perhaps no place for connoisseurs—no plate lunch place is. But as an opportunity to try food you may never have encountered, at a price so cheap you don't even have to worry about eating it all, the experience is incomparable.

OAHU OUTSIDE HONOLULU

By John W. Perry

John W. Perry, a contributor to several North American and Asia-Pacific magazines, is a longtime resident of the Pacific area. He lives in Honolulu and travels frequently throughout the South Pacific on assignment.

Charles Nordhoff, a 19th-century journalist (and grandfather of a co-author of the Bligh-Christian saga *Mutiny on the Bounty*), suggested in 1874 that a traveller exploring Oahu outside Honolulu take a pack mule, an English-speaking guide who could cook, and a daily stream bath. The scenic grandeur remains as Nordhoff saw it, but the mule has been replaced by a rental car, baths are taken in beach-park showers, and the guide's great-great-offspring are riding the North Shore's big-wave surf. Nonetheless, a trip outside Honolulu can still be a most rewarding experience for the traveller on Oahu.

An hour's drive from Waikiki, past sugarcane and pineapple fields, are shorelines where Hawaiian royalty vacationed and surfed. Two tunnels (Highways 61 and 63) through the spine of a mountain range lead to a landscape whose natural landmarks and curious place-names figure in ancient Hawaiian legends. Beside quiet bays on Oahu's windward (eastern) side you can feel head-on the trade winds that have blown since an ancient god created the first ancestor of all Hawaiians. On the North Shore, especially around Haleiwa on weekdays, it's difficult to remember that this is Hawaii's capital island and that phone calls to Honolulu are local, not long distance. Along Kamehameha Highway, fruit sellers at makeshift stands hawk papayas and finger-sized bananas, sometimes grown by mom and pop in their front yard.

Always near as you traverse the island are mountains. The Koolau Range, the southern end of which looms over Honolulu, is the remains of an eroded shield volcano and is the site of the Nuuanu Pali Lookout. The Waianae Mountains, on the western side of the island, are home to an Oahu guardian spirit, Kolekole. They are relatively little-travelled and still retain a rustic, old-time-Hawaii atmosphere. It was between the Waianae foothills and Honolulu that carrier-based Japanese aircraft violated Hawaiian airspace and attacked the U.S. Pacific Fleet's battleships at Pearl Harbor in December 1941.

MAJOR INTEREST

Pearl Harbor
USS *Arizona* Memorial
USS *Bowfin* submarine tours

The Southeastern Coast
Scenic grandeur
Hanauma Bay and Koko Head
Whale-watching
Halona Cove and Koko Crater
Bodysurfing at Makapuu Beach
Sea Life Park oceanarium

The Pali Area
Queen Emma Summer Palace
Nuuanu Pali Lookout
Haiku Gardens

The Windward Coast
Kualoa Regional Park's rustic landscape
Polynesian Cultural Center
Eating freshwater prawns

The North Shore
Haleiwa's beaches and art galleries
Eating shave ice
Waimea Bay Beach surfing (world's largest ridable waves)
Full-moon walks in Waimea Falls Park
Sunset Beach surfing contests

The West Coast
Wild West landscape and spirit
Kaneaki Heiau, ancient temple
Kaena Point at land's end

Exploring Oahu outside of Honolulu is a pleasant adventure taking in six separate areas—Pearl Harbor, the southeastern coast, the Pali area, the Windward Coast, the North Shore, and the Waianae (western) Coast—all of which are an easy drive from the city. Our tour starts just west of Honolulu at Pearl Harbor naval base, home of the best-known memorial of World War II. After that we skip east over Honolulu/Waikiki past Diamond Head to Oahu's southeastern toe and visit a pristine bay and a marine park. Turning inland, we drive up into the mountains to the Pali, a cliff famous as a battleground in Hawaiian history, then travel up the Windward Coast to spend an evening at a Polynesian theme park. On the North Shore we stop at a botanical garden noted for its archaeological sites, and on the Waianae Coast, separated from the North Shore by a mountain range, we head into the beautiful Makaha Valley, which shelters a backcountry resort.

PEARL HARBOR

A morning visit to Pearl Harbor's USS *Arizona* Memorial, a monument erected above the remains of a battleship destroyed in the Japanese attack on the harbor, is a dramatic and stirring experience. The immediacy of the ship directly below you, the name list of the dead in the shrine room, the battleship flag flying at full mast can be overwhelming, even to those indifferent to military sites. It is moving to watch handfuls of flower leis drop onto the water and, pulled by the outgoing tide, drift over the remains of the forward gun turret. War and its aftermath make strange bedfellows, and at Pearl Harbor two very dissimilar groups—the U.S. Navy and the National Park Service—act in unison to guide and transport visitors to this underwater cemetery. When naval warships fill the harbor, gunmetal gray and masculine in profile, the memorial, tiny and alone on Battleship Row, is an unforgettable sight.

VISITING THE BASE
The memorial and shoreside visitors' center, located about 10 miles (16 km) west of Waikiki, are both on

Oahu

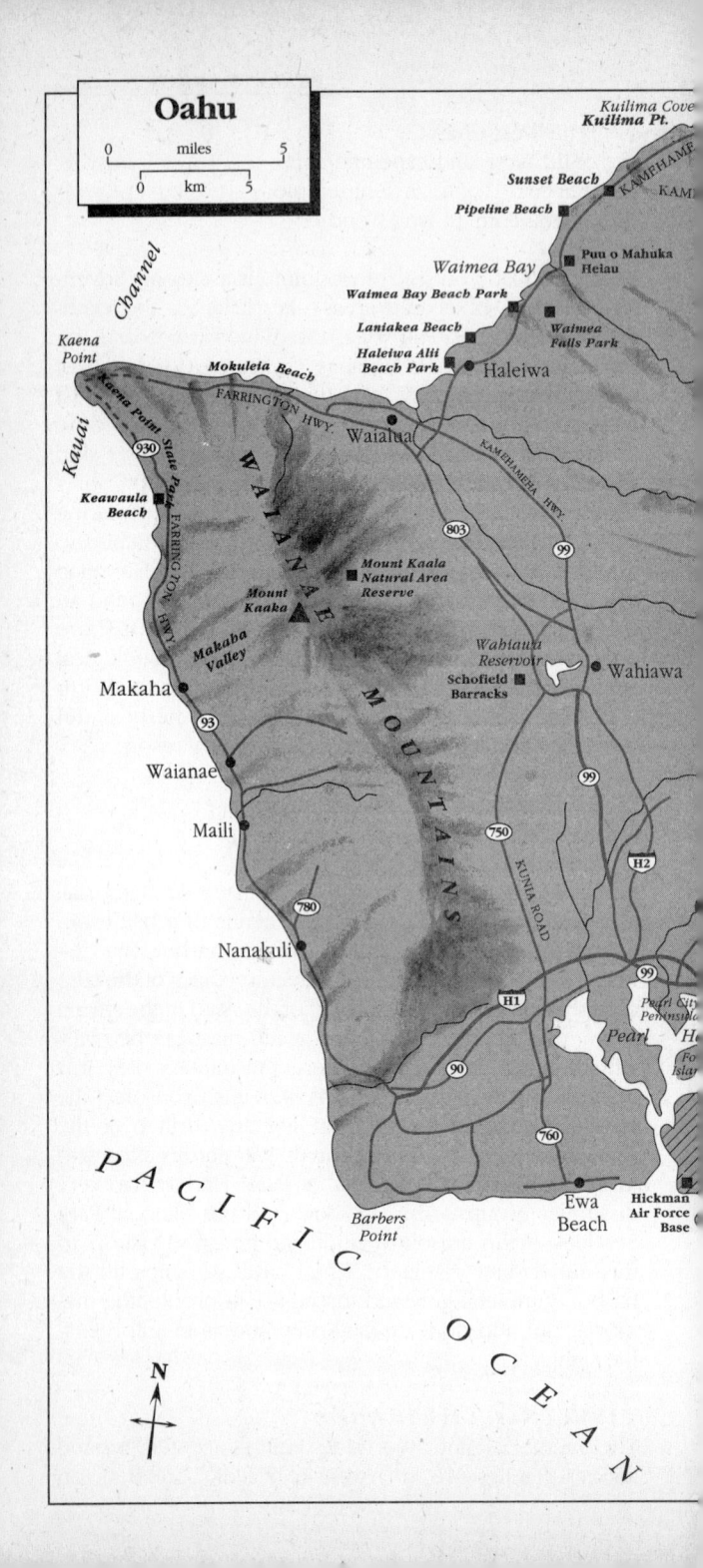

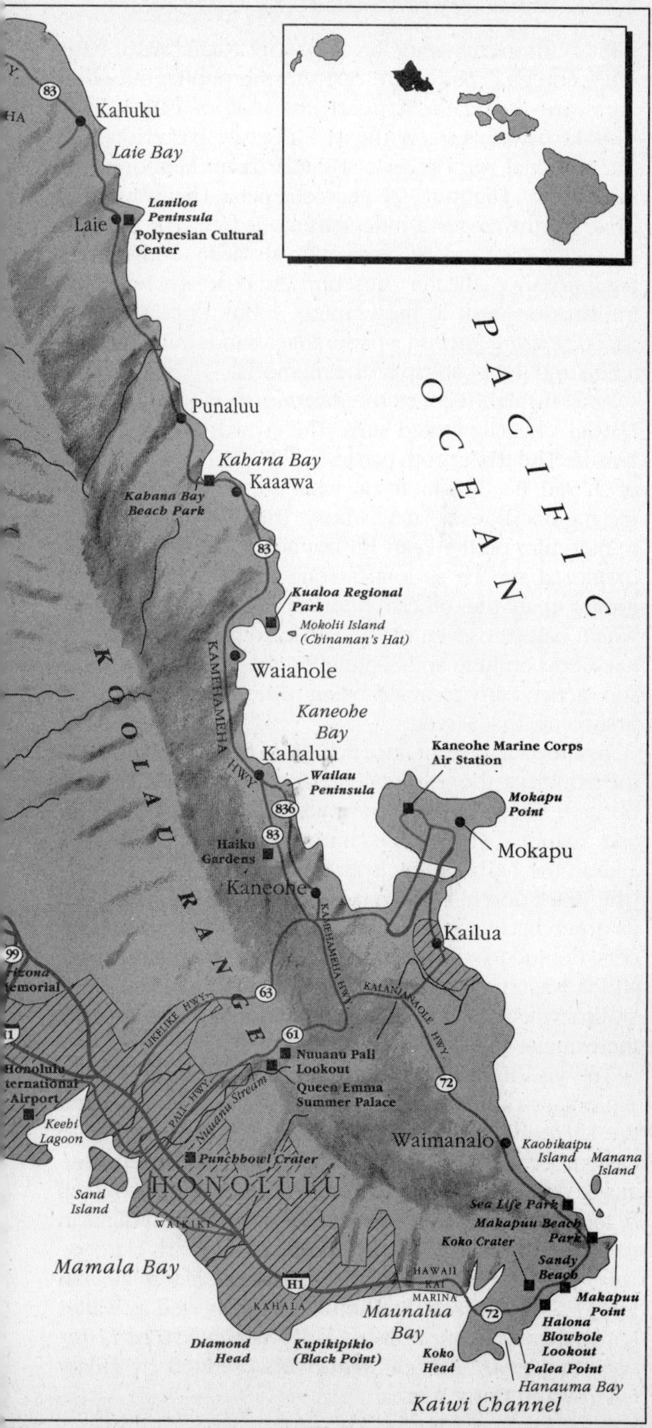

PACIFIC OCEAN
Kahuku
Laie Bay
Laie
Laniloa Peninsula
Polynesian Cultural Center
Punaluu
Kahana Bay
Kaaawa
Kahana Bay Beach Park
Kualoa Regional Park
Mokolii Island (Chinaman's Hat)
Waiahole
KAMEHAMEHA HWY
Kaneohe Bay
Kahaluu
Wailau Peninsula
Kaneohe Marine Corps Air Station
Mokapu Point
Mokapu
Haiku Gardens
Kaneohe
KOOLAU RANGE
Kailua
KALANIANAOLE HWY.
LIKELIKE HWY.
Arizona Memorial
Honolulu International Airport
Keehi Lagoon
Nuuanu Pali Lookout
Queen Emma Summer Palace
PALI HWY.
Nuuanu Stream
Punchbowl Crater
HONOLULU
Sand Island
WAIKIKI
Mamala Bay
Waimanalo
Kaohikaipu Island
Manana Island
Sea Life Park
Makapuu Beach Park
Koko Crater
Sandy Beach
Makapuu Point
Halona Blowhole Lookout
HAWAII KAI MARINA
KAHALA
Maunalua Bay
Diamond Head
Kupikipikio (Black Point)
Koko Head
Palea Point
Hanauma Bay
Kaiwi Channel
83
836
63
61
72
99
H1

military property inside an important Pacific naval base. The center's grounds are open to the public, but other areas are restricted. To reach the visitors' center from Waikiki drive west on the H-1 freeway past Honolulu International Airport, exit at the *Arizona* Memorial off-ramp onto Highway 99 (Kamehameha Highway), and drive northwest for a mile; parking is free. The modern center, opened in 1980, is an open-air facility with a snack bar, bookshop, theater, museum, and boat landing. At the information desk in the entrance lobby, opposite a salvaged *Arizona* anchor, a park ranger hands out tickets for a film and the boat trip to the memorial.

As you might expect, the *Arizona* Memorial is one of Hawaii's heavily visited sites. The crowds are large with reason: The trip is both patriotic (for Americans) and free of charge. It's difficult to say what is the best time to visit the memorial; every day is busy. The wait to see the 25-minute film on the Pearl Harbor attack and then visit the memorial can be as long as one to three hours, often longer than the official hour-and-a-quarter tour itself, which is given seven days a week from 8:00 A.M. to 3:00 P.M. Between June and September, the busy summer season, arrive early to avoid being turned away; tickets are first come, first served.

To alleviate the wait once ticket is in hand, stroll through the exhibits at the visitors' center, opposite the theater, and observe the stern-faced portraits of Admirals Yamamoto and Nagumo, who planned and executed the attack, then take in the harbor view from the center's southern lanai (the "back porch"), which faces toward the memorial and its green backdrop, Ford Island, which houses naval officers. Behind Ford are the distant Waianae Mountains, over which Nagumo's Zeroes and dive-bombers flew. A boatswain's whistle, followed by a tour number, calls visitors to their queue.

The visitors' center's new film, which focuses on the diplomatic ramifications of the attack and how it affected the United States, has replaced the film shown prior to December 7, 1991, the 50th anniversary of the Japanese attack on Pearl Harbor. If you want to prepare yourself before your visit, you can get a thorough grounding in the area's military history by reading Pearl Harbor–related books by Gordon Prange, Michael Slackman, and John J. Stephan (see the Bibliography), as well as Walter Lord's *Day of Infamy,* Blake Clark's *Remember Pearl Harbor!,* and *Pearl Harbor Reexamined,* edited by Hilary Conroy and Harry Wray.

THE USS ARIZONA MEMORIAL

After the film, your group is ready for the trip to the memorial. Because the *Arizona* lies in an aquatic graveyard, the approach is by boat over the often murky waters of Pearl Harbor. The ten-minute ride in a navy-operated shuttle named *Kukui* or *Aloha* or *Nene* is itself worth the wait. Wheelchair visitors are welcome onboard the shuttle, and a 1990 policy change now allows children to visit the memorial. En route a park ranger describes the Pearl Harbor attack, speaking with military precision about the *Arizona* and her memorial: the type of bombs dropped, the number of men killed, and the fuel oil that has leaked from the *Arizona* since the attack at a rate of two drops per minute.

The slender memorial, spanning the *Arizona* amidships like a suspension bridge, was designed by Alfred Preis, a Vienna-born architect. The sagging roofline is symbolic of America's post-attack depression, and the upward-rising ends evoke the high point of World War II—U.S. victory. The sag also distributes weight, and the 21 window openings and the viewing well above the *Arizona* lighten the structure. Preis purposely omitted overtones of sadness to permit visitors to make their own personal responses, such as tossing flowers into the well onto waters where, in the words of Admiral Yamamoto (who opposed starting the war with the United States), Japan "awakened a sleeping giant and filled him with a terrible resolve."

The battleship that lies beneath the memorial, entombing more than one thousand men in a metal sarcophagus, is unrecognizable as a warship. The superstructure is missing, and the deck guns were removed and converted to shore batteries to protect Oahu from further Japanese invasion. What is left is a naked, eerie hull mostly submerged in mud and encrusted with coral. Steel plating more than four inches thick failed to save the *Arizona* from armor-piercing bombs, but tiny coral polyps, fragile as flower petals and as intricate in design as any warship, are entombing the *Arizona* in a cocoon of calcareous skeletons and saving it from saltwater corrosion.

Pearl Harbor Cruises

The park service tour is the only tour that allows you to board the *Arizona* Memorial, but there are a couple of cruises that will take you to see it directly from Honolulu. **Paradise Cruise**'s private tour boat, *Star of Honolulu*, motors near Ford Island, passes another ship destroyed during the attack (USS *Utah*), and pauses near the *Arizona*. The two-and-a-half-hour excursion departs daily at 9:00 A.M. from Fisherman's Wharf at Kewalo Basin, opposite Honolulu's Ward Warehouse shopping center; Tel: 536-3641. **Royal Hawaiian Cruises'** *Navatek I* also embarks on a Pearl Harbor cruise daily, leaving at 8:30 A.M. from Pier 6, near Honolulu Harbor's Aloha Tower; Tel: 848-6360. The *Navatek*, with a special hull designed for a smooth, stable voyage, is recommended for landlubbers prone to seasickness.

USS BOWFIN

To immerse yourself in more naval memorabilia of the World War II variety, walk from the *Arizona* Memorial's shoreside visitors' center to the nearby USS *Bowfin*, a retired combat submarine floating at harbor's edge. Unlike the *Arizona*, destroyed in the first moments of conflict, the *Bowfin* conducted nine war patrols and sank 44 ships. Speed is what visitors ask about: the *Bowfin* went 21 knots surfaced, 10 submerged, the reverse of nuclear subs, which are faster submerged than surfaced. The walk through the brightly lit interior is a delightful experience as the carry-on headphones, activated as you enter each compartment, play a recorded message describing the sub's interior anatomy from torpedo room to captain's quarters. Because of the tightly confined space no one is allowed inside the conning tower—the brain of the sub's combat operations—but the conning tower of the *Bowfin*'s sister sub, *Parche*, can be seen in nearby Bowfin Park (be sure to look through the periscope). Time spent on board the *Bowfin* complements an *Arizona* visit by enabling you to see firsthand a naval vessel that fought a war denied the *Arizona* and its crew.

PACIFIC SUBMARINE MUSEUM

The Pacific Submarine Museum, adjacent to the *Bowfin*, is worth a walk through; most interesting are the cutaway models of modern subs and the hands-on displays of electrical devices used to locate enemy targets. The open-air snack area, surrounded by cigar-shaped torpedoes, is a shady spot to pause and reflect on naval history. Along with the *Bowfin*, the museum is a memorial to the 3,500 U.S. submariners who, like *Nautilus*'s Captain Nemo in Jules Verne's *Twenty Thousand Leagues under the Sea*, lie submerged forever in dark waters.

THE SOUTHEASTERN COAST

In dramatic contrast to Pearl Harbor's naval landscape are the beautiful oceanside parklands on the opposite side of Honolulu, east of Waikiki and Diamond Head, along Kalanianaole Highway (Highway 72). The highway rims Hanauma Bay, parallels a shore of lava cliffs, coral-sand beaches, and tiny coves, then curves past a picturesque red-topped lighthouse on Makapuu Point, Oahu's easternmost tip. The reward for exploring this shoreline is a sense of geographical wildness almost within shouting distance of Honolulu itself.

Hanauma Bay

A topographical oddity, Hanauma is a volcanic crater with a bay inside, formed when ocean waves eroded the crater's seaward rim and created an amphitheater of coral and sand. Because Hanauma is only 7 miles (11 km) east of Diamond Head (past Honolulu's exclusive Kahala district, Maunalua Bay, and Hawaii Kai Marina), it's very popular with Honolulu residents and visitors alike, so arrive early for a choice beach spot. On holidays thousands descend into the crater, forcing lifeguards to cordon off their square of sand with conical traffic dividers. Historically you will be in good company here, because in the old days royal day-trippers from Honolulu came to this beach, and King Kamehameha V fished in the bay itself. The bay is now an underwater marine park, which means the beach, sea floor, water, and marine life are protected by state law from public and commercial abuse—no fishing, collecting, or killing is permitted.

Perhaps Hanauma's most striking feature from a beach sitter's point of view is **Koko Head**, a volcanic tuff cone rising above the bay's rim and forming a rugged backdrop for snorkelers on their downward trek from the parking lot. Koko Head's highest point (642 feet), Kuamoo Kane, which means "backbone of the god Kane," is a 30-minute hike from a trail head near the bay's parking lot. (If other place-name connotations interest you, try arm wrestling—a sport of ancient Hawaii—atop a picnic table here; Hanauma means "hand-wrestling bay.")

Even veteran lifeguards are awestruck by Hanauma Bay's topography, which is, without exaggeration, ethereal: Clusters of coconut trees sway above a white-sand beach; the turquoise bay is ringed by steep cliffs over which fly seabirds—brown boobies and kite-like frigate birds—in search of marine snacks. Within the bay are three distinctive features: Witches' Brew, where strong surf boils in caldronlike swirls; Toilet Bowl, a pool that flushes like a bathroom commode; and Keyhole, a swimming area where the reef is shaped like an Alice-in-Wonderland peephole. Keyhole is a popular fish-feeding area; a new restriction at the bay prohibits feeding the fish anything except "naturally balanced fish food" available from the park's concession stand.

Be forewarned that drownings do occur here, about ten a year, most of the victims being Japanese snorkelers unfamiliar with bay water. Hanauma's three best-known landmarks—Witches' Brew, Toilet Bowl, and Keyhole—are the places where lifeguards most frequently find swimmers in trouble: Stay within the bay to avoid the notorious Molokai Express, a strong current that will take you not to Molokai but on a one-way trip to meet the god of waters.

Because of the adverse impact on the beach and bay by large numbers of visitors, the park has banned tour buses from the area. Beach-goers must now arrive by car, public bus (number 22), or taxi. This restriction has reduced the human congestion on the beach. The park has also cut the Wednesday hours to noon to 6:00 P.M.; other days the hours remain 6:00 A.M. to 6:00 P.M.

Halona

The short and scenic drive from Hanauma east to Halona Cove is stunning, making it difficult to keep an eye on traffic. Overhead looms Koko Crater, and below Kaiwi Channel's incoming surf collides head-on with a shoreline of ancient lava. During the breeding and calving season (December to April), pods of humpback whales blow and breach, some cruising near Hanauma Bay. On the horizon, beyond the farthest visible humpback, a group of neighboring islands, Molokai, Lanai, and Maui, is visible.

Halona Blowhole Lookout, though crowded between 9:00 and 11:00 A.M. with tour buses, tee-shirt hawkers, and Krishna devotees offering vegetarian snacks and guru guidebooks, is an enjoyable stop. The name Halona means "peering place." The blowhole, an appropriate landmark on this whale-watching coast, expels sea spray with the same dramatic showmanship with which a whale exhales breath. Opposite the blowhole is **Halona Cove**, wedged between ocean-cut cliffs and capped with a white-sand beach. In this romantic spot, reached by a downward winding trail, filmmakers shot scenes for *From Here to Eternity*.

KOKO CRATER

Opposite the blowhole, on the *mauka* (inland) side of the road, rise the outer walls of Koko Crater, a valley formed by volcanic tuff cones. Within the valley is **Koko Crater Botanical Garden**, an undeveloped garden with a few walking trails and unpaved roads. The crater floor is covered with a thick growth of dryland plants including *kiawe* (mesquite) and *wiliwili*, a tree from which Hawaiians used to make surfboards. Koko Crater has a curious Hawaiian name, Kohelepelepe, which means labia minora. According to Hawaiian myth, after the goddess Pele was attacked by Kamapuaa, the pig man, Pele's sister, Kapo, had her vagina placed inside the crater to lure him away. To reach the botanical garden from Halona Blowhole Lookout, drive past Sandy Beach Park, turn left onto Kealahou Street and follow the sign for Koko Crater Stables, which is near the garden.

The Makapuu Point Area

After rounding Makapuu point, where Hawaiian fishermen once made seaweed offerings to the gods, **Makapuu Beach Park**, one of Oahu's best-known bodysurfing beaches, is visible: a pocket of sand alongside the highway overlooked by the point's lighthouse. The surf's slow roll and excellent shorebreak make it ideal for bodysurfing, and the sport is so popular here that board surfing is prohibited. A red flag signals offshore risk; when it is posted ask a lifeguard for the safest place to swim. The two offshore islands are Kaohikaipu and Manana (the larger, which is nicknamed "Rabbit Island" because a plantation owner once raised rabbits here). Both are bird sanctuaries where thousands of seabirds nest and breed.

The Koolau Range runs along the coast here. At **Kamehame Ridge**, opposite Manana Island, the range rises sharply and dramatically from the shoreline to form the awesome "Green Wall," a favorite hang-glider launching spot. Gliders sailing off the wall share the trade winds of Makapuu and **Waimanalo Beach** (to the north) with black-winged frigate birds and white-tailed tropic birds.

SEA LIFE PARK

If you plan to visit the North Shore's Waimea Falls Park (see below) and wish to complement your resulting cache of botanical knowledge with insights into marine biology and whale ecology, Waimea's sister park, Sea Life Park, is within walking distance of Makapuu's beach, and is the main man-made attraction on this coast. Besides the usual oceanarium entertainment—splashing dolphins, sleeping turtles, waddling penguins—numerous informative lectures are scheduled throughout the day explaining the fascinating marine environment that surrounds Hawaii.

A one-room museum devoted to the Pacific whaling era is next to the **Rabbit Island Bar & Grill**. The aptly named **Sea Lion Café**, with a view toward the sea lions' feeding pool, is open for lunch every day and for dinner on Fridays. A Friday-night Hawaiian plate includes such victuals as long rice, *lomilomi* salmon, and a local favorite, *poi* (taro), very edible and nutritious but disliked by many *haole,* including Mark Twain: "A villainous mixture, almost tasteless before it ferments and too sour for a luxury afterwards."

A worthwhile excursion is Sea Life's behind-the-scenes tour, offered five times daily and limited to 16 people per tour (first come, first served). The tour enters off-limits areas where dolphins and other marine creatures reside, watched over by trainers carrying buckets of herring and smelt. Visitors get a close-up look at the day-to-day workings of the park and tour the facilities used by trainers to teach new tricks to false killer whales, dolphins, and sea lions. Of special interest are the newborn dolphins in the maternity tanks. A knowledgeable guide answers questions about marine life: What marine creatures can see ultraviolet light underwater? (Sea turtles.) Is a penguin really a bird? (Yes.) How large is a dolphin's brain? (The size of a human being's.)

The tour's top attraction is Kekaimalu (Peaceful Sea), a hybrid cross between an Atlantic bottle-nosed dolphin and a false killer whale. Called a wholphin, Kekaimalu, a *wahine* (female), has characteristics of both her dolphin mother and torpedo-shaped father. Circling in her tank, she frequently breaches to eye onlookers. In early 1992 she gave birth to a baby fathered by a Pacific bottle-nose dolphin. Kekaimalu and her baby can be viewed on a limited basis.

Undersea marine life, once Hawaii's best-kept secret, is no longer the exclusive domain of snorkelers and scuba divers; at Sea Life landlubbers can view in comfort as they descend three fathoms on the aquarium's spiral ramp and view Hawaiian reef fish swimming behind acrylic windows. The colorful *uhu* (parrot fish) swims here (oldtime fishermen climbed the cliffs below Makapuu's lighthouse to make offerings to a stone image devoted to uhu, a fish favored by the gods). Primeval hammerhead sharks also circle the aquarium, eyeballs set at head's edge— they are fitting residents for Makapuu, which means "bulging eye." (It is said that the mother of King Kamehameha I, when she was pregnant, had an appetite for raw sharks' eyes.)

Be sure also to look for a native Hawaiian fish whose shape resembles a human nose, in particular that of Captain Cook, Hawaii's European discoverer. A pre–World War II song sung to tourists immortalized the triggerfish's name: "I want to go back to my little grass shack in Ke-ala-ke-kua Hawaii where the *humuhumunukunukuapuaa* go swimming by."

From Sea Life Park it is possible to continue around the island by driving northward on Kalanianaole Highway (Highway 72) as far as Kailua, then along the Windward Coast to the North Shore by way of Kamehameha Highway (Highway 83), making stops at roadside beach parks or the Polynesian Cultural Center in Laie (see the Windward Coast and North Shore sections below). You may also return to Honolulu from the Kailua area on the Pali Highway (Highway 61), which passes the Pali Lookout, also easily reached from Honolulu.

THE PALI LOOKOUT AREA

On the northern outskirts of Honolulu, past Punchbowl Crater and the Royal Mausoleum (see the Honolulu chapter), the **Pali Highway** (Highway 61) on its upward journey into the Koolau Range parallels Nuuanu Stream, which flows seaward through dense rain forest thick with tree-climbing vines, the last refuge of Oahu's endemic land birds.

QUEEN EMMA SUMMER PALACE

A right turn near Nuuanu Park leads to the Queen Emma Summer Palace, a wood-shuttered house with a wide verandah supported by six Doric columns and surrounded by rain forest as green as Maori jade. Here Emma Rooke, who married King Kamehameha IV in 1856, escaped from Honolulu's summer heat and enjoyed short reprieves from downtown court life that (by her design) resembled the court etiquette of Europe. Nowadays visitors to her cozy retreat are confronted with visual reminders of monarchical Europe's strong influence on Hawaiian royalty, and especially on Queen Emma, who named her son Albert after a prince of England.

A house tour offers a brief glimpse of Hawaii's own Victorian era. Knowledgeable Daughters of Hawaii, charmingly enthusiastic about Queen Emma and her vanished world, guide you room to room, chatting about unusual vases, koa-wood furniture, and deceased kings and queens. Some of the mementos Queen Emma kept are her son's wooden cradle (shaped like a canoe), her first piano, built in 1801, and gifts from European aristocrats, including Queen Victoria, whom she met in 1865 at Windsor Castle. A special keepsake is a locket bracelet containing a picture of the English queen and a lock of her hair. Outside the house are the stone remains of the palace kitchen, now carpeted by an overgrowth of vines. Viewed from the bench beneath a nearby rainbow shower tree, the ruins resemble a green Victorian hedge.

Nuuanu Pali Lookout

Returning to the Pali Highway, Oahu's landmark viewpoint, Nuuanu Pali Lookout, is only minutes away, reached by an uphill side road lined with ironwood trees. "The celebrated view," wrote Victorian traveller Isabella Bird, "burst on us with overwhelming effect."

The view faces the island's Windward Coast. The steep walls of the Koolau mountains rise up to the extreme left and right, and the green Haiku Valley, on the left, stretches seaward toward the blue bay of Kaneohe and the distant shoreline. Straight ahead is Mokapu peninsula, separating the twin towns of Kaneohe (left) and Kailua (right), each spread like an aerial reconnaissance map on the flatlands below. On the peninsula is Kaneohe Marine Corps Air Station, built on the site where Kane, one of Polynesia's most powerful gods, is said to have created the first Hawaiian. To the right of Kailua is Mount Olomana. (You'll better enjoy the view if you dress for the strong winds that funnel through here—it can get quite cold.)

Some historians claim that an entire army of Oahu defenders tumbled over this thousand-foot precipice in 1795. Fighting with their faces toward present-day Honolulu Harbor—hidden from view to the west—they were forced backward and upward by the warriors and European gunners of the invading Kamehameha, Hawaii's great warrior-king. Puiwa ("to startle"), a lane near Emma's palace, is a subtle reminder of the battle, the name referring to the noise made by Kamehameha's cannon, fired by John Young, Emma's grandfather.

Haiku Gardens

A drive east down past the lookout and then north to Haiku Gardens, on Haiku Road in Kaneohe, is a perfect conclusion to an over-the-*pali* excursion. The **Chart House** restaurant, which overlooks the garden, is open for dinner (steak and seafood), but the garden, not the food, is the attraction. Although the place is well known to Oahuans, you will be certain that you have discovered a private oasis known only to bridal couples and botanists. Saturday is the best day to observe the weddings held in thatched-roof huts that are hidden in vegetation. Even if you don't eat at the restaurant, make the five-minute walk around the garden; the view from the dense foliage upward toward the Koolau Range is astonishing. The bright green breadfruit tree, nature's edible gift to the Polynesians, grows near the pond, sharing the garden's coolness with an over-the-water gazebo. The fruit has a texture like bread when baked or roasted. Seedling breadfruit trees were the cargo carried on board William Bligh's HMS *Bounty.*

(The Haiku Gardens can also be a stop if you are driving from Honolulu to the Windward Coast on the coastal highway east around Makapuu Point.)

THE WINDWARD COAST

Viewed from the Nuuanu Pali Lookout, the distant Windward Coast headlands to the north of Kaneohe Bay appear both remote and mysterious, a place where legend pinpoints the birth of Oahu itself. The island's creation, the main event in the mythology of this eastern Oahu coastline, occurred long before the arrival of the first voyaging canoes from present-day French Polynesia. A brother and sister with magical hands locked fingers and united the Koolau and Waianae mountain ranges, creating Oahu and a shoreline of beaches and bays.

Today, this coastline, still rich in legends, shelters the

bays of Laie, Kahana, and Kaneohe, cooled by Windward Oahu's trademark, the incoming trade winds. To reach the Windward Coast from Honolulu, take the Likelike Highway (Highway 63) or, more roundabout, the Pali Highway (Highway 61; see also the Pali Lookout section, above) or the Kalanianaole Highway (discussed above in the Southeastern Coast section).

Kahaluu

Named "the diving place" by old-time fishermen, Kahaluu, north of Kaneohe, is a welcome escape from the hustle and bustle (and concrete) of Waikiki for those wishing to feel the Windward Coast's trade winds and enjoy the area's frequent rain showers. Kahaluu's **Wailau Peninsula**, a finger of land jutting northward into Kaneohe Bay, has a tiny oceanside park (no beach).

Overnight accommodations can be found at the ▶ **Windward Marine Resort**, a rural, low-rise hotel with a flock of free-roaming ducks. The pleasant rooms have separate lanais, and at night if you listen carefully you can hear fish splashing in the bay from your room. The hotel has no on-site restaurant, but there are kitchens in the rooms as well as outdoor barbecue grills and picnic tables. Dinner at the Chart House at Haiku Gardens (see above) is a nice conclusion to a carefree evening of shore walking or swimming in the resort's pool.

Only minutes away by car from the resort, at 47-754 Lamaula Road, is the **Hart, Tagami and Powell Gallery and Gardens**, a tiny oasis of art and flora in the lush Kahaluu Valley. The gallery is Japanese in design, featuring original oils, watercolors, and mixed-media paintings by Hiroshi Tagami and Michael Powell, as well as wooden bowls and ceramics by other local artists. A stroll through the gardens, filled with heliconia, ginger, and other exotic plants, is a refreshing complement to the indoor artwork. Open Saturdays, Sundays, and Mondays, by appointment only; Tel: 239-8146.

Kualoa Regional Park

North of Kaneohe and Kahaluu along Kamehameha Highway is Kualoa Regional Park, a favorite hangout of Hawaiians who prefer the simple amenities of fresh water, park toilets, picnic tables, and isolation from fast-food stops and gas stations.

As you enter Kualoa on Kamehameha Highway notice the Hawaii Visitors Bureau's historical marker—a cloaked Hawaiian—calling attention to the beach from which the double-hulled canoe *Hokulea* was launched in 1976. When *Hokulea* ("star of gladness") returned to Kualoa in 1987 after several successful Polynesian voyages, a Hawaiian chanter welcomed it ashore: "Arise and look to the faraway seas... here comes the worthy canoe." Because chiefs' children were taught beside the beach here, canoes of yesteryear lowered their sails in reverence when passing.

The circular lava wall at the end of the parking lot protects an ancient **fishpond**, purposely camouflaged beneath trees to discourage human intrusion, much to the delight of songbirds nesting among the branches. Earlier generations of Hawaiians created several types of fishponds; some were inland brackish-water ponds, while others, called *loko kuapa,* were constructed by enclosing small coves with sea walls, hard labor that required hundreds of workmen to pass stones hand-to-hand over long distances. Such ponds were filled with mullet and milkfish, favorite foods of Hawaiian chiefs, who believed guardian water spirits, called *moo* (MO-oh), inhabited fishponds and appeared as beautiful girls or mermaids combing their hair. In precontact times the open land around Kualoa was known as Apua, the fish basket.

The offshore island of Mokolii ("Little Dragon") dominates the ocean view from Kualoa park. In Hawaiian mythology, Hiiaka, a sister of Pele, killed a water dragon, cut off its tail, and cast it seaward, creating the island. The most popular non-Hawaiian name for this island, nonetheless, is **Chinaman's Hat**. Artist Dean Howell's painting of a gargantuan Chinese submerged beneath the island, his hat protruding above the waterline and humpback whales feeding from his rice bowl, colorfully visualizes Mokolii's nickname. A table beside Kualoa's Hokuleu Beach, facing Mokolii, is a perfect spot for a picnic.

Kaaawa

As you leave Kualoa and drive north toward Kahana Bay, the surrounding landscape is called Kaaawa, named after a yellow reef fish in the family Labridae. Four roadside parks flank the roadway. This is "night marcher" country, where, centuries before Halloween's ghosts and goblins captured Hawaii's fancy, processions of dead spirits were thought to walk at night, and human beings who happened to block their passage or addressed them without humility died before sunrise.

Today the tiny community of Kaaawa hosts health-minded visitors at the ▶ **Plantation Spa**. The health spa, at 51-550 Kamehameha Highway, near Swanzy Beach Park, is on the grounds of an old plantation estate and is affiliated with the Halsohem-Masesgarden spa near Stockholm, Sweden. The program includes morning walks, aerobics, tai chi, beach excursions, and water volleyball. Vegetarian meals, with fresh fruit from the spa's garden, are provided. Though hardly a wilderness retreat, the spa offers backcountry serenity amid tropical flora and is only 26 miles (42 km) from Waikiki. The ocean is nearby, though across Kamehameha Highway, which, at times, can be busy with traffic. A century ago when horse-drawn carriages passed this way, the spa's grounds served as a watering stop halfway between Kaneohe and Kahuku. The estate's original carriage house is now the spa's gymnasium.

As you pass Kaaawa, disregard Nordhoff's outdated advice to travel with a cook outside Honolulu and stop to eat at the **Crouching Lion Inn** (a short drive up the coast from Kaaawa town), a restaurant with a bar and souvenir shop named after a lion-faced rock on an overhead cliff. Formerly a family residence, the inn dates from 1927 and is built from U.S. West Coast timber shipped to Hawaii aboard one of the Islands' last lumber schooners. Try the restaurant's "mile-high" coconut pie, *pau niu,* which is really only four inches high. Be warned that the crowd is not local—it's usually Japanese, American, and Canadian—and at noon a procession of tour buses and rental cars arrives. Nonetheless, there is decent food here at reasonable prices, friendly service, and an ocean view, all of which overshadow the heavy tourist trade. Reservations are recommended for dinner; Tel: 237-8511. A converted four-car garage next door houses a gift shop selling Waikiki-style souvenirs—aloha shirts and non-Hawaiian handicrafts. Skip it and chat with the yardman or friendly neighbors who people-watch on the premises.

Kahana Bay Area

A lovely curve farther north along the highway brings you to **Kahana Bay Beach Park** on the shores of a cozy bay fronting an undeveloped state park. Immediately apparent is the same kind of engulfing coolness that you would feel entering a rain forest. Kahana is a place to sit quietly on the beach and meditate. The Hawaiians who once lived in the valley behind the beach netted *akule* (big-eyed scad), one of Hawaii's most delicious fish, from canoes and built fishing shrines on bluffs surrounding the bay. A dense thicket of ironwood trees—the same species seen in Honolulu's Kapiolani Park—shades the beach, making this a fine spot to read Jack London's short story "The Water Baby," in which London and a Hawaiian fisherman talk dreams while afloat in a canoe: "Perhaps it is that you are a dream," remarks London, "and that I and sky and sea and the iron-hard land are dreams, all dreams." Few visitors know that fishponds once flanked Kahana Bay and the remains of one, Huilua, can still be seen.

The shoreline north of Kahana Bay, **Papaakoko** (which means "secured blood"), is an ancient place of refuge, where *kahuna* (priests) gave sanctuary to defeated warriors and lawbreakers who reached its lifesaving boundary.

STAYING IN THE KAHANA BAY AREA

Those wishing to overnight on this part of the Windward Coast will find ▶ **Pat's at Punaluu** (53-567 Kamehameha Highway), about 3 miles (5 km) north of Kahana Bay Beach Park, a comfortable, off-the-beaten-path stopover. The condominium-hotel and its restaurant, **Banana Beach Bar & Grill**, are at beachside, surrounded by homes of country-living Hawaiians. The restaurant, on the bottom floor of the multistoried condominium, is open for lunch and dinner and is a favorite eating spot of longtime visitors to Oahu who relish the guava-glazed lamb.

The Polynesian Cultural Center

It's a 7-mile (11-km) drive from the Paniolo, past Punaluu Beach Park and Pat's at Punaluu, to Laie's sober Polynesian Cultural Center, a money-making theme park run by the Church of Jesus Christ of Latter-day Saints (familiarly, the Mormons). This is sanitized Polynesia, blemish free and highly manicured, yet exceptionally educational, even for veteran Pacific travellers weaned on Frederick O'Brien's *White Shadows in the South Seas* and *Atolls of the Sun*. More than a passing glimpse is demanded here, as the showcase is Polynesia-wide, containing seven re-created villages (six Polynesian, one Melanesian), each with its own cultural uniqueness. Even the movie is big here—an ultra-large screen featuring a South Pacific travelogue, *Polynesian Odyssey,* that is grander, the gods of Polynesia might think, than Odysseus's original Mediterranean voyage.

Despite a smorgasbord of dance extravaganzas, exotic-food tastings, and canoe rides (which can be shoulder to shoulder, sardine style), the cultural center's real Polynesian experience is simply walking from village to village, over waterways and bridges, observing the excellent thatch-and-wood craftsmanship of the dwellings, and listening to a Samoan, Tongan, or Hawaiian explain the foods and handicrafts native to his or her homeland. Some of the highlights are seeing a fire started by rubbing sticks, a Maori war canoe that was carved for King George V of England, and a paper mulberry tree, used to make *kapa* (bark cloth). Always popular is the Tahitian village, where dancers who fulfill the Western idea of South Seas beauty do the hip-shaking *tamure.* (One guidebook to Hawaii recently featured a Tahitian dancer on its title page.)

The Marquesan village will be of special interest to travellers familiar with Herman Melville's *Typee: A Peep at Polynesian Life,* which recounts his stay in the cannibalistic Marquesas in the 1840s. His island sweetheart was the enchanting Fayaway, who rode naked in the bow of his canoe, transforming her *kahu* (robe) into a sail—a literary scene that has bred generations of South Seas romantics. You won't find Fayaway in this re-created village, but the elderly ladies weaving palm-leaf baskets near the tattooing hut will answer questions. Strangely, a blowup portrait of a tattooed Marquesan displayed inside the tattooing hut is not a Marquesan at all, but the French beachcomber Jean Cabri, whom the Marquesans tattooed on face as well as body. When Cabri returned to Europe, he performed Polynesian dances and exhibited his tattoos but denied eating "long pig," a Marquesan hors d'oeuvre made from sliced human flesh wrapped in leaves and baked in earth ovens.

An all-you-can-eat dinner (no "long pig," however) is served at the center's **Gateway Restaurant**, a massive eatery decorated with Maori birdman figures and replicas of Easter Island stone sculptures. There is also a fancy luau with an *imu* (earth oven) ceremony, roast pig, Hawaiian music, and hula dancing, the evening ending with a 90-minute Polynesian revue with flashy stage effects. The downside of all this is the sheer tourist volume, and a *kapu* (taboo) on alcoholic beverages, including *kava,* the mouth-numbing elixir made from a pepper-plant root and renowned as the national drink of Polynesia and Melanesia. Called *awa* in old-time Hawaii, kava is no longer consumed by Hawaiians but remains the favorite beverage of tradition-minded Fijians. Of course you couldn't drive, or even find your car, after drinking from two or three kava-filled coconut shells; kava is notorious for encouraging the left leg to travel north while the right proceeds south.

Set aside ample time and money to explore the cultural center's many attractions; a visit can quickly become an all-afternoon experience, continuing until sunset or even moonrise depending on the ticket you have bought. Gates open at 12:30 P.M., Mondays through Saturdays; closed Sundays. Reservations required for some packages; Tel: 293-3333; elsewhere in U.S., (800) 367-7060.

STAYING NEAR THE POLYNESIAN CULTURAL CENTER

Within walking distance of the Polynesian Cultural Center, at 55-109 Laniloa Street in Laie, is ▶ **Laniloa Hotel**, the accommodations closest to the famous cultural attraction. The low-rise units, each with a lanai, are near a sandy beach leading to **Laniloa Peninsula**, which has five offshore islets created, according to Hawaiian mythology, when demigods butchered a water monster and threw the remains into the sea. The islets are now seabird sanctuaries.

Kahuku

Beyond the cultural center on Kamehameha Highway, where northernmost Oahu bends around to the west toward the North Shore's Sunset Beach, is the old sugar-plantation town of Kahuku. The town's charm lies in its atmosphere of remoteness, that far-from-the-freeway feeling worth its weight in traveller's checks. The main reason to stop here is to buy Island-grown shrimp and prawns at **Amorient Aquafarm**. The shrimp (saltwater) and prawns (freshwater) come cooked or uncooked, fresh from the ponds. You can buy them to go or to eat at picnic tables on the premises (bring your own beverages). The roadside store, with a backdrop of aquaculture ponds and crustacean-stealing birds, is labeled "Royal Hawaiian Shrimp & Prawns" and flies the U.S. and Hawaiian flags. It's easy to find, on the outskirts of Kahuku. Outback Oahu? This is as close as it gets.

THE NORTH SHORE

The North Shore, the Windward Coast's neighboring shoreline, is beach, surf, and shave-ice country, where the surf rises in 30-foot "monster" waves, and where on weekends escapists from Honolulu come to enjoy the laid-back, suntanned atmosphere and "talk story" about the shore's choice surfing spots—Rocky Point, Off-the-Wall, the Banzai Pipeline.

To reach the North Shore direct from Honolulu take H-1 to Pearl Harbor, H-2 to just before Wahiawa, and Highway 99 northward. On this route the nondescript interstate highway skirts military-reservation land and curves past Mililani town and Wheeler Air Force Base before joining Highway 99 in central Oahu. The route then crosses open fields of pineapple and sugarcane between Wahiawa and Haleiwa by the sea. The inland drive, however, is not as scenic or romantic as the route along Oahu's Windward Coast.

Haleiwa

The main village in this area is Haleiwa, a town of rustic charm struggling to cope with weekend crowds, its growing fame as Oahu's last historic town, and the difficult task of keeping the country in its country atmosphere. At sunrise, visitors departing from the Turtle Bay Hilton to the northeast, or early-bird arrivals from Honolulu, can hear roosters crow beside the Haleiwa post office while they breakfast across the street at **Café Haleiwa**, an unpretentious place with handwritten breakfast specials thumbtacked to the front door. A snapshot of a record-holding snow skier who stopped for pancakes decorates the wall; the windows look out on western Oahu's Waianae Mountains. The conversation is surfing, and the breakfast large.

Haleiwa is a growing art community, with two galleries to occupy time off the beach. **Kaala Art**, next door to Café Haleiwa, has artworks by several area artists, and a short ride away, opposite the Haleiwa Shopping Plaza, is the **Wyland Galleries of Hawaii**, opened in 1988 by Hawaii's mural-painter Wyland. Wyland's themes are marine, and he is noted for his "whaling walls," several large outdoor murals on Oahu.

The town's heartland is the area around **Haleiwa Alii Beach Park**, with its well-known surf break. An hour can be spent simply watching the surf from shore or walking the black-rock jetty sprinkled with fishermen, where views of beach, surfers, and the Waianae Mountains fading seaward toward Kaena Point are superb.

One of Haleiwa's charming sights is **Liliuokalani Protestant Church** (on Kamehameha Highway), erected where the North Shore's first missionary church stood. Enter beneath the lava-rock archway leading into the churchyard and walk to the cemetery, where gravestones, some garlanded with wilted leis, some tumbledown, memorialize North Shore citizens who died as long ago as 1830. Inside the church is a clock presented in 1892 by Hawaii's last monarch, Queen Liliuokalani, who wrote the soft farewell "Aloha Oe." The clock's hours are represented by the 12 letters of her name, N minutes to K is five minutes to seven o'clock. Outside, look at the church's steeple: The metal bird atop the weather vane is a frigate bird.

DINING IN HALEIWA

Between Haleiwa Alii Beach Park and Anahulu Bridge is the **Chart House** restaurant, serving locally caught fish but offering almost no sea view. Historically, what's of interest here isn't the food or the view but real estate: The restaurant is built on the site of the long-demolished Haleiwa Hotel (1899 to 1928), which made the town's name (which means "house of the frigate bird") famous. This was Oahu's first luxury accommodation, accessible by train from Honolulu on a railroad that circled Kaena Point. Nothing remains of the hotel.

Nearby is **Jameson's by the Sea**, offering a menu of fish entrées. Local fishermen provide the catch, which includes *ulua* (crevalle; old-time Hawaiians preferred the liquid around the eyeballs), *opakapaka* (blue snapper, a deep-sea fish favored by foreigners), and *mahimahi* (dolphinfish). The lanai fronting the bar has an ocean view, and the colorful sunset, not listed among the entrées, is free.

Shave Ice

Visiting Haleiwa and not eating shave ice is as criminal as touring Burgundy or Tuscany and refusing wine. Each day in quaint stores fronting the highway skilled shave-ice makers crush ice into finely shaved crystals, compress it into snowballs, and drench it with flavored syrup. Just about everyone goes for shave ice to **M. Matsumoto Grocery Store** (on Kamehameha Highway), king of North Shore shave ice since 1951. Inside are an antique-looking ice machine, a hand-pull adding machine, and old-fashioned glass display cases filled with candy and sundries. On rainy days newspapers carpet the floor. Artist Guy Buffet, known for his whimsical watercolors, captures the charm of Matsumoto's in a painting of the store's shave-ice clientele: surfers, tourists, and shark-jaw sellers. Try the strawberry or shave ice with sweet *azuki* beans, and be sure you ask for ice cream at the bottom of your shave ice.

Even though one of Oahu's earliest hotels was built in Haleiwa, today no hotel rooms are available here. Those wishing to overnight in or near Haleiwa must rely on bed-and-breakfast accommodations available through the reservation services listed at the chapter's end.

West of Haleiwa

WAIALUA

To discover your basic, down-home country bar and back-street, mom-and-pop grocery store, drive south of Haleiwa on Highway 83 to Waialua Beach Road, which leads west to Waialua, an old sugar-plantation town hidden in a sea of sugarcane. Daily, like clockwork, regulars assemble at the **Sugar Bar and Restaurant** inside a restored bank building shaded by monkeypod and *kukui* (candlenut) trees. The regulars like to joke that the bar stores its brews in the bank's vault, safe from bandits. A grouchy-looking bust of Ludwig van Beethoven, the owner's favorite composer, stares out at the customers, who prefer country-and-western and Hawaiian music.

A few streets away, within smelling distance of a sugar mill that still sounds the old curfew whistle at 8:00 P.M., is **R. Fujioka & Sons Ltd.**, a family-run grocery store with road dust on the canned beans and a church pew beside the doorway offering soda-pop drinkers a fine view of the nearby Buddhist temple. Like native land birds, the mom-and-pop store is an endangered species on Oahu, and survivors such as Fujioka are state treasures, a world apart from Waikiki's convenience groceries.

MOKULEIA BEACH

The best-known beach park between Fujioka's grocery store and land's end at Kaena Point is Mokuleia, about 4 miles (6½ km) away via the Farrington Highway. The park is the only developed public area along the six-mile stretch of Mokuleia beach and has rest rooms, a grassy playground for kids, and picnic facilities. This shoreline once housed a school devoted to an ancient martial art called *lua,* a type of dangerous hand-to-hand combat in which the fighters broke bones and dislocated arms and legs. The best *lua* artists were bodyguards to chiefs.

Waimea Bay

WAIMEA BAY BEACH PARK
Northeast of Haleiwa, across the 1921 Anahulu Bridge (continue east to a horseshoe bend in the road), is Waimea Bay Beach Park, a small, intimate place where newlyweds smooch beneath coconut trees and, when the waves are high, Hawaii's best surfers challenge the world's largest ridable waves, the "cathedral peaks" of this sport. Waimea Bay's beach and shorebreak are spectacular—deep white sand rimming a blue bay that in winter months rises skyward in 30-foot waves. Once you've seen Waimea, you'll never forget it. Centuries ago no Hawaiians swam here, fearing the wrath of the gods; only the nocturnal *menehune,* mythical sprites, ventured onto the bay to fish (their night-lights are still visible to those area residents who believe strongly enough). The tan-colored landmark nearby is the bell tower of Saints Peter and Paul's Mission Church. The tower is a former storage bin for the gray-blue lava rocks quarried from the Waimea shoreline; inside are piles of stones left over from the tower's rock-crushing past. The mission's name is a volcanic tribute to Apostles Peter and Paul, the "rocks" of Christianity.

WAIMEA FALLS PARK
Waimea Falls Park, tucked in the valley behind the bay, is an arboretum and botanical garden built around Hawaiian historical sites. Archaeologists, digging in remote valley locations in the park, probe temple foundations and the remains of chiefs' residences for clues to the North Shore's ancient past, while visitors attend Hawaiian cultural performances and view endangered plant species along the scenic trails between the visitors' center and Waimea Falls. Peacocks, show-offs not native to Oahu, strut the grounds in front of the **Proud Peacock Restaurant**, open for dinner only. The restaurant, serving up seafood and steaks, overlooks a meadow filled with wildlife and exotic flora. During the day, soups and sand-

wiches are available at the adjoining **Pikake Pavilion**, named for the Arabian jasmine, *pikake,* a fragrant flower used for leis. *Pikake* also happens to be the Hawaiian word for peacock. Hawaii's state flower, the hibiscus, grows in abundance nearby, and a fragrant garden has lei flowers from each island. Ask to see the yellow *ilima,* Oahu's official lei flower, once worn by Hawaiian royalty.

A must for an autumn itinerary is the annual **Makahiki Festival**, a two-day celebration at Waimea Falls Park with ancient-style hula, lei making, and Hawaiian games held the first weekend in October. Captain Cook first came to the island of Hawaii during a *makahiki* festival devoted to Lono, a fertility god who carried in his penis the sweet potato's sweetness. The park cultivates sweet potatoes, and there are reconstructed potato mounds (an old cultivation method) near a burial temple.

Once they've checked into the Turtle Bay Hilton (see below) and dined, perhaps at the Proud Peacock, those visitors who enjoy moonbeams in a tropical setting shouldn't miss the park's **full-moon walk** each month. Moonwalkers stroll past night-blooming plants, croaking frogs, and nocturnal birds on a one-hour safari to the park's waterfall, used in daytime for Acapulco-style diving shows. Two rules apply: no nude dancing in moonbeams and no skinny-dipping under the falls (there's no lifeguard). Crowds can be large, mosquitoes troublesome (take repellent), but the moonlight on the waterfall will delight the romantic—and, of course, the lunatic. A donation to the Waimea Arboretum Foundation is requested for the walks.

PUU O MAHUKA HEIAU

Above the park, on a *pali* (cliff) behind the Peter and Paul tower, is Puu o Mahuka Heiau (Hill of Escape), Oahu's largest sacrificial *heiau* (temple). As meaningful to ancient Hawaiians as St. Peter's basilica in Rome is to modern Roman Catholics, this heiau, though now reduced to knee-high walls of rubble, remains an active spiritual center for many Hawaiians. To find the heiau, turn right off Kamehameha Highway onto Pupukea Road (beside the Foodland supermarket), drive the curved road to the heiau turnoff sign, and minutes later disembark at this sacred destination. The site affords a superb view of Waimea Beach and is a cliff-top listening post where, Hawaiians say, you can hear the voices of sacrificial priests that still haunt the countryside. In 1792 several

British seamen, captured while taking water from the Waimea River, died here, victims of sacrifice.

Sunset Beach

If you prefer sand, another fine surfing beach, Sunset Beach, is 3 miles (5 km) up the coast (northeast) from Puu O Mahuka Heiau, overlooked by a COMSAT satellite station and a stone that president-minded cartographers believe resembles a toothless George Washington. Like other big-wave beaches, happiness at Sunset is measured in surf footage and in the frequency with which surf championships occur here, such as the Hard Rock Café's World Cup of Surfing, Marui Pipeline Masters, and Billabong Pro. To find out about upcoming surf events, ask at a surf shop, call a radio station's surf line (KPOI, Tel: 521-7873, is good), read the sports pages of the *Honolulu Advertiser* or *Honolulu Star-Bulletin,* or check for contest listings in the *Waikiki Beach Press,* free in sidewalk racks in Waikiki.

At Sunset Beach, the precontact Hawaiians who invented surfing (they called it *hee nalu,* wave sliding) paddled seaward on huge koa-wood boards and risked their bodies in high water. Today a nearby chiropractic clinic (the sign has a life-size image of a man's back) cares for Sunset's victims. Even if you don't surf, ask a lifeguard about swimming conditions, which may be hazardous. These tower-sitting watermen are paid to protect you, and their main complaint is that people seldom ask for advice—or ignore it when it's offered. Also keep in mind that weekend traffic between Sunset Beach and Haleiwa is a growing problem, and on a crowded Saturday, with surfers' cars jammed along the roadside and Honolulu day-trippers escaping from the city, the Haleiwa to Waimea Bay to Sunset Beach drive can be frustratingly slow, even bumper-to-bumper during midday. For years a highway bypass has been planned to free Haleiwa of the heavy northbound traffic, but no construction has been started. In the meantime, unless you prefer the auto-congested atmosphere of weekends, the best time to visit is on weekdays.

Kuilima Point

Farther north of Sunset Beach is Kuilima Point, a finger of grass-covered lava that supports on its back, like a mythical tortoise, the ▶ **Turtle Bay Hilton** (off the Kamehameha Highway), the only resort hotel on the North Shore. There's nothing special architecturally about the hotel's three-wing main structure, but the location is remote—it's as far north as you can drive—and the isolated, yet still posh, environment is appealing to those who prefer a low-keyed, outback accommodation.

Kuilima Cove, beside the hotel, has a fine white-sand beach, and its name has a special meaning for honeymooners (Kuilima means "to hold hands"). The backcountry ambience is ideal for horseback riding and jogging, and several miles of shoreline beaches allow for long, lazy walks in a landscape of sand dunes, tidal pools, and shoreside ironwood trees. A night or two here is an excellent way to explore the North Shore in detail, allowing for early morning drives to Haleiwa and the shore's beaches, or a leisurely afternoon visit to the Polynesian Cultural Center in Laie (see the Windward Coast section, above).

The hotel's **Palm Terrace** restaurant and the **Hang Ten! Surf Bar** are welcome retreats after a beach stroll at Kuilima Cove or a golf game played on a course approved by Arnold Palmer. The restaurant overlooks the bay and the distant hills spiked with white propellers converting wind power into electricity. The bartender at the Hang Ten!, which is located beside the swimming pool fronting the Palm Terrace, makes an exotic cocktail called a turtle, a blend of blue curaçao, pineapple juice, and Hawaiian rum. The cocktail's (and the hotel's) reptilian namesake, *honu,* the green sea turtle, is an endangered species in Hawaii; should you see a bay-swimming honu, consider yourself blessed by sea gods.

OAHU'S WEST
The Ewa Coast

West of Pearl Harbor, at the southern foot of west Oahu's Waianae mountain range, is an elbow-shaped coastline that is home to an industrial park, a naval station, an interstate highway, and Oahu's newest seaside hotel, the ▶ **Ihilani Resort and Spa**. Part of the massive Ko Olina resort complex, the 15-story, 390-room Ihilani (which means "heavenly splendor") is the most expensive hotel on the island outside of Waikiki. The guest rooms are equipped with marble bathrooms and deep soaking tubs, and the hotel's spa has therapeutic hydro treatments.

Nearby is an arcade of shops and the 18-hole **Ko Olina Golf Club**. The sunsets at Lanikuhonua Beach are spectacular. Guests reside on property where Kaahumanu, a wife of Kamehameha I, once bathed and performed religious rites. The hotel is a 25-minutes drive from Honolulu International Airport; take H-1 west to the Ko Olina exit.

The Waianae Coast

Dry and rocky, Oahu's west coast, Waianae, doesn't evoke love at first sight or dazzle the senses with postcard lushness. Endearment to its benefits takes time. The area stretches from Nanakuli in the south to Kaena Point in the north and is reached from Honolulu by the H-1 freeway, which loops around Pearl Harbor and intersects Highway 93 (Farrington Highway) south of Nanakuli. If you are driving from the North Shore, take Highway 99 (Kamehameha Highway) to the H-2 freeway, continue on H-2 as if returning to Honolulu, then exit onto H-1 (westbound) near Pearl Harbor.

The key words to remember when travelling here are *makaha* (savage) and *kaena* (heat). As these ancient names indicate, the Waianae Coast is Oahu's "Wild West," the last bastion of the rough-and-ready spirit that has disappeared from the island's more populated areas. There is a profusion of army and navy installations in the area, and many tourist luaus take place near an industrial park here. Nevertheless, independent travellers can find diversions on the Waianae Coast: golfing, surf-watching, and simply touring the area by car. Because this *is* a rough-and-ready area, though, *haole* should take precautions to avoid car theft: Lock your car whenever you leave it and take valuables with you or lock them in the trunk.

MAKAHA BEACH

Makaha is *the* beach here, though compared to the North Shore's most attractive beaches it appears rather ragged, and butts close against Farrington Highway. During winter months the beach suffers from erosion caused by the heavy surf, but in summer the sand returns, rejuvenating the shoreline. For years Makaha hosted a big-wave surf contest, but that event faded, replaced by a community benefit called Buffalo's Big Board Surfing Classic, named for local surfer Richard "Buffalo" Keaulana, who crewed on *Hokulea,* the replica Polynesian voyaging canoe. The long-board competition is held in February or March, depending on surf conditions. This is a back-to-yesterday event, a fun affair replaying the era when long boards (ten feet plus) cruised the surf unleashed to ankles, and top surfers won waxes and boards, not prize money and photogenic kisses from bikini-clad models.

MAKAHA VALLEY

Directly inland of the beach is Makaha Valley, its centuries-old rock walls sheltering the ▶ **Sheraton Makaha Resort** and surrounding golf course. The valley owes its name, which means "savage," to a community of bandits who preyed in ancient times on west-coast wayfarers. Lookouts shouted "High tide!" when travel groups too strong to rob approached and "Low tide!" for likely victims. Nowadays the valley's loudest shouts are golf warnings ("Fore!") and quacks from the ducks floating in the pond beside the hotel's driving range.

The hidden Sheraton Makaha is a sophisticated oasis of palm trees surrounding open-air pavilions and low-rise cottages with private lanais. The surrounding cliffs are a mountain-watcher's delight—they may make you forget that planned drive to nearby Makaha Beach as you stroll the grounds with an eye toward the skyline.

For a quiet drink, share the lobby lounge with returning horseback riders fresh from trails circling the remains of a coffee plantation and *paniolo* (cowboy) ranch; for lunch try the **Pikake Café**, beside the swimming pool; and for dinner the elegant **Kaala Room**, named after Waianae's highest mountain peak. Though the hotel is strong on tennis and horseback riding, guests are rather golfish, and café chitchat centers on tees and greens.

A short drive from the Sheraton's parking lot, on Maunaolu Street, is **Kaneaki Heiau**, a 700-year-old Hawaiian temple first used for offerings to agricultural deities and later for human sacrifices to war gods. The stones that enclose the heiau form Oahu's best-preserved example of a precontact religious site, restored between 1969 and 1970. Visitors must arrive at the heiau in a vehicle; walking or hiking in is not allowed. Open 10:00 A.M. to 2:00 P.M. daily except Mondays; closed on rainy, muddy, or windy days.

KAENA POINT

A short drive north beyond Makaha leads to **Kaena Point State Park**, site of rustic **Keawaula Beach**, the last beachhead before land's end. Waikiki sand is far away, and your beach neighbors will mostly be locals. Elder Oahuans call this beach "Yokohama," after a railroad man who worked for the now-defunct Oahu Railroad, which looped Kaena from 1895 to 1947. Don't expect to ride a steam engine, cross the railroad tracks, or meet the switchman—all are gone. The point of land fading into the ocean is Oahu's western tip, Kaena Point. Standing on the beach facing the point, you can almost hear the words of a Hawaiian chant: "Kaena, salty and barren, now throbs with the blaze of the sun; the rocks are consumed by the heat."

At point's end, a battery-powered light inside a miniature lighthouse sends an eight-mile beam into the night, searching, perhaps, for the souls of pre-Christian Hawaiians who departed from the rocky shore on an eternal voyage to the netherworld. The spot from which a soul exited Kaena is Leinaakauhane, **Ghosts' Leap**. Here, among the black-lava rocks overlooked by the lighthouse, Oahu's homeless spirits gathered like travellers awaiting a ferryboat to nowhere. According to William Westervelt's *Legends of Gods and Ghosts,* such spirits had no friends and owned no property during their residence in a Hawaiian's body; when the body perished, they became outcasts who wandered about like hobos, searching for Kaena Point.

SHOPS AND SHOPPING

Shopping outside of Honolulu is much easier now than in 1875, when visitors on horseback shopped for fish and fruit, and *The Hawaiian Guide Book,* published by a Honolulu newspaperman, apologized that milk cost eight cents a quart, a whole cow ten dollars, and a goat fifty cents. "These luxuries," wrote the author, "are always more expensive in Hawaii than elsewhere." Although nearly everything a traveller might wish to purchase on Oahu can be bought in Honolulu, shopping on location for a field-fresh pineapple or for a war souvenir at a battlefield is always more enjoyable than in-town buying or impersonal purchases by mail order.

Produce and Coffee
The recently remodeled **Dole Plantation** (64-1550 Kamehameha Highway/Highway 99), an off-road shop 3 miles (5 km) north of Wahiawa in the Dole pineapple fields, has take-home pineapple packs and assorted snacks. Aprons, cooking mitts, and even yoyos are for sale, all emblazoned with the Dole logo. Here in central Oahu in 1901 pineapples became an exportable product when

James D. Dole organized the Hawaiian Pineapple Company and canned this strange fruit brought to Hawaii in 1813. The plantation shop is a 40-mile (64-km) drive from Waikiki.

In Haleiwa, the **Coffee Gallery**, its ceiling bedecked with coffee-bean sacks, roasts a large selection of gourmet coffees, including Hawaiian Kona coffee (grown only on the slopes of Mauna Loa on Hawaii's Big Island). Kona coffee has a royal ancestry: The seedling trees came to Kona from Brazil in the 1800s, and the trees in Brazil had come from the botanical gardens of King Louis XIV of France.

World War II Memorabilia

The *Arizona* Memorial Museum Association bookstore at the **USS Arizona Memorial Visitors' Center** is a treasure trove for collectors of Pearl Harbor attack memorabilia. World War II buffs will find plastic models of the *Arizona*, a "Day of Infamy" cassette tape featuring radio broadcasts about the attack—hear the U.S. Congress voting on the declaration of war—and a "Remember Pearl Harbor" videotape narrated by actor Telly Savalas. A popular item is a U.S. flag that has been raised and lowered over the *Arizona,* including a certificate (mailed) confirming the day the flag was hoisted. A large selection of books about the attack are available, from John Toland's *Infamy* to Hiroyuki Agawa's *The Reluctant Admiral,* a biography of Isoroku Yamamoto, who planned the air raid. The bookstore is run in cooperation with the National Park Service.

Souvenirs and Books

The **Market Place** at the Polynesian Cultural Center in Laie has authentic South Pacific handicrafts, both imported and handmade at the center by Polynesians. New Zealand sheepskins are always a good buy as are the *taiaha,* traditional Maori war clubs similar to English quarterstaffs and used nowadays as dance ornaments. Other Polynesian items are hand-dyed *pareu* (sarongs) from Tahiti, Tongan wood carvings, and Hawaii-made *kukui*-nut leis strung from the polished nuts of the candlenut tree (these oil-rich nuts were once chewed and spat into the sea by Hawaiian fishermen to calm the water).

Charlie's Country Store, at Waimea Falls Park near Waimea Bay, has Hawaii books, videotapes, and island handicrafts, plus feed for the park's birds. The **Sea Life General Store**, at Sea Life Park at Makapuu Point, has a large selection of island gifts and souvenirs in a marine-world setting; the park's **Pacific Whaling Museum** gift shop, near a reconstructed skeleton of a 36-foot sperm whale, also has unusual items for whale lovers.

A large selection of Hawaii books, both new and out of print, are available at Kailua's **Tusitala Bookshop**, which also has hard-to-find books on the South Seas. The bookshop, at 116 Hekili Street, is named after Robert Louis Stevenson's Samoan nickname, *Tusitala,* "teller of tales." Open seven days a week.

GOLF COURSES

Oahu is by far the most visited Hawaiian island, so it is not surprising that tee times here are hard to come by. While there are some 30 courses on Oahu, many are restricted, such as the eight military courses and four highly exclusive private clubs, and a number of courses cater to large tour groups. Others are simply packed with people; Oahu's Ala Wai Municipal is the busiest golf course in the world.

Nevertheless, you can still have a highly enjoyable experience golfing on Oahu. First, avoid the municipal courses. Tee times are impossible to get and, with the exception of **West Loch Municipal Golf Course** (91-1126 Okupe Street, Ewa Beach; Tel: 296-5624), not worth the headache. The resort courses are expensive, but well worth playing. Always book ahead. Make tee times before arriving in Hawaii if possible, because all golf courses on Oahu are busy all the time.

Public Courses
The best bets for a good round of golf at a mid-level price are Pearl Country Club, Makaha Valley Country Club, and Olomana Golf Links. All cost $65 to $100 for out-of-state visitors.

Pearl Country Club, 98-535 Kaonohi Street in Aiea, is situated just above Pearl Harbor. Playing 6,230 yards (white tees), it is not an overly long course, but golfers will find plenty of challenges in many different guises, such as wind—the course sits at the mouth of a valley—hilly terrain, and tricky greens. You'll love every minute of it, though, particularly the magnificent views. Tel: 487-3802.

Just about the same description applies to **Makaha Valley Country Club**, 84-627 Makaha Valley Road, Waianae, an hour's drive west of Honolulu by way of Highway 93. Situated at the mouth of a valley—meaning some wind and occasional showers (we call them blessings in Hawaii)—the course has beautiful ocean views. Makaha Valley, which measures 6,091 yards (white tees), is a little kinder to your handicap than Pearl Country Club, as it is generally flatter. Tel: 695-9578.

Olomana Golf Links, 41-1801 Kalanianaole Highway, Waimanalo, on the other side of the Koolau Range from Honolulu (drive over the Pali Highway and then south or take Highway 72 east out of Honolulu, then follow it around the island's southeastern tip), is the shortest of the three, measuring only 5,887 yards (white tees). But don't take it lightly, because there are many hazards to cross on this layout. Water comes into play on every hole on the back nine and there are thoughtful challenges throughout. Tel: 259-7926.

Resort Courses

There are some wonderful resort courses on Oahu. The new **Hawaii Prince Golf Club**, 92-1220 Aliinue Drive, West Beach (take H-1 west out of Honolulu to the Ewa exit), opened 27 holes designed by Arnold Palmer and Ed Seay in mid-1992. Working with a basically flat piece of land, the designers introduced an abundance of fairway mounding to add some mischief. As this course matures it will get better and better. Tel: 956-1111 or 944-4567.

Ko Olina Golf Club, 3733 Alii Drive, West Beach (take H-1 west out of Honolulu to the Ko Olina exit), opened in 1990 with a wide-open course that is always well groomed designed by Ted Robinson. Gorgeous water features define the course, which plays a long 6,324 yards. On the 12th hole, for instance, you drive under a waterfall to get to the tee box, and on the 18th you must make your way over a large lake to reach the green. Tel: 676-5300.

Sheraton Makaha Resort and Country Club, which is next door to the Makaha Valley Country Club on Oahu's western coast (84-626 Makaha Valley Road, Waianae), has been considered one of the best courses on the island since it opened in 1967. Striking views of the Pacific and the green folds of the Waianae Mountains distinguish this course, which is always in top shape. Although it's pricey, at $140 for nonresident, non-hotel-guest players, it's definitely worth playing. Tel: 695-9544.

Turtle Bay Country Club, an hour's drive from Honolulu in Kahuku on the North Shore, is receiving positive reviews on its courses including a new 18-hole course, designed by Palmer and Seay. The Links at Kuilima, the Turtle Bay's original course, is undergoing a renovation and is expected to reopen in 1994. Tel: 293-8574.

Military Courses

If you are active or retired military, you can play Oahu's military courses. **Hickam Mamala Bay Golf Course**, at Hickam Air Force Base, west of Honolulu and south of Pearl Harbor (Tel: 449-6490), and **Kaneohe Klipper Golf Course**, at Kaneohe Marine Corps Air Station, on the Windward Coast (Tel: 254-2107), are seaside, offering delightful scenery as well as some challenging golf. **Leilehua Golf Course** (Tel: 655-4653) is inland, next to Wheeler Air Force Base and Schofield Barracks in the center of Oahu. But it is perhaps the most beautiful of the three, lush with flowering trees and well-kept fairways and surrounded by the bright green mountains of the Koolau Range on one side and the Waianae Mountains on the other.

—*George Fuller*

GETTING AROUND

Car Rentals

A rental car is the most convenient transport outside Honolulu. Car travellers will find the *Oahu Drive Guide*, which comes in every rental car, valuable. For strong cartographic detail, James A. Bier's two-part reference map, *Oahu 1* and *Oahu 2*, is also recommended. These maps, available in most bookstores and in Waikiki shops, plus a rental car, put outback Oahu within your reach.

Public Transportation

Daily public-bus service (number 20, always crowded) is available to the *Arizona* Memorial Visitors' Center from Waikiki (TheBus; Tel: 848-5555). The *Arizona* Memorial Shuttle (Tel: 839-0911) also provides round-trip transportation from Honolulu to the memorial's visitors' center.

A public bus (number 22) runs between Waikiki and Hanauma Bay daily, and there are buses that circle the island, both clockwise (number 52) and counterclockwise (number 55), leaving from Ala Moana Center. An intrepid traveller prepared to wait at roadside bus stops can travel around Oahu by bus; the round trip, without leaving the bus, takes about four hours (buses run every half hour during the day). An easy around-the-island day trip by bus might be to ride from Ala Moana Center to Waimea Bay in the morning (bypassing Haleiwa), then back to Haleiwa for lunch, go from Haleiwa to the Polynesian Cultural Center in Laie in the afternoon, and return directly to Honolulu that evening; total bus fare at 60¢ per ride: $2.40. (Call TheBus for schedules; Tel: 848-5555.) For those planning daily bus-riding excursions on Oahu a monthly bus pass ($15 per adult) is sold by all 7-Eleven stores and is valid from the first to the last day of the month. Bus information booklets are available in bookstores for those with the required time and patience.

Oahu's Roadways

For those driving, a profusion and confusion of Hawaiian highway names and route numbers clutter Oahu's highway maps. The Kamehameha Highway, for example, is Highway 830 and Highway 83 along the Windward Coast and the North Shore as far as Haleiwa, but is Highway 99 and Highway 80 on its inland leg (parallel to H-2) to the North Shore. But the main highways are actually laid out fairly simply. The Koolau Mountains are encircled by one roadway, with two over-the-*pali* (cliff) highways cutting through the range's southern end. No road suitable for rental cars circles the Waianae Mountains. All the major regional areas outside of Honolulu, except the Waianae Coast, can be reached by around-the-island driving, which means around the Koolau Mountains.

The section of the Windward Coast from Kualoa Regional Park to Kahuku, for example, can be reached by four routes. The most direct is the over-the-*pali* Likelike Highway (Highway 63), through the Wilson Tunnel into Kaneohe, and onto northward-bound Kamehameha Highway (Highway 83); more roundabout is the Pali Highway (Highway 61) past the Queen Emma Summer Palace and Nuuanu Pali Lookout, joining the northbound Highway 83 in the Kailua-Kaneohe area. And by travelling either clockwise or counterclockwise around the mountain range you will, of course, also enter this coastal area.

The H-1 freeway running eastbound from Honolulu into Kalanianaole Highway (Highway 72) is the traffic artery leading to the southeastern coast and Hanauma Bay, while westbound H-1 is the departure point for Pearl Harbor, the Waianae Coast, and, north of Pearl Harbor, the northbound H-2 freeway to central Oahu and the Kamehameha Highway (Highway 99), which leads to the North Shore.

ACCOMMODATIONS REFERENCE

The rates given here are projections for winter 1993–1994. Unless otherwise indicated, rates are for double room, double occupancy. Hawaii's telephone area code is 808.

- **Ihilani Resort and Spa.** 92-1001 Olani Street, Honolulu, HI 96707. Tel: 679-0079; Fax: 679-0080; elsewhere in U.S. and Canada, Tel: (800) 626-4446. $275–$425; suites $600–$5,000.
- **Laniloa Hotel.** 55-109 Laniloa Street, Laie, HI 96762. Tel: 293-9282; Fax: 293-8115; elsewhere in U.S., Tel: (800) LANILOA. $84–$110.
- **Pat's at Punaluu.** P.O. Box 359, Hauula, HI 96717. Tel: 293-8111; Fax: 293-9322; elsewhere in U.S., Tel: (800) 845-8799. $76–$140.
- **Plantation Spa.** 51-550 Kamehameha Highway, Kaaawa, HI 96730. Tel: 237-8685; Fax: 947-1866; elsewhere in U.S. and Canada, Tel: (800) 422-0307. $1,254 per person per week; includes accommodations, meals, and activities.
- **Sheraton Makaha Resort and Country Club.** 84-626 Makaha Valley Road, Waianae, HI 96792. Tel: 695-9511; Fax: 695-5806; elsewhere in U.S., Tel: (800) 325-3535. $110–$170; suites $260–$360.
- **Turtle Bay Hilton Golf and Tennis Resort.** P.O. Box 187, Kahuku, HI 96731. Tel: 293-8811; Fax: 293-9147; elsewhere in U.S., Tel: (800) HILTONS. $170–$320; suites $370–$1,550.
- **Windward Marine Resort.** 47-039 Lihikai Drive, Kaneohe, HI 96744. Tel: 239-5711; Fax: 239-6658; elsewhere in U.S., Tel: (800) 735-5711. $70–$300.

BED AND BREAKFASTS

In recent years, a number of bed and breakfasts have opened on Oahu and the Neighbor Islands. The companies below supply information and booking services for B-and-B accommodations in the Islands.

- **All Islands Bed & Breakfast.** 823 Kainui Drive, Kailua, HI 96734. Tel: 263-2342; elsewhere in U.S. and Canada, Tel: (800) 542-0344.
- **Bed & Breakfast Honolulu.** 3242 Kaohinani Drive, Honolulu, HI 96817. Tel: 595-7533; Fax: 595-2030; elsewhere in U.S., Tel: (800) 288-4666.
- **Pacific Hawaii Bed & Breakfast.** 19 Kai Nani Place, Kailua, HI 96734. Tel: 262-6140; Fax: 261-6573; elsewhere in U.S., Tel: (800) 999-6026.

THE BIG ISLAND
HAWAII

By Bill Harby

Bill Harby is associate editor at Island Scene *magazine and a contributing editor at* Honolulu *magazine. Besides various Hawaii publications, he has written for* Details, Modern Bride, *and* Guitar Player *magazines. He has lived in Honolulu for 17 years, and travels often among the six main islands.*

Officially known as the island of Hawaii, the Big Island is the youngest in the Hawaiian chain, less than a million years old and still breathing fire. Nearly twice as large as all the other Hawaiian Islands combined, it is a very big island—more than 4,000 square miles—and a very diverse one, encompassing tropical rain forest, bone-dry lava deserts, alpine heights, rolling green hills, and red-hot lava flows. Its five volcanic peaks include the snow-capped Mauna Kea, taller from its base deep beneath the sea than Everest; Mauna Loa, the single most massive mountain on the planet; and Kilauea, which is still liquid hot.

But while lava bubbles to the surface on one side of the Big Island (the east), on the opposite side the lava flows are all cold, hard, and black. Ancient petroglyphs are scored into the smooth lava—images of sails and warriors—and rock walls and platforms outline the sites of once-thriving fishing villages and temples. Today those villages on the west coast have been replaced by extraordinary resorts fringed with white sand, offering everything from thatched huts to frosty blue drinks to water slides. Broad fields of black lava give way to the lush green fairways of championship golf courses.

The north is cow country, where Hawaiian cowboys tend herds on the largest privately owned spread in the world. On the summit of Mauna Kea astronomers study the night sky; by day a few intrepid skiers try out the novelty of Hawaiian snow.

The Big Island has a wet side (the eastern) and a dry side, luxurious resorts and strenuous hiking trails, convivial bars and restaurants and quiet retreats far from the crowds. It seems to have something for everyone and plenty to keep even the most restless traveller occupied. Take at least a week, better yet, two, and see why other visitors have come and never left.

MAJOR INTEREST

Hilo
Restored downtown
Restaurants and cafés
Lyman Museum
Tropical scenery

Volcano area
Live volcano in Hawaii Volcanoes National Park
Volcano Village artists' community
Bed and breakfasts
Volcano Art Center
Jaggar Museum (volcanology)
Mauna Loa volcano

Kau
Ancient historic sites
Punaluu resort, golf course, and beach
Land's end at South Point
Green-sand beach

Kailua-Kona
Deep-sea fishing
Submarine excursion
Hulihee Palace and Hawaiian history
Oceanfront eating and drinking
Boutique shopping

Holualoa
Artists' community
Galleries
Bed-and-breakfast inn

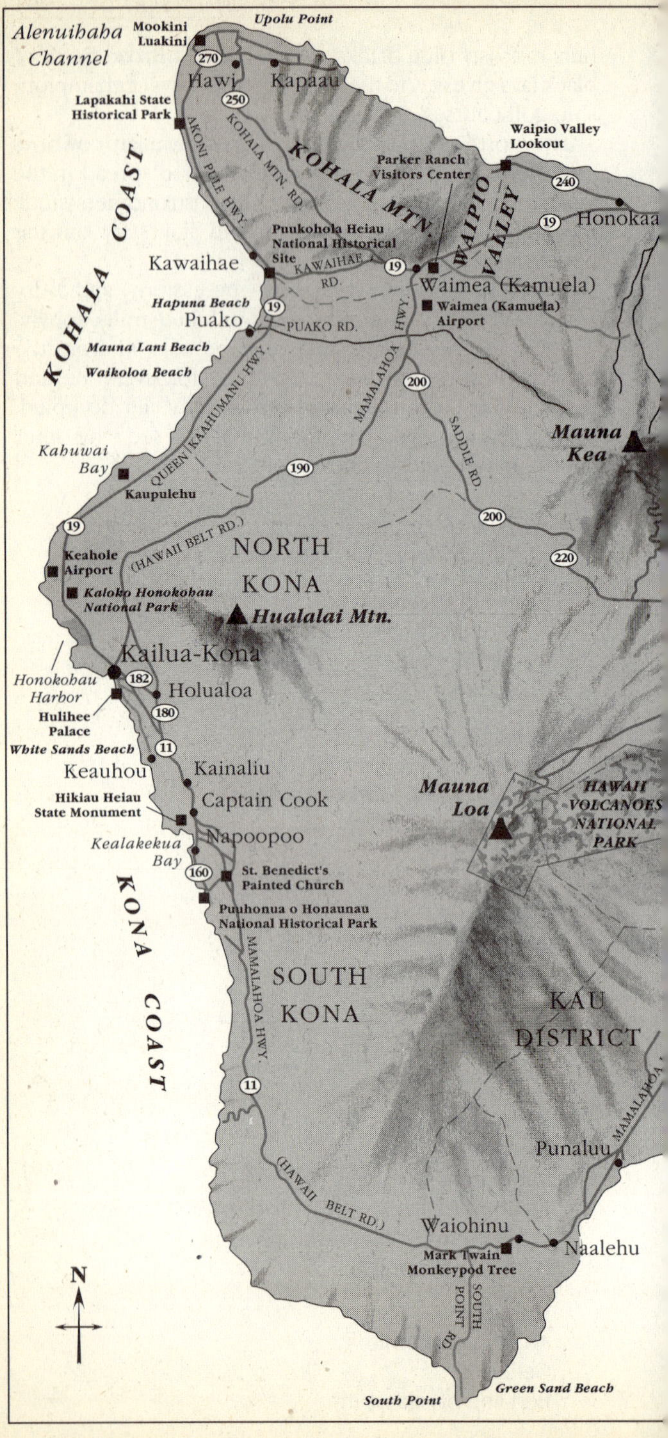

Alenuihaha Channel
Upolu Point
Mookini Luakini
270
Hawi
Kapaau
250
Lapakahi State Historical Park
AKONI PULE HWY.
KOHALA MTN. RD
KOHALA MTN.
Waipio Valley Lookout
Parker Ranch Visitors Center
WAIPIO VALLEY
240
19
Honokaa
KOHALA COAST
Puukohola Heiau National Historical Site
Kawaihae
KAWAIHAE RD.
Waimea (Kamuela)
Waimea (Kamuela) Airport
Hapuna Beach
Puako
PUAKO RD.
MAMALAHOA HWY.
Mauna Lani Beach
Waikoloa Beach
QUEEN KAAHUMANU HWY.
200
SADDLE RD.
Mauna Kea
Kahuwai Bay
Kaupulehu
190
(HAWAII BELT RD.)
NORTH KONA
220
Keahole Airport
Kaloko Honokohau National Park
Hualalai Mtn.
Kailua-Kona
182
Honokohau Harbor
Holualoa
Hulihee Palace
180
White Sands Beach
11
Keauhou
Kainaliu
Hikiau Heiau State Monument
Captain Cook
Mauna Loa
HAWAII VOLCANOES NATIONAL PARK
Kealakekua Bay
Napoopoo
160
St. Benedict's Painted Church
Puuhonua o Honaunau National Historical Park
KONA COAST
SOUTH KONA
KAU DISTRICT
Punaluu
MAMALAHOA
(HAWAII BELT RD.)
Waiohinu
Naalehu
Mark Twain Monkeypod Tree
SOUTH POINT RD.
N
Green Sand Beach
South Point

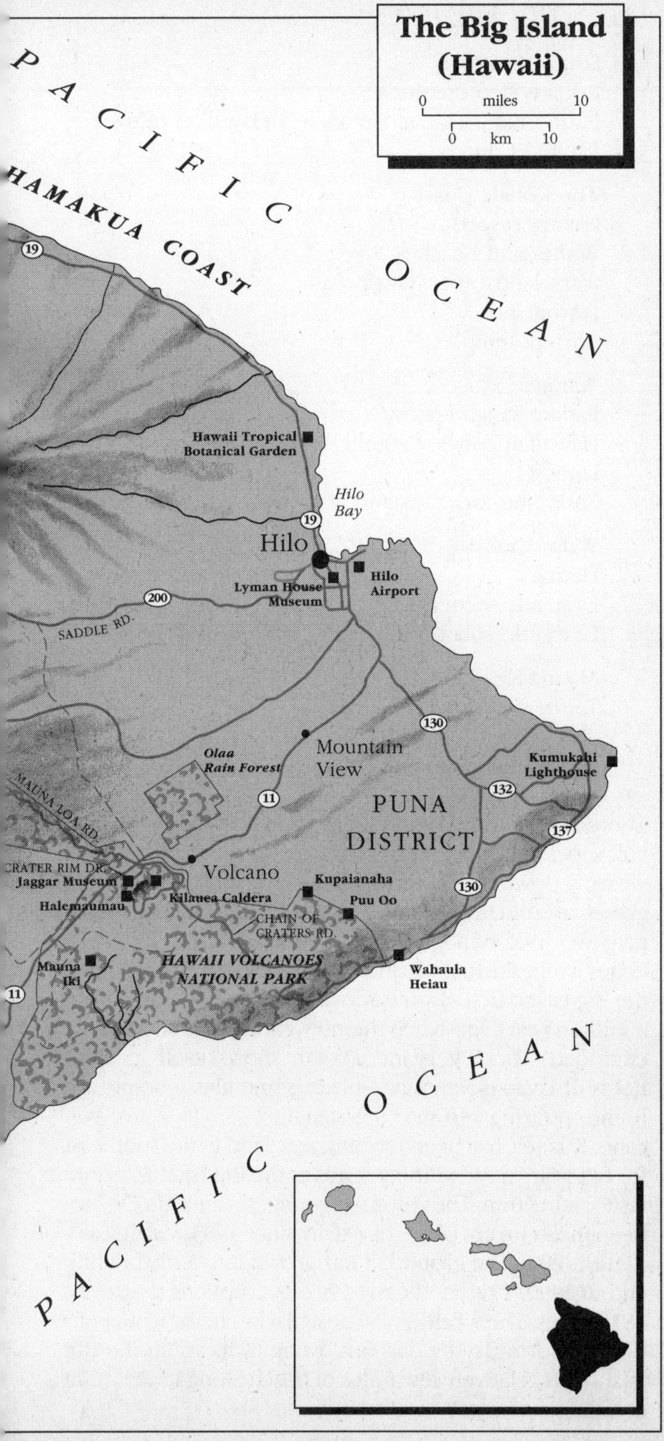

The Big Island (Hawaii)
0 miles 10
0 km 10
PACIFIC OCEAN
HAMAKUA COAST
19
Hawaii Tropical Botanical Garden
Hilo Bay
Hilo
Lyman House Museum
Hilo Airport
200
SADDLE RD.
130
Olaa Rain Forest
Mountain View
Kumukahi Lighthouse
132
11
PUNA DISTRICT
137
MAUNA LOA RD.
Volcano
CRATER RIM DR.
Jaggar Museum
Halemaumau
Kilauea Caldera
Kupaianaha
Puu Oo
130
CHAIN OF CRATERS RD.
HAWAII VOLCANOES NATIONAL PARK
Mauna Iki
11
Wahaula Heiau
OCEAN
PACIFIC

South Kona
Kona coffee orchards
Puuhonua o Honaunau ancient Hawaiian refuge
Painted Church

The Kohala Coast
Luxury resorts
White-sand beaches
Stark landscapes, lava fields
Petroglyphs
Ancient temples

Waimea
Parker Ranch history
Hawaiian cowboy country
Dining
Shopping for crafts and artwork

Waipio Valley
Hiking
Dramatic scenery
Peaceful, isolated valley

Mauna Kea
Tours to summit
Stargazing
Skiing excursions

There is a natural evolution that occurs on islands born of volcanoes. After the lava spews out, a gentle geological wearing down has its way with the land and the coral that grows around it, until the island's interiors become a patchwork of rich greens and reddish browns, and its edges a thin skirting of sand. Born of five volcanic centers, the Big Island first saw life above the ocean's surface about a million years ago when the now-extinct volcano Kohala exploded. The Big Island's youth shows itself in great fields of lava—some matte black, some glassy, some still liquid, pouring red into the steaming sea. Its active volcano, Kilauea, has been forming new land in the southeast for ten years now, winning status as the Big Island's prime visitor attraction. The volcano's youngest vent, Puu Oo, has been in its current phase of activity since 1983. Starting as a mere hole in the ground, it has grown into a sizable hill, and in 1990, 1991, and early 1992 its eruptions destroyed 181 homes. The world's youngest black-sand beaches continue to form day by day. But owing to its youth the Big Island has relatively few miles of beach along its 266-mile coastline.

SCIENTIFIC DEVELOPMENT

Lately the Big Island has seen quite a bit of controversy because of its scientific potential. Environmentalists and native Hawaiians are pitted against geologists and certain state politicians who would like to exploit the island's geothermal energy sources. The environmentalists and natives claim that tapping into the volcano for its steam energy would destroy one of Hawaii's last natural rain forests—and anger Pele, the goddess of volcanoes, besides. The geologists maintain that there are plenty of rain forests remaining and that geothermal power is an earth-friendly way to provide cheap, efficient energy. The state has given its go-ahead to the scientists, but accidents at the drill sites that released toxic fumes have given the activists more ammunition to get the drilling halted. A similar conflict is brewing over a possible rocket-launching site at South Point, whose residents can hardly bear the thought of their sleepy community being used for this purpose. Native Hawaiians, who want their fishing grounds and historic sites left untouched, have a stake here, too.

EXPLORING THE BIG ISLAND

It's only to be expected that an island this large and this diverse would have several nicknames. Its real name is Hawaii, but to avoid confusion with the state's name locals started calling it the Big Island. The tourism industry likes to use more romantic monikers, such as "The Volcano Isle" or "The Orchid Isle," but it is "The Big Island" that sticks.

The Big Island's sparse population is divided by the huge volcanic mountains running north–south down the center. These two groups differ in character: The people of West Hawaii's Kona and Kohala coasts bring home the bacon for the island, but those of East Hawaii control the budget—a situation guaranteed to generate a few family rifts.

East Hawaii claims the majority of the Big Island's residents—the island's county seat is in Hilo—but has relatively few overnight visitors; too many visitors see only Volcanoes National Park on the east side, bypassing the area's many other attractions. This is their loss: East Hawaii—which, being on the windward side of the island's mountains, gets most of the rain—has a tropical charm not to be found on the Big Island's western shores. We strongly recommend beginning a visit to the Big Island on the east side. When you land at Hilo Airport the surrounding landscape *looks* like what you imagined Hawaii to be. **Hilo** is a warm, friendly, accessible town, a relaxing place to unwind for a day or two before you head for the volcanoes, south of Hilo, and on around the island to the dry western shores.

West Hawaii is where the island's tourism industry is concentrated—which at first glance is somewhat surprising, as the land here seems so stark and uninviting. But people are enterprising on this side of the Big Island, and have worked hard at making this area as attractive as possible to those—nearly a million visitors each year—who travel to this coast for the endless sun and bone-dry days. In West Hawaii, some of the state's finest resorts have carved lush oases out of the lava fields of the southern **Kohala Coast**, establishing a niche in the market with their careful attention to service and amenities.

The Big Island's north and south are as different in ambience as east is from west. In the northern coast's growing community of **Waimea**, where cowboys mingle with rich kids, artists, astronomers, and restaurateurs, the pace is easy and friendly. (As Waimea is easily accessible from the Kohala Coast, it is covered in the West Hawaii section.) South Hawaii's **Kau** district, a rural outpost whose residents are farmers and pioneers, has little population. It is the least visited of any area on the Big Island, and most islanders would rather just leave it that way. (Kau is covered in the East Hawaii section.)

Driving around the Island

The major highways follow the perimeter of the Big Island, which means you have to circle the isle to get from east to west. Driving time between the two major towns—Hilo on the east and Kailua-Kona on the west—is about three hours, whether you travel the southern or northern route. From Hilo, the southern route passes through the volcano area and the rugged Kau district, rounds the southern part of the island, then heads up the South Kona Coast to Kailua-Kona. The northern route back to Hilo takes you up the North Kona and Kohala coasts to the island's northern tip, then down into Waimea and east to the Hamakua Coast, which stretches down to Hilo.

EAST HAWAII

East Hawaii does not have the luxury resorts that its western counterpart has, but it does have the delightful town of Hilo, as well as Hawaii Volcanoes National Park, where all the current volcanic activity is. Hilo is a good place to start your Big Island visit; and after a day or two there you can head south to the volcano area and then continue on down the slopes of Mauna Loa to the rugged Kau district, the tip of which is the southernmost land in the United States.

Hilo

Most who live in Hilo, the Big Island county seat (population 37,800), have been here all their lives, descendants of immigrants from Japan, China, or Portugal who came to work on the sugar plantations. Many residents work in county or state government offices or are merchants who own the mom-and-pop establishments that have lined Hilo's streets for decades. Not too many years ago, Hilo, largely left out of the state's booming tourist trade, seemed to be on an inevitable downslide into abject dilapidation. About the only reason visitors lingered in town was to experience the **Merrie Monarch Festival**, the state's most prestigious hula competition, held each year in late March or early April. (Tickets go on sale in early January and sell out quickly. Write to: Merrie Monarch Festival, 400 Hualani, Hilo, HI, 96720, or Tel: 935-9168.)

Several years ago merchants and local government decided to tap the area's potential. They reclaimed their town and began inspired renovation efforts, many of which have won state preservation awards. Thanks to such tending, downtown Hilo has become a lively center for strollers, shoppers, and those looking for a good meal.

DOWNTOWN HILO

With its yesterday feel and clapboard character, downtown Hilo—a ten-minute drive from the airport, north on Highway 11, then west on Highway 19—is made for pedestrians. (For 25 cents you can park your rental car on the street for two hours.) Make your first stop at the Hilo Main Street office in the newly spruced up historic S. Hata Building (on Kamehameha Avenue, which runs east–west along Hilo Bay, between Mamo and Furneaux streets) to pick up a free map to guide you on a historic walking tour of downtown. This building also houses **Café Pesto** (gourmet pizza), an art gallery, a health food store, a Hawaiian heirloom jewelry shop, and professional offices. If you begin your walk on a Wednesday or Saturday morning, you'll be drawn to the corner of Mamo and Kamehameha, west of the Hata Building, and the bustling **Hilo Farmers' Market**, where vendors hawk local produce (spiky, leafy greens and pale, oblong vegetables you never knew existed), flowers, crafts, and Kona coffee (at about the best price on the island). Fine old gents sing and play Hawaiian music for donations.

Keawe Street, which is another street made for strolling, runs parallel to Kamehameha a block inland. Within a few blocks of each other on Keawe, heading west, are **Elsie's**, a soda fountain that has been in business for more than 50 years; the incense-laden **Gamelan Gallery**, featuring Indonesian and Balinese folk art; **Pescatore**, a good Italian restaurant (try the *carpaccio de pesce*—thin strips of sashimi sprinkled with balsamic vinegar, capers, garlic, and fresh-grated parmesan cheese); the **Spencer Health & Fitness Center**, a bright, clean workout room with day rates; **Bear's Coffee**, where you can stop to sip cappuccino on the sidewalk outside; and **Roussel's**, an excellent French-Creole restaurant housed in an elegant old bank building (the owner helped create Hilo's own mini Mardi Gras celebration, now an annual event).

About a block toward the bay from Roussel's, down Waianuenue Avenue, is **Basically Books**, a little shop rich in Hawaiian fact and fiction, international travel guidebooks, and maps—including basketballs painted with the globe. On the same block, down on the corner of Kamehameha, **Lehua's Bay City Bar and Grill** draws Hilo's happening crowd for breakfast, lunch, and dinner (the spicy waffle french fries are a specialty). On weekends live jazz, blues, or reggae keeps the dance floor hopping, and on Wednesdays you can join the Boot Stompers' Club for a night of country-and-western dancing. Two blocks east, on Haili Street, are the fine old **Palace Theater**, under renovation and enjoying its second childhood as a home for community theater, and, across the street, the **Paramount Grill**, a little local café with stainless steel stools, a Formica counter, and arguably the best fried rice on the island.

A few blocks farther up Haili Street is the **Lyman Museum and Mission House**. This was the home of the Reverend David Belden Lyman and his wife, Sarah, missionaries from Boston who came to Hilo in 1832 to run a school for boys. The original house, with period furniture, is open for guided tours, and there is a museum in a contemporary building adjoining the old home, with such displays as a complete Taoist shrine carried piecemeal to Hawaii in the luggage of Chinese immigrants around 1850; the Earth's Heritage Gallery, which explains volcanology; and exhibits of cut glass, art glass, pressed glass, international ceramics, and Asian teak furniture.

BANYAN DRIVE

Five minutes away from downtown is Banyan Drive—take Highway 19 east, it's on the left—a bayside circle on which most of Hilo's decidedly unremarkable hotels are tucked away. Make the drive anyway to stroll through the Japanese-style **Liliuokalani Gardens**, with its fine views of Hilo Bay and a teahouse, a gift from the emperor of Japan. Gazing at the calm waters, it's difficult to picture the 30-foot *tsunami* (tidal waves) that swept over Hilo in 1946 (83 deaths) and again in 1960 (61 deaths), leveling whole blocks of the waterfront. Just west of the gardens is the site of a daily Hilo ritual, the **Suisan fish auction**. Each morning at about seven, fishing boats pull into the harbor and the day's catch of *ahi, opakapaka,* and smaller reef fish is auctioned off. It's a lively, multilingual bit of local color.

NORTH OF DOWNTOWN

Hilo's position, curled around the bay where Mauna Kea meets Mauna Loa, means it gets the bulk of the island's rain. That extra precipitation gives the area its abundant flora (and saves it from being overrun with visitors), including the fields of orchids and anthuriums that carpet the surroundings. About 4 miles (6 km) north of Hilo off Highway 19, the **Hawaii Tropical Botanical Garden** produces a wild variety of flora in a 17-acre valley. Torch ginger, heliconia, hibiscus, and flowering bromeliads are only a few of the several thousand species on display along the paths. On the opposite side of Hilo the 20-acre **Nani Maui Gardens**, at 421 Makalika Street near Hilo Airport, features a more manicured presentation of local foliage, along with a tram ride and a restaurant.

STAYING IN HILO

Forgo Hilo's mediocre hotels and consider staying in one of the bed and breakfasts on the outskirts of town. ▶ **Hale Paliku**, near downtown, is an airy, spacious, two-room suite in a house built in the 1930s. ▶ **Hale Kai Bed and Breakfast** is in a residential area less than a ten-minute drive from downtown. What it lacks in local character it makes up for in contemporary creature comforts, affable hosts, lavish breakfasts, and incredible views of the bay, where whales frolic in the winter. Another option is to spend the night up the hill, 45 minutes away, in Volcano Village, which offers a growing selection of fine B and Bs (see below).

The Volcano Area

Kilauea Volcano has been spurting lava virtually without pause since January 3, 1983, when a new vent opened and soon created the cindercone that came to be known as **Puu Oo** (Poo-oo Oh-oh). Periods of intense activity, manifested by broad viscous tongues of splattering lava pouring overland into the steaming ocean, alternate with lulls during which the lava creeps through a system of subterranean tubes, sometimes hardening, sometimes breaking through to the surface near the sea. As it seeps into the water, the lava adds acreage to the Big Island inch by molten inch (more than 300 acres since 1983).

The **Puna** district—the knob of land sticking out of the island's eastern side, south of Hilo—is the smaller of the Big Island's two volcanic areas (the other is Kau), but the recipient of just about all the activity. The major road that once ran along the coast here (Highway 130/137) was partly covered by lava in 1987, making it impassable in one section. It is where the road comes to a dead end that much of the excitement occurs. All along this coast black-sand beaches attest to the district's intimacy with lava, as these are young beaches, many newly formed by the eruptions. Here and there the black stone walls of a *heiau* (temple) and segments of ancient trails still survive between the old flows.

Pele is the fire goddess of the ancient Hawaiians, and it is no wonder that some modern-day Big Islanders still hear her voice and see her visage in the shifting landscape. The most storied, most volatile member of the Hawaiian pantheon, Pele gives life and takes it away. Those who live in her path, on the ground she laid down for them in a prior age, come to accept this—or else they don't live downslope for long.

For the folks who live in this area, volcanic activity is of course serious, sometimes tragic, business. Many homes still survive in the little Puna district communities through which fingers of lava have flowed over the last few years. But not all. The village of Kalapana and its famous black-sand beach were smothered in 1990 and 1991; 181 houses destroyed to date. Some people dismantled their houses and trucked them away, while others resigned themselves to Pele as their homes (often uninsured) burned to coals before being blanketed. (This threat is why Puna still has the cheapest land values in the state.) More fortunate home owners watched as the flow stopped just short of their backyards. The owner of Kalapana's only store offered a bottle of gin each day to Pele, who is said to have a taste for this particular firewater. One day he neglected the offering, however, and his market was swallowed up. On a helicopter ride over the flow, the rusted hulks of a school bus and a tin roof can be seen poking out of the now-hardened lava.

SEEING VOLCANIC ACTIVITY

Despite its awesome destructive power, the volcano is the Big Island's major tourist attraction—albeit one that must never be taken lightly. If the lava is flowing, the best places to see it can change each day. Sometimes visitors can walk right up to the lava as it flows into the ocean at the end of Chain of Craters Road (see below). For the best viewpoint, and for safety's sake, get up-to-date information on volcanic activity from the 24-hour hotline (Tel: 967-7977) or from the National Park Service (Tel: 967-7311).

An exhilarating, if environmentally questionable, way to see what the volcano has wrought is by helicopter. About half a dozen companies offer volcano flyovers, some leaving from Hilo, some from Waikoloa, and one from the Volcano Golf Course. **Papillon Hawaiian Helicopters** has an especially good narrated tour that flies directly over the active Puu Oo vent and travels down to the sea (Tel: 329-0551). **Kenai Helicopters Hawaii** also has an excellent tour (Tel: 329-7424). These flights can be expensive; they start at $100 for a 30-minute flight. However, conservationists have a quarrel with helicopters flying low over wildlife preserves. Hawaii's native bird population is dwindling, and biologists claim that the noise of the choppers disturbs mating rituals and thereby contributes to the demise of fragile species. Also, hikers and campers resent making their way miles into "remote" areas to be with the volcano only to find themselves under a helicopter flight path.

SOUTH FROM HILO

The entrance to Hawaii Volcanoes National Park is up the gradual slope of Kilauea on Highway 11 at the 29-mile marker (take Highway 11 south out of Hilo). There are a couple of interesting stops along the way. Past the 12-mile marker is **Tinny Fisher's Antique Shop**, a two-story ramshackle old house brimming with everything from Indonesian swords and priceless Chinese furniture to a player piano. Another mile or so up the hill on Highway 11 is the **Mountain View Bakery**, which has become one of Hawaii's favorite excuses for *omiyagi,* the Japanese-influenced Island tradition that says you must take something home—preferably food—to those who couldn't make the trip. This little home-style establishment specializes in hard, bland biscuits suitably called stone cookies. The ten dozen or so stone cookies pulled out of the ovens each morning are soon snatched up. They're an acquired taste—but they grow on you. Some Islanders are so hooked on stone cookies that they can't make a trip to the Big Island without stopping for a munch in Mountain View.

Volcano Village

Continuing about 15 miles (24 km) along Highway 11 from Mountain View, you reach the village of Volcano, the entryway to Hawaii Volcanoes National Park. Locals cross paths and stop to "talk story" at the general store, which stocks all the essentials as well as fresh-cut tropical flowers, such as orchid sprays and anthuriums, and calla lilies at probably the lowest price in the state—starting at three dollars a dozen.

Volcano is something of an artists' community, and its permanent residents include ceramicists, painters, and sculptors, some of whom open their studios to visitors by appointment. For a peek inside the Volcano artistic life, check out the studios of mask maker and mixed-media artist **Ira Ono** (Tel: 967-7261) and fiber artist **Pam Barton** (Tel: 967-7247), who fashions natural materials into baskets, hangings, and sculpture. If you stop in at the stunning Japanese-style studio of ceramicist **Chiu Leong** be prepared—he may challenge you to a hot game of Ping-Pong. You can also ask Chiu about art workshops. Area artists sometimes use his studio and thhe surrounding rain forest to teach their craft (Tel: 967-7637).

STAYING IN THE VOLCANO AREA

Until a few years ago, visitors wanting to stay at the volcano opted for ▶ **Volcano House**, the 1920s inn perched on the edge of Kilauea Caldera (crater) inside the national park. Back then, when the Halemaumau vent was more active, guests delighted in watching it steam and sometimes become a molten lake while they sipped a cup of hot coffee near the stone fireplace. Volcano House still rents rooms, but the grande dame has been surpassed in reputation—partly because of its fondness for the ubiquitous tour bus—by several establishments in the village proper. Although none can boast the incomparable crater views of the best Volcano House rooms, these new lodgings are gaining clientele by offering higher quality.

▶ **Kilauea Lodge and Restaurant**, one block off Highway 11 on Wright Road, is a former YMCA camp that Lorna and Albert Jeyte turned into a fine restaurant and bed-and-breakfast inn. Nonguests are welcome for dinner in the homey 50-year-old lodge, which is served at tables set around the immense "fireplace of friendship," a constantly crackling hearth built of rocks donated by civic and youth organizations from 32 countries around the Pacific. In the kitchen, Albert puts his masterful touch on such entrées as veal Milanese and seafood Mauna Kea. In addition to four rooms that come with a fireplace and skylighted bathroom, a small cottage and seven newer rooms are designed and decorated to evoke the sense of quiet mountain comfort. A full breakfast is included in the lodge's reasonable rates.

The three-story, three-bedroom ▶ **Volcano Bed & Breakfast** is a simpler alternative for those on a tighter budget. Jim and Sandy Pedersen have turned their home into a haven for visitors who enjoy basic country charm and friendly hosts. A Big Island native, Sandy offers a wealth of good advice on where to go and what to see during your visit. The Pedersens lend guests the use of their VCR and their stock of tapes, including some they filmed themselves of the Merrie Monarch Festival as well as documentaries on the area.

▶ **Hydrangea Cottage**, also in Volcano village, offers a more secluded, upscale hideaway. On a three-acre landscaped estate surrounded by a fern forest, this little house is so inviting that it's tempting to forget about exploring the Volcano area and just enjoy the homey hospitality. With its understated contemporary decor, redwood paneling, a white enamel wood stove for those chilly nights, a full kitchen (stocked with the makings for breakfast), a washer and dryer, and two beautiful Japanese kimonos, Hydrangea Cottage is one of the best B and Bs on the island. It shares the property with ▶ **Mountain House**, a spacious, luxuriously appointed house with beds for five and additional futons to lay out on the floor for guests. Mountain House also boasts a gourmet kitchen complete with two warming ovens (a steamer and a crisper), a gas wok, gas grill, and two dishwashers. Rich furnishings crafted from native koa wood complement the Asian cabinetry and partitions. From the bed in the master suite, you can gaze out at Mauna Loa and imagine staying forever.

Hawaii Volcanoes National Park

Just down Highway 11 past the village is the entrance to Hawaii Volcanoes National Park. Admission costs five dollars per car (a pittance with all the park has to offer), which includes an excellent annotated map of the park and its points of interest. The **visitors' center**, just within the gate, should be the first stop. Here you'll find more maps, books, a film, and exhibits that explain the workings of the volcano and the surrounding forest.

Next door, the **Volcano Art Center** shows a large collection of local art in a restored 1877 mountain lodge. The original Volcano House, this building once hosted adventurous overnight visitors at its former rimside location. When the new hotel was erected in 1921, this edition was moved into a field and left for scrap—until the park service and a group of local residents rescued it in the mid-1970s. Now it serves as a gallery for Volcano artists selling paintings, pottery, baskets, batik, photographs, and sculpture. Among the favorites are Dietrich Varez's brown-and-white Hawaiian block prints, G. Brad Lewis's striking color photographs of volcanic eruptions, Marian Berger's watercolors depicting a range of Hawaiian wildlife, and Chiu Leong's dramatic *raku* pottery. The art center also maintains an aggressive schedule of classes in all kinds of visual and performing media, as well as concerts, dance programs, writers' and artists' retreats, lecture series, and rotating exhibits. Like all the others in the upper reaches of the Volcano area, the art center's stone fireplace is often crackling and glowing, and flute or guitar music enhances the mood.

CRATER RIM DRIVE

Past the art center on Crater Rim Drive, which encircles Kilauea Caldera, the pine trees give way to scrub-covered lava fields. Scenic lookouts along the drive are terrific vantage points from which to view this huge hole, which once bubbled and spurted lava. One of the best lookouts is at the **Thomas A. Jaggar Museum**, along the caldera rim about midway between the art center and Halemaumau.

This park service museum, next door to the Volcano Observatory, brings the geological phenomenon to life with displays of Hawaiian volcanology. The museum gives a complete account of eruption history and forecasts for the Big Island, offers exhibits on seismic activity, demonstrates data-gathering equipment, and shows volcanic landform models. There are also plenty of photos of previous eruptions, and a videotape keeps visitors up to date on the latest volcanic activity—sometimes with footage shot only hours earlier.

Park rangers lead several daily walks from the museum and give lectures about the park. Some hikes get close to current lava flows, while others focus on the plants and animals that thrive on these volcanic slopes.

Farther east around Crater Rim Drive is the main stopping point on the rim of **Halemaumau**—a crater within Kilauea Caldera known as "the fire pit" because it was the site of spectacular activity in the early 1900s. The sulfuric fumes are particularly noxious here, and warning signs advise that caution be exercised, especially by those with respiratory problems.

Continuing along the park road you can circle the entire crater in your car, making several interesting stops on the circuit. **Devastation Trail** is a 30-minute stroll along a boardwalk that traverses a forbidding landscape of black cinders and the skeletal remains of trees that succumbed to the 1959 Kilauea Iki eruption. The **Kilauea Iki Trail** (park at the Thurston Lava Tube entrance) is an easy hike (about three miles) first through fern forest and a grove of bright red flowering *Ohia lehua* trees, then down a short switchback to the crater floor. Though the surface lava is now hard, small fissures releasing steam attest to the still-molten bowels beneath. You can walk up to the hole from which shot the 1,900-foot fountains of lava (the highest on record) in 1959. Another switchback on the other end of the crater leads back to the parking lot.

Cross the street and follow the path through the **Thurston Lava Tube**. This short tunnel, lit by electric lights, is one of many formed on the Islands when rivers of flowing lava begin to cool at the edges then harden, building up the tube's walls and ceiling. When the flow stops, the tube empties of molten lava, leaving the cylindrical form. Beyond the point where the stairs lead up and out of the tube, you can see the tunnel continue on into the darkness. Those with strong flashlights and a sense of adventure might want to explore the dark passage for a vivid subterranean experience—at the risk of annoying the park rangers. The floor is mostly flat, but watch out for rough spots and places where the ceiling gets low.

CHAIN OF CRATERS ROAD

Back on Crater Rim Drive, you'll come to the turnoff for Chain of Craters Road, which heads seaward and ends abruptly 20 miles (32 km) later at the western side of the 1993 lava flows that blocked Highways 130/137. Chain of Craters Road is a well-paved, two-lane blacktop cutting through flows from 1969, 1974, and 1982, among other years. The road winds past little craters and mounds formed by volcanic activity on a meandering path to the ocean. One of the better shorter walks along here is over the cinder path to the base of **Mauna Ulu** (about two miles), a low *puu* (hill) created from a 1969–1974 eruption. Some hikers venture right up to the rim of the sleeping mound, but the walk over uneven, crumbly lava is only for the surefooted. There are plenty of other places along Chain of Craters Road to pull over and walk onto the old flows, where you'll see the two types of lava: *aa,* which is jagged and rough, and *pahoehoe,* which is glassy, smooth, and ropy.

Kipuka Nene campground (take Hilina Pali Road off Chain of Craters Road) is fairly secluded and is the starting point for several rigorous hikes to craters and the ocean. For information about the campground, contact Hawaii Volcanoes National Park, P.O. Box 52, Volcanoes National Park, HI 96718; Tel: 967-7311. No fee or permit is required.

At the coast Chain of Craters Road runs east along the ocean a couple of miles before ending in a dam of lava rock. The nearby **Wahaula Heiau**, an ancient Hawaiian temple built in 1275, has so far been spared by the volcano, but just barely. A 1990 flow, which destroyed the adjacent visitors' center, came right up against the wall of the temple, then turned and went around it.

From the end of Chain of Craters Road you may be able to see active flows—sometimes right at your feet. Hikers love this region for the trails through the lava to secret coves and beaches. These are major forays, not day hikes, and best left to experienced hikers. Talk to the park service (Tel: 967-7311) about trails and conditions (you are required to register with them if you go on certain trails) or consult Craig Chisholm's *Hawaiian Hiking Trails.* By car the only way out of this area is back the way you came, along Chain of Craters Road and around Kilauea Caldera to the park entrance.

MAUNA LOA

About 2 miles (3 km) past the entrance to Volcanoes Park, going southwest on Highway 11, you will come to Mauna Loa Road, which leads to Mauna Loa, a gigantic shield volcano—and the mountain with the greatest mass on the planet—that last erupted in 1984, its flows coming within scant miles of Hilo's outskirts.

Truly serious hikers interested in reaching the summit of Mauna Loa can take Mauna Loa Road about 13 miles (21 km) from Volcanoes Park until it dead-ends at a lookout. A seven-and-a-half mile trail leads from there to Red Hill, where you will find a cabin to overnight (all cabins and campgrounds are free). Another ten strenuous miles past cones and craters leads to **North Pit**, a section of Makuaweoweo Caldera. Numerous splatter cones lie inside this mammoth volcanic indentation. The summit trail ends two and a half miles past North Pit, at an altitude of 13,677 feet. A cabin stands on the opposite rim of the caldera; for information and cabin reservations contact Hawaii Volcanoes National Park, P.O. Box 52, Volcanoes National Park, HI 96718; Tel: 967-7311.

The Kau District

Adventurers who can't leave a stone unturned may want to continue on around the Big Island's southern half to the Kau (KAH-ooh) district. This area is usually bypassed, even though it has some of the island's most dramatic and historic coastline—including a green-sand beach. The steadily descending drive southwest on Highway 11 from Hawaii Volcanoes National Park passes through a landscape of rough, matte-black lava sparsely covered with gnarly, stunted *ohia* trees and low scrub.

KAU DESERT TRAIL

After the 37-mile marker (about 11 miles/18 km past the town of Volcano) a sign indicates the **Kau Desert Trail**. Besides offering an interesting walk through a glassy black landscape, the trail passes by what are believed to be 18th-century footprints pressed into clay, evidence of a deadly moment in Hawaii's volcanic history. In 1790, when an army was marching here enroute to battle Kamehameha, the young warrior chief who would later unite the Islands under his rule, Kilauea Volcano let loose with a rare explosive eruption that sent massive clouds of volcanic ash into the air. As the ash fell, it mixed with moisture in the air and deposited a layer of clay on the ground. Some 80 people reportedly succumbed to the suffocating gases and ash; it is believed that the footprints embedded in the clay show where they took their last steps.

THE PUNALUU AREA

The tiny communities that populate the southern section of Highway 11 were born in the plantation days (generally from the 1890s to the 1970s), when workers needed a place to live and owners gave them one "near the office." Scenery here remains much as it was in those heady times—sagging storefronts and frame houses splashed with a hopeful coat of colorful paint.

For years the area's most important sugar manufacturer has been C. Brewer & Company, which decided in the 1970s to take some of its vast land holdings out of sugar and put them into the resort business. That was when the company, once a member of the Big Five (the corporate quintet that ruled the Islands in the first half of the 20th century), opened ▶ SeaMountain at Punaluu to serve as the hub of the area's low-key tourist activity. A 450-acre oasis, SeaMountain (on Highway 11) has 76 condominiums in secluded low-rise buildings. The rolling 18-hole golf course is consistently packed with folks who winter at the resort. Others find their way to the resort because of the Aspen Institute–Hawaii conference facility on the property, a cerebral center for humanistic professional, government, and business conclaves.

Kau's most famous beach is the black sands of **Punaluu**. "Punaluu," which means "diving spring," is blessed with one of the area's numerous freshwater springs, some of which bubble up at sea's edge, some beneath the sea. Hawaiians used to dive down off Punaluu Beach with stoppered calabash gourds to get drinking water. When they felt the cold fresh water surging up, they would uncork the gourds and let them fill.

SOUTH POINT

Several more miles down the hill is South Point, the southernmost point of land in the United States. To get there you must trundle 12 miles (20 km) down a narrow paved road through pastureland. (Don't bother stopping for the Mark Twain Monkeypod Tree. Despite its intriguing name it probably has nothing at all to do with Twain.) Take the turnoff after the village of Naalehu (watch for the sign saying "South Point") to approach the broad, flat, windy plain of South Point. Just before you come to the coast you'll see the wind farm—a spread of about 30 giant, white, high-tech windmills. At the end of the road there is nothing but breathtaking, rugged coastline and a subtle sense of history. According to tradition, some of the earliest voyaging Polynesians (perhaps 350 A.D.) first made landfall in Hawaii at Ka Lae—the Hawaiian name for South Point. Ancient canoe moorings carved into the lava rock testify to Ka Lae's importance as a rich fishing ground in old Hawaii. And it remains so today. Because the water drops to great depths right off shore, fishermen can cast from shore for such deep-sea fish as *mahimahi* and *ulua*. A number of local residents make their living fishing off Kau. It is these folks who generally disagree with plans for a possible commercial rocket launching facility in the area.

About 2½ miles (4 km) northeast of the boat ramp at South Point is **Green Sand Beach**. This is the most concentrated deposit of glassy olivine granules along the Kau coastline. To see it you have to either walk the bumpy trail or have a sturdy four-wheel-drive vehicle.

From South Point you can continue west-northwest along Highway 11 to the South Kona Coast (covered in the West Hawaii section). It's a leisurely drive along the lower slopes of Mauna Loa through pasturelands and past grazing cattle on decent roads. From South Point to South Kona's Puuhonua o Honaunau National Historical Park is a 38-mile (61-km) drive.

WEST HAWAII

Seen from the air as you fly in, Keahole Airport, 6 miles (10 km) north of the west-coast town of Kailua-Kona, brings to mind the stark, lifeless landscape of another planet. Runways smoothly stripe the hard black lava fields, which seem to cover the ground in every direction. This forbidding scenery—in sharp contrast to the lush tropical greenery of Hilo—is not what most visitors to Hawaii expect, but it is, after all what the islands are made of.

From the airport you may simply continue north on the Queen Kaahumanu Highway (Highway 19), past messages written with white coral ("Derek loves Lani") along the lava roadsides, to the toney resorts that line the North Kona and South Kohala coasts—from the Kona Village and Waikoloa beach resorts up to the Mauna Lani and Mauna Kea resorts. Or you may wish to check out the action in Kailua-Kona, the island's one unadulterated tourist town, and opt to stay in one of the little condos, hotels, or guest houses that have sprung up there.

We begin our West Hawaii coverage in Kailua-Kona, right in the middle of the western coast. Heading south, we explore some of the ancient historical legacy of the Kona Coast down to South Kona, then return to the area north of Kailua-Kona: the Kohala Coast, where all the super-luxury resorts are. Rounding the northern tip of the island we visit the rustic town of Waimea and the isolated Waipio Valley, followed by an excursion up Mauna Kea, which, while not technically in West Hawaii, is most easily accessible from that side of the island.

Kailua-Kona

West Hawaii's major metropolis is actually named Kailua, but because a more populated town on the island of Oahu bears the same name, this little town of 9,100 tacked on the name of its district and is known as Kailua-Kona, or sometimes simply Kona. Locals call it Kailua or Kailua Town.

ALII DRIVE

Alii Drive, Kailua's main drag, is a long strip of boutiques, souvenir shops, restaurants, and watering holes interspersed with a few historical sites. A cynic might call it a poor man's Waikiki. At the northern end of the street, near the Hotel King Kamehameha, is Kailua's one little patch of beach and **Kailua Pier**, where excursion boats pick up guests for deep-sea fishing, scuba diving, parasailing, and even a commercial submarine ride. Ocean activities are Kailua Town's forte. The deep-sea fishing in Kona waters is the best in Hawaii, and the billfish (marlin) tournament that operates out of Kailua each August draws teams from all over the world. At the pier in the late afternoon boats dock and weigh their catches on the huge scales. Numerous charter boats are available year-round; get in touch with the Kona Activities Center, Tel: 329-3171; or the Kona Charter Skippers Association, Tel: 329-3600. (Many of the boats leave out of **Honokohau Harbor**, about 2 miles/3 km north of town.)

The odd white vessel bobbing low in the water not far offshore in Kailua Bay is the **Atlantis**, a submarine designed purely for sightseeing. Passengers are ferried out by surface boat and transferred to the sub, which descends to about 90 feet and slowly trolls the bottom. Everyone has a window seat with large portholes through which to see the fish attracted by the diver accompanying the sub with a bag of food. For reservations, Tel: 329-6626; Fax: 329-3177; elsewhere in U.S., Tel: (800) 548-6262.

By the water next to the Hotel King Kamehameha are two of Kailua-Kona's historical sites: **Kamakahonu**, once a compound of houses, gardens, and fishponds for royalty, where Kamehameha the Great died peacefully in 1819, and **Ahuena Heiau**, an ancient temple. Though a few plaques explain the historical significance of the location, the heiau and adjacent huts appear a little forlorn surrounded by sunbathers and the hustle-bustle of the pier.

Farther south, on the bay, is **Hulihee Palace**, a stately two-story seaside house with coral-and-lava walls built in 1838 by Governor John Adams Kuakini. Now open to visitors each day, it contains a collection of furniture and artifacts owned by Hawaiian royalty before the Islands were made a U.S. territory in 1898. Hawaii's last king, Kalakaua, used the house for his summer palace. Hulihee is run by the Daughters of Hawaii, all of whom are at least part Hawaiian. Directly across Alii Drive sits **Mokuaikaua Church**, erected in 1823 and rebuilt in 1836 by the island's first Christians.

SHOPPING AND DINING IN KAILUA-KONA

There are plenty of casual places along Alii Drive to grab a meal and a cold beer. One of the most intriguing is the **Sibu Café**, a sidewalk spot in the Banyan Court, a small alcove of shops. The café serves huge portions of exotic Indonesian dishes. A few minutes' walk south, on the other side of the street, is the historic **Kona Inn**, originally a hostelry for 19th-century sailors, now a collection of restaurants, bars, and shops selling everything from six-foot-long stuffed-fabric lizards to silk tie-dye and imported batik clothing.

A few more minutes walking south brings you to **Waterfront Row**, another covey of shops and restaurants, including **Phillip Paolo's** (Tel: 329-4436), serving fine Italian fare. There's beachfront dining and drinking at **Jameson's**

by the Sea (Tel: 329-3195), at 77-6452 Alii Drive, just south of town at White Sands Beach (also called Magic Sands and Vanishing Sands, for obvious reasons).

One of the most unexpected dining pleasures in Kailua is **La Bourgogne** (Tel: 329-6711), a cozy French restaurant run by French chef Guy Chatelard and his wife, Jutta. It's just south of town at 77-6400 Nalani Street, on the road to Captain Cook. Some visitors will surely find this small, quiet bistro, with its elegant Continental menu, a welcome respite from all the Kailua commotion.

KEAUHOU

Hardly anyone who has been to the Big Island looks for lodgings in Kailua itself. Instead, repeat visitors often stay in the Keauhou resort area, 5 miles (8 km) to the south, most notably at the ▶ **Keauhou Beach Hotel**, one of the southernmost properties on the strip of condos and hotels in the Kailua-Kona area. The Keauhou Beach has been partly refurbished and its public rooms have been opened to the ocean view. Despite the hotel's name, there's not much of a beach at the Keauhou Beach, but the ocean borders the property rather dramatically.

The town of Keauhou has a golf course and a gallery or two, but its greatest attraction is the snorkeling and scuba boats that set sail from its harbor. One good diving excursion is with the trimaran **Fair Wind**. The boat sails down the coast to Kealakekua Bay, the site of Captain Cook's death (a monument on shore commemorates him) and a marine preserve teeming with fish.

The area's nightlife offerings are meager, but the **Kona Comedy Club**, presenting a revolving lineup of top-notch Mainland comics on Tuesday nights at the Kona Surf Resort and Country Club (74-28 Ehukai Street, on the south side of Keauhou Bay; Tel: 322-3411), is one worthwhile diversion.

Holualoa

Inland above Kailua Town, on the slope of a mountain, is the little village of Holualoa, a gathering place for artists, especially during the past several years with the opening of at least five art galleries along the town's main drag. The art movement really started here some 25 years ago when two California art teachers, Bob and Carol Rogers, bought the dilapidated Kona Coffee Mill, renamed it the **Kona Arts Center**, and started offering classes there. For two decades the couple gave lessons in pottery, batik, basketry, painting, and other media in their active and colorful Coffee Mill Workshop, but rumors were circulating in 1993 that the Rogerses were considering turning the center over to local artists, who would convert it to gallery space. In the meantime, art snobs put off by naïve watercolors, neighborhood gossip, and students passing around cookies and coffee should skip the Rogerses' homey salon. Others will want to peruse the works for sale—or ask about the next painting class. (For information write to P.O. Box 272, Holualoa, HI 96725.)

Following the success of the Kona Arts Center, other galleries started opening their doors in Holualoa. One of the Rogerses' former students, Hiroki Morinoue, specializes in contemporary monotypes and woodblock prints in his **Studio 7 Gallery**, just up the road. His work, the ceramics of his wife, Setsuko, and the pieces of other Island artists make this the most progressive gallery in the village.

STAYING IN HOLUALOA

Holualoa is also home to the extraordinary ▶ **Holualoa Inn**, a 14-year-old red-cedar mansion owned by the Twigg-Smith family of Honolulu. Thurston Twigg-Smith, who built the house, publishes one of Honolulu's two daily newspapers and is a great patron of contemporary art. The 5,000-square-foot inn, now owned by his nephew Desmond, reflects this. Large, fantastical paintings cover many walls, offering intriguing counterpoint to the unfinished cedar paneling and polished eucalyptus floors. Only four bedrooms are available, but there is a swimming pool and guests (predominantly from Europe and North America's West Coast) can talk or play billiards in several living areas. Breakfast comes with the room, but guests are on their own for other dining and drinking. The views at the inn are fabulous, spanning the entire Kona district from the airport south to Kealakekua Bay—and there is a rooftop gazebo to capitalize on them. Bring a jacket (and perhaps a bottle of cognac) and spend a crisp evening in the lantern-lit gazebo gazing down at the twinkling coastal lights. Three suites feature private Jacuzzis that face the same view.

Holualoa's ▶ **Kona Hotel**, just up the street from the inn, was once popular with adventurous travellers who thought they had stumbled upon a bare-bones, back-roads experience. But the Manago Hotel in the town of Captain Cook (see below) now offers a better experience of the same type. Nonetheless, you can't beat the Kona's rates

($15 for a single, $23 for a double), but you'll share a bathroom with construction workers, bargain-hunting Island families, and backpackers from around the world. Admittedly, the bathroom perched at the end of a long open catwalk boasts the best panorama of its type in the Islands.

SOUTH OF HOLUALOA

Heading south from Holualoa on the Mamalahoa Highway (Highway 180), you'll come to the **Fuku-Bonsai Center**, near the intersection with Highway 11. This newly opened attraction, featuring nine different theme gardens, started as a collection and research center for the dwarf Japanese trees.

A little farther south is the little village of **Kainaliu**, where the 1932 Aloha Theater houses the **Aloha Café**, a casual eatery serving up delicious homemade pastries, soups, fresh local fish, other tasty entrées, and sandwiches. With breezy seating on a covered porch, the café is open for breakfast, lunch, and dinner.

South Kona

KONA COFFEE

Continuing south along the Kona Coast, you enter Kona coffee territory. The heaviest growing areas start around the village of **Captain Cook** (about 8 miles/13 km south of Holualoa) and stretch to the south. The famous Kona variety has flourished on this western slope of Mauna Loa for more than 150 years, the delicate bean coddled by the generally dry air and cool temperatures. Coffee isn't an easy crop to grow; the beans must be handpicked when they're exactly the right ripeness, and more beans ripen every day. Most coffee farmers on the Big Island do it part-time; they are families who inherited their tiny two- or three-acre spreads, or they do the work for the extra money. On a Saturday you might see them out with their bags plucking the coffee and tending their fields.

About 6 miles (10 km) south of Captain Cook is a road marked "**Coffee Mill**" veering off Highway 11 toward the ocean. While a working coffee mill does indeed sit at the bottom of the two-lane switchbacks that amble through the coffee orchards, what is open to the public is largely a tourist display and gift shop. It's of mild interest to see how the mill roasts and dries the coffee. Prices here, close to the source, are not any better than at anyplace else in the Kona district. (In fact, the best prices for 100 percent Kona coffee are often found at the Hilo farmers' market.)

THE CAPTAIN COOK AREA

Before coffee arrived, the area around the village of Captain Cook was visited by English explorer James Cook. West of the village, the **Hikiau Heiau** marks the site on Kealakekua Bay where Cook was honored by the Hawaiians as the god Lono, when he arrived in 1779 during the *makahiki* festival—the most important celebration of the year—established, according to legend, by Lono himself. About a month later, forced back by foul weather, Cook returned to the bay, not knowing the makahiki had ended, and this time the Hawaiians were not so receptive. The English explorers' need for supplies strained the Hawaiian hospitality, and cultural differences made the foreigners seem less and less godlike to the Hawaiians. When Cook and his shore party tried to hold a chief hostage until a missing boat was returned, a confrontation turned violent, and Cook, four of his men, and about a dozen Hawaiians were killed.

In the town of Captain Cook is the funky ▶ **Manago Hotel**, which features some standard dormitory-type rooms with a shared bath as well as individual accommodations in a newer wing. A third-floor room, dedicated to the hotel's founders, is the most comfortable. Japanese in decor, it is furnished with tatami mats, a deep *ofuro* for bathing, and a futon for sleeping. The hotel's dining room serves hearty home-style meals that attract crowds from around the island, so in the hotel bar you might hear some local yarn spinning.

SOUTH FROM CAPTAIN COOK

From Captain Cook continue south on Highway 11 about 7 miles (11 km) and then drive toward the ocean a few miles to find one of the Big Island's most accessible and interesting pieces of cultural history, **Puuhonua o Honaunau National Historical Park**, whose name means "place of refuge at Honaunau." This was a sort of "no-tag zone" for the ancient Hawaiians. Warriors defeated in battle could find sanctuary until the storm passed, or a woman could come here if she'd broken one of the sacred *kapu* (taboos) that governed so much of her behavior—eating with the men, for example. Also strictly kapu, for both men and women, was standing in the shadow of a royal. The trick was that the kapu-breaker had to get here first, often with others in hot pursuit. Upon reaching the *puuhonua,* he or she could be absolved by a *kahuna* (priest).

What gave the puuhonua its power was the *heiau* (temple) that housed the royal bones (the ancient Hawaiians believed each person's spirit lived in his or her bones). Within the Puuhonua o Honaunau are two heiau built around 1550 and another that dates from about 1650. The newer one, which served as a temple and mausoleum until 1818, harbored the bones of at least 23 chiefs, giving this particular puuhonua power that went beyond any other. In 1820 King Kamehameha II abolished the kapu system and there was no more need for places of refuge. This puuhonua, however, has been carefully rebuilt and maintained ever since as an important part of Hawaiian history, and looks much the way all the Islands did before the advent of Western ways. Hawaiian arts and crafts are sometimes exhibited on the grounds, which also contain several reconstructions of Hawaiian thatched huts, idols, and canoes.

Inland from Puuhonua o Honaunau is St. Benedict's, a simple wooden structure most affectionately called the **Painted Church**. St. Benedict's interior was painted with Renaissance-style murals around 1900 by its priest, who wanted to show his congregation what Europe's grand and glorious cathedrals looked like—if only in a small way. Unfortunately, the church has been the target of vandalism over the years, sometimes forcing its closure.

If you continue south on Highway 11, rounding the southern tip of the Big Island, you will enter the two volcano districts, Kau and Puna (both of which are covered in our East Hawaii section, above).

The Kohala Coast

North of Kailua-Kona is the Big Island's Kohala Coast, where many of the island's luxury resorts are carved into the lava. This is the driest, sunniest part of the Big Island, and you are almost guaranteed good weather here. One resort, the Mauna Kea Beach Hotel, even offers a free night's stay on your next visit if it rains for 30 continuous minutes or more while you're booked at the hotel.

Lava no longer flows onto this upper-left quadrant of the Big Island, but the Kohala Coast wears its past on its sleeve, as ancient Hawaiian heiau, petroglyphs, and the rock ruins of villages poke up unexpectedly here and there between aprons of hardened lava. Even more startling are the monuments to the present that began nestling amongst the lava fields in the early 1960s and now constitute one of the finest coveys of luxury hotels in the world.

THE RESORTS

North Kona
Although technically in the North Kona district, south of Kohala, the ▶ **Kona Village Resort** easily compares with its sister properties in southern Kohala in terms of service and price. Five miles (8 km) north of Keahole Airport off the Queen Kaahumanu Highway (Highway 19), Kona Village consistently opts for the understatement, starting with its thatched-hut security gate set back 50 feet from the road. There's no sign, no way for the uninformed to guess what lies beyond. The wealthy families who come back year after year for another dose of Kona Village's restorative powers, the couples who honeymoon in seclusion here, and the harried executives and celebrities who know they'll get some peace at this outpost don't need any further advertisement. The likes of Lou Rawls, Shelly Duvall, and novelist Michael Crichton simply want to sit unnoticed behind their sunglasses.

After a 2-mile (3 km) drive over a narrow, bumpy road, Kona Village guests find 125 individual *hale* (thatched bungalows), where they can cozy up in privacy. There are no phones in the rooms here, no televisions, and jackets and ties are not allowed. There's also no golf course, but visitors can play tennis, sail, scuba dive, sign up for sportfishing, learn traditional Hawaiian crafts or simply lounge on the black-and-white sand beach or by one of the two pools. And they can eat and eat and eat. All meals at the village are included in the price, with dining choices in one of two charming establishments on the property. On Friday nights the hotel holds a luau, setting out *lomilomi* salmon, *kalua* pig, *haupia, tako,* and *opihi,* with the smiling staffers standing by with a handy definition.

Three new hotels are in various planning and building stages nearby. Just what effect they will have on Kona Village's exclusive atmosphere remains to be seen.

Waikoloa
Another 10 miles (16 km) north is the southern Kohala Coast's most self-consciously opulent luxury resort. The ▶ **Hyatt Regency Waikoloa** was the idea of Honolulu developer Christopher Hemmeter, who wanted to "create

a fantasy," but then unleashed a fantasy far from what most folks in Hawaii would imagine for their islands. Opened in September 1988, the 1,241-room property met with disdain from vacationers accustomed to resorts with more pedigree, while less snooty families splurged a little and tried out the place as kind of an arty alternative to Disneyland. Guests are transported about the sprawling oceanfront grounds (62 acres) by monorail or by boats that run on tracks through man-made canals while a pilot in a crisp white hat with gold braiding pretends to steer. The decor includes seven-foot-tall, blue-glazed Chinese vases with gold scrollwork, huge stucco pillars, large rainbow-feathered parrots and macaws perched on brass rings, a thatched hut from Papua New Guinea in an alcove near designer shops, and a painting of a Balinese fishing village. At the foot of the grand staircase is a life-size bronze carriage and six horses frozen midstride—part of the extensive art collection displayed throughout the resort.

Perhaps the Hyatt's most unusual feature is its variety of water activities. One long, curving pool has a steady current built in that draws swimmers downstream. Another receives crashing waterfalls and a long water slide that's as close to a bobsled run as you'll ride in a bathing suit. Jacuzzi's are tucked here and there in grottoes and gardens. The man-made lagoon is home to six resident dolphins, part of a program called Dolphin Quest, which allows visitors (guests and nonguests) chosen by a daily lottery to hop into the water with them. It's a closely controlled shake-hands, rub tummies, feed-them-fish meeting that has some people crying exploitation while others say it's creating a tribe of dolphin devotees newly sensitive to the animal's needs. Hotel guests can decide for themselves. (It costs about $65 per adult; $40 for kids.)

The Hyatt Regency Waikoloa also offers several dining options, with six restaurants and a luau. **Donatoni's** sophisticated northern Italian menu is enhanced by high ceilings and open-air design. **Imari**, a Japanese restaurant, serves teppanyaki and sushi in a quiet tea garden setting. You can work off extra calories on one of the two championship golf courses, the tennis courts, or in the sprawling 25,000-square-foot spa, and there are plenty of activities for kids.

When the Hyatt began taking reservations there was only one other hotel operating in the Waikoloa resort area: the ▶ **Royal Waikoloan**. Not as elaborately endowed or flashy as its neighbor, the Royal attracts low-key guests who want the relaxation of the Kohala Coast but not the steep prices charged by the other hotels here. The entire Waikoloa resort area sits amidst tide pools and ancient fishponds, and the Royal Waikoloan has done the better job of wrapping its hotel around the Hawaiianness of the geography and capturing its essence.

Mauna Lani

Only a few miles north, the Mauna Lani Resort, on some 2,300 acres of stark lava purchased back in 1972 by the Tokyu Group, is one of Hawaii's earliest examples of Japanese investment outside Waikiki. It was ten years before the company even broke ground on its first hotel, but when it did, the resulting ▶ **Mauna Lani Bay Hotel & Bungalows** was a stunner: white stucco with bougainvillaea tumbling from the balconies and a lavishly tropical courtyard complete with meandering pools inhabited by the same species of fish that snorkelers find offshore. The rooms—accented with teak furnishings and wallcoverings of traditional Hawaiian woven mats—manage to be both casual and quietly elegant.

This area's original inhabitants were Hawaiians who fished the ancient ponds on the property. Around 1930 a noted Hawaiian businessman and sportsman, Francis Ii Brown, took title and built a compound fit for Hawaiian royalty: simple wood buildings and a spring-fed pond for his beloved, Winona. Brown would be the last individual owner of the Mauna Lani area, which Hawaiians called Kalahuipuaa. His nephew Kenneth, however, remains as president of Mauna Lani Resort, a decision that means the developers intend to preserve some semblance of Hawaiian spirit. One of Francis Brown's cottages has been restored and is accessible to the public on a limited basis. There are also five 4,000-square-foot bungalows available, each of which comes with its own pool and butler—at a price that limits guests mostly to celebrities, CEOs, and lottery winners.

Although owned by Japanese—and reflecting their characteristic attention to detail and presentation—the Mauna Lani hasn't turned out to be a haven for visitors from the Far East. North American businesspeople on holiday with their families, many of them repeat visitors, favor the hotel. The restaurant **Le Soleil**, serving local fish and produce with a Mediterranean touch, is one of the coast's finest restaurants, and the open-air **CanoeHouse** has established itself as a pacesetter for Pacific Rim cuisine. Both welcome guests from other hotels (Tel: 885-6622 for reservations at both restaurants).

The Mauna Lani's famous golf course, named for Francis Ii Brown, is carved out of the surrounding lava. The 18 holes are among the most photographed in the golfing world, particularly the number 6 hole, which requires hopeful duffers to drive the ball across more than 100 yards of raging ocean. Other hazards along the course are also of the natural variety: dozens of free-form lava mounds were left as they were found. (Although this area hasn't seen volcanic activity since the mid-1850s, the landscape is still mostly broad fields of black lava.)

Sharing the golf course with the Mauna Lani is the ▶ **Ritz-Carlton Mauna Lani**, which opened in 1990 on a 32-acre beachfront spot. This was the Ritz-Carlton's first Hawaiian property, and the company's legendary European-style service and elegance are always evident—sometimes at the expense of Hawaii's casual ambience. The Ritz touch is seen in gestures small and large: from the ice water cheerfully offered poolside to the complimentary spa, the deluxe rooms, concierge staff, and exclusive lounge of the Ritz-Carlton Club.

The decor is not your typical tropical look. Dark mahogany four-posters and armoires dominate the rooms while deep shades of green and rose in bedspreads, wallpaper, and carpets provide color. Marble bathrooms with double vanities provide a second phone for those inspired to make inconveniently timed calls. Outside, a 10,000-square-foot pool is the centerpiece in a landscape of rambling pathways, flora tumbling into a courtyard area, and private nooks set with colorful tables and umbrellas.

Mauna Kea

Several miles up the road, the ▶ **Mauna Kea Beach Hotel** (off Highway 19) has been the doyenne of Kohala Coast resorts for a full quarter-century. Conceived and built by Laurance Rockefeller in the early 1960s, the property, with its broad white-sand beach, has been a faithful vacation home for those to whom Rockefeller most wanted to appeal: folks just like himself. The toney hotel, embellished with a dazzling collection of Asian and Pacific art, is one of the nation's first examples of a corporate art program. Twice-weekly art tours led by professor Don Aanavi are among the hotel's more unusual amenities. The dapper art historian explains the subtleties of the collection, which ranges from an early seventh-century granite Indian Buddha to late 19th-century Japanese garments, and from New Guinea ritual masks to 30 Hawaiian quilts Rockefeller commissioned for the hotel's opening. Without the tour, the significance of the artworks might go unnoticed, because there are no ropes or signs (Rockefeller didn't want his place to look like a museum).

Hawaii's mistress of lei making, **Barbara Meheula**, is ensconced at the hotel. Meheula specializes in customizing each lei according to the occasion or the wearer's clothing or sensitivities, using Big Island plants and flowers as well as an occasional bloom from a Neighbor Island. Orders for Meheula's leis must be placed through the Mauna Kea.

Nearly 75 percent of those who take a room at this fairly formal hotel have been here before. Once the enclave of blue bloods who could take a three-month holiday during the winter, then check in again with the kids for the summer, the Mauna Kea is now heavily visited by those children, who have grown and are married themselves. This relatively younger crowd inspired the hotel to develop more activity-oriented facilities, such as a two-mile jogging path and an 18-station running and exercise course to complement tennis courts and a golf course annually rated as one of the best in the country by *Golf Digest*. Rooms at the Mauna Kea are breezy affairs furnished in teak, cane, and colorful Thai cottons.

The **Garden**, one of five restaurants on the property, is formal—jackets are required for men—yet relaxed. It serves inventive dishes such as lamb smoked with guava wood and Kona coffee beans. The **Batik Room**, also formal, glows with candlelight and serves fine Continental cuisine. Right outside the mood is more casual as a Hawaiian trio lazily serenades those stopping by for a romantic dance under the stars. Mauna Kea revelers often cap off the night with a stroll along the beachside path to watch massive manta rays hunt for food around an underwater light the hotel installed to attract smaller fish.

EXPLORING THE KOHALA COAST

When you are ready to leave your hotel, there are several interesting, natural historical, and cultural sights in the Kohala region.

Puako

Up the coast from the Mauna Lani Resort, the tiny village of Puako keeps its own counsel as the quiet, seldom-visited site of one of the state's oldest and most extensive

petroglyph fields, spared by the later lava flows. A new, well-marked road that bypasses Puako altogether has improved accessibility to the site. Enter the Mauna Lani Resort and watch for the sign. At the site, prehistoric carvings of warriors, turtles, fish, and boats, mysterious even to archaeologists who have studied them, crowd acres of lava. Archaeology buffs can pass an hour or more walking through the fields, although the entire trek is manageable in 20 minutes.

Hapuna Beach
Only two beaches away to the north, Hapuna Beach, the Big Island's widest white-sand crescent, lures swimmers, bodysurfers, and picnickers (during the winter months beware of the dangerous undertows and riptides here). A new hotel, the ▶ **Hapuna Beach Prince**, is slated to open here in mid-1993. On the beach the hotel's guests will be joined by the usual bunch, people who live on the Big Island or those staying elsewhere who simply need a wet respite along the road. Covered tables on the grassy slope offer spots for shady picnicking. A snack bar sells cold soft drinks, hamburgers, and local-style plate lunches, and rents snorkeling gear.

Kawaihae
Just south of the small industrial town of Kawaihae, about 2 miles (3 km) north of the Mauna Kea Beach Hotel, the **Puukohola Heiau**, a temple built by Kamehameha in 1790–1791 before he was king, today welcomes visitors in a far friendlier fashion than its original owner did. Stop in at the visitors' center and the ranger will tell you how Kamehameha eliminated his rival, Keona Kuahuula, who came to help dedicate the temple and ended up being sacrificed there. An imposing structure, Puukohola Heiau is now a national historic site.

Another mile up the coast, at the only shopping center in the uninteresting town of Kawaihae, is the diner **Café Pesto**, Pizza lovers while away whole afternoons here, downing gourmet Italian pies and calzones. The food is so good that some of the Kohala Coast hotels fill their own orders from Café Pesto.

Lapakahi Park
About 11 miles (18 km) farther north, along the dry, hot eastern coast of the North Kohala district is Lapakahi State Historical Park, where the ruins of an ancient fishing

village—first settled during the 14th century and still thriving into the 19th century—have been restored as an outdoor museum. A caretaker answers questions and provides a brochure that outlines a walking tour past surviving stone platforms and walls where houses and canoe huts once stood. The face of a fishing god is carved in a seaside rock, and various plants and trees that were used by old-time Hawaiians for food, medicine, and building materials still grow along the paths. Visitors are invited to play traditional Hawaiian games.

Mookini Luakini

About 6 miles (10 km) north of Lapakahi Park, at the Big Island's northernmost tip, is another historical site, Mookini Luakini. A *luakini* was a heiau of human sacrifice. Dating from the fifth century, Mookini Luakini is the oldest known temple in the islands. In front, a low wall of pale green, lichen-covered rocks marks the room where the body gatherer, who brought the sacrificial victims, stayed. Outside the temple walls sits the rock where sacrifices—usually prisoners of war or kapu-breakers—were slain. Though no one is sacrificed at Mookini anymore, of course, it is still very much a living temple, overseen by its *kuhuna nui* (high priest), Leimomi Mo'okini Lum, a direct descendant of the family line that has protected the luakini since it was built.

A short drive down the dirt road are two low rock walls that Lum and Hawaiians in the community built in 1978 around the birthplace of Kamehameha the Great. Tradition says he was born just offshore in a canoe bringing his mother from Maui. He and his mother were secreted away to nearby caves to avoid capture by the local chief, who had been warned of an arriving infant who would one day usurp him.

Kapaau

Around the northern point of the North Kohala district, about 3 miles (5 km) beyond Mookini Luakini, in the tiny town of Kapaau, is the workshop of master guitar-maker **David Gomes**. Although he learned his craft in Spain, Gomes has developed his own way of shaping and bending his guitars and ukuleles. Gomes takes orders from those truly interested in owning one of these prize instruments—a uke will cost its buyer nearly $600 and a classical guitar about $1,400. Delivery may take a year.

Waimea

If the Big Island's credo is diversity, then consider the scenic contrast between the hot, dry, largely barren Kohala Coast and the inland town of Waimea, surrounded by lush pastureland and often shaded by low passing clouds. Also called **Kamuela** to avoid confusion with the town called Waimea on Kauai, the Big Island's Waimea nestles in the saddle between Kohala Mountain and Mauna Kea at an elevation of about 2,700 feet. To reach Waimea from the South Kohala resorts, head north on Highway 19, then follow that same road east (it's also called Kawaihae Road on this stretch) 8 miles (13 km) to Waimea. If you are up on the North Kohala coast, you can either head south to Highway 19 or go north on Highway 270 to the town of Hawi, then south about 20 miles (32 km) on Highway 250, known as the Mountain Road, a beautiful, scenic drive.

Waimea rests on land owned by **Parker Ranch**, the largest individually held spread in America, founded in 1847 by John Palmer Parker. His great-great-great-grandson and heir to the ranch, Richard Smart, also had a profound impact on Waimea. Until his recent death, Smart, who loved the arts, imbued his town with a sense of culture that has made it much more than a cow town. He built the Kahilu Theatre, and occasionally donned costume and stage makeup to act in a community production.

One of the state's most prestigious private schools, the Hawaii Preparatory Academy, brings students to Waimea from around the world. Some of their parents have moved in as well, shipping over their Mercedes and furs, better to tame the wilds of the Big Island.

Waimea is a town in transition, as rocketing property values show all too clearly. Its cool climate and gorgeous setting have drawn movers-and-shakers from the resorts down on the Kohala Coast, expatriates from the Honolulu business community, and astronomers who work in the observatories atop Mauna Kea, which, snowcapped during winter, provides a majestic backdrop for the town.

AROUND IN WAIMEA

Despite the proliferation of the new (and trendy), Parker Ranch remains the foundation on which Waimea was built and still dominates the town. Glimpses into the ranch's history and influence can be had at a couple of places. A **visitors' center** and small **ranching museum** are located within the Parker Ranch Shopping Center in the heart of town at the junction of Highways 19 and 190. Also in the shopping center is the **Parker Ranch Broiler**, with its ranch decor and delicious steaks cooked on a kiawewood broiler, recalling Waimea's old rustic days.

About a mile south of the shopping center (take Highway 190) is Smart's century-old family home, **Puuopelu** (open for tours), with elegant furnishings and an impressive collection of Impressionist art. Next door is a fine replica of ranch patriarch Parker's home, **Mana**, built of native koa wood and filled with period furniture and displays of photos and artifacts from the family's history. Some of the historic photographs show *paniolo* (cowboys) at work. *Paniolo* is a local derivative of the word *español,* the language spoken by the first cowboys brought from then Mexican-owned California in 1832 to domesticate the wild cattle herds.

Another Parker descendant founded her own memorabilia repository, the **Kamuela Museum** (Highway 19 at the entrance to Waimea). Harriet Solomon and her husband, Albert, have crammed their large home with some of the most curious stuff in Hawaii, thousands of items they've put together during the past 50 years from family collections, estate sales, private auctions, and dealers looking to unload their wares. Some of it is valuable: the only known ancient Hawaiian canoe buster (a weapon for destroying canoes), for example, and a five-foot-high wooden Hawaiian idol. But some is just quirky: ostrich eggs, a pen filled with black dirt inscribed "Mt. St. Helen's Ash May 18, 1980," a Czechoslovakian machine gun, and a stuffed black bear shot by a Mrs. Gay Wilfong in British Columbia in 1965. There's no order in this museum, no rhyme or reason to the exhibits—simply meeting the eccentric Solomons is worth the admission.

SHOPPING IN WAIMEA

Some of the island's finest art galleries are in Waimea, displaying the work of painters, weavers, and woodcarvers. Jane Curtis at **Topstitch Fiber Arts** in Parker Ranch Shopping Center works directly with Hawaiian quilters to commission the large appliquéd covers that take up to a year to make and set buyers back about $3,000 to $4,000. In Parker Square, on Highway 19 opposite Merriman's (see below), the **Gallery of Great Things** specializes in the works of Island artists. Their collection includes paintings and a selection of koa (a dark, rich wood) and rare-wood furniture, rockers, desks, bowls, and chairs crafted in Hawaii. They also have museum-quality items from other Pacific islands, such as the New Hebrides (Vanuatu), New Guinea, and the Philippines.

DINING IN WAIMEA

Waimea's allure has also given rise to several interesting restaurants. Formerly a Parker Ranch property, the **Hale Kea** (half a mile west of town on Highway 19), built in the 1890s for ranch manager A. W. Carter, has a restaurant called **Hartwell's** in the main house (Tel: 885-6094). It serves steak, seafood, sandwiches, and occasionally wild game (boar or venison) within the intimate library, the glassed-in porch, and the "cowboy" room. Shops in the handsome estate's outbuildings sell artful collectibles. (Be forewarned: Hale Kea has of late been overrun by tour buses at midday.)

Another intriguing restaurant is the cozy **Edelweiss**. A little red-frame building in the middle of town (Highway 19), Edelweiss successfully blends cultural incongruities: Hawaiian waitresses in German dirndls, Viennese waltzes for entertainment, and Big Island anthuriums and koa-wood walls for decor. The food is similarly blended, Hawaiian fish specialties such as *opakapaka* and *mahi-mahi* side by side on the menu with schnitzel and pot roast. Tel: 885-6800.

Down the street, chef Peter Merriman made his entrepreneurial foray four years ago with his restaurant **Merriman's**, featuring regional Pacific cuisine (Tel: 885-6822). The chef's inventive dishes are made with fresh local products such as lamb from nearby Kahua Ranch and fish from Kawaihae boats, as well as produce from small independent farmers. Across the street from Merriman's, there's gourmet takeout at **Mean Cuisine**—prepared boxed lunches include such delectable dishes as *mahi-mahi* with cashews, Mexican cheese chicken, and roast pork tenderloin. A selection of fresh salads, pies, pastries, chilled wine, Champagne, juices, and soft drinks are also available.

STAYING IN WAIMEA

Most visitors to this part of the Big Island don't overnight here, mainly because until recently there simply weren't many lodging choices. In 1988, however, rancher Carolyn Cascavilla bought the once-dumpy ▶ **Kamuela Inn**, on the north side of Highway 19, and renovated it in oak, turn-of-the-century antiques, and calico fabrics. She serves a Continental breakfast each morning in a sprightly first-floor room and keeps a pot of coffee on for the magazine readers who drop in during the day. The inn's third-floor penthouse, actually two suites that can be rented separately, has expansive views of Mauna Kea. The penthouse provides several sleeping areas as well as a kitchen and wet bar outside. Edelweiss and Merriman's restaurants (see above) are within a two-minute walk down the forested path to the main road.

Waimea has also become quite the spot for quality bed-and-breakfast lodging. ▶ **Puu Manu Cottage** is a lovely little house with a fireplace on a dead-end road surrounded by pasture. ▶ **Waimea Gardens Cottage** also offers privacy and country charm. At ▶ **Waimea Countree Bed & Breakfast** host Balbi Brooks rents two rooms of her beautiful house, which is rich with koa-wood furnishings and tastefully and whimsically decorated. Balbi's breakfasts of fresh fruit, granola, waffles, juice, coffee, and more are a fine way to start the day.

Waipio Valley

After a relaxing day in Waimea, you might like to try an easy but dramatic hike to the rim of Waipio Valley, a north-shore enclave that was the island's seat of power from the 14th through the 16th centuries.

SEEING THE VALLEY

Just out of Waimea on Highway 19 heading east (toward Hilo), a few hundred yards across a pasture on the left, is a grass berm topped with a fence. Leading up to it is a narrow paved road; follow the road to its end (less than half a mile) and park. Walk through the gate, pass the reservoir, and follow the path through the forest as it crosses the aqueduct. After about a half-hour walk you'll suddenly come upon the incomparable view at the rim of Waipio Valley. Furry green cliffs are striped by skinny waterfalls threading their way 2,000 feet to the valley floor. The trail continues around the rim of the cliff; follow it at least to the very back of the valley, through the misty bog and the bamboo grove. From there you can see all the way along the ambling valley to the sea miles away.

There is another Waipio Valley lookout—an easily accessible one—west of Waimea, past the town of Honokaa, at the end of Highway 240. From there you can see waterfalls cascading down the 2,000-foot wall opposite the lookout, and taro fields laid out in patchwork far below. You can also drive down into the valley if you're in a four-wheel-drive vehicle with a good driver. Several companies offer a Waipio tour past homesteads, across riverbeds, and onto the state's largest black-sand beach. **Waipio Valley Wagon Tours**, started in 1988 by Englishman Peter Tobin and his Maui-born wife, Makaala, offers mule-driven covered wagon tours (Tel: 775-9518), and **Waipio Valley Shuttle** makes the trip in four-wheel-drive vans and Land Rovers (Tel: 775-7121). If you'd like to try the trip on a horse, contact **Waipio Naalapa** (Tel: 775-0419) or **Waipio on Horseback** (Tel: 775-7291).

STAYING IN WAIPIO VALLEY

If you've fallen in love with the scenery and the peace and quiet you can even stay over in this secluded rural valley. Camp out in Tom Araki's tiny hotel, which although familiarly known as the ▶ **Waipio Hotel**, doesn't actually have a name. It does have five rooms, each with a bed, a nightstand, and a kerosene lamp. A communal kitchen provides a place to cook your own food (there are no stores in the valley, so you must shop for groceries before going in). If you're lucky you'll enjoy a visit on the porch with the 84-year-old proprietor, a taro farmer who's got some great stories but just can't seem to get around to naming his hotel.

For ten times what Araki gets for his rooms, you can play Tarzan in the ▶ **Waipio Treehouse**, a little dwelling in the branches of a sturdy monkeypod tree. The hut has a refrigerator, gas stove, cold running water, electric lights, a flush toilet, and the damp, glistening forest all around. On the same property there's also ▶ **The Hale**, with a full kitchen and hot running water. Guests at either place can use the hot tub and enjoy a shower in the waterfall down the path.

Mauna Kea

On the northeastern coast of the Big Island, east of Waipio Valley, the **Hamakua Coast** stretches toward Hilo. Vast fields of sugarcane extend from the ocean up onto the slopes of Mauna Kea. The sugarcane looks like very tall grass and makes a soft rustling sound in the wind. The mountain that gives it nourishment is Mauna Kea, at 13,769 feet, the state's highest.

REACHING THE SUMMIT

The preferred way to visit the summit of Mauna Kea is by four-wheel-drive vehicle with an official tour guide, because the only access road, the **Saddle Road**, is off limits to rental cars, some of whose drivers make the trip anyway because of the dazzling, shifting scenery—upcountry pastureland, barren lava fields, and ruddy cinder cones (if the car breaks down, however, it means a tow charge of at least $75). Pat Wright (Paradise Safaris, Tel: 322-2366) will take small groups to the summit for stargazing, as will the Waipio Valley Shuttle (see above), but there are no facilities whatsoever for visitors at the summit. To reach the Saddle Road, head south of Waimea on Hawaii 190 about 6 miles (10 km); the Saddle Road (Highway 200) will be on your left.

At any time of year the nine telescopes perched on Mauna Kea's summit are a moving sight. Scientists from around the world converge on this facility to scan the heavens. The University of Hawaii gives tours showing its 88-inch **telescope** on Saturday and Sunday afternoons. Tel: 961-2180 for directions and mountain conditions.

During the winter there's also a ski tour of Mauna Kea. **Ski Guides Hawaii** (Tel: 885-4188) supplies the gear and the four-wheel-drive jeeps to the summit. The novelty of Hawaiian corn snow will hold little interest for experienced skiers, but it's impossible not to be awed by the panorama of snow fields, black cinders, blue sky, and blue sea. From here there's a profound sense of just how big—and how remarkable—the Big Island is.

GOLF COURSES

The Big Island's stark contrasts are especially apparent from a golfer's perspective, especially at the courses of the Kona and Kohala coasts—bright green islands in the middle of the hard black lava fields that blanket West Hawaii.

Resort Courses
The first course to be constructed in the unusual volcanic surroundings of East Hawaii was the **Mauna Kea Golf Course**, off Highway 19 on the Kohala Coast. Designed by Robert Trent Jones, Sr., in 1964, it is still one of the top three layouts in Hawaii. Under the direction of effervescent PGA professional J. D. Ebersberger, Mauna Kea prides itself on offering top-quality service from golf shop to locker room. It is remarkable how well the resort's low-key elegance has withstood the passage of years. The

golf course itself is highlighted by the picturesque third hole, which shoots from one Pacific promontory to its green on another, with nothing between but 200 yards of ocean—and a few hundred thousand golf balls.

Mauna Kea's new 18-hole **Hapuna Golf Course**, designed by Arnold Palmer, is built into the slopes above the existing layout. Taking a "hands off" approach to design, this course ambles over the terrain, preserving much of the rough, natural look of the landscape. Palmer has gone so far as to create "target" golf in quite a few areas, where the rough is basically unkempt. Tel: 882-7222 for Mauna Kea; 882-1035 for Hapuna.

Just 5 miles (8 km) away, **Mauna Lani Resort** has recently added 18 holes to the original **Francis H. Ii Brown Golf Course**, which has been divided in two, with nine new holes added to each half. The contrast of dark lava against bright green grass still defines the Mauna Lani courses, now called the North Course and the South Course, and it is lava that presents the main threat to your handicap as well. The sharp volcanic rocks—and there are lots of them—delineate out-of-bounds. Thus, accuracy is the operative word: Keep your ball in the fairway, even if you must sacrifice some distance, and you'll do fine. Tel: 885-6655.

The other exquisite golf resort along the golf-crazy Kohala Coast is the **Waikoloa Resort**, with three top-notch 18-hole courses. The first to be built was the **Waikoloa Village Golf Club**, by Robert Trent Jones, Jr., in 1972. It's a little off the beaten resort track, located 6 miles (10 km) up the hill from Waikoloa's hotels, but is definitely a course you'll want to play. Tel: 883-9621.

In 1981 the **Waikoloa Beach Golf Club** opened a good resort-style course that plays well for those with high handicaps. The Beach is a visually beautiful course with quite a number of fascinating lava formations, such as that at the 12th hole, which plays down to the waterfront and culminates on a lava outcropping next to the Hyatt Regency Waikoloa. Tel: 885-6060.

The third course at Waikoloa is the **Waikoloa Kings' Golf Club**, designed by Tom Weiskopf and Jay Moorish in 1990. The Kings' is the most demanding of the three Waikoloa choices, playing 7,074 yards with a rating of 75 from the back tees. It is a course on which you can play conservatively or, if you're feeling lucky, you can go for broke. The latter approach will present you with some real challenges and, possibly, some real rewards. Tel: 88-KINGS.

Public Courses

The Big Island has some interesting public golf courses, but, because of the size of the island, they're rather far-flung.

Kona Country Club, 78-7000 Alii Drive on the Kona Coast, has recently added nine new holes to its Mauka course, and now has two full 18-hole courses: Mauka and Alii Country Club. You can count on a good game on either course. Tel: 322-2595.

Volcano Golf and Country Club has one of the most unusual settings in the world, right on the side of the active volcano Kilauea, within Hawaii Volcanoes National Park. Of course, you're in no danger—Kilauea issues what is called a "friendly flow" by volcanologists—and this is a moderately challenging and well-maintained course. Tel: 967-7331.

—*George Fuller*

GETTING AROUND

Arrival by Air

United Airlines flies nonstop to the Big Island's Keahole Airport (at Kona) from San Francisco, and to Keahole via Honolulu from Los Angeles, Denver, Philadelphia, New York, Chicago, and most other major North American cities. Other airlines require a separate interisland flight.

From Honolulu, as well as from the Neighbor Islands, Hawaiian Airlines and Aloha Airlines have frequent daily flights to both Hilo and Kona airports on the Big Island. United has interisland service for local travellers, but the flights are so few and far between (two or three a day) that you are better off just hopping on one of the local companies' flights, which leave with the regularity and ease of shuttle buses. Interisland flights usually take 20 to 30 minutes.

If you're staying at one of the big Kohala Coast resorts and you choose not to rent a car, your hotel can arrange for a shuttle to pick you up from Keahole Airport in Kona.

Driving on the Big Island

Reserve a car in advance at whichever airport and, once you've retrieved your luggage, proceed to the car-rental buildings, which are across the road from the terminal at both major airports. All the big-name agencies, as well as some less-expensive, locally run companies, maintain operations on the Big Island—National and Tropical, among the most notable.

Be sure to pick up the *Island of Hawaii Drive Guide* at car-rental desks; it has a complete set of maps with close-ups of selected areas. Except for the Saddle Road—an east–west route out of Hilo upon which car-rental companies forbid travel—roads do not traverse the Big Island but circle it along the coast.

ACCOMMODATIONS REFERENCE

The rates given here are projections for winter 1993–1994. Unless otherwise indicated, rates are for double room, double occupancy. Hawaii's telephone area code is 808.

▶ **The Hale. Waipio Valley.** P.O. Box 5086, Honokaa, HI 96727. Tel: 775-7160. $200 for one night; $150 per night for two or more nights.

▶ **Hapuna Beach Prince Hotel.** One Mauna Kea Drive, **Kamuela**, HI 96743. Tel: 882-1111; Fax: 882-1174; elsewhere in U.S., Tel: (800) 735-1111. $325; suites $800.

▶ **Hyatt Regency Waikoloa.** Waikoloa Beach Resort, HC02, P.O. Box 5500, **Waikoloa**, HI 96743. Tel: 885-1234; Fax: 885-5337; elsewhere in U.S., Tel: (800) 233-1234. $250–$350; suites $575–$3,000.

▶ **Kamuela Inn.** P.O. Box 1994, **Kamuela**, HI 96743. Tel: 885-4243; Fax: 885-8857. $54–$79; suites $83; penthouse $165.

▶ **Keauhou Beach Hotel.** 78-6740 Alii Drive, **Kailua-Kona** HI 96740. Tel: 322-3441; Fax: 322-6586; interisland, Tel: (800) 462-3491; elsewhere in U.S., Tel: (800) 367-6025. $95–$160; suites $230–$400.

▶ **Kilauea Lodge.** P.O. Box 116, **Volcano**, HI 96785. Tel: 967-7366; Fax: 967-7367. $85–$105.

▶ **Kona Hotel.** P.O. Box 342, **Holualoa**, HI 96725. Tel: 324-1155. $23.

▶ **Kona Village Resort.** P.O. Box 1299, **Kailua-Kona**, HI 96745. Tel: 325-5555; Fax: 325-5124; interisland; Tel: (800) 432-5450; elsewhere in U.S., Tel: (800) 367-5290. $375–$650.

▶ **Manago Hotel.** P.O. Box 145, **Captain Cook**, HI 96704. Tel: 323-2642. $25–$55.

▶ **Mauna Kea Beach Hotel.** 1 Mauna Kea Beach Drive, **Kohala Coast**, HI 96743-9706. Tel: 882-7222; Fax: 882-7657; elsewhere in U.S., Tel: (800) 882-6060. $260–$450.

▶ **Mauna Lani Bay Hotel & Bungalows.** 1 Mauna Lani Drive, **Kohala Coast**, HI 96743-4000. Tel: 885-6622; Fax: 885-4556; elsewhere in U.S., Tel: (800) 367-2323. $275–$425; suites $465–$725; bungalows $2,500–$3,000.

- ▶ **Ritz-Carlton Mauna Lani.** 1 North Kaniku Drive, **Kohala Coast**, HI 96743. Tel: 885-2000; Fax: 885-1064; elsewhere in U.S., Tel: (800) 845-9905. $285–$495; suites $625–$2,800.
- ▶ **Royal Waikoloan.** HC02, P.O. Box 5300, **Kohala Coast**, HI 96743. Tel: 885-6789; Fax: 885-7852; elsewhere in U.S., Tel: (800) 462-6262. $99–$250; suites $350–$750.
- ▶ **SeaMountain at Punaluu** (Colony One Condominiums). P.O. Box 70, **Pahala**, HI 96777. Tel: 928-8301; Fax: 928-8008; elsewhere in U.S., Tel: (800) 488-8301. $86–$157.
- ▶ **Volcano Bed & Breakfast.** P.O. Box 22, **Volcano**, HI 96785. Tel: 967-7779; Fax: 967-7619. $55–$70.
- ▶ **Volcano House.** P.O. Box 53, **Hawaii Volcanoes National Park**, HI 96718. Tel: 967-7321; Fax: 967-8429. $79–$131.
- ▶ **Waipio Hotel. Waipio Valley.** Tom Araki, 25 Malama Place, Hilo, HI 96720. Tel: 935-7466 or 775-0368. $30.
- ▶ **Waipio Treehouse. Waipio Valley.** P.O. Box 5086, Honokaa, HI 96727. Tel: 775-7160. $200 for one night; $150 per night for two or more nights.

BED AND BREAKFASTS

- ▶ **Hawaii's Best Bed and Breakfasts.** P.O. Box 563, Kamuela, HI 96743. Tel: 885-4550; Fax: 885-0550; elsewhere in U.S., Tel: (800) 262-9912. The following can be reserved through this agency:
- ▶ **Hale Kai.** Hilo. $95–$120.
- ▶ **Hale Paliku.** Hilo. $90.
- ▶ **Holualoa Inn.** Holualoa. $100–$150.
- ▶ **Hydrangea Cottage.** Volcano. $100.
- ▶ **Mountain House.** Volcano. $170 per couple (two couples minimum) per night (three-night minimum).
- ▶ **Puu Manu Cottage.** Waimea. $105.
- ▶ **Waimea Countree Bed & Breakfast.** Waimea. $60.
- ▶ **Waimea Gardens Cottage.** Waimea. $90–$95.

For information about other bed-and-breakfast accommodations in the Hawaiian Islands see the Oahu Outside Honolulu Accommodations Reference.

MAUI

By John Heckathorn and Bill Harby

humuhumunukunukuapua'a

There is no other way to say it: Maui has glamour, the same glamour that in the 1930s and 1940s used to cling to Waikiki. To those shivering in colder climes the name Maui inspires images of lush foliage, warm rain showers, rainbows, sunshine, and white-sand beaches. Maui is like one of those aloha shirts that reproduces a prewar pattern in the hottest up-to-date colors: It is gentle Hawaii with a modern edge, casual yet with a kind of tropical chic.

It's hard to pinpoint the source of Maui's power over the imagination. Perhaps it is the brooding volcanic presence of Haleakala or the vast green agricultural areas along its eastern slope. Perhaps Maui's glamour emanates from the wealth of sparkling beaches along the Kaanapali, Kihei, and Wailea resort areas. Perhaps it prevails in the wide-open waterfront spirit of the old whaling port of Lahaina—despite the souvenir shops and overpriced eateries.

Maui's triumph could be the result of a self-fulfilling prophecy. Once Maui became glamorous—through a combination of clever marketing and intelligent resort development that managed to avoid the worst excesses of Waikiki—it began to attract artists, artisans, writers, and the sort of folks who have turned the island into Hawaii's closest approximation to trendy California. Maui is now a thriving arts colony, as the abundance of galleries attests.

But Maui is no longer the place to go if you are looking for a beach without a footprint on it. Its success as a trendy tourist destination came with a price: crowds and traffic. Still, the congestion is largely contained within Lahaina and along the Kaanapali resort strip with their concentration of popular attractions. And in the end, Maui is much less urban and congested than Oahu. (In fact, Maui residents who fly to Honolulu to shop deplore the crowds and traffic there.) By any reasonable standard,

Maui is still quite livable and drivable. Anyone who commutes in a major metropolitan area will laugh at the notion that Maui's two-lane road traffic is terrible.

What Maui has done best is separate its primary tourist areas from its workaday towns and its more remote agricultural stretches. Its resorts were designed to be largely self-contained, with shopping, dining, and all sorts of recreational attractions (from the usual, such as golf, tennis, swimming, and diving, to the unusual, like gazing through a telescope or soaking in a herbal bath). In other words, Maui is a place where those in the pursuit of either rural or resort-type pleasure are not likely to be distracted. And that, ultimately, may be the key to Maui's glamour: You can have a lot of fun here.

MAJOR INTEREST

Lahaina
Historical sites
Art galleries
Restaurants and nightlife
Sailing and boating excursions

West Maui outside Lahaina
Luxury resorts at Kaanapali and Kapalua
Beaches and bays
Old Hawaiian fishing village at Kahakuloa

Central Maui
Historic town of Wailuku
Kepaniwai Park, site of Hawaiian battle and
  melting-pot memorial
Iao Valley scenery

South Maui
Luxury resorts in Kihei, Wailea, and Makena
Beaches
Winter whale-watching from shore

Haleakala and Upcountry
Hikes and tours of the volcano crater
Rural scenery
Winery tour
Protea gardens
Cowboy town of Makawao

East Maui
Lush scenery along Hana Highway
Hana town's quiet Hawaiian charm
Seven Pools

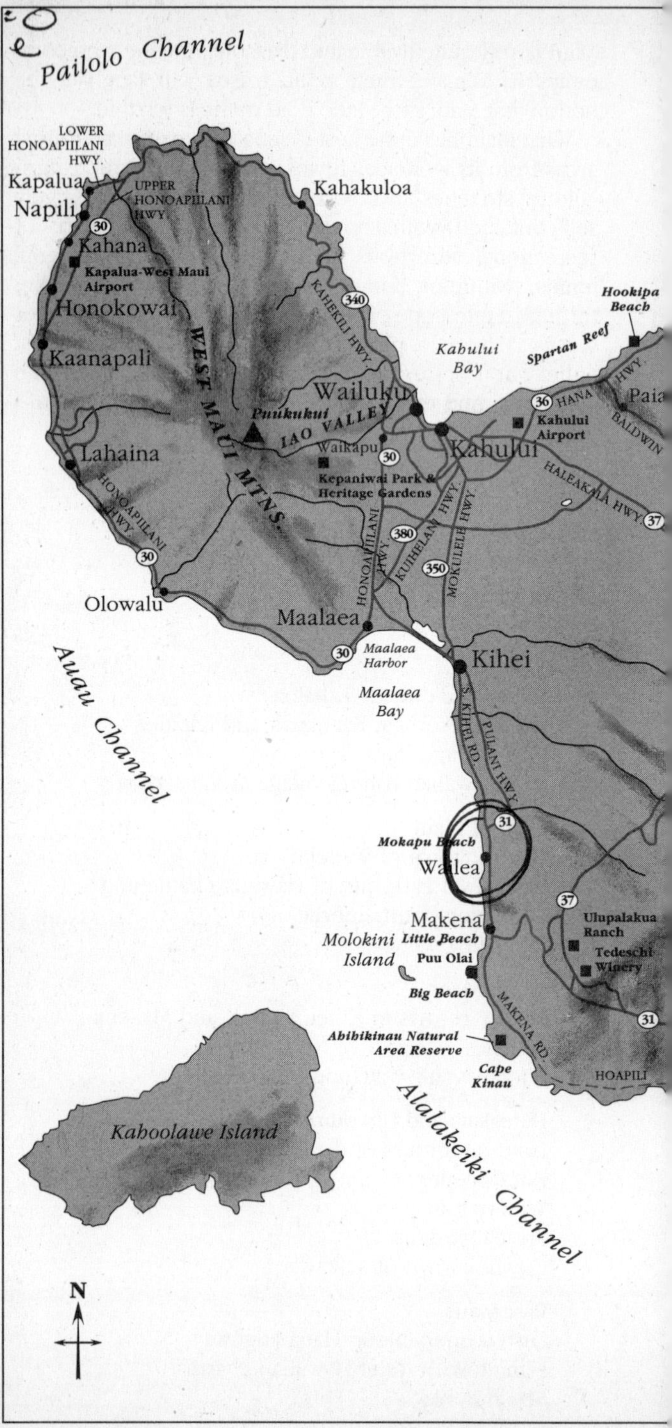
Pailolo Channel
LOWER HONOAPIILANI HWY.
Kapalua
Napili
UPPER HONOAPIILANI HWY.
Kahakuloa
30
Kahana
Kapalua-West Maui Airport
Honokowai
KAHEKILI HWY.
340
Hookipa Beach
Kaanapali
WEST MAUI MTNS.
Kahului Bay
Spartan Reef
Wailuku
HANA HWY.
36
Paia
Kahului Airport
BALDWIN
Puukukui
IAO VALLEY
Waikapu
Kahului
Kepaniwai Park & Heritage Gardens
Lahaina
HONOAPIILANI HWY.
HALEAKALA HWY.
37
HONOAPIILANI HWY.
KUIHELANI HWY.
MOKULELE HWY.
380
350
Olowalu
Maalaea
Maalaea Harbor
Kihei
Auau Channel
Maalaea Bay
S. KIHEI RD.
PULANI HWY.
31
Mokapu Beach
Wailea
Makena
Molokini Island
Little Beach
Puu Olai
Big Beach
Ulupalakua Ranch
Tedeschi Winery
MAKENA RD
Ahihikinau Natural Area Reserve
Cape Kinau
HOAPILI
Kahoolawe Island
Alalakeiki Channel
N

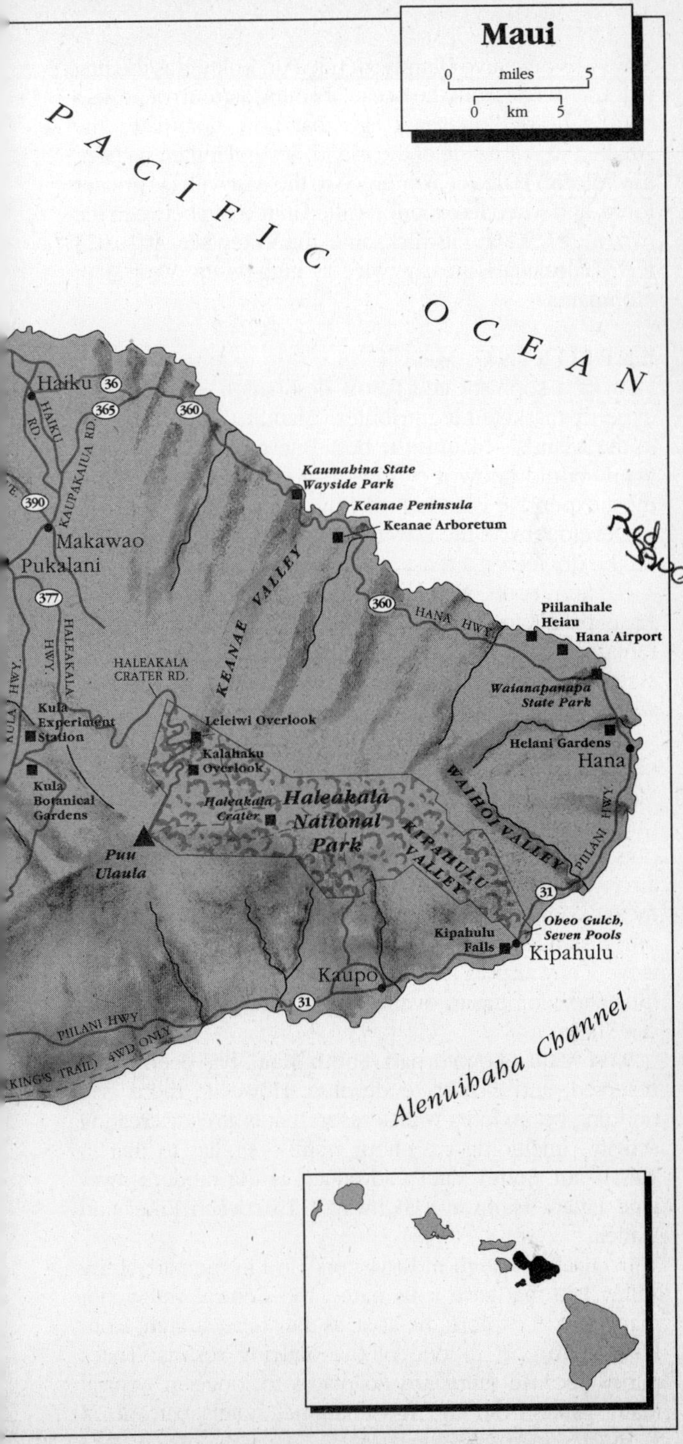
Maui
0 miles 5
0 km 5
PACIFIC OCEAN
Haiku
36
365
360
HAIKU RD.
KAUPAKAIUA RD.
390
Makawao
Pukalani
377
HALEAKALA HWY.
KULA HWY.
HALEAKALA CRATER RD.
Kula Experiment Station
Kula Botanical Gardens
Puu Ulaula
Kaumahina State Wayside Park
Keanae Peninsula
Keanae Arboretum
KEANAE VALLEY
360
HANA HWY.
Piilanihale Heiau
Hana Airport
Waianapanapa State Park
Helani Gardens
Hana
PIILANI HWY.
Leleiwi Overlook
Kalahaku Overlook
Haleakala Crater
Haleakala National Park
KIPAHULU VALLEY
WAIHOI VALLEY
31
Obeo Gulch, Seven Pools
Kipahulu Falls
Kipahulu
Kaupo
31
PIILANI HWY
KING'S TRAIL 4WD ONLY
Alenuihaha Channel

Maui was once two islands. Gentle Puu Kukui was the first volcano to rise from the ocean, forming a group of peaks a couple of million years ago that now dominates the smaller, western side of the island. Several millennia later, the volcano Haleakala emerged to the east with far greater force, and when its eruptions filled in the gap between the two, they left Maui its nickname, the Valley Isle. At 10,023 feet, Haleakala is nearly twice as high as the West Maui Mountains.

EXPLORING MAUI

Maui is a sophisticated resort destination, one that has expertly marketed its attributes. "Maui *no ka oi*," they say in the Islands—Maui is the best. But travellers bound for Maui should know they must pay for the best; it is the most expensive island in the Hawaiian chain.

Developers on the Hawaiian Islands build their resorts on the dry leeward coasts, and Maui was blessed with two such sunny spots, West Maui and South Maui. **West Maui**— Kaanapali, Kapalua—is older, with more hotels, restaurants, activities, and people. It was a natural development, since the old West Maui port at Lahaina had been attracting visitors for years before the jet-travel boom.

West Maui is about a 30-minute drive from Kahului, site of Maui's major airport, where direct flights from the Mainland can land. Those who book a room in West Maui might find that flying into the Kapalua–West Maui Airport puts them closer to their hotel, but only some interisland aircraft can land on that airport's short runway, so it means coming to Maui by way of Honolulu or one of the other islands. The Kapalua–West Maui facility has the best view of any airport in the state, as planes land high in the hills after coming in over acres of pineapple and sugarcane fields.

West Maui's counterpart, **South Maui**, has been quiet, reserved, and slower to develop. However, there is a building boom in its Wailea resort that is already creating activity—including rush-hour traffic—similar to that in West Maui. South Maui's advantage is the modern, two-lane Piilani Highway (Highway 31) between Kihei and Wailea.

Ironically, though most visitors land in the part of the Valley Isle that gave it its name, the **Central Valley**, not many stay to explore the area, as they head straight from Kahului Airport to one of the outlying resorts. That's partly because there are no places to lodge in Central Maui, aside from the few marginal hotels patronized mostly by interisland businesspeople who need to stay close to clients or by people who bought the cheapest package deal. Central Maui is home to most of Maui's residents and, as such, tends to cater to their needs rather than to the visitor's. Kahului Airport itself is large and efficient, and a ten-year renovation completed a few years ago has made it even better.

Haleakala in **Upcountry Maui** attracts day-trippers and overnight campers who come to explore the rural atmosphere along the mountain's slopes. An increasing number of Mainlanders who first found West Maui to their liking are building homes in the Upcountry area, enjoying the solitude, the country lifestyle, and the cooler, albeit wetter, weather.

In **East Maui**, the town of Hana, long famous for its difficult access, lures people brave enough to make the drive (or brave enough to sign up for the daylong van ride from West or Central Maui). Contrary to what you may have heard, the road to Hana (Highway 36/360) is mostly smooth and well maintained—but it *is* narrow, with twists and turns every inch of the way. Some local residents can go the distance from Kahului in under two hours; the average driver will need three to four hours. Along the way, the lush scenery on the northeastern coast more than makes up for the inconvenience of hundreds of hairpin turns and dozens of narrow bridges. And once you've arrived you'll find a Hawaiian town that will take you back to a simpler time in the island's history.

The ideal way to get around Maui is in a rental car, because there is no reliable island-wide public transportation. The roads are easy to use, even though most are only two lanes, and travel time between major towns is only an hour or two. While you could in theory see much of Maui in two or three days, you would probably want to allow two or three times that length of time for a more enjoyable visit.

WEST MAUI
Lahaina

West Maui draws most of the Valley Isle's visitors. The Hawaiian Islands' first capital city, Lahaina, dominates West Maui with its honky-tonk **Front Street**, bustling harbor, and eclectic mix of bronzed surfers, old salts, and sun worshipers clad in neon-bright bikinis. The old whaling port has a magnetic effect on most people, even those who try just to drive by. Throughout Lahaina's past, hardly anyone has been able to resist her charms.

Hawaiian royalty were perhaps the most important group attracted to Lahaina, especially after 1810 when Kamehameha unified the Islands, naming himself king in the process, and made centrally located Lahaina his capital. He also built himself a brick palace—though he never lived in it—near the spot now occupied by the Pioneer Inn. The king was from the Big Island, but his favorite wife, Kaahumanu, and his most sacred wife, Keopuolani, were both Maui natives. Nevertheless, King Kamehameha and his 21 spouses soon moved to the more exciting town of Honolulu, although the capital stayed officially in Lahaina through the reigns of two more kings.

Foreigners also loved Lahaina. After Captain James Cook came to Hawaii in 1778, more and more Europeans found their way to the Sandwich Islands, anchoring off Lahaina for a little R and R with the native women. By the early 1820s word of the Islands had spread to whalers, who began sailing toward Maui. At about the same time, missionaries set on educating the heathens also alighted in Lahaina. The resulting blend of hell-bent rowdies and savage-saving Christians gave everyone a reason to live and set the town's character.

Lahaina later fell into disrepair, like so many towns whose residents can't quite remember the former significance of the ramshackle buildings that lean on every corner. In 1966, however, a 37-acre parcel of town land was declared a national historic landmark, and renovation then started in earnest through the efforts of the Lahaina Restoration Foundation. The foundation now publishes a free map and has installed signs pointing out the 31 stops on a self-guided walking tour of the town. The map is available at most site locations throughout Lahaina, in most West Maui hotels, and from the Hawaii Visitors Bureau in Kahului.

AROUND IN LAHAINA

It's worth devoting an hour or two to the walking tour of Lahaina's historical sites, if only to get a sense that Lahaina was not always a place where merchants vied with each other to extract dollars from tourist pockets. Lahaina was a center of 19th-century life in the islands, a place where native Hawaiians encountered the West in both missionaries and whaling crews and where modern Hawaii was formed.

Some of the points along the tour are of only passing

interest (such as the lawn in front of the present-day Lahaina library, which was a thriving taro patch in the old days when Lahaina was a place of many waterways, streams, ponds, and flooded taro fields). But other stops are worth devoting a little more time to. The **Baldwin Home Museum**, on Front Street at Dickenson Street, for instance, is the oldest standing building in Lahaina, built in 1834 of coral, stone, and hand-hewn timbers for missionary and physician Dwight Baldwin and his family, who lived in the house until 1871. Kings and queens of old Hawaii were entertained here, as were ship captains, consuls, and other weary travellers. The home is open daily as a museum.

Nearby, in the harbor, the brig **Carthaginian**, a replica of the kind of 19th-century freighter that first brought commerce to Hawaii, is a reminder that Lahaina was once a major island seaport. The only authentically restored brig in the world, *Carthaginian* now houses an exhibit on whales and whaling, complete with audiovisual displays. Turn-of-the-century Lahaina is captured just inland at the **Pioneer Inn**, built in 1901 and still operating as a hotel after 92 years, and at **Wo Wing Temple**, farther north up Front Street, built as a fraternal hall for the first Chinese contract laborers who came to work Maui's sugar plantations. In addition to displays on the history of the Chinese in Lahaina, the temple offers continuous showings of films taken in Hawaii by crews Thomas Edison sent in 1898 and 1903 to record a visual history.

LAHAINA'S ART GALLERIES

Lahaina has become a major art center in recent years, with many new galleries opening (and some then rapidly closing). Not surprisingly, much of the art in Lahaina is focused on the ocean and marine life, most notably at the new **Galerie Lassen** (844 Front Street), featuring the work of Christian Riese Lassen. The eponymous owner of the two **Wyland** galleries has made an international reputation for himself painting whales and dolphins. Other galleries try for a more unusual mix. **Hanson Art Galleries** (839 Front) offers huge Colleen Ross acrylics and a significant collection of Peter Max prints and Erte sculptures. **Madaline Michaels** features whimsical sculptures by Todd Warner and the wacky paintings of Peter and Madeline Powell, among other artists with an eccentric flair at her gallery at 900 Front Street. **Martin Lawrence Galleries**, 126 Lahaina Luna Road, offers works ranging from traditional Guy Buffets to bright and movable folk-art sculptures by the late Keith Haring. Together, Lahaina's 20 galleries stage the weekly "Friday Night is Art Night," with roving entertainment, special showings, and other hoopla.

RESTAURANTS AND NIGHTLIFE IN LAHAINA

Part of Lahaina's charisma comes not from its past, but from its present. Nightlife runs through this old port's veins just as demon rum was once the lifeblood of its sea dogs. Tucked in amongst Front Street's many altars to retailing are several pleasant spots to while away an evening or watch the setting sun. **Kimo's Restaurant** (number 845) calls to a comfortable crowd that wants more than oceanfront: The bar places you right over the water. From Kimo's you can watch the sun sink quietly behind the island of Lanai, to the west.

Similar views and an even more relaxed atmosphere are available at **JJ's** and **Old Lahaina Café**, both at 505 Front. Those who like their action a little more lively might try **Cheeseburgers in Paradise** (811 Front), a wild and woolly burger joint that takes its name from a Jimmy Buffet song, or **Moondoggies** (666 Front), which features live entertainment in the early evening. There's nothing placid, either, about the **Hard Rock Café**, the newest addition to Lahaina's night scene, at 900 Front Street. The first Neighbor Island outpost of the famous chain, the bar and grill now dominates the newly built Lahaina Center.

For a more traditional Island nightlife try the **Old Lahaina Luau**, on the beach at 505 Front Street. Here the food is Hawaiian—the *kalua* pork is actually cooked in an underground *imu* (the more usual practice these days is to roast it in an oven and add "liquid smoke" flavoring); interested guests can stop by early in the morning to watch the lava-rock *imu* being heated. The food is adequate: teriyaki steak, chicken long rice, and such real Hawaiian delicacies as *poke* (raw fish and seaweed) and *haupia* (a coconut pudding). An attempt is made to make the entertainment authentically Hawaiian (no Tahitian hula here), and the Old Lahaina Luau has the reputation of being the best on the island. That's true, but the competition isn't keen. The key is to reserve ahead, arrive early, and have a drink at the Old Lahaina Café. That way you avoid the lines and get a better table. Tel: 667-1998.

Lahaina has also attracted a large number of more refined restaurants, such as the trendy **Avalon Restaurant & Bar** in Mariner's Alley at 844 Front Street. Opened in

1988, Avalon has drawn hordes of celebrities and other beautiful people to feast on the bistro's Pacific Rim menu, with dishes from California, Mexico, Indonesia, Thailand, Japan, Vietnam, and, of course, Hawaii. That range gives the chef, Mark Ellman, lots of license: His signature specials include a roast duck with plum sauce and Chinese steamed dumplings; guacamole made tableside; and Caramel Miranda, a dessert of fresh exotic fruits with caramel sauce, sour cream, and brown sugar. Designer-clad diners sup from fiestaware, music plays softly, and bold 1940s-style Hawaiian tropical prints lend a suitable decor to the patio brasserie.

A few buildings to the northwest, at 888 Front Street, **Longhi's** has practiced its kicky approach to dining since 1976. There are no menus here; sun-bronzed waiters or waitresses simply pull up a chair and tell you the day's selections, including prices. Such dishes as prawns Amaretto, veal Marsala, and shrimp Longhi have made Longhi's famous. Breakfast is popular here, too—at least ten cases of oranges are squeezed each morning. Longhi's is busy night and day.

Other Lahaina eateries include **Tasca's** (608 Front Street), a Mediterranean bistro that patterns itself after a Spanish *tasca,* serving hors d'oeuvre–size portions of Spanish, French, Italian, and Greek cuisine, and **Compadres** (located at Lahaina Cannery), the newest link in a successful chain of Mexican food joints that started in Honolulu.

More genteel gourmands take their evening meals at one of Lahaina's French restaurants. One of them, **Gerard's Restaurant**, has captured an ardent following with chef Gerard Reversade's sumptuous menu, a bill of fare that includes such delectables as medallions of veal Normande, noisette of venison, and confit of duck. Set in the lobby and on the verandah of the Victorian-style Plantation Inn (a block and a half from the ocean at 174 Lahaina Luna Road), Gerard's milieu is as exquisite as the food: Rich oak walls, brass appointments, and crystal chandeliers provide a homey atmosphere for the tall, white wicker chairs and country-print linen-covered tables that are also set out on the breezy porch. Tables are close enough that neighboring diners sometimes find themselves exclaiming over the meal together.

STAYING IN LAHAINA

Some of Gerard's revelers are guests of the ▶ **Plantation Inn**, the first truly decent hotel in Lahaina. With 18 rooms, this bed-and-breakfast inn was designed by owners of Lahaina's Central Pacific Divers, who decided to build a place where scuba divers could lodge locally. Soon after opening in 1987, however, the group discovered the crying need for attractive quarters in Lahaina, and now regularly books nondivers as well, including honeymooners and couples who love the inn's romantic atmosphere.

The Plantation Inn has the look of an old, renovated inn, but in fact its two buildings are brand new—with modern plumbing, roomy closets, and lights and fans operated by remote control. Each room received special attention: One has a canopy bed set next to French double doors with gauzy curtains; another has a maple four-poster and a crewel-covered divan. Guests are treated to a lavish breakfast buffet at Gerard's (included in the rate), as well as a 20 percent discount on dinner there. The inn also has a pool. The Plantation Inn doesn't advertise; all guests are strictly word-of-mouth referrals—and a place like this gets recommended enthusiastically.

A similar restaurant-inn arrangement has been set up down the street with the opening of **David Paul's Lahaina Grill** in the new ▶ **Lahaina Hotel** (127 Lahainaluna Road). Two bon-vivant Honolulu businessmen have intricately restored a former flophouse and biker bar into an Old World inn and Southwestern-style restaurant. Restaurant owner and chef David Paul calls his type of cooking New American cuisine. Ingredients from Thai, Chinese, and other Asian specialties are combined in sizzling dishes presented with Southwestern flair. Paul is happy to recommend complementary wines from his well-stocked cellar. Hotel owner Rick Ralston made his fortune selling decorated tee-shirts and seems to have spent it on collectibles, many of which have ended up in the hotel. Flowered wallpaper decorates the walls above the wainscoting, Oriental rugs cover the rich wood floors, and each small room has its own theme and its own individually controlled air conditioner.

CRUISES AND EXCURSIONS

Lahaina's harbor provides plenty of opportunities to engage in water activities. You can take a **whale-watching cruise** between December and April, when the humpbacks journey to the Islands to calve. (Whale-watching boats also leave from **Maalaea Harbor**, about a 45-minute drive from Lahaina toward South Maui.) The behemoths often spout and breach near the boats, which, by law, must keep their distance. **Pacific Whale Foundation** (Tel:

879-8811) and **Captain Nemo's Ocean Emporium** (Tel: 661-5555) are probably the best Lahaina-based whale-watching companies. From Maalaea, try **Ocean Activities Center** (Tel: 869-4485).

Lahaina also provides anchorage for sailboats bound for other islands, such as Lanai immediately to the west, and is the jumping-off point for various interisland excursions. **Club Lanai** (Tel: 871-1144), for example, takes visitors from here to its private eight-acre beachfront retreat on Lanai for a day of sunning, bicycling, eating, and drinking from the open bar. A more informative Lanai trip, but completely dry because the owners are Seventh-Day Adventists, is **Trilogy Excursions** (Tel: 661-4743). Once the tour reaches the little island, Trilogy's sailing Coon family (which is how this bunch actually bills itself) takes its charges for a tour of Lanai City, the island's only town, before snorkeling and lunch at Hulopoe Bay. Trilogy also offers whale-watching tours.

Other boating trips that leave from Lahaina include one to Molokai on the ferry *Maui Princess* (Tel: 661-8397), and sunset, snorkeling, and fishing excursions. You can find companies that offer these trips listed in the Yellow Pages or in the free visitors' publications available throughout Lahaina. Or you can simply walk along Lahaina Harbor past the desks set up on the dock; the captains and crews will be more than happy to book you then and there.

Kaanapali

The **Kaanapali Beach Resort**, 2 miles (3 km) north of Lahaina, is the state's oldest master-planned destination resort (Waikiki obviously had *no* plan). Now, more than 25 years later, the resort boasts flashy hotels, pricey condominiums, and toney boutiques. Nothing about Kaanapali will fit into an average budget, but as Hawaii's other booming luxury resorts become more and more expensive, Kaanapali is starting to seem more affordable. All told, Kaanapali's owner, Amfac Resorts Hawaii, lays claim to some 15,000 acres on Maui, but in the nearly three decades since this former Big Five company first went about the business of turning land unsuitable for agriculture into the Kaanapali resort, only 600 acres have been incorporated into the West Maui enclave. Another 1,200 acres, however, are scheduled for development. This could make the West Maui traffic, which was somewhat relieved by the addition of a third lane on the highway, return to its former heavy condition.

STAYING IN KAANAPALI

Within the confines of the Kaanapali resort as it now exists are six hotels and five condos. First out of the blocks was the Royal Lahaina (see below), followed within months by the ▶ **Sheraton Maui**, which continues to be a comfortable hotel (although it is in need of some redecorating). The construction that followed was mostly unremarkable until 1980, when Christopher Hemmeter took his Hyatt Regency Waikiki success story and extended it to the ▶ **Hyatt Regency Maui** hotel. In Waikiki the young developer had installed a giant waterfall cascading into a shallow courtyard pool and decorated the walls and corners with tasteful selections of South Pacific art. In the Maui Hyatt, Hemmeter went for *nine* waterfalls and a 750,000-gallon swimming pool; stocked the grounds with peacocks and flamingos; and placed Asian bronze sculpture, granite statuary, and other *objets d'art* throughout the property. More recently, the Hyatt installed a telescope on its roof and offers a nightly complimentary stargazing program.

The Hyatt remains the best of Kaanapali, although Hemmeter had another shot at a resort in 1984, when he bought the sagging Maui Surf hotel three doors down. In three years he transformed it—with the aid of many tens of millions of dollars—into the ▶ **Westin Maui**. Waterfalls here are too numerous even to count; one begins its descent from a two-story, lava-rock cliff guarded by a lighted Buddha ensconced in a niche, then splashes into a palm-rimmed lagoon festooned with swans and mandarin ducks. Within the grounds are five interlocking swimming pools and gurgling streams overlooking the beach, while the collection of Oriental and European art has starred in its own lavish coffee-table book. The Westin has distinguished itself as one of Kaanapali's premier hotels, although many of its rooms are small. But the suites are quite roomy and lavish—art collections, marble Jacuzzis, and all.

Many island residents swear by the ▶ **Maui Marriott Resort**, a rose-colored medium-rise hotel next door to the Hyatt. The decor is low-key, the staff is helpful, and the junior suites are huge—with fine views. Its *teppanyaki* restaurant, **Nikko**, is so good that Japanese visitors come from across the island to eat here. Families staying in Kaanapali tend to choose the ▶ **Kaanapali Alii** condominium with its separate bedrooms and well-stocked kitchens, although the decor is much too uptown for sandy, wet kids after the beach—artwork, carpeting, and fine upholstery create a rather genteel beachside environment. Honeymooners may opt for a cottage at the ▶ **Royal Lahaina**, a laid-back property at the far end of Kaanapali. They sometimes choose the Royal Suite, which has its own pool and waterfall.

SHOPPING IN KAANAPALI

Some visitors come to Kaanapali to play golf on the resort's two championship courses, the Royal Kaanapali North and South, featured on nationally televised tournaments (see Golf Courses, below). Others find some of the 57 shops at **Whalers Village** more enticing. Located right on the beach between the Westin Maui and the Whaler condominium, Whalers Village has a number of art galleries, including the well-respected **Lahaina Printsellers**, and a whole list of stores with custom resortwear, including **Blue Ginger** for women, **Kula Bay Clothing** for men, and **Superwhale Boutique** for children. (The Whalers Village restaurants, however, are best avoided.)

Whalers Village also houses the **Whalers Village Museum**, a collection of memorabilia that illustrates the industry once so predominant in the area, with ship models, scrimshaw, and photographs as well as films and lectures. Still other visitors prefer simply to hang out on **Kaanapali Beach**, a wide, three-mile-long strip that is one of the most glorious people-watching spots on Maui.

Kapalua and Northwest Maui

NORTH FROM KAANAPALI

The Lower Honoapiilani Highway (Highway 30) continues north from Kaanapali past the towns of Honokowai, Kahana, and Napili, which lie along the lower beachside road. This is condo city: nicely landscaped, but with buildings close together. The ▶ **Papakea Resort**, just north of Embassy Suites, has good tennis courts within its oceanfront acreage, and once a week it hosts a farmers' market in its parking lot. The comfy ▶ **Napili Kai Beach Club**, farther north near the town of Kapalua, is probably the best bet in the area. Along the Upper Honoapiilani Highway (slightly inland from the lower highway), strip shopping is the architecture of choice these days.

The brightest spot along the highway is the new **Roy's Kahana Bar & Grill**, in the Kahana Gateway shopping center (4405 Honoapiilani Highway). The first Neighbor Island outpost in the growing empire of hot young Honolulu chef Roy Yamaguchi, Roy's Kahana is built around a display kitchen with a massive copper-clad chimney. The restaurant is more casual than the Honolulu original and even noisier. As soon as it opened a couple of years ago it was filled every night with patrons sampling such East-West fare as salmon on fresh sprouts with shoyu-miringinger sauce. Tel: 669-6999.

KAPALUA

Past these little towns on the Upper Honoapiilani Highway (also called Highway 30), the turn-off for the **Kapalua Bay Resort** beckons with its sedate sign. Inside is the ▶ **Kapalua Bay Hotel and Villas**, West Maui's understated major accommodation, with only 194 rooms. Built in 1978 by Maui Land & Pineapple (which owns and operates all the pineapple fields on Maui), the hotel seems to grow naturally out of its environment. It's all low-rise buildings of off-white stucco with polished wood and open views to the ocean. It's heavily landscaped and filled with the wild, colorful flower paintings of Maui artist Jan Kasprzycki. The rooms are all identical and feature spacious his-and-her bathrooms, which, were they standard in all dwellings, would probably make marriage a less perilous institution.

Lacking the glitz and glitter of its Kaanapali cousins, the hotel was not immediately successful, so it was forced to come up with the novel events that are now cornerstones for the resort. Each summer, the **Kapalua Wine Symposium** lures wine lovers for two days of tastings and seminars by some of the wine world's greats, such as Robert Mondavi and Andre Tchelistcheff. Some guests come for the summer **Kapalua Music Festival**, an event that has now become a working vacation for musicians from the Juilliard School and the Chicago and New York philharmonics as well as the Tokyo and Israel symphonies. The widely televised **Kapalua International Championship of Golf** was started in the early 1980s.

Kapalua has become a favored hideaway for many who want luxury and seclusion. The resort now administers rentals of 141 privately owned one- and two-bedroom villas with fully equipped kitchens and laundry facilities. Villa guests enjoy full resort privileges, including golf and tennis. For those who really need space, three-bedroom luxury homes are also available. Many show-biz people are repeat guests in the spacious condominium units.

Kapalua's shops have also gained a reputation, even with shoppers who aren't guests at the resort. The resort's distinctive butterfly logo is so popular it has spawned not one, but three shops: the **Kapalua Logo Shop**, **Kapalua Kids**, and **Kapalua Designs**. **Reyn's** and **Mandalay** offer upscale resortwear without logos. There are several jewelry stores, an art gallery, and the **Market Café**, where you can get a decent sandwich and cappuccino.

Last year a second resort opened at Kapalua, Hawaii's second Ritz-Carlton (the first is at Mauna Lani, on the Kohala coast of the Big Island). Although at 550 rooms the ▶ **Ritz-Carlton-Kapalua** is more than twice the size of the Kapalua Bay Hotel, it was built with a reasonable amount of environmental sensitivity. (And also cultural sensitivity: The original plans for the resort had to be redrawn when preliminary excavations uncovered a traditional Hawaiian burial ground. The resort was also careful not to disturb a historic church and general store.) Although Ritz-Carltons tend toward the generic, the Kapalua branch looks much more like Hawaii than the Big Island's Ritz-Carlton. It provides a high level of luxury and contains 58 suites and 72 club rooms, the latter with exclusive lounges offering complimentary food and beverage service. With the Kapalua Bay Hotel the new Ritz-Carlton shares 54 holes of golf and one of Maui's most beautiful white-sand beaches, **Fleming Beach**.

Visitors to Kapalua with a car and $174 to spare can have a personalized tour of the Valley Isle with **Local Guides of Maui** (Tel: 877-4042). Following the tour, many drive down the long driveway between rows of ironwood trees to **Plantation House**, 2000 Plantation Club Drive, to dine on such colorful local dishes as honey-guava scallops, mixed grill with fresh fish and curried chicken sausage, or prawns wok-fried with Maui onions, local tomatoes, and serrano peppers, all at fairly reasonable prices; Tel: 669-6299.

West Maui's Northern and Southern Coasts

THE NORTH COAST

Along the stretch of Highway 30 past Kapalua to the north and around to the east, you'll find a whole series of isolated bays, some of them marine preserves, that are popular with snorkelers and surfers. The farther you go along this narrow, winding road, the more deserted the area becomes. Points of interest are unmarked—you'll want a good map—but you'll want to include the light station at **Nakalele Point** and the blowhole at **Mokolea** in your explorations. About 12 miles (19 km) in you wind down a steep hillside to find **Kahakuloa Village**, a small encampment of houses, taro terraces, an 1832 Catholic mission, and a brightly painted village church, all clustered around a ragged semicircle of rugged, rocky beach. This is one of the few truly Hawaiian places left. It does not really welcome visitors, although it's possible to stop at the church, but those searching out the remote and the authentic may wish to see it.

From Kahakuloa, the road winds up a massive rocky outcropping called **Kahakuloa Head** and continues, a slender thread of asphalt, through miles of ranches and stunning coastal views all the way to Wailuku. Most car-rental maps maintain that the whole coastal road is unpaved and warn that driving over it violates your rental contract. The road is paved all the way, although it's so narrow in spots that when two cars meet, one has to pull off onto the dirt shoulder to let the other pass. But if you run into car trouble, the car-rental company will make you pay for the tow truck. This is a drive only for travellers with hours to spare and a sense of adventure.

THE SOUTH COAST

Around the southern end of West Maui, south from Kapalua and Lahaina toward Maalaea, the mountains bend the road (Highway 30, the Honoapiilani Highway) first toward the flat island of Kahoolawe (an uninhabited island used for many years by the U.S. Navy for bombing practice) and then into Maui's interior. There are plenty of places on this stretch where drivers can stop to watch the whales that breach in these waters regularly from December to April. The big black mammals love this protected bay. If you spot one, pull over, because it's easy to lose track of the winding road. Usually, if you see a number of people standing beside their cars looking out over the ocean you can be sure a whale has been spotted. (For whale-watching cruises from Maalaea, see Lahaina, above.)

The small-boat harbor at **Maalaea** does contain one relatively undiscovered treasure, a restaurant called the **Waterfront**, located on Hauoli Street in the Milowai Condominium. Here the wine list is first class and reasonably priced, and the fresh fish is served nine different ways. Visitors to Maui often suspect there must be one restaurant that's not trendy but simply good, a restaurant that Maui residents keep to themselves. This is it. Tel: 244-9028.

CENTRAL MAUI

Many Maui visitors don't bother exploring the rather uninteresting central part of the Valley Isle, passing through only on their way to or from the airport in Kahului or to the heavily advertised **Maui Tropical Plantation** in Waikapu, a few miles south of Wailuku on the Honoapiilani Highway (Highway 30). In only a few short years, the plantation has become Maui's most popular paid visitor attraction. Although advertised as a free attraction, only the huge gift shop and a few displays are free. Visitors who want to take the tram ride through the fields of tropical fruits and vegetables, see coconut-husking demonstrations, or get lei-making instructions, have to pay eight dollars apiece for the privilege.

Wailuku

Located on the valley's north shore is Wailuku, Maui's county seat (Maui County also includes the islands of Molokai, Lanai, and Kahoolawe). This humble, historic town, located on the northern coast below the West Maui mountains, doesn't try to be anything it's not. A recently activated Main Street program has begun the tedious task of turning some of the town's old buildings along Vineyard and Market streets into functional edifices.

MARKET STREET

Wailuku's most photographed landmark, the pink **Iao Theater**, stands proudly at the head of Market Street, almost daring anyone who admires its Art Deco architecture to presume to enter. Built in 1927 as a movie house, the Iao is home to the Maui Community Theater—which opens the theater only when a play is running—until it moves to a more modern art center in Kahului in 1994 or 1995. A new owner may then turn the theater into a more accessible visitor attraction.

Along Market Street a few intrepid shopkeepers selling antiques and unusual collectibles set out their signs. **Memory Lane** stocks a healthy collection of antique aloha shirts, old Hawaiian sheet music, and such oddities as "Legalize Pot" bumper stickers. Nearby, **Hula Moons** features similar Hawaiian memorabilia—and even has a chartreuse grass skirt and bra for those who can wear that color. **Helen's Treasures**, with its vintage glass, and **Alii Antiques** both have their followers. **Wailuku Gallery** features such Maui artists as Don Jusko, whose acrylic and watercolor landscapes are big sellers. **Traders of the Lost Art** sells vintage aloha shirts, exotic furniture, and the primitive wood sculpture, masks, rugs, and baskets the proprietor Tye Hartall collects from trips to New Guinea and other exotic locales throughout Oceania. Hartall's shop is open only by appointment or by chance; Tel: 242-7753.

Siam Thai, also on Market Street, dishes up the island's best Thai cuisine. Robert Redford's autographed eight-by-ten glossy hanging on the wall may attest to that diner's impeccable taste; reports claim that Harrison Ford took his family there three times during one Valley Isle visit.

WAILUKU'S MISSION BUILDINGS

Some of Wailuku's edifices go back to the time of the missionaries who journeyed to the Sandwich Islands and to one group in particular that settled in Central Maui. In 1833 the Reverend Jonathan Green first set foot on the Valley Isle, founding the Central Maui Mission Station on a choice piece of Wailuku land that Maui governor Hoapili had given to Green's employer, the American Board of Commissioners for Foreign Missions. The lush property was in the Wailuku foothills, at the entrance to Iao Valley, and had an expansive view all the way to Kahului Bay. Green also established the Wailuku Female Seminary in 1837, wherein girls were trained in the feminine arts, in the building at the corner of Main and High streets that is now **Kaahumanu Church**.

In 1840 missionary Edward Bailey and his wife, Caroline, moved to Maui to teach at the seminary. Eventually (after the reverend left the board of commissioners because it refused to stop accepting funds from slave states) the Baileys moved into the Greens' home. In time the old timber-and-stone house at 2375-A Main Street became known as the **Bailey House**, or Hale Hoikeike, and the Maui Historical Society now runs a museum there. The upper floors look much as they might have back in Bailey's day: A canopied bed dominates one room, while clothing from the period hangs in the closet. In the top-floor sitting room a koa-wood dining table made for President Ulysses S. Grant reminds visitors just how far away and distinct from the United States Hawaii once was:

The president had to refuse the table because he couldn't accept gifts from foreign nations.

Downstairs are Hawaiian artifacts from the days before the white man's arrival: Stone tools, dog-tooth necklaces, *kapa* (cloth made from bark), and fishing gear are only some of the items the society has on display. In the basement the museum's small shop stocks a good selection of Hawaiian gifts, from quilt kits to note cards to books on Hawaiian culture. The Bailey House grounds show that its proprietor also had commercial vision: Bailey was fascinated by sugar cultivation, perhaps suspecting he wouldn't always be principal of the Wailuku Female Seminary (which was, indeed, finally shut down). Sugar industry relics sit around the property as testimony to the missionary who had prepared himself to be the first manager of the Wailuku Sugar Company.

WEST FROM WAILUKU

Long before the Greens or the Baileys ever dreamed of Maui, the Wailuku area was the scene of a bloody battle. At the site of **Kepaniwai Park and Heritage Gardens**, on Iao Valley Road a few miles west of Wailuku, Kamehameha and his troops engaged in an intense struggle for domination of Maui in 1790. When it was over, bodies blocked the normally rushing Iao Stream, giving the village downstream its name: Wailuku means "water of destruction."

Kepaniwai Park belies its violent past; the small pavilions that memorialize Maui's melting pot provide a peaceful setting for a picnic or a stroll. Within the state park, visitors follow paths that lead past an early Hawaiian thatched house and a taro field; a Japanese teahouse and gardens surrounded by ponds filled with *koi* (carp); a Portuguese villa fronted by arbors and a statue of the Madonna; and a white clapboard New England saltbox. The Chinese and Filipinos are also represented, as are present-day local folk, who often reserve one of the large picnic pavilions for a party.

Just a few miles farther on you will see signs pointing out a rock promontory called the John F. Kennedy Profile. It's supposed to look like our 35th president—it doesn't much.

Right around the corner is **Iao Needle**, a stone spire rising dramatically some 1,200 feet from the valley floor. Erosion gave this outcropping its pointed shape, and when the mists roll in off the north shore they create an eerie effect. There are several easy hikes here in the Iao

Valley State Park, originating in its parking lot. There are also more difficult ones, although frequent rains tend to force walkers to stay on paved trails and out of the mud. But all that precipitation is responsible for the lush fern and philodendron forests that hikers find themselves in.

Kahului

Central Maui cradles one other major town: Kahului. Except to residents, who love having the island's largest mall, the most movie theaters, the major airport, and a pivotal location, there's not much to recommend the town. Created by Alexander & Baldwin when its workers wanted to launch themselves into the happy state of home ownership, Kahului is still called "Dream City" by those who remember its beginnings as a company town.

One resident with a memory now runs the **Alexander & Baldwin Sugar Museum** in a renovated plantation manager's home just outside Kahului. Although small, the museum, next door to the still-belching Hawaiian Commercial & Sugar Company refinery in Puunene, captivates the crowds with such exhibits as a working model of a sugar mill. Already offering an absorbing presentation, the museum plans to unveil its restored locomotive sometime this year. Originally the number one engine on the Kahului Railroad, the vintage train is one of the oldest restored locomotives in the United States.

Kahului locals gather *pau hana* (after work) at the **Chart House** (500 North Puunene Avenue), where the drinks come with a generous view of the harbor.

SOUTH MAUI

For a while, it was only West Maui that was booming. Now the shore that hugs Haleakala's western slopes, known as South Maui, is having its own construction explosion, particularly in its far southern reaches, where a battle rages for the upscale market. New hotels have gone up at breakneck speed, competing for the all-important ocean view.

KIHEI

South Maui also contains the island's low-rent district. From Maalaea Bay south for about 10 miles (16 km), the beach town of Kihei controls the coast with its hodgepodge of (mostly budget) condominiums. Determined travellers can find decent lodging in Kihei—clean and reasonably priced—but the overall atmosphere borders on the tacky. Strip shopping centers and fast-food joints have been given far too much rein.

The best place to stay in Kihei is just before Wailea at the ▶ **Mana Kai Maui Resort**. This little hostelry looks out at the same beaches that you'll pay top dollar for down the road, and you can get studios or one- or two-bedroom units. Some rates even include a compact rental car. The decor isn't fancy, but the views are great and there's a decent restaurant on the premises. The formerly run-down Surf & Sand, nearby, has been spruced up and renamed the ▶ **Wailea Oceanfront Hotel**. The rooms are still small and plain, but the beach is grand.

The three best places to eat in Kihei are all located in the same shopping center, Kai Nani Village, located across from Kamaole Beach at 2511 South Kihei Road. They are the inexpensive Mexican eatery **La Bahia**, the art-filled **Kihei Prime Rib and Seafood**, and, a local favorite, the **Greek Bistro**. Local Kihei residents also swear by **Shaka Pizza**, a storefront take-out place in Paradise Plaza shopping center, at 1295 South Kihei Road. (Shaka is hard to find, and as it delivers, it may make more sense to have them find you; Tel: 874-0331.)

Wailea

Wailea, some 7 miles (11 km) south of Kihei, got off to a late start, but it seems destined to replace Kaanapali as Maui's premium resort destination. Wailea is quieter than Kaanapali, and has three things Kaanapali does not: the agricultural lands of Ulupalakua Ranch surrounding it; a stunning succession of white-sand crescent beaches; and three of Maui's newest and most pleasurable resorts.

WAILEA'S RESORTS

The first of the new resorts to open was the ▶ **Four Seasons**, one of the few newer Hawaii resorts that manages to be elegant without being grandiose. Most hotel entries are designed to impress. The Four Seasons introduces you by way of a side entrance, which keeps you from noticing how big the 380-room hotel really is. The focus is not on the building, but on the hotel pool with its large fountain and the beach beyond. Pleasantly enough, the resort does not charge extra for many amenities, from the daily children's program to the iced towels and Evian spritz poolside.

Another major draw: The Four Seasons has the best food in Wailea, if not in all of Maui. Both dining rooms, the informal **Pacific Grill** and the dressier **Seasons** restaurant (jackets required for gentlemen), are oceanfront and largely open-air. The fare at both restaurants presents inventive Pacific Rim cuisine: Asian specialties such as Vietnamese spring rolls and charred Korean beef at Pacific Grill; and such items as pan-seared *opakapaka* with a vegetable strudel and lychee-papaya relish, or lamb with a hazelnut crust served with lasagna made from Japanese eggplant and feta cheese upstairs at Seasons. You can eat very well here.

The Four Seasons is flanked on both sides by two of the most stunning resorts ever built in Hawaii, and in the 1990s that's saying something. To the north is the 787-room ▶ **Grand Wailea** (formerly the Grand Hyatt Wailea). According to some reports, the $600-million resort is so extravagant it may never pay back its Japanese investors, but that shouldn't keep you from enjoying it. It has become fashionable to decry the Grand Wailea as *de trop*—and of course it *is* too much—but the whole intention was to create "hotel as entertainment." The resort has $30 million worth of art, including a wonderful collection of non-hotel-style sculptures by Fernando Botero. There are a seaside wedding chapel with commissioned Hawaiian-theme stained-glass windows on all four walls and a Japanese restaurant surrounded by rocks brought in from Mount Fuji for authenticity. The 2,000-foot-long swimming pool has locks, slides, cocktail lounges, a scuba diving area, and a sandy beach outlet. (That's besides the 15,000-square-foot decorative mosaic pool in the lobby.)

There's so much in the Grand Wailea that it's hard to know which details would appeal to which visitor. But two features clearly emerge. Most Hawaii resorts have a room devoted to children's activities. The Grand Wailea has not only a room, but also a whale-shaped children's pool and outdoor playground, a video-game room, a science classroom, ceramics studio, children's theater, and restaurant. All this, and daily child care for those who like to travel with children but not to spend all day with them. The second standout is the Grand Wailea's spa, the largest in Hawaii, 50,000 square feet of massage rooms, mineral, mud, and aromatic baths, sonic relaxation studios, and even real workout equipment for those whose devotion to health includes working up a sweat.

None of this should obscure the fact that the Grand Wailea is a comfortable place to stay. Outside of a few large oceanfront suites, the rooms are comfortable and attractive rather than grand. And the hotel maintains an unpretentious level of service that enables you to simply relax and enjoy the resort's more elaborate trappings.

The Grand Wailea boasts a number of restaurants. The most touted is the spa restaurant, **Café Kula**, where the fare is more low-fat than palatable and the service awful, especially since the café was an afterthought and is located in—to put it bluntly—a busy corridor. Far less publicized but exponentially better is the hotel's Japanese restaurant, **Kincha**. Built to emulate a traditional Japanese teahouse, Kincha is not only the most beautiful and most tranquil Japanese restaurant in the Islands, it is also the best. It's quite expensive, but, then again, "inexpensive Japanese restaurant" is an oxymoron. For the best combination of quality and value, order the *kaiseki* dinner of the day. Since kaiseki is supposed to include the best and freshest seasonal ingredients anyway, the more expensive dinners are not likely to be much better than the chef's daily special.

The third of the new Wailea resorts is the ▶ **Kea Lani**, located just south of the Four Seasons (separated only by ▶ **Grand Champions Golf and Tennis Villas**, a condominium that shares its 14-court tennis complex with the Wailea resorts). Group 70, a well-known Honolulu architectural firm, designed the Kea Lani to give the appearance of an Arabian castle—the turrets, domes, and sweeping curves look as if they were carved out of white icing. What also sets the Kea Lani apart is that all the rooms are suites, with separate bedroom, full entertainment unit (two TVs, a VCR, and a laser-disk player), marble bath, and mini-kitchen. In addition to these standard suites there are a number of two- and three-bedroom oceanfront villas, each with a private sundeck and swimming pool. Although room service is available, each villa comes with a functional kitchen, and a basic stock of groceries is included in the room rate. As is standard with the new Wailea resorts, Kea Lani has a two-level pool, a health spa, and a wonderful crescent of white sand where snorkeling, windsurfing, sailing, and scuba lessons are offered.

Makena

Maui's baby resort lies down the beach a piece from Wailea, about 3 miles (5 km) south over the winding Wailea Alanui Road, lined by scrubby *kiawe* trees (more commonly called mesquite on the Mainland). In fact, if it weren't for prodigious watering, all the land along Maui's southeastern coast would look this arid and unappealing. In the distance, finally, a three-story white hotel—the Maui Prince—appears in the vast field to the right. Beyond, the red cinder cone of the volcanic vent Puu Olai stands sentinel to this rural frontier, while offshore the crescent tip of Molokini, an underwater volcano, gives shelter to dozens of snorkelers' boats. And, past that, Kahoolawe, the uninhabited island once used by the U.S. Navy for bombing practice, stops the eye from venturing any farther over the horizon.

Inside, the ▶ **Maui Prince Hotel** is mannerly, reflecting its Asian owner's ideas about hospitality: A Japanese rock garden fills the interior courtyard; a small stream ripples between the temple statuary and tiny, meticulously tended trees. Front-desk attendants graciously proffer hot washcloths at check-in so that guests can wipe away the dust of travel. And each evening three musicians dressed in symphony black set up their chairs and stringed instruments beside the brook to play classical selections.

Rooms at the Prince are simple, one prosaic print per chamber. The hotel's lavish Sunday brunch, however, an all-you-can-eat affair featuring sideboards heaped with seafood and salads and omelets cooked to order, is anything but simple. Afterwards guests can head out for the nearby golf course, which boasts Maui's lowest greens fees. The Maui Prince is oceanfront, but a tree-lined berm separates the beach from the hotel, inhibiting views but not access.

South of Makena

On the coast road exactly one mile south of the Maui Prince turnoff is the first of several unmarked rights-of-way to the huge sand expanse lovingly called **Big Beach**. At the far northern end of Big Beach (to the right as you face the water), a trail leads over a rock embankment to what's even more affectionately called **Little Beach**, the favorite strand for locals who'd rather go suitless. Big Beach is frequented by families, as well as some guests of the Maui Prince who prefer the more ample acreage they find here. Some 3,000 feet long and 100 feet deep, Big Beach rarely looks crowded, even with kids darting between their sand castles and the ocean. Little Beach is probably the better-maintained of the two, however, because a group of regulars polices the area, keeping the place clean and monitoring rowdy behavior. Officially, Hawaii outlaws nude sunbathing, so locals try to be extra careful about the comings and goings on this beach.

Beyond the beaches, Makena Road soon becomes the Hoapili, or **King's Trail**. A path used by ancient Hawaiians to travel around the island's southern shore to Hana, the extremely rough road now goes through—and sometimes under—Maui's last lava flow, spit out by Haleakala back in 1790 and covering portions of the trail and some ancient *heiau* (temples). Eventually, the trail joins the Piilani Highway and continues the journey east to Hana along Maui's southern coast on extremely bad "roads."

HALEAKALA CRATER

One trip was all it took for Mark Twain, who years after his 1866 visit wrote to a friend, "If the house would only burn down, we would move to the isles of the blest, and shut ourselves up in the healing solitudes of Haleakala." More than a century later Haleakala still inspires such feelings in the visitors and residents of its slopes.

Haleakala stands 10,023 feet tall, and although it hasn't spewed lava in 200 years is considered dormant, not extinct. But there doesn't seem to be any imminent danger of an eruption.

Once every few years snow falls on the peak, and local families rush up to play in the white stuff before it melts, usually within a few hours. The air at the summit can be crisp and crystalline. Often though, clouds gather early on, covering the mountain's upper half by midday. On overcast days Haleakala goes completely into hiding, giving a shock when she finally does appear to visitors who arrived when she was invisible. Cloudy days on Haleakala are better left for exploring Maui's other environs, because visibility downward is just as poor as visibility upward.

GETTING TO THE SUMMIT

It's best to start the drive up to Haleakala's summit early in the morning. Sunrise from the peak ranks as one of the natural wonders of the world. Launch yourself into the car and onto the Crater Road (number 378), off Haleakala Highway/Highway 37/377 by about 4:00 A.M. Be sure to take long pants and a jacket or sweater, as early-morning temperatures occasionally drop to freezing. It's not uncommon to see visitors who didn't bring their winter wear to Hawaii wrapped up in blankets they've borrowed from hotel beds (though the hotels frown on this).

If you are racing to see the sunrise don't stop until you reach the **Puu Ulaula Overlook**, the highest lookout, a glass enclosure that perches right at the pinnacle and offers stunning 360-degree views. About 2,000 feet below the lookout sprawls the dark earth crater with an area of 19 square miles and a circumference of 21 miles—nearly big enough to hold the island of Manhattan. When the sun begins to peek above the crater rim, the great bowl gradually fills with golden light, and black and ruddy cinder cones throw long shadows on the crater floor.

Haleakala may look like a classic Hawaiian volcano crater, but it's not. Some 800,000 years ago rivers began to cut wide valleys into Haleakala's summit. Over the millennia the erosion formed what geologists call an "erosional depression"—not a true volcanic crater, although subsequent eruptions that partially filled the valleys with lava flows and cinder cones certainly made it look like one. But let the rock hounds call it what they may. For the rest of us peering down on the hardened flows and stout cinder cones encircled by high ridges, the word "crater" suits just fine.

Just down the road from the summit is a small enclosed visitors' center with more stunning views into the crater. It also has a few simple displays, including one that tells the myth of how the demigod Maui captured the sun from within the crater of Haleakala ("House of the Sun"), and forced it to go more slowly across the heavens so Maui's mother's *kapa* cloth would have time to dry. Rangers are posted at the summit observation shelter to answer questions every morning at 9:30, 10:30, and 11:30, and they give brief, informative talks on park geology and natural history.

The 27,284-acre national park, which was dedicated in 1961 to preserve Haleakala's natural resources, is open round the clock. (During daylight hours there is an admission fee per car.) From the Hosmer Grove Campground, a few miles before park headquarters at 7,000 feet elevation, the park service leads a three-hour hike every Monday and Thursday morning at 9:00, pointing out native Hawaiian birds and plants along the way. Park headquarters (Tel: 572-9306) traces Haleakala's volcanic origins and eruption history through a series of exhibits and lectures. And at the visitors' center of Haleakala at 10:00

A.M. Tuesdays and Fridays rangers lead hikers on a moderately strenuous two-mile hike into the crater along the **Sliding Sands Trail**. The bed of loose cinders, crunching underfoot like icy old snow, cushions each step as you make your way down. The panorama from Sliding Sands is almost too spectacular to absorb. Against a curving canvas of matte black and sky blue, goliath brush strokes of earth tones and green accent the topography. Rolling plains of rock and cinders make it easy to see why this moonscape was chosen to train the Apollo astronauts before their lunar landings.

On the drive back from the summit there are several lookouts and trails along the way. At about 9,000 feet, the **Kalahaku Overlook** is home to the silversword, a rare plant that grows only in Haleakala. **White Hill**, with its small crater, is an easy walk away. From White Hill there is a good view of Haleakala that reveals the volcano's geological structure. A little farther down the road is **Leleiwi Overlook**, where the **Halemauu Trail** begins a two-mile descent on switchbacks that eventually reach the crater floor. Some people are lucky enough to see the phenomenon known as the Brocken specter at Leleiwi, an optical illusion that sometimes occurs if you are between the sun and a mass of clouds at just the right time, when tricks of light project your much enlarged reflection, sometimes surrounded by rainbow colors, onto the clouds.

CAMPING AT HALEAKALA

Three cabins, at different spots within the crater, can be reserved three months in advance through a lottery system run by the park. Each houses up to 12 people, and stays are limited to two consecutive nights. The cabins contain a wood stove, pressed-wood logs, cooking utensils, and bunk beds. Potable water is available from a catchment tank—it's guaranteed to be just on the liquid side of freezing, chlorinated so as to be safe for drinking and so bad tasting you won't want to. Each cabin has its own outhouse with a diverting view. Tent camping is permitted next to two of the cabins.

Farther down the mountain, just after you exit the park, is **Hosmer Grove**, a small campground (no permit required, stays limited to three days) that is a good staging area for trips into the crater. In 1910 Ralph Hosmer planted several varieties of temperate-zone conifers from Europe, North America, Japan, and Australia on the slopes of Haleakala, with the aim of providing a watershed and a dependable source of commercial-grade lumber. Hosmer's experiment was a failure—the volcanic soil at 7,000 feet was too thin to support strong root systems and the trees often toppled in high winds. But his loss is the camper's gain. Hosmer's efforts survive in the cozy little campground (though it's chilly at this elevation) and half-mile trail through a cosmopolitan sampling of conifers.

See the Accommodations Reference at the end of the chapter for information on reserving a cabin in the park.

UPCOUNTRY

The habitable, western side of Haleakala is called "Upcountry" for obvious reasons. Here, as the elevation progresses ever upward, the air cools and purple-blossomed jacaranda trees dot the landscape. In its higher reaches, Upcountry gives haven to those who need solitude and have chosen one of the long, winding roads for their hideaway estates. The yards of some homesteads along the highway are shared by a horse, some chickens, and a satellite dish. Farmers are busy in the fields, nurturing such diverse crops as carnations, onions, and grapes. One of Hawaii's two wineries cultivates and ferments its harvest on Ulupalakua Ranch land on the southern end of the Kula Highway (Highway 37).

TEDESCHI VINEYARDS

Tedeschi Vineyards was founded in 1974 when Napa Valley winemaker Emil Tedeschi joined the Erdmans of Ulupalakua in testing California and European grapes here. The climate and soil were found to be most suitable for the carnelian grape (a hybrid of cabernet sauvignon, grenache, and carignane). Soon the winery was in business, producing both still and sparkling wines from grapes, as well as a very popular dry wine from pineapples grown on the island. Now open daily, the winery's tasting room was built by James Makee, who called his spread Rose Ranch when he founded it in the 1850s. He raised cattle, but kept himself busy importing as many varieties of the blooming beauties as he could get. Between 9:30 A.M. and 2:30 P.M. vineyard staffers give behind-the-scenes tours of the wine-making equipment, and also lead a stroll around the grounds, which still have their original landscaping, including a 100-year-old camphor tree and a healthy stand of Norfolk Island pine.

Up the Kula Highway

The Kula Highway goes north from Tedeschi Vineyards up the western face of Haleakala to Pukalani. Some 5 miles (8 km) from the winery, is the tiny village of **Keokea**, more or less the hub of the area. Stop in for locally grown and roasted coffee at **Grandma's**, a homey little place with lion tamer chairs, watercolors of cowboys, and rows of mugs painted with the names of regulars. You can also get homemade pastries, cookies, sandwiches, and cold drinks here.

KULA BOTANICAL GARDENS

Gardeners will want to visit the Kula Botanical Gardens on Upper Kula Road about 10 miles (16 km) northeast of the winery. It features a "Taboo Garden" of poisonous plants. The University of Hawaii's **Kula Experiment Station** on Mauna Place is easily reached just off the Kula Highway (Highway 37) on Copp Road. The gardens may be seen in a relaxed 30-minute walk beside koa and *kukui* trees, ginger and orchid blooms, and the exotic protea shrub. Protea, whose immense blossoms seem straight from the plains of Venus (but actually come from Australia), were first introduced to the Islands at this station. More than 300 varieties grow here, in colors from blushing pink to fireball red and flaming orange, and with fanciful names to match: Sunburst Pincushion, Pink Mink, and Hawaii Gold. Several nurseries in the area will pack protea for shipping anywhere in the world.

STAYING IN THE AREA

Down the road, the ▶ **Kula Lodge and Restaurant** looks out over the protea fields and onto the valley below. Both a restaurant and an inn, the lodge has become a favorite breakfast spot for trekkers in need of sustenance after a trip up to the Haleakala summit for the sunrise. The view is especially great for those who can't quite tear themselves away from the urge to merge with nature. Tables sit next to huge banks of windows, and on misty days when there is a fire in the fireplace this could be heaven. The restaurant also serves lunch and dinner. At the bottom of a winding stone stairway, the lodge houses the **Curtis Wilson Cost Gallery**, featuring pastoral paintings and ethereal background music.

The lodge has a few "chalets" with wonderful views for overnight guests, but a few bed and breakfasts in the area

offer more interesting hospitality. One of the best is
▶ **Bloom Cottage**, on Highway 37 about 10 miles (16 km) south from Pukalani. The homey little house is filled with grace notes of comfort, including a four-poster bed covered with a Hawaiian quilt and dried aromatic herbs to throw in the fireplace.

Makawao

Other pockets of Upcountry Maui are also appealing. The little town of Makawao, just a couple of miles northeast from Pukalani between Haleakala and Kahului, was once a typical western burg, its sagging storefronts along the lone main thoroughfare selling such no-nonsense staples as saddles, hard tack, and *palaka*-print work shirts (*palaka* is a plaid favored by Island plantation workers). Settled by Portuguese immigrants who took up working the nearby ranches after their sugar plantation contracts ran out, Makawao was the Maui version of the Old West. Now the once rough-and-tumble cowboy hangout is home also to longhair farmers, artists, and upwardly mobile merchants and businesspeople who work down in Kahului. A few art galleries, boutiques, and cafés have made themselves part of the community as well.

SHOPPING IN MAKAWAO

Makawao's cowpokes probably don't shop at the town's tiny clothing and knickknack emporiums anymore, but the buildings, both inside and out, remain true to their origins. Meet one of Makawao's local characters at **Silversword Stove and Fireplace**, Gary Moore, an Oregon transplant who is one of the people most responsible for restoring this little town. Stop in his shop to see the antique stove or to choose from his wide selection of other wood stoves—he ships all over the world. A chat with him guarantees you'll get the real lowdown on Makawao. In the town's other renovated clapboard storefronts you'll find everything from a general store and old-fashioned barbershop to health food, holistic medicine, and little shops selling crystals, incense, medicinal herbs, and tie-dye. In one store you might share the aisle with a big friendly dog, in another you'll find the latest fashions from Santa Fe. A sidewalk bulletin board advertises things like used cars, upcoming concerts, psychic healers, and home delivery of fresh coconuts.

In a breezy, tin-roofed dwelling, **Collections** has unusual baskets, colorful woven rugs, and clothes imported from places like Cyprus and Guam, as well as delightful jewelry. **Coconut Classics** is a wood-frame store stuffed with antique aloha shirts, old books, and oddball Hawaiian collectibles. **Maui Child Toys & Books** is perhaps one of Hawaii's finest toy stores, with quality playthings and a healthy selection of beautifully illustrated reading material. A new gallery, **Viewpoints Gallery Maui Artists Collective**, has opened in the renovated Makawao Theatre on Baldwin Avenue. Artists represented range from photographer Steven Minkowski to sculptor Savra Posey.

Nonetheless, Makawao has not given up its roots: The centerpiece for this wide spot in the road is still the venerable general store called **T. Komoda Store & Bakery**, where for six decades a crew of women has baked fabulous pastries—the cream puffs are especially popular—that have consistently drawn crowds. Although baked goods get the most attention, Komoda's also stocks an assortment of fabric and other necessities.

Down the street, Norman and Patty Diego run **Tack 'n Things** for the diehard cowboys who still need bridles and stirrups, many of whom also compete in the annual **Makawao Rodeo**. Held each Fourth of July, this riding and roping event draws thousands to the Upcountry fairgrounds.

DINING IN MAKAWAO

Dining choices in town include the **Makawao Steak & Fish House**, a dark-paneled restaurant that serves up thick slabs of expertly grilled beef. A livelier crowd opts for **Polli's Mexican Restaurant**, where proprietor Polli Smith serves vegetarian Mexican dishes and margaritas. **Casanova Italian Restaurant & Deli** has seductive pasta; many patrons drive from Maui's lower elevations just for the ravioli or rigatoni (open for lunch and dinner). After 10:00 P.M. the place becomes Upcountry's one and only nightclub, sometimes featuring intimate live performances by international name acts (John Mayall, Dave Mason, Mose Allison, Taj Mahal).

NORTHWEST FROM MAKAWAO

As Baldwin Avenue winds downhill from Makawao on its way north toward the beachside town of Paia, it gives shelter on a gentle curve to the **Hui Noeau Visual Arts Center**, set back off the road behind a simple stone gate. The pink, tile-roofed Mediterranean mansion was once the home of Ethel Baldwin, who founded the Hui—the Hawaiian word for "group"—in 1934, holding meetings and ceramics classes at the estate she and her husband called Kaluanui. About 14 years ago descendant Colin Cameron (who built Kapalua Bay Hotel) gave the home to the Hui, and the association now holds workshops here, open to the public, on a wide range of subjects, including drawing, photography, ceramics, and design (Tel: 572-6560). Each spring the Hui also opens its grounds to **Art Maui**, the Valley Isle's only juried art show. About 250 artists participate in the event; some donate their time to lead tours through the exhibits.

Some of the area's artists hang out at Beverly Gannon's **Haliimaile General Store**, off Baldwin Avenue on Haliimaile Road. Once a market for workers from the pineapple plantation that surrounds it, the Gannons' reincarnation is a hip restaurant, its peach, green, and white exterior a stylish anomaly in its out-in-the-middle-of-nowhere location. Inside, the Gannons employ a casually elegant decor—pastels, wood, and large paintings decorating expansive walls—while the menu, which changes every two weeks, includes such staples as barbecued ribs, smoked chicken, and duck with various sauces.

A long deli case lining one wall serves as a reminder of the Gannons' success story: Beverly was running a little catering company, cooking for a few clients, when she decided to open a deli in the old general store and put in eight tables and some shelves offering fiestaware, baskets, and cooking gear for sale. Before long her business doubled, then tripled. It is easy to taste why.

EAST MAUI

East Maui, the wet, windward side of the island, is probably best known for the Hana Highway, a narrow, twisting, scenic road that skirts the coastline from Kahului to Hana, on the island's far eastern coast. The town of Paia, a good place to start the drive, is a funky artists' community. At the other end is Hana, a beautiful, get-away-from-it-all spot with a remoteness that is all too hard to find elsewhere in Maui these days.

Paia

Paia, 7 miles (11 km) up Baldwin Avenue from Makawao and about 6 miles (10 km) northeast from Kahului, has come a long way since its early days as the retailing headquarters for an Alexander & Baldwin sugar operation. During World War II marines pitched their tents nearby, and for a while the town really boomed, but the marines soon left. A & B also decided that its unprofitable Paia operation should come to an end. Many Paia residents took advantage of the opportunity to buy their own homes in Kahului, the town created by A & B in Central Maui, which further depleted the population.

In the 1960s Paia was psychedelic; hippies hung out in the little town, running funky shops and organic restaurants. Windsurfers became the predominant group in the late 1970s, with the discovery that **Hookipa**, a bay a mile past town, is one of the best-winded places in the world. Artists and craftspeople have also been drawn to Paia, and recently boutiques have moved in, too. **Summer House** (83 Hana Highway) and **Nuage Bleu** (down the road at number 76) both carry unusual women's apparel and gift items, ranging from sequined belt packs to Tavros leatherware to Euroshoes.

ART GALLERIES IN PAIA

The work of local artists can be seen at the **Maui Crafts Guild**, located in an old green building at the entrance to town. The wares include unusual baskets woven from twigs, leaves, and boughs; mystical *raku* pottery subtly featuring the female form; and tie-dyed *pareu* (sarongs) suitable for wearing. The artists staff the guild, so you might ask the person behind the desk to point out his or her work.

Artist **Eddie Flotte**, who paints precise watercolors, welcomes visitors to his gallery on the ocean side of the highway. He's often out on location painting, but his friend, Sandy Cotton, watches the shop. Flotte paints Maui scenes—interesting storefronts, expressive old faces, and weather-worn boats—in a painstaking style that captures every detail. He also has a collection of subjects he painted in Greece and France, and plans to release limited-edition prints of selected works.

Another studio to visit in Paia is that of **Piero Resta**, an Italian painter (call first; Tel: 575-2203). Set in the old Pauwala Cannery in Haiku (about 5 miles/8 km beyond Paia, then up Haiku Road), Resta's workplace vibrates with inviting creativity. He and his son, Luigi, show the artist's extraordinary works—large canvases abandoned to color that reflect Piero's travels around the world. You might be asked to drink a glass of wine or a cup of espresso with the whole family. Once a restaurateur, Resta still has the gracious hospitality of someone who wants you to come in, have a seat, and rest your feet.

Hana Highway

Some travellers react to a ride on the Hana Highway (Highway 360; but note that it is called Highway 36 on the stretch from Kahului to Twin Falls) as if it were the Coney Island roller coaster; they wear cartoony "I Survived the Hana Highway" tee-shirts to proclaim their bravery. With 600 hairpin curves and 65 narrow bridges, it challenges even the most careful driver to stay focused on the ribbon ahead. But no one should let this put the brakes on a Hana Highway adventure.

True, the road that traverses the distance from Kahului east to Hana along Maui's north coast demands attention, but no more than the scenery that surrounds it. The Hana Highway route is characterized by abundant waterfalls, tropical rain forests, and secluded trails. Along its entire 55-mile (88-km) length the highway to Hana is well paved. Drivers are more likely to pull over to snap a quick photo than to stop from exhaustion. And when it rains the resulting rivulets give the coastline a mystical appearance.

Hana does have a small airport, but only those who plan to spend their entire vacation in Hana opt to use it. Far more visitors drive out on the Hana Highway, some taking a leisurely day to make the round trip (starting pretty early in the morning), others spending a night or two in Hana.

Paia might be thought of as the last outpost before the Hana Highway really begins. As for filling your tank, that's true, because you'll find no gas stations until you reach Hana. **Picnics**, a hole-in-the-wall spot on Baldwin Avenue in Paia, is the place to pick up snacks to eat along the way. Picnics packs simple lunches that include sandwiches, fresh fruit, cookies, and drinks, as well as the more extravagant Executive Picnic: slices of ham, beef, turkey, and a split kiawe-roasted chicken, along with cheeses, wheat buns, chips, fresh fruit, nut bread, drinks, and condiments. Picnics also provides ice chests and tablecloths.

Once you've actually made the commitment to leave civilization and head for Hana, the twists, turns, and waterfalls really kick in. The countryside is lush with huge mango trees and groves of bamboo. It's no wonder the Hana Coast used to be Maui's prime marijuana-growing area before the authorities cracked down. Along the Hana Highway you can stop at **Kaumahina State Wayside Park** (bathrooms), right after mile marker 12, for a look at the rugged Hana coastline, with Keanae Peninsula and its old village and patchwork of taro fields in the distance. The **Keanae Arboretum**, just past mile marker 16, is a well-laid-out garden with trees and plants from tropical regions around the world. A couple of trails lead deeper into the valley. For an hour's detour, drive down on to the peninsula to the rocky coast and explore the tidepools. Back up on the highway continue on to the Waianu Fruit Stand and then **Uncle Harry's**, near the halfway spot, marker 20, which sells fresh fruit, home-baked breads, and the requisite souvenirs.

Hana

Hana itself sneaks up on you. First-time visitors might wonder if they've even reached the place. Indeed, it has to be said that in terms of excitement the drive to Hana is more than half the fun. Those looking for man-made excitement stay in Lahaina. Yet Hana has a quiet charm that cajoles guests into adapting to its pace.

A couple of miles before town are **Kahanu Gardens**, the National Tropical Botanical Garden's 120-acre preserve, where ethnobotany is a special focus. The gardens are closed to the public at present, but may reopen in 1994. Also on the grounds is **Piilanihale Heiau,** a 15th-century Hawaiian temple with 50-foot-high walls. It is the largest heiau in the state—and what it was used for no one really knows.

Farther along the highway, about a mile before town, are the 60-acre is **Helani Gardens**, the creation of Hana native Howard Cooper, who labeled the gardens' many tropical plants and put up signs bearing odd aphorisms. The gardens are now under new ownership, and parts are under renovation, but the public is still welcome to drive through.

Hana itself is heavily Hawaiian, and distinctly rural. (The local bank opens from 3 P.M. to 4:30 P.M. Monday through Thursday; Fridays it stays open all the way until 6 P.M.) Many Hana people are natives; others are seekers of tranquillity. Jim Nabors has a macadamia-nut farm right outside town. Other celebrity residents of the Hana Coast include Carol Burnett, Kris Kristofferson, and George Harrison, though they're rarely seen, having chosen the area for its privacy and seclusion.

For an introduction to Hana's history, head to the **Hana Cultural Center**, a one-room museum right in town, chock-full of artifacts: *kapa* cloth and *kapa* beaters, a huge *poi* board and *poi* pounders, a fertility symbol in the form of a phallic stone, fishhooks, adzes (cutting tools), an old steel guitar, historic photos, and several exquisite Hawaiian quilts.

STAYING IN HANA

The town's present-day history is made at the graceful ▶ **Hotel Hana-Maui**, which isn't just *in* the center of town, it *is* the center of town, both geographically and emotionally. If there's anything you need or want to know in Hana, just ask at the hotel—they will be more than happy to oblige you. Low-rise and low-key, the small hotel was renovated by Caroline Hunt's Rosewood Hotels (the same company that runs the Bel-Air Hotel in Los Angeles). When Hunt's company purchased the hotel and the 7,000-acre ranch that surrounds it in 1986, the property had been operating for 30 years. True, it was run-down, but it employed about a third of Hana's 700 residents. There was natural suspicion about an outsider taking over the hotel. In the end, Rosewood's dedication to fine lodging blended well with Hana's family-style atmosphere, but when Rosewood sold the hotel to a Japanese company, the locals became edgy again. The new owners made Sheraton Hotels manager to improve its booking and reservations system. It seems Sheraton is fitting in well with the good-neighbor policy, but service to guests, unfortunately, is sometimes uneven, with less than professional courtesy by the occasional waiter or housekeeper.

Nevertheless, the hotel provides a most memorable vacation for those who seek out the secluded hostelry. People who enjoy the Hotel Hana-Maui most are those who want to relax and entertain themselves. Each room and suite is dominated by a giant bed frame made of sturdy, fat bamboo staves. Amenities include a bowl of fresh fruit at check-in and coffee beans, grinder, and maker. The hotel is not on the ocean, it has no golf course, and there is no nightlife here to speak of, but the hotel has come up with a wide range of things to do: tennis, golfing (at three chipping/putting practice holes), sand volleyball, croquet, snorkeling, fishing, swimming in heated pools or freshwater natural ponds, horseback riding, hiking, biking, hula and ukulele lessons, lei-making, historical and botanical tours, jeep tours, and a ranch tour. The hotel also runs the **Wellness Center**, a fitness facility with an open-air workout room, a pool, a Jacuzzi, and a running trail through Hana Ranch pastureland. Activities include aerobics and yoga classes, facial and body massage, and hiking excursions. Special Wellness Center menus are available in the hotel dining room.

When sugar dominated the Hana lifestyle the town was far larger. But the last plantation finally went sour in the 1940s, and many people left in search of new jobs. Several years back, when Rosewood decided to add some new guest accommodations to the Hotel Hana-Maui, its executives looked to the town's sweeter days and erected 24 duplex buildings—called the ▶ **Sea Ranch Cottages**—on land where one of the town's last plantation housing camps had been. Moreover, they had their architect research the style of those old buildings and duplicate their simple shapes: post-and-beam structures with tin roofs and generous decks. Then they painted the outside in the once-pervasive "plantation green," the color favored by plantation owners, probably because it was cheap and readily available. Rosewood also declined to landscape the grounds, so the cottages look as if they've been here for years, set among the native Hawaiian plants and wind-whipped sea grass.

The cottages' exteriors also belie their interiors, for once you go inside you find the same understated decor as in the rooms throughout the rest of the hotel. A distinct advantage of the cottages, however, is the views: The retreats perch near a cliff with the ocean boiling and crashing against the rock outcroppings below. Some of the units have hot tubs on the porch, some have living rooms; all are quietly comfortable and well appointed.

Many Hana travellers who can't afford the steep rates at the Hotel Hana-Maui check in at Fusae Nakamura's ▶ **Aloha Cottages** (just north of the Hotel Hana-Maui), a four-room hostelry that's basic, clean, and inexpensive. Mrs. Nakamura offers the fruit off her trees and has been known to wash her guests' laundry so they can see the sights around Hana. Tasty meals can be had at the **Hana Ranch Restaurant** (just off the town's main street), which features breakfast and lunch daily, pizza Thursday nights, and full dinners Fridays and Saturdays. Its well-lit, rustic character makes it equally well suited as a watering hole or a family restaurant. The lunch buffet with barbecued chicken and ribs and baked beans is popular with visitors passing through.

The comfortable and reasonably priced ▶ **Hana Kai-**

Maui Resort Condominium is the only Hana accommodation that's actually on the oceanfront. A few cabins at the ▶ **Waianapanapa State Park** are also near the ocean, though they're pretty spartan. Several miles before Hana town, Waianapanapa's rustic setting appeals to those who want to get back to nature but don't want to rough it totally. Cabins are spacious and come with linens and kitchen gear, available from the state, at $5 to $10 per person a night. (There are also campsites at Waianapanapa.) The park has a beautiful little black-sand beach, and the bay offers good snorkeling. Trails lead past old Hawaiian burial sites. A cave half filled with frigid brackish water is the site where, legend says, the wife of a cruel chief was murdered by her husband when he wrongly suspected her of unfaithfulness. To this day the waters sometimes turn red, recalling the woman's bloody death.

SOUTH FROM HANA

Just south of Hana the highway becomes rough. Many temples were built by ancient Hawaiians in this area, but they are difficult to find because there are few roads crossing the private land here. The traffic traversing the 10 miles (16 km) from Hana to **Oheo Gulch** can get heavy in spite of the difficulty in making the passage. Most people are on their way to **Seven Pools** at Oheo Gulch (sometimes called Seven Sacred Pools). No one is quite sure how the pools acquired their revered status; Hawaiian mythology does not consider them sacred. It is commonly believed that overzealous tourism promoters probably made the whole thing up and it sounded too good to change. Anyway, Seven Pools (there are actually nearly two dozen pools along the cascade down the hill to the ocean) is a delightful place to swim, sun, and picnic on the rock ledges that seem tailor-made for lounging. After heavy rains the pools can rise quickly and become dangerous, however. There's no ocean beach here, but the rocky shore is dramatic, especially the view from the grassy ruins of an ancient village by the lower pools. You can also hike up the trail to **Waimoku Falls** (one and a half miles), through forest thick with mango, monkeypod, breadfruit, ginger, and bamboo.

One of Hana's most respected former residents lies in the small **Palapala Hoomau Congregational Church** graveyard about a mile past Oheo Gulch. Charles Lindbergh and his wife, Anne Morrow Lindbergh, loved Hana and built a home there so Charles could spend his last years in the secluded village. When he died in 1974 he was buried in Hana, as he had requested. The dirt road to the church is narrow, leading toward the ocean through a grove of trees. County officials and residents are protective of Lindbergh's grave, which is understandable since vandals have left the site in a shambles several times. As a result, the sign that directs visitors there often disappears. If you don't see it, chances are you can ask five residents for directions and you'll get five different answers—and they'll all be evasive.

KIPAHULU AND WEST

Beyond the Hoomau church, Kipahulu Falls mark the opening to one of Maui's most beautiful—and rarely visited—valleys, **Kipahulu**. You must find someone knowledgeable to take you back into the wilds; the trails are rough—overgrown with native *ohia* and kiawe trees and studded with enormous rocks—and most easily traversed on horseback. There are no organized tours into Kipahulu Valley, but if you are interested you might try asking at the Hotel Hana-Maui.

Along the coast road farther west are numerous heiau and the 1859 Huialoha Church, renovated in the early 1970s. The village of Kaupo comes up shortly, with another of Hawaii's venerable general stores. Eventually this road, the Piilani Highway (Highway 31), comes out in South Maui at Ulupalakua Ranch near Makena. This route, however, is Maui's greatest driving challenge, particularly if you do not have a four-wheel-drive vehicle. For the most part, it's best not to attempt this stretch. Rental cars are forbidden for good reason. You would be likely to get stuck where the road is washed out, or you could damage the undercarriage.

GOLF COURSES

You'll love Maui with or without your golf clubs, but if you're an avid golfer you'll not forgive yourself if you don't take them along. There are 16 courses on the island, the best of which are resort courses.

Resort Courses
Ever since the **Kapalua Golf Club**, 300 Kapalua Drive, in West Maui's northwestern corner, opened its Bay Course in 1975 and its Village Course five years later, it has been known throughout the golfing world as a supreme club.

Both those courses remain exquisite golfing experiences, but now Kapalua has a third layout—the Plantation, which can be described with one word: demanding. Opening to rave reviews in May 1991, the Plantation Course is a Ben Crenshaw/Bill Coore design that stretches out more than 7,200 yards from the back tees and is rated an intimidating 74.6 from there (par is 73). In addition to being long, the Plantation is a big course, built upon 240 acres of rolling land that was formerly a pineapple field. The course plays around, over, and through a massive ravine on the front nine, creating some dramatic scenery as well as some challenging golf holes. Wind, blind tee and fairway shots, wild, rough, and slick greens make the Plantation one of Hawaii's toughest tracts. Tel: 669-8044.

The resort area of Wailea, in South Maui, is also a great golf mecca. Three courses—the Blue, the Orange, and the Gold—form **Wailea Golf Club**, 120 Kaukahi Street, Wailea. The Blue Course has been one of the favorite designs in Hawaii since it opened in 1972. All three courses are in excellent shape year round and will give you a challenging round of golf while providing some picture-postcard views of the mid-Hawaiian islands. Tel: 879-2966.

South of Wailea, next to the Maui Prince Hotel, is the **Makena Golf Club** (5415 Makena Alanui). Robert Trent Jones, Jr., recently created a new design at this course, which had featured one delightful layout since 1981. He's split the existing course in two and added nine holes on either side to create a lower, seaside layout, called the South Course, and an upper, mountainous layout, the North Course. The South Course is a draw for visitors, but the dramatic scenery from the upper course is equally rewarding, and many of the holes are constructed on the side of a mountain, such as the 14th hole, from which you fire down from a 200-foot elevation to a par-five fairway overlooking an expanse of the Pacific and the islands of Kahoolawe and Molokini. Tel: 879-3344.

Other Maui resort courses that you'll want to play include the new **Waikapu Valley Country Club** course, tucked into the upper hemline of the West Maui Mountains (at 2500 Honoapiilani Highway; Tel: 244-7888) and offering a wonderful perspective of the Valley Isle that no other course can match, and the two well-kept resort designs at the **Royal Kaanapali Resort** (in the Kaanapali Beach Resort, north of Lahaina; Tel: 661-3691), at which the Kaanapali Seniors Classic is held each year.

Public Courses

While unable to match the perfection (or the prices) of the resort courses, Maui's best public courses are the refreshing, Upcountry **Pukalani Country Club**, built on the side of Haleakala Volcano at 360 Pukalani Street, Pukalani (Tel: 572-1314), and **Silversword Golf Club**, located inland of Kihei at 1345 Piilani Highway (Tel: 874-0777).

—*George Fuller*

GETTING AROUND

Arrival by Air

All direct flights to Maui from the U.S. Mainland land at Kahului Airport. United Airlines flies nonstop each day from Los Angeles and San Francisco, with service via Honolulu from Chicago. Delta Airlines flies daily to Kahului from Los Angeles, with service from Atlanta, San Francisco, San Diego, and Dallas. American Airlines lands in Kahului via Honolulu from New York, Chicago, St. Louis, Detroit, Montreal, Houston, Dallas, and Los Angeles. The interisland flight from Honolulu or from one of the other islands is a short, 20- to 30-minute hop. Hawaiian Airlines, Aloha Airlines, and Aloha IslandAir all fly to Kahului.

If you want to touch down at the Kapalua–West Maui Airport you must fly on either Hawaiian Airlines or Aloha IslandAir. This route uses smaller, slower, noisier planes, but you can't beat the convenience if you're staying in West Maui. Interisland flights arrive and depart about every 30 minutes at Maui's two main airports.

Hana Airport is serviced only by Aloha IslandAir. There are relatively few flights per day, just five from Honolulu.

Around on the Island

If you're staying at the Kaanapali or Kapalua resorts, you can catch a free car/van shuttle to your hotel or condominium from the Kapalua–West Maui Airport, or you can rent a car from one of the companies with desks at the airports. All the big-name agencies maintain operations at Kahului, as well as some less-expensive, locally run companies. Be sure to pick up a *Maui Drive Guide* at car-rental desks, which will give you a complete set of maps with close-ups of selected areas.

If you're staying at the Hotel Hana-Maui and land at the Hana Airport, the hotel will pick you up. Or you can reserve a car ahead of time with Dollar Rent A Car. Do not wait until arrival to book a car. The supply is limited, and there are no car-rental desks at Hana Airport.

ACCOMMODATIONS REFERENCE

The rate ranges given here are projections for winter 1993–1994. Unless otherwise indicated, rates are for double room, double occupancy. Hawaii's telephone area code is 808.

- ▶ **Aloha Cottages.** P.O. Box 205, **Hana**, HI 96713. Tel: 248-8420. $55–$80.
- ▶ **Four Seasons Resort.** 3900 Wailea Alanui Drive, **Wailea**, HI 96753. Tel: 874-8000; Fax: 874-6449; elsewhere in U.S., Tel: (800) 334-6284. $300–$600; suites $750–$5,000.
- ▶ **Grand Champions Golf and Tennis Villas.** 3750 Wailea Alanui Drive, **Wailea**, HI 96753. Tel: 879-1595; Fax: 874-3554; elsewhere in U.S., Tel: (800) 367-5246. One and two bedrooms $120–$200.
- ▶ **Grand Wailea Resort & Spa.** 3850 Wailea Alanui Drive, **Wailea**, HI 96753. Tel: 875-1234; Fax: 879-4077; elsewhere in U.S., Tel: (800) 233-1234. $350–$525; suites $750–$8,000.
- ▶ **Haleakala National Park Cabins.** P.O. Box 369, **Makawao**, HI 96788. Tel: 572-9306.
- ▶ **Hana Kai-Maui Resort Condominium.** P.O. Box 38, **Hana**, HI 96713. Tel: 248-8426, 248-7506, or 248-7507; Fax: 248-7482; elsewhere in U.S., Tel: (800) 346-2772. $110–$125.
- ▶ **Hotel Hana-Maui.** Highway 360, P.O. Box 9, **Hana**, HI 96713. Tel: 248-8211; Fax: 248-7202; elsewhere in U.S., Tel: (800) 321-HANA. $305–$525; Sea Ranch Cottages $425–$795.
- ▶ **Hyatt Regency Maui.** 200 Nohea Kai Drive, **Lahaina**, HI 96761. Tel: 661-1234; Fax: 667-4499; elsewhere in U.S., Tel: (800) 233-1234. $240–$430; suites $600–$3,000.
- ▶ **Kaanapali Alii.** 50 Nohea Kai Drive, **Lahaina**, HI 96761. Tel: 667-1400; Fax: 661-0147; elsewhere in U.S., Tel: (800) 642-MAUI. One bedroom $156–$295; two bedrooms $225–$650.
- ▶ **Kapalua Bay Hotel and Villas.** One Bay Drive, **Lahaina**, HI 96761. Tel: 669-5656; Fax: 669-4694; elsewhere in U.S., Tel: (800) 367-8000. $215–$415; one-bedroom villas $275–$375; two-bedroom villas $375–$475.
- ▶ **Kea Lani Hotel.** 4100 Wailea Alanui Drive, **Wailea** HI 96753. Tel: 875-4100; Fax: 875-1200; elsewhere in U.S., Tel: (800) 659-4100. Suites $225–$375; villas $695–$995.
- ▶ **Kula Lodge.** Highway 377, RR 1, Box 475, **Kula**, HI

96790. Tel: 878-1535; Fax: 878-2518; elsewhere in U.S., Tel: (800) 233-1535. $120–$150.

▶ **Lahaina Hotel.** 127 Lahainaluna Road, Lahaina, HI 96761. Tel: 661-0577; Fax: 667-9480; elsewhere in U.S., Tel: (800) 669-3444. $89–$129.

▶ **Mana Kai Maui Resort.** 2960 South Kihei Road, Kihei, HI 96753. Tel: 879-1561; Fax: 874-5042; elsewhere in U.S., Tel: (800) 525-2025. $95–$195.

▶ **Maui Marriott Resort.** 100 Nohea Kai Drive, Lahaina, HI 96761. Tel: 667-1200; Fax: 667-0692; elsewhere in U.S., Tel: (800) 228-9290. $185–$260; suites $400–$1,000.

▶ **Maui Prince Hotel.** 5400 Makena Alanui Drive, Kihei, HI 96753. Tel: 874-1111; Fax: 879-0082; elsewhere in U.S., Tel: (800) 321-MAUI; Fax: (800) 338-8763. $220–$350; suites $400–$800.

▶ **Napili Kai Beach Club.** 5900 Honoapiilani Highway, Lahaina, HI 96761. Tel: 669-6271; Fax: 669-5740; elsewhere in U.S., Tel: (800) 367-5030. $155–$220; suites $220–$295.

▶ **Papakea Resort.** 3543 Lower Honoapiilani Road, Lahaina, HI 96761. Tel: 669-4848; Fax: 669-0061; elsewhere in U.S., Tel: (800) 367-7052. $120–$225.

▶ **Plantation Inn.** 174 Lahainaluna Road, Lahaina, HI 96761. Tel: 667-9225; Fax: 667-9293; elsewhere in U.S., Tel: (800) 433-6815. $99–$175.

▶ **Ritz-Carlton Kapalua.** One Ritz-Carlton Drive, Kapalua, HI 96761. Tel: 669-6200; Fax: 669-3908; elsewhere in U.S., Tel: (800) 241-3333. $285–$495; suites $625–$2,800.

▶ **Royal Lahaina.** 2780 Kekaa Drive, Lahaina, HI 96761. Tel: 661-3611; Fax: 661-6150; elsewhere in U.S., Tel: (800) 447-6925. $130–$265; cottages $225–$295; suites $475–$1,500.

▶ **Sheraton Maui.** 2605 Kaanapali Parkway, Lahaina, HI 96761. Tel: 661-0031; Fax: 661-0458; elsewhere in U.S., Tel: (800) 325-3535. $129–$600.

▶ **Waianapanapa State Park Cabins.** To reserve a cabin, write several months in advance to the Department of Land and Natural Resources, Division of State Parks, 54 South High Street, Wailuku, HI 96793. $5–$10 per person.

▶ **Wailea Oceanfront Hotel.** 2980 South Kihei Road, Kihei, HI 96753. Tel: 879-7744; Fax: 874-0145; interisland, Tel: (800) 272-5275; elsewhere in U.S. and in Canada, Tel: (800) 367-5004; Fax (800) 477-2329. $85–$100.

▶ **Westin Maui.** 2365 Kaanapali Parkway, Lahaina, HI 96761. Tel: 667-2525; Fax: 661-5831; elsewhere in U.S., Tel: (800) 228-3000. $199–$395; suites $500–$2,000.

BED AND BREAKFASTS
▶ **Bloom Cottage**. RR2, Box 229, **Kula**, HI 96790. Tel: 878-1425. $90.

For information about other bed-and-breakfast accommodations on the Hawaiian Islands see the Oahu Outside Honolulu Accommodations Reference.

MOLOKAI

By Thelma Chang

Thelma Chang is a Honolulu-based writer specializing in travel and human-interest stories. She is the author of "I Can Never Forget": Men of the 100th/442nd, *a history of the much-decorated Japanese-American regimental combat team of World War II. Her articles have appeared in such publications as* Westways, Essence, *and the Smithsonian's* Air and Space *magazine.*

Molokai may be only a 15-minute flight east of Honolulu's hustle and bustle, but it is one of the few places in the Islands that remains steeped in the spirituality of its Polynesian past.

It's no wonder that the "Friendly Isle" is a favorite weekend retreat for many refugees from Honolulu seeking escape from Oahu's crowds and traffic jams. On this narrow island—38 miles long from east to west and only 10 miles wide—you won't find such modern trappings as fancy stores, movie theaters, elevators, and high-rises. Instead, you'll see acres of open plains and rolling hills. You'll also discover that a large number of Molokai's 6,500 residents are native Hawaiians who like their traditional, close-to-nature lifestyle. There is physical and psychological balm in the easygoing pace of an island that discourages complicated lists of "things to do." Yet, Molokai unfolds its beauty in a complicated way.

The central plain connects Molokai's two major land masses, volcanic mountains that rose from sea depths about one and a half million years ago—Maunaloa in the west and Kamakou in the east. Over time, streams carved huge canyons on the east side of Molokai, marine erosion created high sea cliffs on the island's windward, northeast-

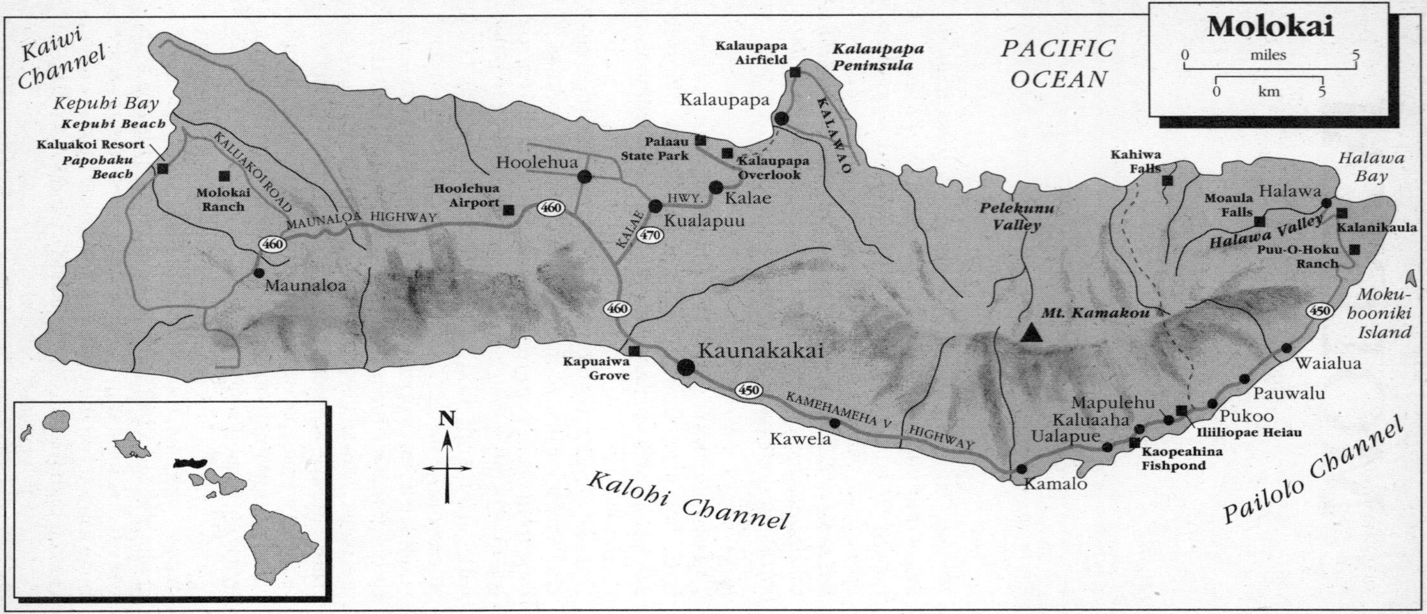
Molokai
0 miles 5
0 km 5
PACIFIC OCEAN
Kaiwi Channel
Kepuhi Bay
Kepuhi Beach
Kaluakoi Resort
Papohaku Beach
Molokai Ranch
KALUAKOI ROAD
MAUNALOA HIGHWAY
460
Maunaloa
Hoolehua
Hoolehua Airport
460
KALAE
HWY.
470
Kualapuu
Kalae
Palaau State Park
Kalaupapa Overlook
Kalaupapa
Kalaupapa Airfield
Kalaupapa Peninsula
KALAWAO
460
Kapuaiwa Grove
Kaunakakai
450
KAMEHAMEHA V HIGHWAY
Kawela
Pelekunu Valley
Mt. Kamakou
Kahiwa Falls
Moaula Falls
Halawa
Halawa Bay
Halawa Valley
Kalanikaula
Puu-O-Hoku Ranch
Moku-hooniki Island
450
Waialua
Pauwalu
Pukoo
Iliiliopae Heiau
Mapulehu
Kaluaaha
Ualapue
Kaopeahina Fishpond
Kamalo
N
Kalohi Channel
Pailolo Channel

ern coast, and a subsequent, smaller eruption produced Kalaupapa Peninsula.

On the western side, giraffes and other exotic creatures roam a wildlife park that borders a resort complex. A bit farther to the east, the fertile plains of Hoolehua (also the location of Molokai's airport) bloom with fields of watermelons, sweet potatoes, onions, and bell peppers—reflecting the people's hope that tourism will be balanced by diversified agriculture after the recent departure of the island's once thriving pineapple industry.

The island's main town, Kaunakakai, sitting by the southern central shoreline, is home to quaint shops, local-style eateries, and people who gather to "talk story." East of Kaunakakai, the island offers spiritually powerful vistas: ancient fishponds, a well-preserved *heiau* (ancient place of worship), coconut groves, tiny churches, country scenes, and unexpected small sandy beaches.

On the North Shore, also known as the "back side," rough seas and sheer cliffs border the hauntingly beautiful area of Kalaupapa (which means "the flat plain").

This last site is one facet of the dramatic past of the island long known as "Molokai Puleoo"—Molokai, place of matured prayer—in reference to the effectiveness of rituals practiced on the island. Precontact Molokai was once a center of ancient learning and a bastion of *kahuna* (priests) who protected the island from invasion, partly through spiritual prestige. Later, in one of the saddest chapters of Island history, Molokai became synonymous with its Hansen's disease (then called leprosy) colony at Kalaupapa. Torn from their families, leprosy patients of the 1800s were dumped at this isolated spot to suffer their pain in loneliness under very harsh conditions. Their despair was eventually alleviated somewhat by the care of many Samaritans, the best known of whom was Father Damien de Veuster. The carpenter-priest dressed open sores, buried the dead, and built shelters, churches, and coffins until he, too, was ravaged by the disease.

MAJOR INTEREST

The West Side
The relaxed atmosphere of Kaluakoi Resort
Sandy beaches
Molokai Ranch Wildlife Park
Maunaloa town

Central Molokai
Kaunakakai, Molokai's charming "trading post" town
Farms and farmland

The East Side
Dramatic and spiritual beauty
Ancient fishponds
Iliiliopae Heiau
The East Molokai Mountains
Pristine bays and beaches
Lush Halawa Valley and Moaula Falls

Kalaupapa
A beautiful site with a tragic history
Kalaupapa Overlook from "topside" Molokai

THE WEST SIDE

KALUAKOI

About 12 miles (19 km) west of Molokai's Hoolehua Airport lies the 6,800-acre resort–residential community of Kaluakoi, set in a somewhat dry terrain that is nonetheless surrounded by rolling hills and green pastures. This oasis includes the luxurious 175-room ▶ **Colony's Kaluakoi Hotel & Golf Club** on Kepuhi Beach, three resort condominiums with fully equipped apartments (the ▶ **Paniolo Hale**, the ▶ **Ke Nani Kai**, and the ▶ **Kaluakoi Villas**), and a championship 18-hole golf course.

Colony's Kaluakoi Hotel has a wide range of accommodations, from modest-sized rooms to suites and cottages with kitchenettes and marvelous views of the ocean and the golf course. The hotel also offers tennis courts that are lit at night, a good restaurant, and other amenities. (No need for air-conditioning here; the wind sometimes comes roaring through your room.) The hotel fronts **Kepuhi Beach**, a wonderful stretch of white sand that is a fine spot for beachcombing, jogging, and suntanning. Swimming and snorkeling may be enjoyed here during calmer seasons, namely summers. (It is always advisable to check with people who know the local waters before venturing offshore.). If you walk the beach on a clear night you will see the bright lights of Oahu, 25 miles away.

South of the hotel are Hawaii's largest white-sand beach, **Papohaku**, and a ten-acre beach park complete with showers and picnic spots. Papohaku's often turbulent sea and pounding waves are tricky, however, and it is wise to stay away from them.

MOLOKAI RANCH
Unlike Molokai's eastern side, which experiences frequent rainfall, the western side is generally dry and sunny. Take advantage of this area's usually bright days by contacting the travel reservations desk at Colony's Kaluakoi Hotel and joining the **Molokai Ranch Wildlife Park Safari**. It's an exciting way to see and photograph zebras, giraffes, axis deer, and many other resident animals, numbering 1,000, who greet the tour director for "snacks." You can also see part of the 52,000-acre Molokai Ranch, the island's largest private landholder.

MAUNALOA
From the resort, a ten-minute drive up Kaluakoi Road, then southwest on the Maunaloa Highway (Highway 460), will take you to Maunaloa, a former pineapple plantation town that is home today to just a few stores, houses, and a restaurant. One of the most intriguing shops here is the **Big Wind Kite Factory**, filled with international kites of all sizes, shapes, and colors. If you feel you're being stared at, you are; on the ceiling huge kites in the shapes of bats, butterflies, and other creatures peer down at you. Next door is the **Plantation Gallery**, crammed with knick-knacks ranging from local handicrafts, books, and cards to jewelry, Indonesian fabric, and little wooden animals from Bali. Hungry shoppers may stop and rest nearby at **Jojo's Café**, a spot known locally for its fresh fish dishes.

KAUNAKAKAI

To drive from Hoolehua Airport to the main town of Kaunakakai, follow Highway 460 east, then south toward the ocean. Watch for **Kapuaiwa Coconut Grove**, once the site of a thousand coconut trees planted by King Kamehameha V in the 1860s. Though reduced in size today, the grove presents a pretty picture of old Hawaii. If you walk through the grove, keep alert for falling coconuts, and try to find the freshwater spring bubbling at the ocean's edge.

Kaunakakai resembles a trading post straight out of the Old West. Cowboys (*paniolo*) and fishermen join grandmas, grandpas, dogs, and store proprietors at wooden false-front buildings for the latest news. Shopping is very limited, but the town is a wonderful place to mingle with the people, learn about Molokai—stop by the **Molokai Fish & Dive** shop and ask about snorkeling or sailing cruises from Kaunakakai Wharf—and taste some local fare. **Kanemitsu Bakery**, one of the island's oldest establishments, is the source of the popular Molokai bread, fresh-baked cookies, and local-style meals, such as teriyaki steak and rice. Other options for dining include Filipino dishes at **Oviedo's** and take-out food at **Rabang's** or **Outpost Natural Foods**. The well-loved Mid Nite Inn burned down early in 1992; there's talk of rebuilding, but no definite plans yet.

Kaunakakai's shoreline is graced by two cottage-style hotels: the ► **Pau Hana Inn** and the ► **Hotel Molokai**—comfortable, no-frills havens with lots of Island atmosphere. Sandy beaches front the hotel, but the water here is too murky and shallow for swimming. There are also fully equipped vacation apartments at the oceanfront ► **Molokai Shores**, which is surrounded by tropical gardens.

Like a lifelong friend, the Pau Hana Inn, Molokai's oldest existing hotel, is a popular end-of-day gathering spot (*pau hana* means "finished with work") for fun-loving islanders, who unwind at the hotel's outdoor bar under the benevolence of a century-old banyan tree. For oceanside dining try the **Holoholo Kai Restaurant** at the Hotel Molokai, where you can enjoy a (daylight) view of Lanai across the sea.

THE EAST SIDE

A 30-mile (48-km) stretch of the Kamehameha V Highway (Highway 450) leads east, then northeast, from Kaunakakai to lush Halawa Valley. Pack a snack, check your gas tank, and allow at least half a lazy day for a round trip that takes in much scenic and spiritual beauty. The road hugs a southern shore fringed with ancient Hawaiian fishponds that deserve more than passing mention.

Conceived in the 1400s, the fishponds were a natural yet sophisticated kind of aquaculture. Like other early Hawaiian inventions, they illustrate the people's intelligent and sensitive approach to gathering sustenance for survival from their environment.

Typically, the Hawaiians built the fishponds by constructing an encircling wall of stone or coral in the sea or by connecting two points of land with a wall. Wooden grates were placed at strategic points in the ponds to ensure circulation and the entrance of young fish, which eventually grew too fat to escape. Some ponds remain, while others have been destroyed by silt, tidal action, and people.

EAST TO HALAWA

A significant event in Hawaiian history took place at **Kawela** ("the heat of battle"), about 3 miles (5 km) east of Kaunakakai. Near Kawela is the site where Hawaii's King Kamehameha I won a battle in the 1790s that placed Molokai under his reign. (No doubt part of the king's overall military success in placing the Islands under one chief was his acquisition of the cannons and other weapons brought by Westerners.)

Western impact can also be seen farther east on the Kamehameha V Highway at **Kamalo**, where Father Damien erected St. Joseph's Church, a tiny chapel with a tall steeple, one of three surviving churches the priest built on Molokai. From the church, look toward the East Molokai Mountains and the pristine beauty of **Mount Kamakou**, the island's highest elevation at 4,970 feet—a dreamlike sight that has inspired numerous oil and watercolor artists.

Images of local life are probably the most enchanting part about the drive to and from Halawa Valley. Chickens, ducks, and roosters scamper alongside the road, pecking at the dirt; a horse munches on grass; an egret sits contentedly. Old and new houses in east Molokai reflect the subtle changes taking place. At one turn, there's a series of ramshackle wooden homes in need of paint and fixing up; at the next turn, modern, almost luxurious, beach houses loom into view. And all along, pockets of sandy beach dot the shoreline.

The spiritual presence of early Hawaiians can be felt at Mapulehu, site of the magnificent 13th-century **Iliiliopae Heiau**. About the size of a football field, the *heiau* is a platform consisting of numerous rocks. Legend says the heiau was constructed by Hawaiian *menehune,* little people not unlike the Irish leprechauns. According to the legend, the menehune formed a chain of many miles, passing the rocks hand to hand from the beach at Wailau on the island's north coast through rough, steep terrain inland.

You can get to the heiau by means of the **Molokai Wagon Ride**, a horse-and-wagon journey that bumps and grinds through bramble bushes and the Mapulehu Mango

Grove. Wear comfortable clothing and footwear, because the trip involves a short hike and the crossing of a streambed. If you really want to be prepared, bring a raincoat or umbrella. The wagon ride leaves from the 15-mile marker on Highway 450, one mile short of Pukoo.

Conducted by lifelong Molokai residents, the tour offers visitors a chance to meet locals who love their island—Larry Helm and his partners in the tour operation will regale you with song, dance, and Island stories. As an option, you can combine the tour with a special luau lunch at the Hotel Molokai in Kaunakakai. Tel: 558-8380 or 567-6773.

The road then twists and climbs to the private Puu-O-Hoku Ranch ("hill of stars"). The top of this bluff boasts gorgeous views of west Maui and Mokuhooniki Island, the latter used for bombing practice by the U.S. military during World War II. Past the ranch's entrance, on private property, is **Kalanikaula**, a sacred *kukui* (candlenut) grove that once surrounded the home of a powerful *kahuna* (priest) whose *mana* (spiritual force) continues to be respected; the grove is one of the most sacred places in Hawaii.

STAYING ON THE EAST SIDE

If you wish to stay on the east side you might rent a vacation apartment at the ▶ **Wavecrest Resort** in Ualapue, a short distance east of Kamalo. Just past Ualapue, at Kaluaaha, there's another church built by Damien, Our Lady of Seven Sorrows. Across the way is **Kaopeahina**, a well-preserved fishpond.

Up the coast from Iliiliopae Heiau are Pukoo Lagoon and a real get-away-from-it-all rental opportunity: ▶ **Pukoo Vacation Rental**, the second floor of Diane and Larry Swenson's beachfront cottage, complete with kitchen and views of the ocean and Maui island.

HALAWA VALLEY

A few more zigzags on the road and Halawa Valley—the oldest recorded inhabited area on Molokai—unfolds its beauty. Far below, a W-shaped bay fronts the grassy plains of this valley, which is home to only a few people. Inland, the thick tropical jungle with waterfalls is visited only by the hikers who come to this place for its utter seclusion.

The 3-mile (5-km) descent into the valley on a narrow road can be a hairy one, most people honking their horns when they hit blind curves. Still, the valley is popular with picnickers and nature lovers, who sometimes trek into the jungle—take mosquito repellent—to see the 250-

foot-high **Moaula Falls**, legendary home of a giant sea dragon. It's a complicated trail that requires the crossing of a stream or two that can be waist or shoulder high after a rain, so it's best to inquire locally first about safety conditions. You may phone Zachary Helm, head of Molokai's Department of Parks and Recreation, for more information; Tel: 553-5141. (In any case, let people at your hotel know about any plans for going off the beaten track.)

THE NORTH SHORE

Beyond Halawa Valley lie the North Shore and some of the most spectacular, hidden parts of Molokai: awesome 3,300-foot sea cliffs (among the world's highest) and wilderness areas that may be seen only by prearranged boat, helicopter, or kayak tours. The seas here are so rough that even kayaks are restricted to summer months, and then only when weather permits. Kalaupapa is the only place on the North Shore that may be visited throughout the year. (See Getting Around for excursions to all of these destinations.)

Kalaupapa

The history of this lovely, lonely peninsula at the bottom of rugged sea cliffs in the middle of the North Shore sparked strong emotion in author James Michener: "In the previous history of the world no such hellish spot had ever stood in such heavenly surroundings."

In these "heavenly surroundings," leprosy devastated the lives of more than 8,000 people who had been separated from their families and brought here from the mid-1800s to the early 1900s. Afflicted native Hawaiians, who had historically lived in a communal culture of extended families, could not understand the imposed Western value of isolation. Lonely and lacking adequate food or shelter, the first patients died quickly from despair and the harsh elements. (The powerful, howling winds at Kalaupapa can move people and make missiles out of objects.)

Mercifully, improvements came with such caretakers as Father Damien, Mother Marianne Cope, and Brother Joseph Dutton, who fought the bureaucracy and worked tirelessly for their patients. (The Roman Catholic church has placed Father Damien in its canonization process.)

Today, more than 100 years after the first ships dumped their patients here, Kalaupapa looks like the pristine paradise it was meant to be.

From "topside" Molokai ("topside" is local parlance for the upper, or elevated, part of the island) there are two ways to visit Kalaupapa Peninsula, which is located at the bottom of steep cliffs: by air or on foot. No matter which method you choose, there's only one daily tour of the peninsula itself—it starts in the morning and will take most of the day, so coordinate your independent plans with Richard Marks at **Damien Molokai Tours** (see Getting Around)—and pack a lunch. (There used to be a mule train that took visitors to the peninsula below, but the rough trail and liability problems have for now eliminated this unforgettable way of reaching Kalaupapa.)

THE ROUTE TO KALAUPAPA

For a spectacular bird's-eye view of what's entailed if you hike to Kalaupapa Peninsula, drive to **Kalaupapa Overlook**, about 20 minutes from Kaunakakai. Go northwest on Highway 460 (Maunaloa Highway), take the right fork, which is the Kalae Highway (Highway 470), and head north. The highway meanders through **Kualapuu**, the former Del Monte plantation town, and passes several other attractions before it reaches the overlook. The **Cook House**, known for its home-style food, and **Purdy's Natural Macadamia Nut Farm** (also known as Purdy's Nuts), are just off the highway. Look for the sign that says "Farrington," and make a left turn; the Cook House (Tel: 567-6185) will be on your right. Purdy's (Tel: 567-6601 or 567-6495) is just up the road from the Cook House.

Back on Kalae Highway, still heading north, you'll come across an access road on the left that leads to the newly refurbished nine-hole Ironwood Hills Golf Course. If you stay on the highway, the **Meyer Sugar Mill** (Tel: 587-6436), an authentic restoration of the only surviving 19th-century sugar mill in Hawaii, soon appears on the left side. The road continues to Palaau State Park and the parking lot at the end of the highway. The trail to the north leads to the 1,600-foot-high overlook and a sight to behold: the North Shore, its 3,000-foot cliffs, and, a tiny dot below, Kalaupapa town.

VISITING KALAUPAPA

Weather permitting (we don't recommend the hike if it's rainy), the hike down into Kalaupapa is an unforgettable experience. From topside the trail meanders down **Kalau-**

papa Trail more than three miles and 26 switchbacks to the settlement below. This rough trail cuts through rain forest and sharp drop-offs, but your nerves are soothed with vistas of the distant peninsula and the Pacific Ocean—fabulous scenery as far as the eye can see.

At the bottom, you're likely to join others who've hiked down or taken the three-minute topside-to-Kalaupapa flight on IslandAir or Air Molokai.

The bumpy daily bus tour of the peninsula treks through the tiny town of Kalaupapa, a beautiful rain forest, and green valleys. Almost like a movie setting of a late-1800s Old West outpost, the town itself appears devoid of people and frozen in time. However, it is home to some 95 people, several churches of different denominations, a general store, and a post office, most of which are off-limits to visitors. Nearly 11,000 acres of Kalaupapa, including three valleys, were declared a national historical park in 1980.

Certainly a highlight is a visit to the windy and rocky east side, **Kalawao**, where crashing waves serve as a background to Father Damien's newly restored church, St. Philomena, the only structure left from the settlement's early days. Throughout the tour, marked and unmarked grave sites remind you of Kalaupapa's grim past.

Although Kalaupapa's remaining 95 residents are free to come and go—sulfone drugs cured and arrested the disease in the 1940s—most are old and choose to spend their later years in this quiet village.

GOLF COURSES

Molokai is proudly undeveloped, with but a few lodging choices and only two golf courses. It is a wound-down island and that's its charm; be prepared to relax.

Resort Courses

Kaluakoi Golf Course, next to Colony's Kaluakoi Hotel, on the island's west coast, designed in 1977 by Ted Robinson, is one of the hidden golf gems of Hawaii. No other course can top it for sheer beauty. On the first hole, for example, you'll find yourself doing what may be two of your favorite things—going to the beach and playing golf at the same time. The hole is bordered all along one side by the waves and white sand of Kepuhi Beach. A beautiful course throughout, Kaluakoi boasts a strong finishing trio, with the par three 16th shooting over a yawning, 190-

yard V-shaped ravine, and the 17th and 18th firing blind from the tee. Tel: 552-2739.

Public Courses
Once you've played your fill at Kaluakoi—which could take quite a few games—you must try **Ironwood Hills Golf Course**, a charming, local-style nine-hole layout on the island's top side off Highway 470 between Kualapuu and Kalaupapa. Ironwood Hills is a fun course in good condition. Tel: 567-6000.

—George Fuller

GETTING AROUND

Arrival by Air
Molokai is served by Hawaiian Airlines, Air Molokai, and IslandAir, with frequent daily flights from Oahu and Maui. Molokai's airport, Hoolehua, is located in the central part of the island. IslandAir provides service between "topside" Hoolehua Airport and Kalaupapa.

Around on the Island
There's no bus service on Molokai, but there are three taxi companies: Molokai Taxi, Molokai Off-Road Tours & Taxi, and Kukui Tours & Limousine. The island deserves a leisurely pace, so it's advisable to rent a car. There are several auto rentals on Molokai, including Budget; Tel: 567-6877. Note: Most gas stations on Molokai are closed on Sundays.

Touring and Trekking Outfits
For information about the **Molokai Wagon Ride**, contact Larry Helm, P.O. Box 56, Hoolehua, Molokai 96729; Tel: 558-8380 or 567-6773. The tour leaves at noon from a spot along Highway 450, 15 miles (24 km) east of Kaunakakai, marked by their sign.

Kayaking treks to Molokai's North Shore may be arranged with Kayak Kauai, P.O. Box 508, Hanalei, HI 96714, Tel: 826-9844. For up-to-the-minute information on sailing, sightseeing, air, and fishing cruises, contact the Destination Molokai Association; Tel: 553-3876; elsewhere in U.S., (800) 800-6367.

If you wish to see Molokai's North Shore by air, contact Papillon Hawaiian Helicopters, P.O. Box 1690, Lahaina, Maui 96761, Tel: 669-4884; elsewhere in U.S., (800) 367-7095. Papillon offers North Shore tours from Oahu and

Maui. (At this time Molokai has no island-based helicopter service.)

Some restrictions apply if you go to Kalaupapa. Visitors must be over 16 and all tours of the area must be escorted. Cameras are permitted, but pictures of residents are not allowed. As there are no overnight accommodations at Kalaupapa, it is advisable to have confirmed departure reservations if you plan to leave by air. For more particulars about the hike or fly-in packages to Kalaupapa, contact tour operator Richard Marks at **Damien Molokai Tours**, P.O. Box 1, Kalaupapa, HI 96742, Tel: 567-6171.

ACCOMMODATIONS REFERENCE

The rate ranges given here are projections for winter 1993–1994. Unless otherwise indicated, rates are for double room, double occupancy. Hawaii's telephone area code is 808.

▶ **Colony's Kaluakoi Hotel & Golf Club.** P.O. Box 1977, **Maunaloa**, HI 96770. Tel: 552-2555; Fax: 552-2821; elsewhere in U.S., Tel: (800) 777-1700. $90–$240.

▶ **Kaluakoi Villas.** P.O. Box 200, **Maunaloa**, HI 96770. Tel: 552-2721; Fax: 552-2201; elsewhere in U.S., Tel: (800) 525-1470. $68–$139.

▶ **Ke Nani Kai.** P.O. Box 126, **Maunaloa**, HI 96770. Tel: 552-2761; Fax: 552-0045; elsewhere in U.S., Tel: (800) 888-2791. $105–$150.

▶ **Hotel Molokai.** P.O. Box 546, **Kaunakakai**, HI 96748. Tel: 553-5347; Fax: 531-4004; elsewhere in U.S., Tel: (800) 423-6656. $55–$115.

▶ **Molokai Shores.** P.O. Box 1037, **Kaunakakai**, HI 96748. Tel: 553-5954; Fax: 553-5954; elsewhere in U.S., Tel: (800) 922-9700; internationally, Tel: (800) 367-7042. $85–$115.

▶ **Paniolo Hale.** P.O. Box 190, **Maunaloa**, HI 96770. Tel: 552-2731; Fax: 552-2288; elsewhere in U.S., Tel: (800) 367-2984. $95–$195.

▶ **Pau Hana Inn.** P.O. Box 860, **Kaunakakai**, HI 96748. Tel: 553-5342; Fax: 531-4004; elsewhere in U.S., Tel: (800) 423-6656. $45–$90.

▶ **Pukoo Vacation Rental.** P.O. Box 280, **Kualapuu**, HI 96757. Fax: 567-6721. Tel: 567-9268. $75.

▶ **Wavecrest Resort.** Star Route 155, **Ualapue**, HI 96748. Tel: 558-8103; Fax: 558-8206; elsewhere in U.S., Tel: (800) 367-2980. $85–$115.

BED AND BREAKFASTS
For information about bed-and-breakfast accommodations on the Hawaiian Islands see the Oahu Outside Honolulu Accommodations Reference.

LANAI

By Thelma Chang

Peaceful Lanai is one of those get-away-from-it-all islands that stands on the brink of being "discovered" at several different levels—physically, emotionally, spiritually.

It's easy to see why this small Hawaiian island, just 13 miles wide and 18 miles long, attracts visitors eager to escape today's hectic high-speed world. Long known as the "Pineapple Island," Lanai is now developing a reputation as a serene private island in the face of a changing economy—from pineapples to tourists. It's a change not even Boston businessman James Dole could have foreseen in the early 1900s when he bought virtually all of the island from missionaries, imported workers (mainly from the Philippines), and made the spiny fruit the economic mainstay of Lanai.

However, Lanai is more complex than its visible, gradually changing face. The island unfolds its landscape in a sequence of interesting and sometimes bizarre contrasts, especially when seen from the rain forest of Lanaihale, the island's highest point. At one moment, there are only barren lands where pineapples once thrived; at another, dusty trails and rocky barren surfaces that give way to stunning vistas of steep cliffs, eroded canyons, shimmering bays, and a beautiful sandy beach. A turbulent ocean borders the east side where Lanai keeps its secrets of the past—a *heiau,* a deserted village, and a windswept beach.

Lanai, located about seven miles south of Molokai and west of Maui, has long been the focus of different perceptions. Polynesians avoided the island for centuries, fearing it was inhabited by ghosts. Only when Lanai was deemed safe did Hawaiians migrate to the island, probably in the 1400s. In the late 1700s a European ship circled the island but chose not to land. In ancient chants the

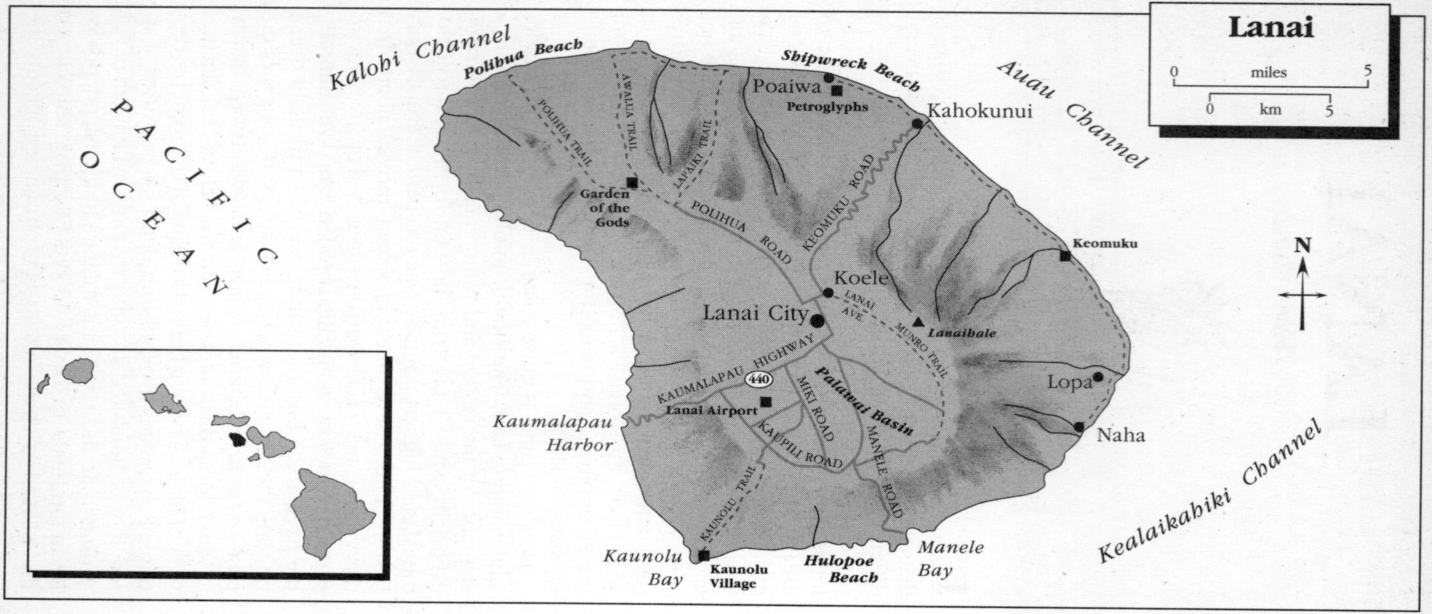

Lanai
0 miles 5
0 km 5
N
PACIFIC OCEAN
Kalohi Channel
Polihua Beach
Shipwreck Beach
Poaiwa
Petroglyphs
Kahokunui
Auau Channel
POLIHUA TRAIL
AWALUA TRAIL
LAPAIKI TRAIL
Garden of the Gods
POLIHUA ROAD
KEOMUKU ROAD
Keomuku
Koele
LANAI AVE.
Lanai City
Lanaihale
MUNRO TRAIL
KAUMALAPAU HIGHWAY
440
Lanai Airport
MIKI ROAD
Palawai Basin
KAUPILI ROAD
MANELE ROAD
Lopa
Naha
Kaumalapau Harbor
KAUNOLU TRAIL
Kaunolu Bay
Kaunolu Village
Hulopoe Beach
Manele Bay
Kealaikahiki Channel

place was called "Red Lanai," referring to the red dirt that flies in the wind and tints everything it touches. Today residents sometimes witness a thick, ghostly mist that covers the fields in **Palawai Basin**, an extinct volcanic crater that is Lanai's best farmland. "It's beautiful in an eerie way," says a lifelong resident of the basin, which is also home to rock formations engraved with early Hawaiian petroglyphs.

Lanai's red dirt, rough terrain, and cool evening temperatures (particularly from November through April) demand common sense, practical clothing, a four-wheel-drive vehicle, and specific directions from old-timers if you plan to go off the beaten track. Vehicle rentals may be arranged directly with or Lanai City Service (see Getting Around) or through the hotels.

MAJOR INTEREST

Relaxed, friendly atmosphere
Small-town Lanai City
Kaumalapau Harbor
Kaunolu Village historic ruins
Hulopoe Beach and Manele Bay small-boat harbor
Lanaihale's summit and sweeping views of neighboring islands
Dramatic historical settings at Keomuku village and Kaiolohia (Shipwreck Beach)

EXPLORING LANAI

For decades the only guest stop in Lanai was the ten-room ▶ **Hotel Lanai**, nestled among pine trees on a hill in tiny Lanai City. It's a pleasant, unpretentious, plantation-style house without television or telephones in its rooms, but with a front porch that invites neighbors to sit and "talk story." There you'll likely see a microcosm of the island's 2,500 residents: Hawaiians, Asians, Caucasians, and a few blacks and Portuguese. And often you'll see visitors with sturdy boots or snorkeling gear, ready for rugged trails and some of the clearest waters Hawaii has to offer.

On Lanai's trails, nature lovers in particular can find something suited to their individual preference—from easy, casual strolls to rough, challenging journeys by four-wheel-drive vehicle or foot. You may, for instance, take a two-mile hike on the Munro Trail (see below), which starts at Koele, and then follow another footpath that circles back to Koele. Serious, hardy hikers who don't mind rocky terrain and bramble bushes may explore such out-of-the-way spots as the Garden of the Gods, northwest of Lanai City.

A short walk down the hill from the Hotel Lanai leads into the island's only town, **Lanai City**, where most of the island's people still live in plantation housing—modest wooden homes erected in the early 1900s. Graced by giant Norfolk Island pines, the homes border the large, grassy town square, a friendly get-together spot for people who stop in town to frequent Lanai City's small eateries and markets, browse through the quaint shops and read the bulletin board at the post office. Blink and you'll pass Lanai's diminutive police station, courtroom, and jail, a sign that Lanai, so far, enjoys a low crime rate.

The town itself, located almost in the geographic center of the island, serves as a handy reference point, because the island's 30-odd miles of paved roads branch from Lanai City to the coast in three main directions: southwest, to Kaumalapau Harbor; south, to Hulopoe Beach; and north, to Kaiolohia, more commonly known as Shipwreck Beach.

Castle & Cooke, Lanai's major landowner since 1961 (owned by businessman David Murdock since the mid-1980s), has essentially phased out its pineapple operation in recent years. Although there are spots where pineapples continue to flourish, dead pineapple fields testify to Lanai's changed economic face. In some areas carrots, onions, and eggplants, grown with organic farming methods, show promise of a viable economic future. Meanwhile, Castle & Cooke's new emphasis on controlled development and tourism can be seen in the firm's two luxury resorts—the 102-room Lodge at Koele and the 250-room Manele Bay Hotel.

STAYING ON LANAI

The ▶ **Manele Bay Hotel**, perched on a terraced cliff overlooking the white-sand beach of Hulopoe on the island's south coast, is a harbinger of the shift in the island's fortunes, as tourism slowly replaces the pineapple industry. The hotel features traditional Island-style architecture set amidst acres of gardens and waterfalls and has an "old Hawaii" atmosphere. Most of the rooms have ocean views. The Manele has three dining spots—the formal Ihilani Dining Room, the casual yet elegant Hulopoe Court and the Pool Grill (reservations recommended for lunch and dinner at all Manele Bay dining rooms; Tel: 565-2290). The Manele's menus highlight freshly grown produce. An 18-hole championship golf course near the Manele Bay Hotel remains in the planning stage.

A 20-minute drive north of Manele Bay, in the center of the island just north of Lanai City, is the ▶ **Lodge at Koele**, a stunning country-style estate. Here, at the cool elevation of 1,700 feet, you'll find turn-of-the-century elegance: massive stone fireplaces, plush couches, Old World antiques, and high-beamed ceilings. The lodge's formal restaurant, known simply as the "formal dining room," specializes in cuisine largely prepared from fresh produce grown on the hotel's 50-acre garden. (Jackets are required for the formal dining room.) A fine but casual dining experience can be enjoyed at the Lodge's Terrace Room (for reservations at both of the Lodge's restaurants, Tel: 565-4580). Golfers will relish the Experience at Koele, a spectacular 18-hole course designed by Greg Norman (see Golf Courses, below). Other amenities include a swimming pool and spa and facilities for croquet and lawn bowling.

Both the Lodge at Koele and the Manele Bay Hotel are managed by Rockresorts and offer guests a wide range of amenities, from tennis and horseback riding to snorkeling and fine dining.

South from Lanai City

Lanai's Highway 440 leads southwest from Lanai City to **Kaumalapau Harbor**, where pineapples used to be loaded on boats for shipment to Honolulu's canneries 60 miles away. This once-thriving industry disappeared from the island in 1992. Off this highway and south around the airport, a jolting drive down bumpy trails takes you to Kaunolu Bay and into Hawaii's past. The ruins of **Kaunolu Village**, King Kamehameha's summer home, offer a complete archaeological site: an abandoned village, house platforms, and gravestones. Locals respect such cultural sites; stories abound of people who have disturbed certain spots, experienced unexplainable events, and quickly returned such "souvenirs" as rocks and plants by air mail.

Hulopoe Bay is a 9-mile (14½ km) drive on Manele Road south from Lanai City. At the end of a scenic ride through former pineapple fields you'll be rewarded by lovely **Hulopoe Beach** and a park with picnic tables and barbecue pits. Snorkeling fans will find some of the clearest waters around.

At nearby **Manele Bay**, to the east, small leisure sailboats bob about, where once only the fishing boats of Lanai's families were moored. This scene is more than symbolic; change is in the air, and it leaves some residents worried about the survival of their cooperative, sharing lifestyle.

Lanaihale

The new hotels and the old pineapple fields, and much more, can be seen from Lanaihale, Lanai's highest ridge. At 3,370 feet, the ridge affords a knock-your-socks-off experience of rain forest and gorgeous views. You get there by means of the **Munro Trail**, named after a naturalist who planted pine trees along the ridgeline in 1910. The trees serve as natural windbreaks around Lanai City and collect moisture from passing clouds, enhancing the island's water supply.

It's wise to allow about a half a day (more if you plan to hike) for a leisurely and bumpy ride to and from Lanaihale's summit. From Lanai City, head north on Lanai Avenue, past the golf course and the Lodge at Koele. At about the point where you see a graveyard to the right, take the middle fork—the Munro Trail—which leads to flat terrain at the top. On your way up, stay on well-travelled track. You'll pass Hookio Ridge, where Lanai's warriors unsuccessfully fought invading forces from the Big Island of Hawaii in 1778. However, it's at the top that you turn your motor off, unwind, and enjoy a dramatic feast for the eyes. The views of the major islands (all of them, except Niihau and Kauai) resemble dreamlike paintings so beautiful you can't take your eyes away. No wonder people often come here at sunrise or sunset, with a snack, coffee, and their thoughts—and the silent rain forest for company.

Windward Lanai

From the ridge you can also see Lanai's northern, or windward, side, which includes the ruins of Keomuku village and Shipwreck Beach, both requiring at least an hour's travel time from Lanai City. From the ridge go back to Lanai Avenue, follow it north to Koele where it connects with Keomuku Road, then take Keomuku to the coastline.

The left fork at the coast leads to the stark beauty of Kaiolohia, familiarly known as **Shipwreck Beach**, where wooden ships and steamers were swept by powerful trade winds and treacherous currents toward Lanai's reef. The beach was used as a convenient dumping ground, where old ships were purposely beached and abandoned. Some shipwrecks are visible, such as the remains of the USS *Liberty*.

A right at the fork leads to the ghost town of **Keomuku** and a bit of Lanai history. The site was once home to a sugar mill and its Asian workers. Hawaiians believe unfortunate events occurred because some stones were removed by *haole* (Westerners) so that a railroad could be built: Not long after the disturbance, the mill's sweet water turned salty, and a plague devastated the population. Before the sugar mill, Keomuku had been inhabited by native Hawaiians, who left behind, among other things, a *heiau* (temple), and it seems to have been this heiau that had been disturbed.

Another facet of Lanai's mysterious past can be found at Kanepuu, also called the **Garden of the Gods**, about 7 miles (11 km) northwest of Lanai City along Polihua Road. It resembles a moonscape, strewn with large boulders and strange lava formations. The rocks look as if some mischievous god playfully dropped them from the sky, letting them fall where they may. Some visitors time their trip so that they can watch the rocks change color with the setting sun. If there is such a thing as an otherworldly spot, this is it.

All over Lanai, such strong spiritual "presence" is what many Lanai residents wish to respect and protect as they face the ever increasing pressures of commercial development.

Golf Courses

Until very recently, few travellers ventured as far afield as the tiny island of Lanai. But with the decline of the pineapple industry the island has begun efforts to attract a modest tourist trade. The new Lodge at Koele and Manele Bay Hotel, ultra-luxurious properties, will both hang their banners on exquisite golf courses.

The first, called the **Experience at Koele**, an upcountry layout, designed by Greg Norman and Ted Robinson next to the Lodge at Koele, is already open. The setting for this course is unlike any other in Hawaii. As you weave your way along the high-mountain ridges of Lanai, where the first nine holes are played, the only sounds you'll hear are the wind blowing softly down the pine-lined slopes and your own sighs of wonder at being in such a magnificent place. Axis deer and wild pheasant can be seen roaming the course. When mature, the Experience at Koele will be considered among the top Hawaii golf courses. Tel: 565-4653.

A Jack Nicklaus course called the **Challenge at Manele**, adjacent to the Manele Bay Hotel, is scheduled to open on Christmas Day 1993. The Challenge measures 7,088 yards from the tips and features three dramatic holes built upon the cliffs above Hulopoe Bay. Tel: 565-3800.

—*George Fuller*

GETTING AROUND

Just 20 minutes flying time from Honolulu, Lanai is served by Hawaiian Airlines, and IslandAir. The island's hotels provide complimentary transit service to and from the airport for their guests. Give them your flight information when you make reservations. Direct arrangements for four-wheel-drive vehicles may be made through your hotel or with Lanai City Service & U Drive, the island's outlet for Dollar Rent A Car (Tel: 565-7227 or 800-376-7006).

Hiking on Lanai

Serious hikers on Lanai may want to pick up Craig Chisholm's 1985 guide *Hawaiian Hiking Trails,* Fernglen Press, Lake Oswego, Oregon. Rockresorts, operator of the Lodge at Koele and the Manele Bay Hotel, has recently published an extensive Lanai guide booklet that includes numerous hiking and driving trails. Inquire at the concierge desk at either hotel.

ACCOMMODATIONS REFERENCE

The rate ranges given here are projections for winter 1993–1994. Unless otherwise indicated, rates are for double room, double occupancy. Hawaii's telephone area code is 808.

▶ **Hotel Lanai**. P.O. Box A-119, **Lanai City**, HI 96763. Tel: 565-7211; Fax: 565-7601; elsewhere in U.S., Tel: (800) 624-8849. $104; suite $135.

▶ **Lodge at Koele**. P.O. Box 774, **Lanai City**, HI 96763. Tel: 565-7300; Fax: 565-4561; elsewhere in U.S., Tel: (800) 321-4666. $295–$350; suites $475–$975.

▶ **Manele Bay Hotel**. P.O. Box 774, **Lanai City**, HI 96763. Tel: 565-7700; Fax: 565-2483; elsewhere in U.S., Tel: (800) 321-4666. $295–$475; suites $595–$2,000.

BED AND BREAKFASTS

For information about bed-and-breakfast accommodations on the Hawaiian Islands see the Oahu Outside Honolulu Accommodations Reference.

KAUAI

By John W. Perry

A Pacific historian partial to Kauai labeled it "a separate kingdom" in recognition of the island's long history of linguistic and cultural separation from the rest of the Hawaiian Islands. Even an attempted invasion from Oahu by Kamehameha the Great failed because of canoe-destroying winds in the channel separating the two islands, and that same geographic isolation—Kauai is Hawaii's northernmost landfall and, with tiny Niihau, stands alone far to the west of Oahu—deflected much of the decimation the post-contact era inflicted on Hawaii's other islands. In many respects Kauai has retained a separateness of spirit, not just place, and, though aptly nicknamed the "Garden Isle," is remembered at journey's end as an island apart, a special port of call outside of Hawaii's mainstream destinations—Oahu, Maui, and the Big Island's Kohala and Kona coasts.

Kauai's physical beauty is stunning, taking a back seat to no other island, not even to Polynesia's "Island of Love" (Tahiti), Micronesia's "Garden Isle" (Pohnpei), or Melanesia's Aoba, fiction's Bali Hai. A popular misconception is that Kauai's major attraction is its resorts, but it is the island itself, with its beauty and splendor, that attracted the resort development and that remains preeminent. Even Kauai's often maligned trademark, *paka ua* (raindrops), the gentle waters that grow the garden in the Garden Isle, has a special significance in Hawaii, having passed into the language as a proverbial saying: *ka ua loku o Hana-lei,* "the pouring rain of Hanalei" (Hanalei being a town on Kauai's north coast). A typical island-wide weather report is "mostly sunny after morning rains," and umbrellas as well as swimsuits are appropriate gifts for Kauai-bound visitors.

Those who like rain, a tropical landscape, and an island wilderness that is still *wilderness* will love Kauai.

MAJOR INTEREST

White-sand beaches
Lush, tropical scenery

Lihue and Environs
Kauai Lagoons resort
Kilohana plantation
Grove Farm Homestead

Poipu and Koloa
Sunny-side resorts
Old Koloa Town restoration

The Waimea Area and the West Coast
Country towns
Allerton Estate botanical garden
Waimea Plantation Cottages
High-country state parks
Waimea Canyon
The spectacular scenery of the Na Pali coast from Kalalau Lookout

Wailua and the Coconut Coast
Coco Palms Resort
Hawaiian legends and history along the Wailua River

The North Shore
Beautiful views and scenery
Kilauea Point lighthouse and wildlife refuge
Princeville's scenic resorts and golf course
Hanalei bayside town
Lumahai Beach
Kalalau foot trail to the Na Pali Coast

TRAVELLING AROUND KAUAI

A traveller's mental map of Kauai, drawn from the east-coast county seat of **Lihue** (which is the site of the main airport), is, like the island itself, almost circular. The **Poipu-Koloa** area, destination of most new arrivals because of its plentiful sun, accommodations, and beach activities, lies to the southwest of Lihue; the coastline west of Koloa is a thoroughfare for cars en route to the backcountry wilderness and high-country parkland above Waimea that delivers green forests, peaceful hiking, rustic cabins, and magnificent views. Those who make the trek west will be charmed along the way by small rural towns such as Hanapepe and Waimea and pleasantly surprised by the expansive, largely undiscovered beaches they'll find on the west coast.

North of Lihue on the east coast is the **Wailua-Kapaa** Coconut Coast region, a way station for those on their way to **Hanalei** and the wet northern coast, or a pleasant stop for those in search of a simpler, local experience (or the Wailua River). The drive to Hanalei and the North Shore, with its Princeville Resort, passes through peaceful small towns, green, undeveloped countryside, and along some of the most beautiful coastline in Hawaii.

The around-the-island coastal roads don't actually go all the way around, but end at Polihale State Park, west of Waimea, and at Haena State Park, west of Hanalei. The road from Waimea ends inland in Kokee State Park. Between these road ends in the island's northwest is the **Na Pali Coast**, accessible only on foot or by tour boat or helicopter. Even more remote—and inaccessible—is the island's center, topped by Mount Waialeale ("rippling water"), which has a yearly rainfall of more than 450 inches, earning it the cartographic label "The Wettest Area on Earth." Atop Waialeale's cloud-covered summit is an ancient altar devoted to Kane, the greatest of Hawaii's gods and, not surprisingly, the deity of rainwater.

HURRICANE INIKI

In mid-afternoon on September 11, 1992, a devastating hurricane with sustained winds of 145 mph and gusts to 175 mph swept across Kauai from south to north. Named Iniki (a Hawaiian word for sharp, piercing wind), the hurricane flattened the island, leaving behind one of Hawaii's worse natural disasters.

Kauai was declared a federal disaster area, and overnight the U.S. military, the Red Cross, and the Salvation Army moved in to aid the stricken island. Three people died, 332 were injured, and 8,000 were left homeless. The immense destruction left 1,444 homes in ruins, 5,261 homes heavily damaged, and the island without electricity as hundreds of telephone and other utility poles toppled onto roadways. Damages totaled an estimated $1.6 billion.

As expected, the recovery of tourist attractions, businesses, and hotels has been slow. In mid-1993, seven months after the storm, most large resorts were still

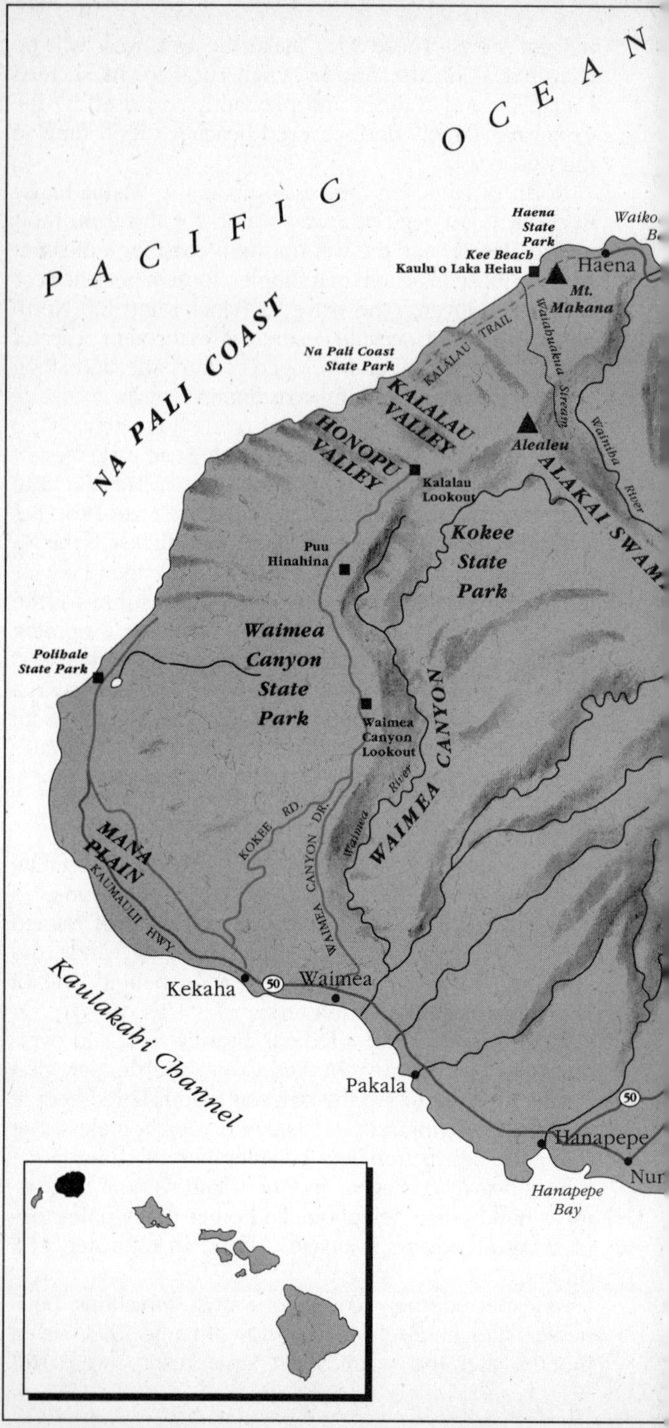
PACIFIC OCEAN
NA PALI COAST
Haena State Park
Kee Beach
Kaulu o Laka Heiau
Haena
Mt. Makana
Waiahuakua Stream
KALALAU TRAIL
Na Pali Coast State Park
KALALAU VALLEY
HONOPU VALLEY
Alealeu
Wainiha River
Kalalau Lookout
ALAKAI SWAM
Kokee State Park
Puu Hinahina
Waimea Canyon State Park
Polihale State Park
Waimea Canyon Lookout
WAIMEA CANYON
Waimea River
KOKEE RD.
WAIMEA CANYON DR.
MANA PLAIN
KAUMAULII HWY.
Kekaha
50
Waimea
Kaulakahi Channel
Pakala
50
Hanapepe
Hanapepe Bay

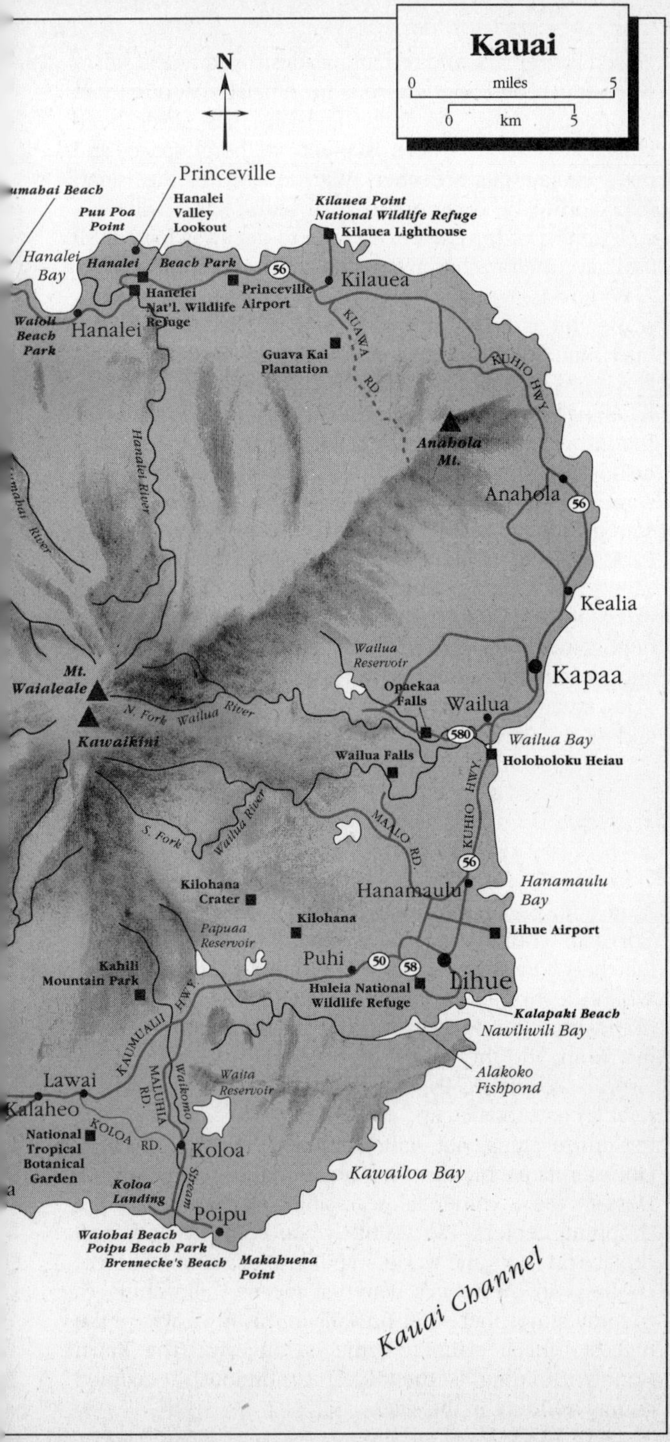
Kauai
miles
0
5
km
0
5
N
Princeville
umahai Beach
Puu Poa Point
Hanalei Valley Lookout
Kilauea Point National Wildlife Refuge
Kilauea Lighthouse
Hanalei Bay
Hanalei
Beach Park
56
Kilauea
Princeville Airport
Hanalei Nat'l. Wildlife Refuge
Waioli Beach Park
Hanalei
Guava Kai Plantation
KUAWA RD
KUHIO HWY
Hanalei River
Anahola Mt.
Anahola
56
River
Kealia
Wailua Reservoir
Kapaa
Mt. Waialeale
Opaekaa Falls
Wailua
N. Fork Wailua River
580
Wailua Bay
Kawaikini
Holoholoku Heiau
Wailua Falls
KUHIO HWY.
MAALO RD.
S. Fork
Wailua River
56
Hanamaulu Bay
Kilohana Crater
Hanamaulu
Kilohana
Lihue Airport
Papuaa Reservoir
Puhi
50
58
Kahili Mountain Park
Huleia National Wildlife Refuge
Lihue
Kalapaki Beach
Nawiliwili Bay
KAUMUALII HWY
MALUHIA RD.
Waikomo
Alakoko Fishpond
Lawai
Waita Reservoir
Kalaheo
KOLOA RD.
National Tropical Botanical Garden
Koloa
Stream
Kawailoa Bay
Koloa Landing
Poipu
Waiohai Beach
Poipu Beach Park
Brennecke's Beach
Makahuena Point
Kauai Channel

closed for repairs, and restaurants destroyed by the storm were still rebuilding. There is no official post-hurricane "reopening date," because the island has never been closed to visitors. There is plenty of hotel space, and many restaurants are open. With tourism to the island expected to be down for several years, Kauai will be a welcome spot for those who want to get away from it all and have the beaches and rain forests to themselves.

With tons of hurricane debris removed from the landscape the island's natural beauty is returning to pre-hurricane conditions as forest canopies thicken and broken trees sprout new limbs. Visitors who travelled on Kauai prior to the hurricane will notice a thinner, leaner island because of the reduced canopy and loss of floral lushness. (A tree-planting program is planned to replace some of the lost foliage.) All state parks reopened in March 1993, including the well-known Na Pali Coast State Park. In Kauai's south-shore resort area, Poipu, the hurricane's 25-foot waves actually enlarged several beaches by carrying sand from the ocean's floor over the reef and depositing it on shore. (Note: Barefooted beach-goers and swimmers should beware that hurricane-scattered glass, metal, and other debris may still exist in beach sand and on the ocean floor.)

LIHUE AND ENVIRONS

A traveller passing through Lihue in 1840 saw only a tiny Christian church, a few banana plants, and a chief's thatched *hale* (house), which he called a "straw palace." When the first hotel opened in the 1890s, featuring an oceanside annex for "sea-bathers," a dentist pulled teeth in his room, and the island's sheriff rented a bed. Now an airport accepts DC-9s, streets once designed for horses now accommodate cars, and the harbor is an anchorage for cruise ships, not sailing canoes. All this reinforces Lihue's relative big-town mystique on this country island. Despite the commercial scars inflicted by nondescript shopping centers—so visible when concrete and steel replace tin roofs and wood—and despite a connotation of coolness in the town's name (it means "cold chill"), a friendly atmosphere still prevails in this town where the biggest official claim to fame is longevity: The Kauai County Building is the oldest continuously occupied county building in the state.

KAUAI MUSEUM

The best introduction to Kauai in "urban" Lihue is the Kauai Museum on Rice Street, a simple repository of artifacts reflecting the island's unpretentious lifestyle. Housed inside a distinctive stone structure with a faded, blue-tile roof is a large collection of Hawaiiana that provides a visual, though rather textbookish, history of Kauai from its volcanic origin six million years ago to the sugar plantation era of modern times. A small exhibit highlights the island's birdlife and plants, including the *mokihana,* a native tree found only on Kauai, whose fruit is strung in leis. Those who admire trees, and artwork made from trees, will treasure the collection of hand-carved *kou*-wood calabashes used to hold *poi* (pounded taro) and fish. *Kou,* today extremely scarce, is a reddish-brown wood that was preferred by ancient Hawaiians, who transformed bowl making into an art form still used here by modern-day craftsmen. Small calabashes made for Hawaiians' favorite children became family heirlooms—a bright mind, bowl makers said, was like a food-filled *kou* bowl. Another interesting exhibit is a model of an old sugarcane plantation house, made from an original home, displaying a plantation worker's living quarters.

KILOHANA PLANTATION

To glimpse more of Kauai life, follow Kaumualii Highway (Highway 50) south and west for 2 miles (3 km) to Kilohana (Hawaiian for "best," "superior"), an old plantation home visible from the highway. Although it sustained severe damage in hurricane Iniki, the plantation plans to reopen, restored to its former conditions.

Plantation owner Gaylord Wilcox lived here in lordly fashion during the 1930s, when sugar was the island's major business, aloha shirts were fashionable, and leis reached to the bottom of a gentleman's double-breasted coat. Once the most expensive home ever built on Kauai, Kilohana became the center of Garden Isle business and social life. Modern restoration has created from it a chic museum that recalls the heyday of sugar. Posh shops with catchy names such as Stones at Kilohana (crafts) and Sea Reflections (a shell store) occupy converted rooms, and the master bedroom is a gallery of works by Hawaiian artists. Throughout the home are furnishings from the 1930s—a piano, floor-to-ceiling beveled mirrors—and out back are the simple houses of the workers who labored in Kilohana's cane fields.

Kilohana's gastronomic centerpiece is **Gaylord's,** a regal restaurant built around a covered courtyard, using, wisely, the museum's furnished interior as a backdrop. On the horizon is Kilohana Crater, where ancient bird hunters captured dark-rumped petrels, an *aumakua* (ancestral spirit) sacred to bird-loving families. In season, vegetables and fruits are picked from Kilohana's gardens, adding a homegrown taste to Gaylord's salads and sandwiches. Lihue business people like to lunch at Gaylord's, and vacationing Hollywood celebs have been known to drop by for dinner to sample the restaurant's prime rib, roast duck, and Alaskan king crab. A special treat is the Sunday brunch, with a menu that includes cheese blintzes with Kauai Portuguese sausage. Reservations recommended for all meals; Tel: 245-9593.

GROVE FARM HOMESTEAD MUSEUM

If you have an unhurried schedule, you might like to complement your visit to Kilohana with a side trip to Grove Farm Homestead Museum, a plantation-life museum also associated with the Wilcox clan. The farm is located off Lihue's Nawiliwili Road (Highway 58), near the Kukui Grove Commercial Village. Compared to Kilohana, Grove Farm is delightfully rural and homespun. Lazy guided strolls take you through a guest cottage, the Wilcoxes' main house and library, and poultry pens with authentic chicken-manure smells. In the farm's antique-looking business office, furnished with a picturesque safe topped with a cannonball, guides show old photos of Wilcox family members, talk about farm life, and tell visitors how the safe's long-lost, but recently discovered, combination (b-a-l-l) explains the cannonball's significance.

Listen for the name Miss Mabel, Grove Farm founder George Wilcox's niece, who in 1971 helped convert the farm into a museum; to some of the tour guides, she's an icon, and "before Miss Mabel left us" was for years a melancholy comment often heard beside the chicken coop or the antique rain gauge. After the tour, tea and cookies are served in the homestead's quaint kitchen. A copy of Miss Mabel's icebox cookies recipe—they are made with raw sugar—is available on request. Your cookies will be good, promises the farm, but not as good as those baked in the homestead's wood stove. Reservations are necessary; Tel: 245-3202.

SOUTH FROM GROVE FARM

On Hulemalu Road, south of Grove Farm Homestead, is **Alakoko Fishpond**, which borders the undeveloped **Hu-**

leia National Wildlife Refuge (neither is open to the public). The roadside view encompasses the whole refuge as well as the fishpond, believed to have been created by the *menehune,* a mythological race of tiny people. Endangered waterbirds at home in Huleia include the *alae keokeo* (Hawaiian coot) and the *koloa maoli* (Hawaiian duck). According to legend, the duck once protected a blind giant, quacking to warn him of attack. Sadly, Hawaii's bird life itself has been under attack since the arrival of the first *haole* (foreigner). So far as birds are concerned, Hawaii is a national disaster area: More bird species have vanished from here than from any other state; in all, about 35 percent of Hawaii's native birds are now extinct, and 31 species are on the brink of extinction, mostly land birds decimated by human encroachment, introduction of pests (such as the mongoose) and non-native birds, and deforestation. In 1992 hurricane Iniki's strong winds stripped away forest foliage and ground cover, exposing bird habitat to additional decimation by the spread of introduced plants harmful to the native forest. Bird watchers will need the Audubon Society's pocket-size book *Hawaii's Birds* or, for the real birder at heart, Andrew J. Berger's authoritative *Hawaiian Birdlife,* both available at local bookstores.

STAYING IN LIHUE

On the outskirts of Lihue, beside a cove fronting Kalapaki Beach on Nawiliwili Bay, is the ▶ **Westin Kauai**, a part of the massive **Kauai Lagoons** resort, a complete travellers' destination with everything a vacationer could need right on the premises. When it opened in 1987 the Westin, with 847 rooms, was a new genre of resort for Kauai, strong on rich appointments and "international" charm—a tropical hybrid somewhere between a private estate and a water-spouting theme park. A herd of marble horses bathed by spraying fountains pranced in the open-air reflecting pool, and a scallop-shaped swimming pool was the structural centerpiece. Fancy shops, an impressive variety of restaurants, nightly entertainment, manmade lagoons, tennis courts, and the hotel's convenient location made the resort a sort of Shangri-La on Kauai. Hurricane Iniki inflicted severe damage on the Westin, however, and the hotel and its restaurants and stores remained closed in 1993. No repair work to the hotel's structural damage had started in mid-1993, fueling speculation whether the hotel will reopen at all.

On the outskirts of southern Lihue, between the Pacific

Ocean Plaza shopping center and the Alakoko Fishpond, is one economically priced accommodation that welcomes visitors with lean pocketbooks and an aversion to expensive, fantasy-land resort hotels. The three-story ▶ **Garden Island Inn**, at 3445 Wilcox Road, is comfortable and convenient and is within walking distance of the Westin Kauai. The hotel is near Nawiliwili Harbor, which was named after a light-wooded tree (*wiliwili*) once used by Hawaiian fishermen to make fishnet floats and canoe outriggers.

Driving north of Lihue you'll find the ▶ **Outrigger Kauai Beach Hotel** (formerly the Kauai Hilton) on Kauai Beach Drive on the oceanside of Highway 56 (Kuhio Highway), 4 miles (7 km) north of Lihue Airport. The Outrigger Kauai has a relaxed, bring-the-family atmosphere that also suits hand-holding honeymooners. Located on not-so-scenic flatlands between Kuhio Highway and Kawailoa ("long water") Bay, the hotel stands rather forlornly on the site of an old dairy farm. A pool surrounded by rock caves and waterfalls is the hotel's outdoor centerpiece. The beach that fronts the bay is a rambling coastline of sand, rugged and wild, not the soft, crescent-shaped beach pictured on Hawaiian postcards. Taking long, lazy beachcombing walks, not beach sitting, is the main activity. The draws here are the cheerful restaurants, the nightclub—**Gilligan's**—and the hotel's proximity to Lihue Airport.

DINING IN LIHUE

While the high-class eateries and cocktail lounges that catered to guests at the Westin may remain closed, the small restaurants and taverns in and around Lihue where locals eat and drink can always be recommended to the visitor looking for the real Hawaii. The best food and prettiest surroundings can be found at **Gaylord's** at Kilohana Plantation (see above). A meal on simple plates, not museum-quality calabashes or hand-painted china, is served in an heirloom atmosphere at **Ma's Family, Inc.**, on Halenani Street, a back street a short drive from the Kauai Museum. The staple diet here consists of pork omelets, papaya pancakes, and *akule*, a delicious frying fish. If Ma is on duty and business is slow she might tell you about the old days when she had only one regular customer for breakfast, a *haole* (white foreigner) who ate eggs and toast—for less than a buck. Never mind that Ma's place isn't included on any travel magazine lists of the top 50 restaurants in Hawaii; you eat at Ma's because someday (perhaps soon) the

Mas of Kauai, like Hawaii's vanishing mom-and-pop grocery stores, will be extinct, replaced by fast-food joints and star-rated resort restaurants.

For *saimin* (a noodle soup), walk around the corner to **Hamura Saimin Stand**, a longtime favorite among Lihue's noodle eaters. No-frills canned beer is on ice at **Hap's Hideaway** on Ewalu Street, site of Kauai's first compact-disk jukebox. More crowded, especially when interisland cruise ships dock at Nawiliwili Harbor, is the **Oar House Saloon**, between the Westin Kauai and the Anchor Cove shopping complex. The crowd is mixed—cruise shippers and locals—with blue-jean-clad waitresses shuffling between poolroom and bar carrying trays of long-neck beer-bottles, hamburgers, and sandwiches.

POIPU AND KOLOA
Poipu

Sixteen miles (26 km) southwest of Lihue Airport, via Kaumualii Highway (Highway 50) and Maluhia Road, is an old sugarcane coast now famous for its more profitable stepchild, Poipu, which, despite hurricane damage to its hotels and beaches, remains Kauai's Waikiki—but one without fast-food stores, traffic jams, and overly crowded beaches. The area's heartland consists of clusters of hotels and condominium resorts sandwiched between the seashore and the parallel Poipu Road and stretching from Makahuena Point (Kauai's southernmost tip, meaning "eyes overflowing with heat") to Koloa Landing, a 19th-century whaleship anchorage. The attraction here is a coastline of beaches (still recovering from hurricane damage)—Poipu Beach Park, Waiohai, Brennecke's Beach—and *sunny* weather on a rainy island. (The annual rainfall at Poipu is only eight inches more than at Waikiki.)

Once revered as a playground for Hawaiian *alii* (royalty), Poipu is best remembered as the birthplace of Prince Jonah Kuhio Kalanianaole, honored every March 26 on Kuhio Day for his achievements as Hawaii's second territorial delegate to the U.S. Congress. A trace of Kuhio's Kauai can still be seen at **Poipu Beach Park**, where Hawaiian fishermen mend their nets and trade stories about sharks, goatfish, and *moi*, a thread fish once reserved for chiefs such as Prince Kuhio. This is Poipu's most popular beach park, heavily used by locals and tourists alike because of the safe swimming area around the tiny beach. A local community association has proposed a plan to restore the beach park to its pre-hurricane attractiveness, but in spring 1993 the park still remained in a hurricane-ravaged condition: littered with rocks, the sand heaped in mounds.

STAYING IN POIPU

Though still low-key and unhurried compared to Waikiki, Poipu is determined to become a major Hawaiian tourist destination though hurricane Iniki crushed that dream for 1993 and 1994. If hurricane insurance settlements are finalized in mid-1993, and if hurricane-damage restoration goes smoothly, Poipu's most upscale beachside address, the ▶ **Stouffer Waiohai Beach Resort**, is to reopen in mid-1994. The W-shaped Waiohai is low-rise and shaded by palms, in keeping with a Poipu ordinance limiting all buildings to the height of a coconut tree: four stories. Guests are greeted with leis in the open-air lobby and escorted to their rattan-furnished rooms by a concierge dressed in a white Hawaiian gown. Quiet suppers with local and international culinary offerings are available in the **Tamarind**, where, by candlelight, you can eat Molokai venison or Kona abalone and drink a distinctive European wine. A fine Sunday Champagne brunch is served in the Waiohai's open-air Waiohai Terrace, overlooking the beach. Meats, seafood, omelets, and salads are served with unlimited pours of Champagne throughout brunch.

An essential ingredient in a fine hotel is its sense of place and history, and the Waiohai has successfully blended itself with the landscape and the area's past. Nestled amid the hotel's foliage is a freshwater spring that fed a long-gone *ohai* (monkeypod tree), the key to understanding Waiohai's place-name, which means "the ohai bush near the fresh water." A restored *heiau* (temple), built from lava rocks in 1600 and dedicated to fishing and agricultural deities, is at beachside, but it suffered damage in the hurricane, and its stones must be reassembled by archaeologists.

Next door to the Waiohai is another Stouffer property, the ▶ **Stouffer Poipu Beach Hotel**, with casual, family-type accommodations right on the beach. Each room has a kitchenette. Candlelit tables in the hotel's **Poipu Beach Café** are perfect for a light dinner for two of perhaps an exotic drink and a sandwich. This property too was damaged in the hurricane and expects to reopen mid-1994.

The nearby ▶ **Sheraton Kauai Beach Resort**, also

closed after the hurricane and planning to reopen in mid-1994, fronts a tiny peninsula of lava rocks that makes a handsome shorefront for any hotel. The guest rooms near the beach are in two- and four-story units; the rest of the hotel's four-story units are set in gardens across Hoonani Road. The Sheraton's most pleasant beachside attraction is the **Outrigger Room**, which, when reopened, will still house its familiar namesake, a *waa*, or outrigger sailing canoe. Right outside Hawaiians hunt among the shore rocks at low tide for the edible *opihi*, a mollusk with a tent-shaped shell that inspired the triangular designs on bark cloth (*kapa*) made in Poipu centuries before resort clothing stores arrived. When the Outrigger reopens with its Friday night seafood buffet, don't expect *opihi* among the offerings, because, being handpicked, it's too expensive. (An ecology-minded traveller will not wish to eat commercially sold *opihi* anyway, as this mollusk declines in numbers yearly; someday, if farsighted legislation is enacted, *opihi* will be limited to noncommercial consumption.)

Poipu's most attractive condominium resort, ▶ **Kiahuna Plantation**, lies camouflaged in tropical foliage between the Sheraton Kauai and the Stouffer Waiohai. The Kiahuna's two- and three-story "plantation-style" units are dispersed over a large acreage and sit on land once part of the Territory of Hawaii's oldest sugarcane plantation. The resort closed after the hurricane and is scheduled to reopen in February 1994.

Inside Kiahuna is the **Plantation Gardens**, a cozy restaurant in a home given as a wedding gift to Alexandra Moir in 1933 by her sugar-growing dad. The open-air restaurant, which will reopen in February 1994 (dinner only; Tel: 742-1695), offers local seafood amidst antique furnishings and an inspiring view of the gardens Alexandra and her husband created over a 35-year period. Paths amble among palm trees, African tulips, monkeypod trees, ferns, and bamboo, and, believe it or not, given Kauai's rainfall—a cactus garden. The secluded gardens, which escaped hurricane damage, are popular with couples who marry in private ceremonies amid the shrubbery, then honeymoon at the resort. "The Hawaiian Wedding Song" is the popular accompaniment.

The ▶ **Hyatt Regency Kauai**, turns back the clock (architecturally speaking) to the pre–World War II era. This low-rise hotel beside Poipu's Keoneloa Bay has an abundance of open-air courtyards and gardens, a style reminiscent of the 1920s and 1930s when travellers arrived in

Hawaii by ship. The Regency is a "complete destination resort"—everything for everybody in one location. It has five acres of saltwater swimming lagoons with private islands and an assortment of theme areas devoted to tropical gardens, beach parties, and luaus. **Keoneloa** ("long sands") **Bay**, which fronts the 605-room hotel, is a spot noted for its bodysurfing, board surfing, and windsurfing. The beach has been nicknamed Shipwreck since a wrecked wooden boat, long ago stripped for its firewood by fishermen and beach-goers, washed up here.

A special attraction at the Hyatt is **Stevenson's Library**, a posh bar with a bookish ambience, complete with a small library, a bar with a large selection of Scotch whiskeys, a billiard table, and newspapers from around the world. It is named after writer Robert Louis Stevenson, who visited Hawaii for five months in 1889. Stevenson's first teenage scribbling was a tale of shipwrecked sailors captured by savage islanders in the South Seas. One of Stevenson's great pleasures was drinking with Hawaiian royalty and discussing Hawaiian folklore.

Visitors to Poipu who like the homely atmosphere of a bed-and-breakfast accommodation will find ▶ **Poipu Bed & Breakfast Inn**, 2720 Hoonani Road, a quaint stopover. The house, built in 1933, has old-fashioned lanais and handcrafted wood interiors. The owner collects wooden carousel horses, several of which are on display. The house sits beside Waikomo Stream, wherein the sleeping forms of several Hawaiian gods are said to be imprinted.

DINING IN POIPU

If you'd like to have a meal or two away from condominium and hotel turf, Poipu has several reliably good restaurants. **Keoki's Paradise** in Poipu Shopping Village, near the Plantation Gardens, features fresh local fish in a tropical setting. Ask your waiter for the seafood special of the day, which may be *ono,* a game fish whose Hawaiian name means "good to eat" (how can you go wrong?), or *au* (swordfish), which was placed with tiger sharks on sacrificial altars in ancient Hawaii. Keoki's has a good selection of Napa Valley wines that is especially strong in Cabernet Sauvignons. After a lengthy closure due to hurricane damage, Keoki's will reopen in late 1993 (Tel: 742-7534). **Café Venturi**, also in Poipu Shopping Village, is a small outdoor restaurant that opened in December 1992. Try the fish and chips for lunch or the baked chicken breast with pasta for dinner. The **House of Seafood**, 1941

Poipu Road, usually offers several varieties of fresh fish nightly, sometimes baked in parchment paper or puff pastry, modern cooking methods unknown to ancient Hawaiians, who preferred to roast fish in *ti* leaves.

Koloa

Less than 3 miles (5 km) inland, north of Poipu Beach Park by way of Poipu Road, is the town of Koloa, which dates back to 1835, when the first sugar mill crushed sugarcane with koa-wood logs, and owners paid workers in scrip redeemable at the mill's grocery store. "Koloa is, and has always been, a delightful place," said a local historian in 1935, when the old town depended on long-jointed sugarcane for its economic livelihood. Now the *new* old town—a restored stretch of shops with bright paint over weathered timber—thrives on tourism generated by the Poipu resorts, and, despite the proliferation of tourists' dollars, remains a delightful road stop. Travellers driving from Lihue to Poipu pass through the town; most continue on to their hotels, then return a day or two later to eat and, after dark, explore the well-lit clothing and gift shops. Today, as in 1935, Koloa's enjoyment is taken slowly.

DINING AND SHOPPING IN KOLOA

The heart of tiny Old Koloa Town is at the intersection of Koloa and Maluhia roads, where there are several eateries. The **Koloa Broiler**, noted for baked beans and broil-your-own steaks, flanks a wooden walkway beside windows that allow passersby to spy on customers seated at the bar. **Lappert's Ice Cream**, the brainchild of a former liquor distiller, is headquarters for local and visiting *aikalima* (ice cream) epicureans. Highly recommended here are mango, passion fruit, and guava cheesecake ice cream, as well as Kauai pie, made from Kona-coffee ice cream, fudge, shredded coconut, and Kauai-grown macadamia nuts.

Old Koloa Town also houses a **Crazy Shirts** outlet that sells high-quality tee-shirts in a restored mom-and-pop store, where for years area schoolchildren stopped to buy dried abalone and coconut candy and watch the gasoline inside the "visible gas" pump. The store, beside a huge monkeypod tree growing from Waikomo Stream, is still a Koloa landmark. Closed for repairs after Iniki, it is expected to reopen in late 1993.

NORTH OF KOLOA

The Koloa area's two most visible landmarks are the **Tree Tunnel** and St. Raphael's Church. The mile-long "tunnel" of trees, near the intersection of Highway 50 (Kaumualii Highway) and Maluhia Road, is a familiar landmark on the Lihue-to-Poipu drive. These eucalyptus trees, also called swamp mahogany, were planted in 1911 by a fruit-and-land company with leftover saplings that survived the hazards of roadside residence. **St. Raphael's Church**, reached from Koloa by way of a road traversed by sugarcane trucks (Hapa Road, off Weliweli Road), is Kauai's oldest Roman Catholic church (1856). The church's walls, built from lava rock that unfortunately is now painted an unattractive white, are three feet thick. Plantation workers and their families are buried in the church's graveyard; one grave (marked "Child Walter") has a plumeria tree growing from its center, the blossoms falling on the aged tombstone like fragrant snowflakes. (Plumeria blossoms, which make a cheap lei, are nicknamed "cemetery flowers.")

North of Koloa, at the end of a sugarcane field, is the ▶ **Kahili Mountain Park**. Operated by the Seventh-Day Adventist Church, the park offers accommodations to campers-at-heart who nonetheless prefer cabins, and to "persons oriented to outdoor activities," such as cool morning walks in the surrounding forested land. Each rustic cabin has a private bathroom (toilet) and outdoor shower. These accommodations are heavily booked, and advance reservations are a must. (See the Accommodations Reference at the end of the chapter.) To reach the park from Koloa, drive north on Maluhia Road to Highway 50, turn left on Highway 50 (westbound), then turn right beyond the seven-mile marker and drive a mile inland on a dirt road.

THE WAIMEA AREA AND THE WEST COAST

West of the Poipu resort area, Kaumualii Highway (Highway 50) cuts through the country towns of Lawai, Kalaheo, and Hanapepe en route to Waimea ("reddish water"), a favorite place-name of ancient Hawaiians. This historic region, first seen by Europeans in 1778 when the ubiquitous Captain Cook arrived, has no fancy resorts or ritzy hotels, only enclaves of workaday Hawaiians living in a landscape blessed with rivers and streams flowing to the ocean. An aura of rebellion and individualism lingers here, for the last battle fought on Kauai occurred near Hanapepe—a revolt against rule by the Kamehameha dynasty—and the rebel island of Niihau, a privately owned domain and last stronghold of Hawaiian-speaking natives, rises forbiddingly on the horizon across the water.

NATIONAL TROPICAL BOTANICAL GARDEN

The garden lushness that is endemic to Kauai is readily experienced about 3 miles (5 km) west of Koloa on the way to Waimea, at Lawai's National Tropical Botanical Garden, home of the beautiful **Allerton Estate**. Plantings in the garden estate (created by philanthropist Robert Allerton and his son John) include plants of medicinal value to ancient (and modern) Hawaiians as well as species that are rare and endangered. A special spot is the *Diana* Fountain, a replica of Antonio Canova's *Diana* standing beside a pavilion and reflecting pool. Film crews find the estate an enchanting backdrop, and scenes in the American TV series "Fantasy Island" and the Walt Disney film *Noah's Last Ark* were shot here.

Hurricane Iniki severely damaged the botanical garden and the Allerton Estate, uprooting trees and plants and blowing a large monkeypod tree into the garden's visitors' center. Cleanup is expected to be completed and the visitors' center repaired and reopened by 1994. An unfortunate victim of the hurricane was **Queen Emma's Summer Cottage**, shattered by high winds and blown from its foundation. It will be rebuilt in the near future. Like modern visitors to the garden, Emma, wife of King Kamehameha IV, seldom escaped the rain: "It has rained all day," wrote a minister in 1871, "but the natives still ride four miles to visit the Queen." When the estate is reopened visitors will be able to walk to her cottage, which can be viewed only from the outside. The exotic plants around the cottage (there's even a Queen Emma lily, *Crinum augustum*) will be recovering from the hurricane for some time.

A tour of the botanical garden and Allerton Estate, which includes a two-mile walk, takes about three hours. Daily tours, by reservation only, depart from the garden's visitors' center at the end of Hailima Road, south of the town of Lawai; Tel: 332-7324. (Some maps still call it Pacific Tropical Botanical Garden, but the name has been

KALAHEO

A likely stop for lunch is the **Camp House Grill**, located at roadside in a brightly colored, plantation-style camp house in Kalaheo, west of Lawai. *Hulihuli* (barbecued) chicken is the house specialty, and chicken eaters from Lawai to Waimea come to nibble on drumsticks. The grill's camp-house look re-creates a bygone time when simple wood-frame camp houses were an integral part of the Kalaheo landscape. Artist **James Hoyle**, who has a gallery in his name in Hanapepe (see below), finds artistic inspiration in the old camp houses and succeeds in preserving them on canvas.

HANAPEPE

A motorist speeding westward to Waimea might easily bypass Hanapepe, though an hour's detour to the town's center, perhaps lunch at the **Green Garden Restaurant** and a stroll through downtown, is a pleasant stop if you want to see a rustic, west-coast Kauai town where the big seller is nuts and bolts at the hardware store. The family-managed Green Garden, opened in 1948, is a converted five-bedroom home decorated with orchids and hanging plants that serves such foods as fresh fish, hamburgers, club sandwiches, and shrimp tempura. The service is still friendly even when the place gets crowded. Be sure to try the homemade pies. You can get a quick bite in town at **Hanapepe Bookstore & Espresso Bar**, featuring cappuccino and pastries and, for the literary-minded, a selection of Hawaiian books.

WAIMEA

The big attraction in Waimea (6 miles/10 km past Hanapepe) is the ▶ **Waimea Plantation Cottages**, a half block west of Waimea Canyon Drive. Each unit is an old sugar-plantation cottage, restored and fitted with modern amenities and named for the the plantation worker who once lived in it: Samio, Alfredo B., Locy, and Cuaresma. No hotel accommodations can duplicate the warm plantation-era atmosphere that pervades the houses with their ceiling fans and mahogany and wicker period furniture.

The cottages border the Waimea shoreline, where Hawaiian kings once lived, and on the premises is a cluster of sugar-camp houses still occupied by Hawaiians and called "our living museum" by the cottages' staff. There are 48 cottages, and several turn-of-the-century houses. An old house that was moved here from Mana—the dry western end of Kauai—is now the cottages' administration office and reception area. The new Grove Dining room, open to the public as well as overnight guests, serves lunch and dinner from a "multicultural" menu in a plantation setting decorated with art work by local artists.

Veteran Kauai travellers stay for weeks at Waimea Plantation Cottages, telling only their closest friends about these special accommodations and hoping no one else discovers them. Reservations are booked months in advance, but cancellations do occur and an on-the-scene traveller may find a vacancy.

The Backcountry Wilderness

"I can feel the spirit of its woodland solitudes," said Mark Twain, "and I can hear the splash of its brooks." Though Twain's 1866 Hawaiian travels didn't include Kauai, his observation about the Islands' outdoors aptly describes Kauai's wilderness areas: Waimea Canyon, Kokee, and Na Pali Coast state parks.

These three high-country state parks, which are interlocked geographically but are dissimilar in terrain—respectively, canyon, mountain woodlands, coastal valleys—form the backcountry's awesome *wao nahele* (wilderness), where a Hawaiian god partial to mortal travellers slew the frightful *akua,* forest spirits that molested intruders. Two roads forming an upside-down Y rise from the coastal Kaumualii Highway (Highway 50) and feed traffic upland to the parks: Kokee Road in Kekaha (about 3½ miles/5 km west of Waimea), the official gateway, and Waimea Canyon Drive in Waimea. The more scenic, and less travelled, is the Waimea Canyon Drive, which intersects the coastal highway near Waimea Plantation Cottages.

WAIMEA CANYON

Those who revere the Colorado River's Grand Canyon will find Kauai's more modest version, Waimea Canyon, nicknamed the "Grand Canyon of the Pacific," lilliputian in comparison, but from an Islander's point of view its beauty and vastness are matchless. The park that bears the canyon's name begins where the Waimea Canyon Drive merges into Kokee Road, some 6 miles (10 km) north of Waimea. The northward drive then leads to two viewpoints, **Waimea Canyon Lookout** and, farther north, **Puu**

Hinahina, both off-road stops with excellent vistas of the mile-wide canyon and the Waimea River, which for a million years has carried water from Mount Waialeale to sculpt this intriguing landscape. A careful observer can see white-tailed tropic birds riding the airways. The extremely long central tail feathers of these tern-like birds were once used to decorate sailors' hats. The canyon was once home to a golden eagle (eagles are not native to Hawaii and this particular bird's origins remain a mystery) that harassed the tourist-filled helicopters that fly here. Sadly, in 1984 the eagle dive-bombed into the blades of a touring copter, leaving only its feathers as souvenirs.

KOKEE STATE PARK

Kokee State Park, north of Waimea Canyon, is the final destination of all visitors to Kauai's high country. Within its boundaries are hiking trails, streams, and a once-dense forest thinned by the hurricane. Camping is permitted in the park, but permits are required (contact Division of State Parks, 3060 Eiwa Street, Lihue, HI 96766; Tel: 241-3444). Rare birds, once hunted by Hawaiian bird catchers to feather royal capes, take refuge deep in the woodlands, camouflaged in *mokihana* and *maile* plants, which are used to make leis. July in Kokee is the plum harvest season, which in its heyday became so popular that hundreds of jam-makers and jelly-heads eagerly awaited the annual shotgun blast that opened the pickings. August and September is fishing season for the rainbow trout that swim in the park's brooks, Hawaii's only trout-fishing area. (The fingerlings are raised on Oahu and carried into Kokee in backpacks.)

The hairy, black wild pigs that roam the woods are significant in Hawaiian history as food, friend, and, along with human beings, sacrificial offerings. Ancient Hawaiians who carried pork after dark risked attack from hungry ghosts, and travellers in Kokee are advised to forget about aluminum foil and wrap ham or bacon picnic sandwiches in *ti* leaves, a traditional anti-ghost protection for *puaa* (pig) meat. Ironically, both the park's fish and plums are imported attractions, not native to Kokee's forest, and the original Polynesian pig exists only in archaeological evidence, having interbred itself out of existence long ago with introduced species.

Hurricane Iniki's immediate impact on Kokee's forest was plainly visible: a reduced canopy and the destruction of larger trees. It's long-term effects could be devastating.

When a forest canopy such as that at Kokee is blown away by a hurricane, a botanical army of introduced weeds and plants harmful to the forest rapidly spreads through the forest's floor preventing the full regrowth of native trees and plants. Some rare plants may not survive the competition for habitat and the forests's rarest birds, so dependent on the canopy, may never be seen again.

Despite the high prices and not-so-exciting reputations of lodges within state and national parks throughout the United States, Kokee's only accommodation, ► **Kokee Lodge**, has a special charm—and price—that makes it a popular year-round hideaway with locals and visitors alike. The cabins sleep three to seven persons and are equipped with basic housekeeping items. The first cabins were built in 1952, constructed from lumber salvaged from the U.S. Army. The lodge's restaurant, originally a country store, is open to guests and non-guests alike for breakfast and lunch daily. The kitchen's fresh-baked corn bread is a backwoods treat. The bar, topped with a slab of *koa* wood cut from a tree felled by a hurricane, is near the fireplace, a comfortable hangout after a forest walk. In ancient times, canoe builders ventured into Kokee to cut *koa* (Hawaiian mahogany) for double-hulled voyaging canoes.

Adjacent to the lodge is the **Kokee Natural History Museum**, with small displays on Kokee weather, plants, and wildlife. A video show about Hawaii's birds is shown on request. A gift shop sells books and maps. The museum is open daily.

KALALAU LOOKOUT

Kalalau Lookout, easily reached by car from the museum or lodge, is among the island's most spectacular viewpoints. It overlooks **Na Pali Coast State Park**, which is inaccessible from Kokee. You have to drive clear around the island and enter by foot from Haena State Park on Kauai's North Shore, at the western end of Kuhio Highway (Highway 56), to the east of Na Pali (discussed below). The lookout also peers into distant **Kalalau Valley**, fronted by a shoreline that can be explored by Zodiacs (the crafts Jacques Cousteau uses) and twin-hulled catamarans departing from Hanalei, also on the North Shore. This beautiful valley holds a tragic tale. A century ago a leper named Koolau refused to be deported to the leper settlement on Molokai. Rifle in hand, he hid in Kalalau, firing at policemen and resisting arrest until his disease killed him. Koolau's tragedy appealed to Jack London, whose short story "Koolau the Leper" glorifies both man and valley.

This valley is only part of the famed Na Pali Coast, noted for its breathtaking beauty. From a helicopter the isolated, rocky crags appear as rugged skyscrapers walling off valley from valley and beach from beach. At Waiahuakua and Alealau the cliffs, sculpted by millions of years of erosion, rise to over 3,800 feet, and at Kalalau to 4,100. When you approach Na Pali by boat, the sea, relentlessly pounding against the shoreline and splashing into mysterious sea caves, adds a chill of excitement to the high-rise landscape of cascading waterfalls and misty peaks. (See the Getting Around section, below, for information on boat and helicopter excursions in the Na Pali area.)

The valley next to Kalalau, not part of the state park, is **Honopu**, the so-called Valley of the Lost Tribe. The discovery years ago of human bones in Honopu led to speculation that the remains of a theretofore undiscovered Hawaiian kingdom had been found. All that is known for certain is that in Hawaiian mythology a tribe of "little people" lived in Honopu and stole campers' food.

WAILUA AND THE COCONUT COAST

Like Kauai's wilderness parks, the Coconut Coast, on the eastern, opposite side of the island, north of Lihue, is rich in mythology, especially the landscape around the Coco Palms Resort at Wailua, 6 miles (10 km) north of Lihue, where Kuhio Highway (Highway 56) intersects Kuamoo Road (Highway 580) beside the Wailua River. Extending for ten miles along Kauai's eastern side, from Lihue to Kapaa, the Coconut Coast takes its name from the coconut groves at the Coco Palms Resort, an area once reserved for Hawaiian royalty. According to legend, on the shores of Wailua Bay where the Wailua River meets the sea, the first *alii* (royalty) from Tahiti beached their double-hulled voyaging canoes, planted *kapu* sticks—no trespassers allowed—and established themselves as masters of Kauai. The area was considered the island's most desirable land, and the river's headwaters and banks became sacred ground, covered with temples and the residences of chiefs, whose *mana* (spiritual power) was second only to that of the gods. Even the beach became a place apart, reserved as a playground for the elite, and *kapu* (taboo) to commoners.

There are two royal birthing stones wedged between the river and Kuamoo Road at **Holoholoku Heiau**. The stones, ancient tumbledown boulders from the hill above, were believed to possess great *mana* to aid in childbirth, and against them rested chiefesses as they gave life to Kauai's royalty. After birth, the child's umbilical cord was hidden nearby. (Mothers seeking good luck for their offspring also hid cords in Captain Cook's ships, thinking them the floating islands of gods.)

STAYING IN WAILUA

Beside the river, and open to commoners and kings alike, is the venerable ▶ **Coco Palms Resort**, which rightly considers itself the *kupuna* (respected elder) among Kauai's resort destinations. At first glance the row of multi-storied units paralleling Kuhio Highway seems rather commonplace, but on the premises a lush landscape of coconut groves and fishponds (called "lagoons" here) reveals itself. Especially charming are the thatched-roof cottages around the ponds. Though beach-goers may find the unromantic amputation of the hotel from nearby Wailua Beach a hardship—you have to cross the highway to get to the beach—the outdoor attractions here are the coconut grove and the ponds, not the beach; the best room views are those that look inland toward the grove.

In the 1840s Deborah Kapule, widow of Kauai's last king, who surrendered his kingdom to Kamehameha in 1810, lived here beneath the cluster of palms, filling the surrounding ponds with fish and feeding them to her distinguished overnight guests. Kauai's early Protestant missionaries, travelling between Waimea and Hanalei, stayed with Kapule, as did the island's first Catholic priest. A canoe carried the visitors across the river while their horses swam behind.

Highly touted is the Coco Palms Resort's nightly torchlighting ceremony, recalling a bygone century when Kapule's guests dined on mullet at her royal table near the torchlit fishponds. After the wail of a conch shell, muscular Hawaiians in red loincloths swinging flaming torches light row after row of torches, brightening the grove. The ceremony begins around sunset. The best tables are in the Lagoon Dining Room and Lagoon Terrace Lounge.

The Coco Palms' grounds, popular with honeymooners, are steeped in TV and movie trivia, a curious fate for an area known to ancient Hawaiians as "Great Sacred Wailua." On this hallowed earth Elvis Presley crooned "The Hawaiian Wedding Song" to Joan Blackman in *Blue Hawaii,* and Mr. Roark (Ricardo Montalban) welcomed deplaning travellers to "Fantasy Island" from a bridge that spans a fishpond. Surprisingly, the most appealing structure in the palm grove is the wedding chapel constructed by Columbia Pictures for the Rita Hayworth film *Sadie Thompson.* The book to read in the chapel is Somerset Maugham's *The Trembling of a Leaf,* which contains the short story "Rain," made into several film versions, one of which was *Sadie Thompson.* Inside are rattan chairs and an altar holding red valentine-shaped anthuriums; the chapel is cooled by wood-bladed ceiling fans.

Closed due to moderate damage inflicted by hurricane Iniki, the Coco Palms is scheduled to reopen by 1994. Some 150 coconut trees were lost in the storm, but they have been replaced by seedlings. The wedding chapel was undamaged and will again welcome couples when the hotel reopens.

An economical alternative to the more luxurious Coco Palms Resort is ▶ **Islander on the Beach**, located at beachside on Wailua Bay, off Kuhio Highway. The Islander sits behind the Coconut Marketplace on the site of an old track used for horse races and polo matches at the turn of the century. A row of ironwood trees separates the hotel from the beach. A short walk away, in the market place, is **Tradewinds**, a friendly, self-proclaimed "South Seas bar" in which locals gather for drinks after work. Notice the large wall photograph of an island cove with sandy beach and coconut trees—it's a Caribbean landfall, not the fabled South Seas.

Near the Wailua River and its lovely fern grotto is the ▶ **Fern Grotto Inn**, at 4561 Kuamoo Road. This relaxing accommodation, which describes itself as a "plantation home on the Wailua River," is surrounded by swaying palm trees. After a night's sleep on white goose-down pillows, you'll wake up to the sound of Wailua's natural music—birdsong.

WAILUA RIVER

The Wailua is the state of Hawaii's only navigable river. **Smith's Motor Boat Service** (Tel: 822-4111) offers excursions from **Wailua River State Park** (if you are headed northbound toward Kapaa, turn left off Highway 56 before crossing the Wailua River). The Smiths are an old-time Kauai family whose ancestors came to the island in the mid-1800s. They started their family-run boat service in 1947, taking tourists on boat trips after finishing their morning fishing and taro-patch chores. Their boats visit the fern grotto, filled with bright green maidenhair ferns—a popular site for weddings—and provide on-board Hawaiian music. The **Wailua Marina Restaurant**, which overlooks the river, is a popular breakfast stop before a mid-morning cruise—it's next door to Smith's.

Kapaa

Wailua's neighboring town, Kapaa, despite its city-size appearance, shoreline location, and weather-beaten rooftops, is mainly a food stop for those travelling to and from Kauai's North Shore. A mainstay in Kappa is **Bubba's**, a burger stand with outdoor umbrella tables. For prime rib, try the **Bull Shed**, located beside the ocean near a seawall. Wall-crashing waves are visible from the window tables. The prime clientele at **Ono Family Restaurant** are moms, pops, and kids partial to the excellent lemonade and the friendly, though unhurried, service. A house specialty is buffalo meat from Kauai and Kansas.

Kapaa's gourmet dining contribution is **A Pacific Café**, in the Kauai Village shopping center. The kitchen is replete with wood-burning grill, rotisserie, and woks. The menu changes daily and might include grilled Japanese eggplant, grilled loin of Australian lamb, or stir-fried chicken with a garlic peanut sauce. Meals are served on polished wood tables set with bamboo placemats. Reservations necessary; Tel: 822-0013. For those with simpler tastes, **Paradise Hot Dogs**, also in the Kauai Village shopping center, has foot-long German franks steamed in beer and served on a sweetbread bun.

THE NORTH SHORE

The drive from Lihue or Wailua to Kauai's North Shore on Kuhio Highway (Highway 56) is a relaxing excursion through green, undulating countryside where cattle egrets—a ubiquitous white bird seen in fields—prowl the landscape looking for insects. The mental restlessness caused by not quite yet being in the Kauai of your imagination, probably detectable in Lihue and even Poipu, fades away as you approach this coast, where most longtime residents will shake their heads in sympathy when you say that you must return south, to the Westin Kauai or a Poipu resort, or to an even more alien destination such as Honolulu. The coastal area's heartland begins at Kilauea and continues along Kuhio Highway west to Princeville, Hanalei, and Kee Beach at road's end. Although Princeville and Hanalei were heavily damaged by hurricane Iniki, the landscape remains rich in scenic grandeur, Hawaiian mythology, rainfall, avian wildlife, and, at Princeville, resorts.

The Kilauea Area

When approaching Kilauea northbound on Highway 56, turn left onto Kuawa Road (about 12 miles/19 km from Kapaa) to reach the area's newest attraction, **Guava Kai Plantation**. The guava trees that cover the landscape are harvested to make jams and jellies and, of course, pink guava juice. After a video show explaining the mechanics of guava harvesting, visitors are given a short tour of the plant and orchards. Guava is not native to Hawaii, having been introduced in the late 1700s, possibly by a Spaniard. The plantation's snack bar has delicious guava treats such as guava ice-cream floats and guava muffins (keep in mind that guavas have five times more vitamin C than oranges). Guava Kai was closed temporarily for replanting and repairs after the hurricane; for information and visiting hours, Tel: 828-1925.

KILAUEA POINT

The island's best bird-watching is atop the steep cliffs of **Kilauea Point National Wildlife Refuge**, a mile north of Kilauea, reached by Kolo and Kilauea roads. The sanctuary is home to large colonies of wedge-tailed shearwaters and red-footed boobies. The sight of a frigate bird—its V-shaped wing tips a favorite tattoo design of yesteryear's Pacific Islanders—riding cushions of air high above the coastline *below* onlookers is unforgettable. Visitors from November through June can also observe the bill-clacking, head-bobbing courtship displays of the Laysan albatross, nicknamed the "gooney bird" during World War II. The refuge's lighthouse, built in 1913, was, by accident, the first Hawaiian landfall—"the light of last resort," said a pilot—for the first transpacific flight from California to Oahu in 1927, which almost missed the Islands entirely. The pilot's three-engine monoplane was aptly named *Bird of Paradise*. Now obsolete, the lighthouse serves in retirement as a picturesque landmark welcoming migrating sea birds and bird watchers. Though visitors are not allowed inside the lighthouse, which still contains a four-ton glass lantern, the oval white tower, called *hale ipukukui* (candlestick house) in Hawaiian, provides a romantic backdrop for snapshots.

Heavily damaged by hurricane Iniki (14 of 20 building were destroyed), the refuge will reopen (Tel: 828-1413). Hurricane winds blew away the visitors' center, but the lighthouse survived, though its doors burst open and the glass lantern inside sustained water damage. The ground nesting sites of the refuge's wedge-tailed shearwaters were destroyed, but luckily those were the only species of seabird nesting when the hurricane struck.

KILAUEA

A pleasant stop after visiting the lighthouse is the Kong Lung Center, a tiny shopping and eating village in Kilauea. **Casa di Amici**, an Italian restaurant open for dinner, has a selection of antipasti, soups and pastas. Reservations recommended; Tel: 828-1388. The wood-frame building that houses the open-air restaurant was once a gas station. In 1881 a Hawaiian princess visited Kilauea, then a sugar plantation town, and hammered (with two blows) the first spike of the plantation's new railroad. **Pau Hana Pizza**, located behind Casa di Amici, is open for lunch and features pizzas made with Kilauea-grown ingredients.

Princeville

From Kilauea, the route westward on Kuhio Highway (about 8 miles/13 km) leads to one of Kauai's most spectacular viewpoints: not a roadside lookout or a mountain watchtower, but, surprisingly, a resort-studded tableland overlooking Hanalei Bay. This is Princeville.

Although the name sounds like a developer's dream, it is rooted in authentic Hawaiian history, being a placename dating to 1860, when Kamehameha IV and his son, Prince Albert, visited the area. First a sugar plantation, then a cattle ranch, and now a resort community, Princeville has its own airport and its own shopping center, a spic-and-span plantation-style complex with supermarket, art galleries, boutiques, restaurants, and a post office. The resorts behind the shopping center encircle the Princeville's Makai golf course (see Golf Courses, below), which has a reputation for being hard on scorecards. Survivors of this course insist that the cannibalistic fairways digest golf balls.

A name you may hear often in Princeville is Bali Hai.

Though romantic in sound, it has no traditional Hawaiian connection, being a fictional place-name in James A. Michener's *Tales of the South Pacific*. The real Bali Hai is Aoba, a small island near Espíritu Santo in the Melanesian nation of Vanuatu, where Michener served as a naval officer in World War II. In 1957 Hollywood filmed *South Pacific,* a musical based on Michener's book, on Kauai. The film immortalized such North Shore locales as Mount Makana, cast as the mysterious Bali Hai, and Lumahai Beach: Both are across Hanalei Bay from Princeville.

STAYING IN PRINCEVILLE

Perhaps Princeville's most eye-catching view of the bay and the "Bali Hai mountains" is from the **Bali Hai Restaurant** at ▶ Hanalei Bay Resort. Even employees from other Princeville resorts come here to breathe in the scenery. A landowner in the 1850s called the area "the most beautiful spot in Hawaii," and seated at the restaurant, with its wraparound lanai overlooking the bay, you will find that observation difficult to refute. The bay fronts a jungle-green valley, often filled with rainbows, and its shoreline is ringed with white-sand beaches and river outlets to the sea. Across the bay the high, green peaks capture the morning and evening sunlight, transforming the landscape into the magical land immortalized in the Peter, Paul, and Mary song, "Puff the Magic Dragon," about a little boy and his best friend, Puff, in a fantasy land called Hanalei.

A $10 million renovation project begun after the hurricane should be completed by September 1993. If you stay at this condominium resort, bring your tennis racket: The rambling collection of pleasant, spacious guest units is erected beside tennis courts. The clientele here is likewise tennis oriented, and even the courts have nice views. No one seems to mind the downslope walk to the beach.

The ▶ **Princeville Hotel** (a Sheraton property), also damaged in the hurricane, expects to be fully restored and open to visitors by 1994. The Princeville has 252 rooms—each with electronic windows that change from white frosted to clear glass with the flick of a switch—including a penthouse with a music room. Built on the slopes of Princeville's Puu Poa Point in three descending terraces, the hotel is the ritziest, and most expensive, place to stay in Princeville. Restaurants, and a cocktail lounge with a wood-burning fireplace, look out on Hanalei Bay (what hoteliers call the "zillion-dollar view"), and elevators carry guests downward to the beach. Escape to

Italy at the Princeville Hotel at **La Cascata**, a restaurant decorated to resemble an Italian village and offering meat and seafood specialties, including swordfish carpaccio seasoned with lime juice.

More low-key is the ▶ **Puu Poa**, a condominium resort sharing the hillside north of the Princeville Hotel, on Princeville's Ka Haku Road. Named for the point of land on which it sits, the Puu Poa's cluster of concrete buildings is designed for those preferring plenty of living space—the luxury of two bedrooms with an expansive lanai and atrium. The condominium sustained light hurricane damage, mainly to stairways, and will reopen in January 1994. A secluded beach is a short hike downhill from the Puu Poa, reached by a concrete walkway beside its sister condominium, the Pali Ke Kua, destroyed by the hurricane (rebuilding is planned to begin in 1994).

The Hanalei Area

Whether you are staying in Princeville, or are just visiting for the views you will want to see the town of Hanalei as well, just minutes to the southwest across the steel-covered Hanalei Bridge. This one-lane bridge, built in 1913, serves as a barrier to large, air-conditioned tour buses and heavy construction vehicles. "When the bridge goes, Hanalei goes," say some locals. But before you reach Hanalei, pull over at the the **Hanalei Valley Lookout**, on the *mauka* (toward the mountains) side of Highway 56 near the Princeville turnoff. The splendid view takes in birds, the Hanalei River, and taro patches. Much of the *poi* (cooked taro, pounded and thinned with water) in Honolulu supermarkets comes from this refuge. (Hurricane Iniki, however, decimated the taro patches, and there is bound to be a poi shortage for a while.) Just off the Highway before Hanalei village is the **Hanalei National Wildlife Refuge**, valley bottomlands split by the Hanalei River. Like the Huleia refuge near Lihue, this wetland also shelters Kauai's endangered waterfowl, especially the black-necked stilt, or *aeo*. Birdlovers can drive along a paved roadway (Ohiki Road) that runs through the refuge and see waterfowl thriving among the taro patches. (Please remain in your car to lessen the human impact on the landscape.) Because of the 1992 hurricane, the refuge's endangered birds have, for the moment, been blown closer to extinction, though, ironically, the hurricane's fury expanded their habitat by creating additional wetlands in Hanalei, an unexpected benefit to the surviving waterfowl.

HANALEI

The village of Hanalei is a hodgepodge of shops, eateries, and residences wedged between Kuhio Highway and Hanalei Bay. The bay, which is shaped like a half-moon (the name means "crescent bay"), is rimmed by Hanalei Beach Park and Waioli Beach Park, both popular surfing areas for Hanalei locals. The village takes its name from the bay, as do the beautiful valley and the Hanalei River, which waters the weeping willows. The Hanalei willows trace their roots to Napoleon's island of exile, Saint Helena, where a 19th-century seaman stole cuttings and carried them to Kauai potted in his shaving mug.

Hanalei village has no real downtown, but Ching Young Village shopping center, a rather nondescript plaza, is where most visitors park. Early arrivals from Princeville or Wailua can extinguish breakfast appetites at the **Village Snack and Bake Shop** in Ching Young Village or at the **Hanalei Gourmet**, across the street (Kuhio Highway) in the Old Hanalei School House. Eating breakfast on the schoolhouse's lanai tables, or indoors beneath the restaurant's ceiling fans if Hanalei's soft rains are falling is a relaxing way to begin a lazy Hanalei morning.

On the opposite end of the town, fronting rain-soaked mountains that sprout falls of "splashing, singing water" (*waioli*), sits **Waioli Mission House Museum**, the residence of American Protestant missionaries between 1837 and 1869. The attractive wood-frame house with a chimney and a second-story lanai was one of the first American-style houses built on Kauai. Friendly docents, sharp on missionary history, conduct a chatty walk through the living room and bedrooms filled with the artifacts of missionary life, such as a bookshelf of bedtime readings (*Annals of the American Pulpit,* for example) and a walking cane with a whale-tooth knob. Hurricane Iniki damaged the house's stairs and ripped away roofing shingles, but the house should reopen (Tel: 245-3202). The beautiful trees that surrounded the house, however, were decimated. Half the tree canopy is gone, leaving an open landscape that will takes years to return to its forest-like greeness. The mission house is behind **Waioli Huiia Church**, a Hanalei landmark nicknamed the "Green Church."

Hanalei's well-loved Tahiti Nui Bar was damaged in the hurricane and as yet has shown no signs of returning to life.

West of Hanalei to the Na Pali Coast

Because the Hanalei area is so wet, the resulting multitude of streams between Hanalei and Kee Beach to the west—road's end—necessitated a series of one-lane bridges. These turn-of-the-century bridges, considered an insult to technological progress by some road builders, are over-the-water treasures acting as traffic dams, slowing movement to the low-keyed pace of North Shore life. Cars must queue to cross each bridge, good news for the aesthetic-minded driver, bad news for the impatient.

LUMAHAI BEACH

Following these bridges westward will bring you to Lumahai Beach, which, thanks to the film *South Pacific,* is the North Shore's best-known seashore. Located on Waikoko Bay, the beach is by the nature of its terrain divided into a western and eastern section; the western end is easily reached by car, with off-road parking in a sandy parking area, but the eastern end, site of the Bali Hai scenes in *South Pacific* (the nurses' beach), is sandwiched between rocky bluffs and is reached only via a downward trek through dense foliage from the roadway. No signs point to this section of the beach, which begins a half mile from the third bridge crossed after leaving Hanalei—the adventure is finding it. To avoid a traffic ticket, be sure to park in the direction of traffic. Because Lumahai Beach has no protective reef to slow ocean waves and currents, swimming is dangerous; many drownings have occurred here. Postcard writing, beach walking, and wave-watching are some of the activities to pursue here.

STAYING NEAR LUMAHAI BEACH

Beyond Lumahai Beach, across the Wainiha River bridge, is Haena Point, site of the ▶ **Hanalei Colony Resort**, the only beachfront resort in the Hanalei area. Two-bedroom units are scattered among the coconut trees and flank a fine beachcombing shoreline. Traffic is minimal here and the beach uncrowded. High surf during the hurricane did not damage the resort's beach but hurricane winds did destroy roofs in the 13-building complex; reopening is set for November 1993.

Honeymooners might be interested in knowing that Haena means "red hot." One famous Kauai honeymooner who fell in love with the area opened **Charo's** (5-7132 Kuhio Highway, Haena) a flashy on-the-beach night spot. Stuffed papayas, macadamia-nut-fried shrimp, and Mexican dishes are on the menu. The restaurant should be fully recovered from hurriance damage by 1994; Tel: 826-6422.

HAENA STATE PARK

At road's end is Haena State Park, mostly undeveloped beachfront land used by Hawaiian fishermen almost a thousand years ago. The park's **Kee Beach** is one of Kauai's best snorkeling sites, home to *manini,* a species of sturgeon fish eaten whole (including entrails) by old-time Hawaiians, and *hinalea,* a colorful fish once offered to the gods by women wishing for children. This is also the homeland of the original *puka*-shell craze of the 1960s, when American hippies strung them together as necklaces and ankle bracelets.

If you do not plan to hike into the Na Pali Coast area, you can still have a dramatic conclusion to your North Shore visit by taking a short, uphill hike from Kee Beach to **Kaulu o Laka Heiau**, a temple dedicated to Laka, goddess of the hula. A trail on the *mauka* (inland) side of Kee Beach—near where the Kalalau foot trail to the Na Pali begins—leads to this dance-inspiring location, once the most important hula site in all Hawaii. Watch your language; crude talk was forbidden here. On special occasions Kauai's hula students still use this platform, where, high on this hill of rain, hula masters of ancient Kauai chanted their devotion to a deity of dance: "Dwelling in the source of the mists, Laka, mistress of the hula; woman, who by strife gained rank in heaven."

NA PALI COAST

The 11-mile-long **Kalalau Trail** into the **Na Pali Coast State Park**, one of Hawaii's best-known hikes, begins at Kee Beach, where the roadway ends, west of Hanalei. Most Kalalau Trail day-trippers leave their cars at Kee Beach and walk the trail's first two miles to **Hanakapiai Valley**, a one- to two-hour trip each way. This is an easy walk, with picturesques views of the Na Pali Coast, passion fruit flowers (named for the passion of Christ), and soaring white-tailed tropic birds. In summer, visitors find an idyllic white-sand beach at Hanakapiai, but in the winter months the surf scoops away the sand, leaving only boulders. Because of the strong surf, swimming here is dangerous.

Beyond Hanakapiai the hike to **Kalalau Valley** becomes a backpacker's adventure, requiring camping equipment, including a rain-proof tent. (Permits are required for overnight stays in Kalalau as well as for hikes beyond Hanakapiai; contact the Division of State Parks, 3060 Eiwa Street, Lihue, HI 96766; Tel: 241-3444.) All fresh water used in Kalalau should be boiled or treated with chemical water purifiers. Swimming is dangerous because of quick drop-offs and underwater currents. For information on foot, sea, and air excursions into Na Pali, see the Getting Around section, below.

The trail is arduous as it winds across cliff faces and descends into several valleys before reaching Kalalau Beach at trail's end, 11 miles from the trail head at Kee Beach. On rainy days it is muddy and slippery. Even though tourist-filled helicopters flightseeing over the coast are a distraction to solitary hikers, the rewards for making Hawaii's most famous wilderness trek include sighting a sea turtle surfacing in the ocean hundreds of feet below the trail, scenic views of a shoreline of undulating hills and tiny coves, and the sheer mental and physical exhilaration the Kalalau Trail evokes. For beach-sitters, the sunset on **Kalalau Beach**, flecked with the silhouettes of seabirds and bats, is unforgettable. The seclusion from urban lights brightens the stars above the beach; watch for rising of the bright star Arcturus, called Hokulea ("star of gladness") by Hawaiians.

SHOPS AND SHOPPING ON KAUAI

In old-time Hawaii the possession of Western trading-ship goods awarded great prestige to the owner. Especially prized were such contraptions as clocks and spyglasses. Kamehameha the Great was Hawaii's first passionate shopper, paying for foreign goods with Island-grown sandalwood, a fragrant wood exported by Westerners to China. Kamehameha liked guns and gentlemen's clothes; he posed for his best-known portrait wearing a red European vest. Nowadays shopping history has reversed itself, and travellers from outside Hawaii seek out Island-made arts, crafts, and products. To go shopping, *kuai hele* in Hawaiian, still adds to one's prestige, even when purchases are made on credit, *kuai hoaie*.

Niihau-Shell Leis

Not simply beautiful shell jewelry, these leis are an art form native to Niihau, Kauai's neighboring island. The refined craft of making shell leis has passed from generation to generation on Niihau, and today Niihau leis are a local status symbol among women of fashion in Hawaii. Three types of tiny beach shells are used: *momi* (pearl), the most commonly used shell, with 20 different variants; *laiki,* which resemble grains of rice; and *kahelelani,* the smallest and most difficult to collect, thus used to make the most expensive leis. The most stately and romantic place on Kauai to buy Niihau-made leis is the **Hawaiian Collection Room** at Kilohana, the restored sugar-plantation estate 2 miles (3 km) south of Lihue. They have a beautiful lei collection and provide knowledgeable, detailed guidance in lei selection and appreciation. A home-display box made of Hawaiian wood is also available to exhibit and protect the lei, which, in time, will become a treasured family heirloom—the essence of Hawaii itself. The shop should reopen with the rest of Kilohana by 1994. **Kauai Gold**, in the Coconut Marketplace on Kuhio Highway between the Wailua River and Kapaa, also sells Niihau leis.

Art and Crafts

The **James Hoyle Gallery** in Hanapepe has oils of old Kauai buildings as well as Kauai nature scenes. **8 Bells**, at Rainbow Plaza in Kalaheo, will frame that Kauai masterpiece. Near Lihue, **Stones at Kilohana**, housed in a 1910 guest cottage behind Kilohana's main house, has beautifully designed handiwork collected from craftspeople throughout Polynesia.

Books

Opened in 1993, Kapaa's delightfully named bookstore, **Tin Can Mailman**, has rare and used books on Hawaiian, South Pacific, and Pacific Rim subjects. The store takes its unusual name from a remote island in Tonga, where the mail is sealed inside tin receptacles, dropped overboard by a passing ship, and retrieved by a swimming mailman. The store is located at 4504 Kukui Street in Kapaa's New Pacific House.

Furniture

Antique and contemporary furniture, as well as such collectibles as plastic hula figurines from the 1940s and old silver candlesticks from England, are available at **Yellowfish Trading Co., located in Kapaa's New Pacific House on the corner of Kukui Street and Kuhio Highway.

Jewelry

The **Black Pearl Collection**, in Poipu Shopping Village, has pearl treasures from the South Seas. Cultured only in French Polynesia, the pearls come from a black-lipped oyster noted for its blackish-green tint. If one is available, you might be allowed to hold a $20,000 black pearl in your hand—perfectly oval, perfectly beautiful. The shop closed after the hurricane but plans to reopen in March 1994.

Clothing

Hilo Hattie's Fashion Center, 3252 Kuhio Highway in Lihue, has muumuus, aloha shirts, and children's wear. The store is named after Clara Nelson's professional moniker, Hilo Hattie, namesake of the tune "When Hilo Hattie Does the Hula Hop."

Fruits

Roadside produce shopping is a fun way for visitors to meet island residents. **Banana Joe's Tropical Fruit Farm**, in Kilauea off Kuhio Highway, specializes in dehydrated tropical fruits, and the owner also makes coconut-leaf baskets and hats. Papayas are always a good buy; pick a yellow and green papaya with a smooth skin that shows no signs of shriveling. Pineapples are popular, of course, though most come from Oahu. To select the best pineapple examine the "eyes," the diamond-shaped figures on the outside. Look for a consistency of size: large, even eye-patterns, from bottom to top, indicate a mature pineapple. The rule for hand-carrying Hawaii pineapples and papayas overseas varies from country to country: New Zealand and Australia, for example, ban pineapples and papayas, while the U.S. Mainland, Canada, Great Britain, and Germany allow them in; France admits pineapples but not papayas. All fruits must be USDA inspected and approved.

Leis

When you place a lei around your neck, remember that Hawaiian children were often called *lei* because their arms encircled their mother's neck like a necklace, or lei. **Greeters of Hawaii**, at the Lihue Airport (under the generic Flower Shop sign), has leis made of *ilima,* a delicate flower whose juice was once used to make a mild laxative for babies. Leis made of *maile,* a periwinkle favored by Laka, goddess of the hula, are made at **Marina Flowers** at Wailua Marina in Wailua, across the river from the Coco Palms Resort.

GOLF COURSES

Bright green Kauai, with its lush and colorful vegetation, has some of the best golfing in Hawaii. This most richly tropical Hawaiian Island boasts 90 holes designed by Robert Trent Jones, Jr. "Clearly, I've had a love affair with an island called Kauai," he has said. "I think it's the best island for golf there is."

Resort Courses

Jones is probably best known for the 45 magnificent holes he designed on the island's North Shore at the **Princeville Resort Kauai**. The Makai Course, consisting of 27 holes, opened in 1972 and has been listed as one of the top 100 courses in the United States most years since then. Jones returned to Princeville in 1990 to open the dramatic Prince Course, which immediately achieved legend status for both its beauty and challenge. The Prince packs a tough 75.6 rating from the back tees and measures more than 7,300 yards. It is designed so that there is no way to play cautiously and score well. You must be accurate, but you must also hit away. Be warned that you're going to lose balls here: Course employees put the average number of "aloha balls" at six per customer. Tel: 826-3580 for the Makai Course; 826-5000 for the Prince Course.

The most prolific golf-course designer to have worked in Hawaii, with ten courses to his credit, Jones also designed courses at the Kiahuna Golf Club and Poipu Bay Resort, both on the opposite side of the island from Princeville in the sunny resort area of Poipu.

Kiahuna Golf Club, 2545 Kiahuna Plantation Drive, is the shorter course, measuring only 6,353 yards from the back tees and 5,631 from the whites. Still, it's one of the most interesting tracts you'll ever play, with such unique hazards as lava rock walls (don't get behind one), lava tubes (forget about your ball), and Hawaiian *heiau* (say your blessings to the golf *kahuna*). Tel: 742-9595.

Poipu Bay Resort, at 2250 Ainako Street, the newest resort course on Kauai (opened in 1991), offers 18 holes of windy, links-style golf in a gorgeous oceanfront setting—from which you may see whales offshore during the winter months. You pretty much have to play Poipu Bay low, except on the handful of holes where the wind is at your back. Twelve holes play into or with a cross wind, with six gracing your play with the wind at your back. You won't lose as many balls here as you might on the Prince but you may not score a heck of a lot better, either. Tel: 742-8711.

Kauai Lagoons Golf and Racquet Club, at Kalapaki Beach in Lihue, features two Jack Nicklaus beauties next door to the Westin Kauai. The signature course at Kauai Lagoons, one of the most beautiful in Hawaii, named Kiele, measures a demanding 7,070 yards from the back tees, with a rating of 73.7. You'll find yourself shooting over ravines thick with mango and guava trees, down from ocean cliffs to tide-pool greens, and past a wedding chapel set on the edge of a lagoon to a green out on a thin finger of land on a hole (the 18th) that Nicklaus calls "one of the best par-fours I've ever built."

The other course at Kauai Lagoons, called the Lagoons Course, is more open and forgiving. It's a true resort course, laid out to accommodate tour groups and golfers with higher handicaps. With plenty of parallel fairways, little water, and quite a bit of sand to slow errant golf balls, the Lagoons design is quite hospitable. Tel: 246-5061; elsewhere in the U.S., (800) 634-6400, for both courses.

Public Courses

For a delightful local-style game, try the best municipal tract in the state, the **Wailua Municipal Golf Course**, just north of Lihue, off Highway 56; Tel: 245-2163.

—*George Fuller*

GETTING AROUND

Arrival by Air

There are two airports on Kauai, one at Lihue, served by Hawaiian Airlines and Aloha Airlines, and a second, smaller one, near Princeville. Flights from Honolulu to Lihue take 27 minutes. If you begin or end your stay in a Princeville resort, Aloha IslandAir (office on Oahu, Tel: 484-1111) has scheduled interisland flights from Honolulu Airport to Princeville Airport on 18-passenger, twin-engine aircraft. Flights take 60 minutes.

Around on the Island

There is limited public bus service in the Lihue-Wailua-Kapaa area (call Kauai Bus for information; Tel: 241-6410). Rental-car is the only way to explore the island well. For the glove compartment, the best map is James A. Bier's *Kauai,* which provides a good overview of the island; it is available in most Kauai bookstores. Because of the rugged terrain, distances and driving times vary dramatically. The Lihue-to-Poipu drive, for instance, is a 16-mile (26-km), half-hour excursion; the 50-mile (80-km) drive from Lihue to Kalalau Lookout in Kokee State Park takes about two hours; and Poipu to Hanalei (54 miles/86 km) takes an hour and a half.

Touring and Trekking Outfits

Pacific Quest, an outdoor-adventure travel company, has multi-island trekking packages that include hiking in backcountry Kauai's Na Pali Coast, Waimea, and Kokee areas; Tel: 638-8338; Fax: 638-8255; elsewhere in U.S., Tel: (800) 776-2518. **Outfitters Kauai** will take you riding through high-forest backroads on mountain bikes or kayaking along the Na Pali Coast; Tel: 742-9667. **Eye of the Whale** leads groups of up to ten on a ten-day hiking odyssey that includes Kauai's Na Pali Coast and Waimea Canyon, plus other Hawaiian islands; Tel: 889-0227; elsewhere in U.S., Tel: (800) 659-3544. **Kauai Mountain Tours'** one-day backcountry excursions aboard four-wheel drive vans are less vigorous. The tour includes a picnic lunch, always welcome while exploring Kauai's magnificent landscape; Tel: 245-7224; elsewhere in U.S., Tel: (800) 452-1113.

A profusion of helicopter and tour-boat operators offers wilderness-area adventures as well. **Bali Hai Helicopter Tours** in Hanapepe, on the southern coast (Tel: 335-3166), flies over both the Waimea Canyon and the Na Pali Coast. **Niihau Helicopters** (Tel: 335-3500) departs from Burns Field outside Hanapepe on a flexible schedule for a 60- to 90-minute flight with two stops on Niihau for $200 per person (four to seven passengers). **Captain Zodiac Raft Expeditions** in Hanalei (Tel: 826-9371) has year-round Na Pali Coast raft trips, plus whale-watching excursions from January to April, when the humpbacks pass through Kauai waters singing their strange songs.

A reminder: Binoculars are useful for enjoying Kauai's spectacular lookouts and wildlife areas.

ACCOMMODATIONS REFERENCE

The rate ranges given here are projections for winter 1993–1994. Unless otherwise indicated, rates are for double room, double occupancy. Hawaii's telephone area code is 808.

- ▶ **Coco Palms Resort.** 241 Kuhio Highway, **Kapaa**, HI 96746-1499. Tel: 947-9477. $110–$160; suites $160–$330; cottages $175–$270.
- ▶ **Fern Grotto Inn.** 4561 Kuamoo Road, **Kapaa**, HI 96746. Tel: 822-2560. $55–$65.
- ▶ **Garden Island Inn.** 3445 Wilcox Road, **Lihue**, HI 96766. Tel: 245-7227; elsewhere in U.S., Tel: (800) 648-0154. $55–$85.
- ▶ **Hanalei Bay Resort.** 5380 Honoiki Road, P.O. Box 220, **Hanalei**, HI 96714. Tel: 826-6522; Fax: 826-6680; interisland, Tel: (800) 221-6061; elsewhere in U.S., Tel: (800) 827-4427. $130–$220; suites $240–$1,000.
- ▶ **Hanalei Colony Resort.** P.O. Box 206, **Hanalei**, HI 96714. Tel: 826-6235; Fax: 826-9893; elsewhere in U.S., Tel: (800) 628-3004. $95–$190 (3-night minimum).
- ▶ **Hyatt Regency Kauai.** 1571 Poipu Road, **Koloa**, Kauai, HI 96756. Tel: 742-1234; Fax: 742-1557; elsewhere in U.S., Tel: (800) 233-1234. $195–$410; suites $475–$1,800.
- ▶ **Islander on the Beach.** 484 Kuhio Highway, **Kapaa**, HI 96746. Tel: 822-7417; Fax: 822-1947; elsewhere in U.S., Tel: (800) 847-7417. $95–$130.
- ▶ **Kahili Mountain Park.** P.O. Box 298, **Koloa**, HI 96756. Tel: 742-9921. $27–$55.
- ▶ **Kiahuna Plantation.** 2253 Poipu Road, **Koloa**, HI 96756. Tel: 742–6411; Fax: 742-7233; elsewhere in U.S. and in Canada, Tel: (800) 367-7052. $155–$400.
- ▶ **Kokee Lodge.** P.O. Box 819, **Waimea**, Kauai, HI 96796. Tel: 335-6061. Cabins $35–$45.
- ▶ **Outrigger Kauai Beach Hotel.** 4331 Kauai Beach Drive, **Lihue**, HI 96766. Tel: 245-1955; Fax: 246-9085; elsewhere in U.S. and Canada, Tel: (800) 462-6262. $125–$160; suites $400–$750.
- ▶ **Poipu Bed & Breakfast Inn.** 2720 Hoonani Road, **Koloa**, HI 96756. Tel: 742-1146; Fax: 742-9417; elsewhere in U.S., Tel: (800) 552-0095. $110–$175.
- ▶ **Princeville Hotel.** P.O. Box 3069, **Princeville**, HI 96722. Tel: 826-9644; Fax: 826-1166; interisland, Tel: (800) 826-4400; elsewhere in U.S., Tel: (800) 325-3535. $265–$495; suites $825–$2,350.

▶ **Puu Poa**. P.O. Box 899, **Hanalei**, HI 96714. Tel: 826-9602; Fax: 922-2421; elsewhere in U.S., Tel: (800) 535-0085. $235–$270.

▶ **Sheraton Kauai Beach Resort**. 2440 Hoonani Road, **Poipu**, HI 96756. Tel: 742-1661; Fax: 742-4053; elsewhere in U.S., Tel: (800) 325-3535. $185–$350; suites $400–$1,350.

▶ **Stouffer Poipu Beach Hotel**. 2251 Poipu Road, **Poipu Beach**, HI 96756. Tel: 742-1681; Fax: 742-7214; elsewhere in U.S., Tel: (800) HOTELS-1. $100–$250.

▶ **Stouffer Waiohai Beach Resort**. 2249 Poipu Road, **Poipu Beach**, HI 96756. Tel: 742-9511; Fax: 742-7214; elsewhere in U.S., Tel: (800) HOTELS-1. $150–$360; suites $465–$1,560.

▶ **Waimea Plantation Cottages**. 9600 Kaumualii Highway, P.O. Box 367, **Waimea**, Kauai, HI 96796. Tel: 338-1625; Fax: 338-2338; elsewhere in U.S. and in Canada, Tel: (800) 9-WAIMEA. $100–$225 (3-night minimum); $525–$2,275 for 7-day stay.

▶ **Westin Kauai**. 3610 Rice Street, **Lihue**, HI 96766. Tel: 245-5050; Fax: 246-5097; elsewhere in U.S. and in Canada, Tel: (800) 228-3000. $175–$345; suites $450–$1,800.

BED AND BREAKFASTS

For information about other bed-and-breakfast accommodations in Kauai, see the Oahu Outside Hawaii Accommodations Reference.

▶ **Bed & Breakfast Hawaii**. P.O. Box 449, Kapaa, HI 96746. Tel: 822-7771; Fax: 822-2723; elsewhere in U.S., Tel: (800) 733-1632.

NIIHAU
THE FORBIDDEN ISLAND

By John W. Perry

The cartographic profile of Niihau looks like an upraised seal peering toward Kauai's western coast, 17 miles away across Kaulakahi Channel. Along the seal's spine, isolated from public Hawaii, is a small, Hawaiian-speaking community of 230 native Hawaiians who live and work on the state's only privately owned island. Most of Niihau is restricted in access to tourists as well as longtime Kauai residents. The closest a visitor can get to Niihau is an airplane flyover or a helicopter tour that lands in two secluded, unpopulated areas. Because of its history of being *kapu* (taboo) for the most part to outsiders, Niihau (pronounced knee-ee-how) is nicknamed the "Forbidden Island," and has for decades retained an aura of seclusion akin to xenophobia. Viewed through rain from a high-country lookout atop Kauai's Waimea Canyon, Niihau—as mysterious to outsiders as King Arthur's fabled Avalon—appears and disappears in the mist, unhurried, seldom visited.

In a state where development is considered by some to be almost divine, many residents and tourists alike shake their heads in disbelief at Niihau's withdrawal from the modern world. The electorate there even voted against statehood, the only precinct to do so. Yet Niihau's isolated lifestyle is considered a blessing, not a hardship. There is no garbage collection, no telephone, no jail. Horseback is a favored mode of transportation, used to herd cattle and chase pigs. Money is earned from ranch work and handicraft (shell leis). Nothing is done on Sundays except going to church and, later, reading wish books: mail-order catalogues.

A Scottish family bought the island from King Kamehameha V in 1864 for $10,000 in gold, and the descendants, the Robinson family, continue to keep it an offshore miracle where the tenet Limited Tourist Access is rigorously enforced and the original language is preserved (as it is in the Kau and Puna districts on the Big Island and in Hana on Maui).

Niihau's most famous unwelcome guest crash-landed in a Zero fighter in December 1941, only hours after the Japanese attack on Pearl Harbor. The bizarre occurrence, known as the Niihau Incident, ended in bloody combat when the pilot shot and wounded a Niihauan. Still conscious, the injured man, used to manhandling sheep, grabbed the pilot, dashed him against a stone wall, and cut his throat with a hunting knife. The pilot's death inspired the patriotic song "They Couldn't Take Niihau Nohow."

Niihau does do trade with the outside world, exporting the most exquisite necklaces made in Hawaii. These delicate shell leis make meaningful—but expensive—souvenirs. Unlike flower leis, the multihued Niihau-shell necklaces are permanent mementos. On Niihau the shells are revered as "island flowers," and are collected by women from the seashore and strung through natural or man-made holes. Old-time hula dancers decorated themselves with these leis, and in the official photographic portraits of Queen Kapiolani and Queen Emma both are wearing ivory-colored Niihau-shell leis to complement their Victorian-style dress. (See Shops and Shopping in the Kauai chapter if you would like to buy one of these precious leis.)

Excursions to Niihau

The only excursions to Niihau are with Niihau Helicopters (Tel: 335-3500), which flies to Niihau Monday through Friday at 9:00 A.M., noon, and 3:00 P.M. The flights depart from Port Allen's Burns Field on Kauai (an old airstrip on Lele Road off Highway 50 outside Hanapepe) and last from 60 to 90 minutes, with two stops on Niihau. The cost is $200 per person, with a minimum of four passengers required and a maximum of seven. The flight is on a two-engine helicopter used to provide emergency medical service for the island, and the airfares help to finance the copter's cost. It lands for 20 minutes at Keanahaki Bay on the island's southern end and for half an hour on the island's remote northern end, avoiding the main village of Puuwai. Visitors are allowed to walk around on a Forbidden Island beach, becoming, for a moment, Niihau's only nonresident beachcombers.

In 1993 **Niihau Safaris** began pig and sheep Qafari hunts on Niihau, each excursion accompanied by a local guide. Hunters are flown to the island by Niihau Helicopters to shoot feral animals that cause damage to the island's native plants. A hunt usually lasts a full day, a sheep taken in the morning, a pig in the afternoon. Excess meat is given to guides and local residents. Tel: 338-9869.

CHRONOLOGY OF THE HISTORY OF HAWAII

Precontact Period

Centuries before the first European explorer sighted Hawaii, the Islanders had evolved a remarkable civilization that embraced a strong seafaring heritage, a pantheon of gods that rivaled those of the Greeks and Romans—Pele (volcanoes), Lono (harvest), Ku (war)—and a strict legal system (*kapu*) that kept order and punished *kapu*-breakers by roasting them in earth ovens until "the body grease dripped." Tribal leaders (*alii*) ruled the common laborers and fishermen, and the *kahuna* (priest) oversaw the religious aspects of daily life. The early Hawaiians were avid surfers, game players, and, like other Polynesians, tellers of tales. Their ancient lifestyle resembled feudal Europe, ancestral homeland of the white foreigners (*haole*) whose arrival in the closing years of the 18th century changed Hawaii forever.

The *pae aina* (archipelago) on which the ancient Hawaiians lived—now America's 50th state—is a landfall of mid-ocean volcanoes both active and extinct forming the most isolated chain of islands in the world. Measured from its submarine base to above-ocean summit, Mauna Kea on the Big Island is the world's highest mountain, rising six miles from the ocean floor. Because of the movement of the earth's crust (plate tectonics) over a volcanic "hot spot" on the ocean floor, the Hawaiian Islands are "drifting" to the northwest, making the westward islands older than the eastward; Kauai, for example, is several million years older than Oahu, and Oahu is older than the Big Island. The hot spot beneath the Big Island is still producing island-building lava, and each eruption of Mauna Loa and Kilauea adds acreage to the state. Near the Big Island, hidden 3,000 feet below sea level, is Loihi, a submerged volcano that rises 13,000 feet above the sea floor. Someday, perhaps in 10,000 years, Loihi will reach the surface, forming yet another Hawaiian island, while wind and rain continue to erode Maui, Oahu, and Kauai, whose eruptive cycles are finished.

In Hawaiian mythology, the islands were created by the demigod Maui, a prankster ("Maui-of-a-thousand-tricks") blessed with extraordinary powers. He "fished up" the Hawaiian Islands from the sea, raised the sky, and regulated the sun's path across the heavens. In addition, Hawaiians had their own creation chant, the *kumulipo* ("origin" or "source of life"), comparable to the Greek creation chants and Genesis in the Bible. Passed from generation to generation, the chant catalogued the creation of the world and the beginning of life on earth: "At the time when the heavens turned about...."

- **c. A.D. 300–850**: Polynesians from the South Pacific, probably the Marquesas Islands northeast of Tahiti, begin migrating to Hawaii in double-hulled voyaging canoes, crossing the world's largest open-water regions; by 850 all the main Hawaiian Islands are occupied.
- **c. 480**: Mookini Luakini, one of Hawaii's first *heiau* (temple), is erected near Upolu Point on the Big Island; Hawaiian chiefs will use it for centuries to offer sacrifices to the gods.
- **c. 1100–1300**: Tahitian explorers arrive, initiating a second wave of immigration; they subdue and enslave the more primitive inhabitants.
- **c. 1400**: The backbone of Hawaiian culture begins to emerge as social classes are established and the islanders split into tribes, adorning themselves with feathered capes and helmets, and jewelry made from shells and human teeth.
- **c. 1758**: Kamehameha the Great, who will unify all Hawaii under his rule, is born on the Big Island's Kohala Coast. According to Hawaiian *kilo hoku* (astronomers), a brilliant celestial "star" appeared in the heavens the year of his birth (probably the 1758 return of Halley's Comet).

Contact and After

- **1778**: English explorer James Cook, commander of HMS *Resolution* and HMS *Discovery*, sights Oahu, Kauai, and Niihau in January. Though Spanish navigators piloting the treasure-laden Manila

- galleons may have sighted Hawaii centuries earlier, Cook retains his fame as the "discoverer" of the Sandwich Islands—as he named them, after the Earl of Sandwich.
- **1779**: In Kona, on the Big Island, Cook unwittingly provokes the Hawaiians at Kealakekua Bay and is killed at water's edge. The Hawaiians, under coercion, return part of his hand to the ship's crew; the rest of Cook's body is butchered for the bones, which are kept as sacred relics. The flesh is burned, buried, or tossed into the sea.
- **1790**: Warriors in the Puna district on the Big Island pause at Kilauea to make offerings to Pele, goddess of volcanoes, and are killed by an eruption of cinders and poisonous gas; footprints in the solidified ash, reputedly those of the warriors, can still be seen.
- **1795**: The Big Island warrior Kamehameha conquers Maui, Lanai, Molokai, and Oahu. His 1796 attempt to invade and conquer Kauai fails, but in 1810 he wins the island by diplomacy, unifying all Hawaii under a single ruler.
- **1819**: Kamehameha I dies in Kona and is buried in a cave beside the seashore. The burial site—"known only to the Morning Star"—has never been discovered. His son and successor, Kamehameha II, overthrows the traditional Hawaiian religion by ordering the destruction of *heiau* and an end to the *kapu* system. The first New England whaleships arrive in September.
- **1820**: The first shipload of American missionaries arrives at Kailua, on the Big Island, on the brig *Thaddeus*. Protestant evangelism in Hawaii begins.
- **1824**: The Christian convert Kapiolani, a high-ranking chief's daughter, stands beside Halemaumau, the fiery pit within Kilauea's crater, and repudiates Pele, winning a victory for the Protestant missionaries. As an act of sacrilege she eats a handful of sacred *ohelo* berries.
- **1826**: Protestant missionaries limit written Hawaiian to the five vowels and seven consonants: *h, k, l, m, n, p,* and *w*. The twelve letters allow all Hawaiian words to be written, making a Hawaiian-language Bible possible.
- **1829**: When a Hawaiian is severely beaten for shooting an Englishman's cow, King Kamehameha

III issues the "Cow Proclamation," warning foreigners not to injure Hawaiians over cow trouble; the wounding or killing of a cow, said the King, is not equal to the wounding or killing of a Hawaiian.
- **1832**: Death of Kaahumanu, Kamehameha I's favorite wife and Hawaii's first regent. Between 1819 and 1832 she virtually ruled Hawaii, with her stepson, Kamehameha II and then his successor, the boy-king Kamehameha III.
- **1842**: U.S. President John Tyler, in a subtle diplomatic move, recognizes the Kingdom of Hawaii by invoking the Monroe Doctrine to discourage intervention by European powers.
- **1843**: When the Hawaiian flag is raised after a British admiral refuses, without authority, to allow it flown, King Kamehameha III, speaking in Hawaiian, gives his kingdom a maxim later to become the state motto: "The life of the land is perpetuated in righteousness." Herman Melville is discharged from a whaleship at Lahaina, Maui.
- **1845**: The Hawaiian capital is in effect moved from the whaling port of Lahaina, Maui, to Honolulu, with its fine harbor.
- **1846–1855**: Decade of the Great Mahele, a land division among the king, his chiefs, Hawaiian commoners, and foreigners that converted native-owned lands to fee-simple title, following the tradition of Western property practices; in short, the long-term disfranchisement of Hawaiians from their lands in favor of whites.
- **1850**: A resolution of Hawaii's Privy Council in August officially designates Honolulu as the capital city; the name means "protected bay." First permanent Mormon missionaries arrive.
- **1852**: First Chinese contract workers arrive.
- **1856**: The first flush toilet in Honolulu is installed in King Kamehameha IV's home on the grounds of the modern-day Iolani Palace.
- **1865**: Singing the antislavery song "John Brown," a procession of Yankee residents marches through Honolulu celebrating the end of the American Civil War.
- **1866**: First leprosy patients are taken to the Kalaupapa Peninsula on Molokai. Mark Twain visits Haleakala on Maui at sunrise and calls it "the sublimest spectacle I ever witnessed."

- **1868**: First Japanese contract laborers arrive. (The Meiji Restoration, signaling the end of feudalism in Japan and the country's entry into the "modern" world, took place in 1867.)
- **1872**: The Hawaiian Hotel, with billiard tables made of California oak, opens on Hotel Street in Honolulu, sporting 42 "sleeping rooms" at $15 per week (extra charge for "ladies' and gentlemen's saddle horses").
- **1873**: Father Damien de Veuster, a Belgian priest, arrives on Molokai to aid leprosy victims; he dies of the disease in 1889.
- **1878**: Charles Dickey installs the Islands' first phone in his home and store in Haiku, Maui, two years after its invention by Alexander Graham Bell.
- **1879**: Portuguese immigrants arrive in Hawaii, bringing with them a small four-string guitar, called *ukulele* (leaping flea) by Hawaiians, the nickname of the quick-fingered Hawaiian who popularized the instrument.
- **1883**: King Kalakaua (the Merrie Monarch) holds a coronation ceremony nine years after his ascension to the throne. The event, held at Kalakaua's newly built residence, Iolani Palace, revives the hula.
- **1889**: Disgruntled Hawaiians, opposed to both Kalakaua and the growing numbers of antimonarchists and reformers, attempt a coup d'etat, which is squashed, leaving several dead. Robert Louis Stevenson, author of *Treasure Island,* arrives in Honolulu and befriends the ill-fated Princess Kaiulani, who dies of rheumatic fever at the age of 23.
- **1891**: King Kalakaua's health deteriorates, and he dies in San Francisco while on a whirlwind tour of the West Coast. Prior to his death he complains that California weather is too cold compared to Hawaii's eternal summer.
- **1893**: Queen Liliuokalani, the last monarch of Hawaii, is deposed by annexationists seeking to further American sugar interests.
- **1894**: The Republic of Hawaii, with Sanford Dole as president, is proclaimed on July 4; U.S. president Grover Cleveland sends a letter of recognition to the new government.
- **1900**: The Territory of Hawaii is inaugurated in the United States in June, following President Wil-

liam McKinley's signing of the Organic Act, which defined the status of the territory and provided for its framework of government; many native-born Hawaiians are appalled.
- **1901**: The Moana, the first large tourist hotel in Waikiki, opens at beachside as a four-story high rise; two additional stories and wings are added in 1918. James Dole, future pineapple magnate, organizes the Hawaiian Pineapple Company.
- **1907**: The College of Agriculture and Mechanic Arts (today the University of Hawaii) begins with twelve faculty members and five students.
- **1908**: Construction of Pearl Harbor begins, disturbing the shark goddess Kaahupahau, who is said to protect the harbor by killing intruders. (In 1913, a dry dock collapses and a *kahuna*, a sorcerer, appeases the goddess with ceremonial blessings.)
- **1912**: Duke Kahanamoku, one of Hawaii's all-time surfing greats, wins a gold medal in the 100-meter freestyle swim at the Olympic Games in Sweden.
- **1925**: Detective writer Earl Derr Biggers' *The House without a Key* is published. Set in Hawaii, the novel introduces the Chinese policeman Charlie Chan, hero of a series of Biggers detective stories set in various parts of the world; Chan is modeled after a real-life Honolulu policeman.
- **1927**: The Royal Hawaiian Hotel, one of the early luxury resorts, opens on Waikiki Beach. First successful nonstop flight from U.S. Mainland to Hawaiian Islands. The National Park Service sanctions a gimmick at Kilauea volcano on the Big Island called "The World's Greatest Hole-in-one Club" that lets tourists (for 50 cents a ball) tee-off into the volcano's Halemaumau crater.
- **1935**: Hawaii-based army aircraft drop 600-pound TNT bombs on a Mauna Loa lava flow to divert its course and protect Hilo (the Big Island) from incineration. The radio program "Hawaii Calls," which will air for 40 years, begins broadcasting from beneath a banyan tree at Waikiki's Moana hotel.
- **1941**: On December 7 (President Roosevelt calls it a day of "infamy") the naval base at Pearl Harbor, Oahu, is attacked by Japan, plunging the United States into World War II. A Japanese pilot sends the message *"Tora! Tora! Tora!"*—code words (*tora* means tiger) to indicate surprise attack achieved.

- **1957:** The *nene,* a rare goose native to the uplands of Maui and the Big Island, is adopted as Hawaii's official bird.
- **1959:** In March Hawaii is admitted to the United States as the 50th state. In August William Quinn takes office as first state governor. The first jetliner lands in Honolulu. Air travel to California is cut to four and a half hours. Ala Moana Center in Honolulu opens.
- **1960:** East-West Center is founded in Honolulu. A 34-foot tidal wave hits Hilo, on the Big Island, killing 61 people.
- **1961:** Elvis Presley begins filming of *Blue Hawaii* on Oahu and Kauai.
- **1962:** The USS *Arizona* Memorial is dedicated on Memorial Day at Pearl Harbor.
- **1963:** The Polynesian Cultural Center opens in Laie on Oahu.
- **1967:** A funeral service is held on Waikiki Beach for well-known beachboy Panama Dave Baptiste, who died of a heart attack while giving a surfing lesson; not long after his death, the coconut hat that he always wore washes ashore at Waikiki.
- **1968:** The first McDonald's outlet in Hawaii opens in Aina Haina on Oahu. The first professional surfing contest—the Duke (Kahanamoku) Classic—is held at Sunset Beach on Oahu's North Shore.
- **1969:** Apollo 12 astronauts make a "moonwalk" in Hawaii Volcanoes National Park on the Big Island, a practice session designed to make them better moon observers. The Palm Tree Inn on Kalakaua Avenue, last of Waikiki's neighborhood saloons and nicknamed the "Poor Man's Pacific Club," closes after 35 years.
- **1973:** The first Honolulu Marathon is run in December with 162 runners.
- **1976:** *Hokulea,* a double-hulled voyaging canoe, departs from Hawaii for Tahiti, renewing interest in Hawaii's Polynesian heritage by retracing the ancient canoe routes between the two island groups.
- **1977:** Marathon runner Jay Longacre ascends Mauna Loa in a brisk gallop of seven hours, twenty minutes. "My Lord!" radios a shocked park employee to headquarters. "Some fellow is climbing Mauna Loa on a dead run."
- **1978:** The Ironman Triathlon, the premiere competition of this grueling three-event sport (swim-

ming, bicycling, running), begins on the Big Island's Kona Coast.
- **1980**: The world's first pineapple sparkling wine is bottled on Maui.
- **1982**: Hurricane Iwa, strongest hurricane to strike the Islands in recorded times, decimates Kauai (the name Iwa means frigate bird, a harbinger of storms when seen over land).
- **1984**: Hawaii's silver jubilee of statehood is celebrated.
- **1986**: John Waihee, first elected governor of Hawaiian ancestry, takes office in December as the fourth governor.
- **1989**: Members of the Elvis Presley Fan Club of Great Britain arrive on Kauai to re-create Presley's wedding scene from the movie *Blue Hawaii*. Research continues on a deep-water cable to transmit volcanic geothermal energy; King Kalakaua originally proposed the idea to inventor Thomas Edison in 1881.
- **1990**: The silver anniversary of the Hawaiian Open is held at the Waialae Country Club Golf Course on Oahu. With a purse of one million dollars, the tournament is Hawaii's top golf attraction. Kilauea Volcano, continuing an eruptive phase that began in 1983, destroys homes and roads, adding acreage to the Big Island's southern coastline; in October lava flows overrun two black-sand beaches, Kalapana and Kaimu.
- **1991**: Astronomers from around the world gather at the observatories atop Mauna Kea on the Big Island of Hawaii to study a total eclipse of the sun in July; scientific studies include solar wind readings and infrared searches for glowing rings of interplanetary dust thought to exist around the sun. The commemoration of the 50th anniversary of the Japanese air attack on December 7, 1941, is held at Pearl Harbor; among those in attendance are members of the Arizona Survivors' Association (sailors assigned to the destroyed ship *Arizona*).
- **1992**: On the Big Island, residents and geothermal developers debate over safety measures taken to prevent blowouts during geothermal drilling in the island's volcano country. How best to control large tiger sharks—the shark responsible for most attacks on humans in Hawaii—occupies marine experts; some native Hawaiians oppose the killing of

tiger sharks because sharks were once *aumakua* (personal gods) of their ancestors. In May the ashes of hermit Bernard Wheatley are buried in Kauai's remote Kalalau Valley, where the so-called hermit of Kalalau spent six years in an isolated cave, which he landscaped to resemble a Zen garden. Hurricane Iniki, with sustained winds of 145 mph, ravages Kauai in September, damaging thousands of homes, injuring and dislocating residents, and curtailing the tourism industry.

- **1993:** January 17 marks the 100th anniversary of the U.S.–backed takeover of the Hawaiian kingdom by businessmen determined to wed Hawaii politically to the United States; the centennial event rekindles the memory of Hawaii's deposed queen Liliuokalani, who is remembered in speech and hula by native-born Hawaiian activists who envision an independent nation of Hawaii.

—*John W. Perry*

INDEX

Academy Shop, 103
Ahuena Heiau, 211
Alakoko Fishpond, 308
Ala Moana, 51 (map), 54
Ala Moana Beach Park, 55
Ala Moana Center, 54, 107
Ala Moana Hotel, 76
Ala Wai Canal, 61
Ala Wai Golf Course, 61
Alexander & Baldwin Sugar Museum, 254
Alfred Dunhill, 98
Alii Antiques, 252
Alii Drive, 210
Aliiolani Hale, 37
Alii Tower, 74
Allerton Estate, 317
All Islands Bed & Breakfast, 189
Aloha Antiques and Collectibles, 100
Aloha Café, 214
Aloha Cottages, 271, 276
Aloha Flea Market, 109
Aloha Friday, 91
Aloha Tower, 33
Amorient Aquafarm, 137, 173
Andrade Sale Studio, 106
Andrew's Italian Restaurant, 54, 89, 134
Angelica's, 45
Anna Bannanas, 89
Ann Tongg Swimwear, 107
Antique Alley, 105
Arizona Memorial, 159, 184
Art Maui, 266
Asian Food Trading Co., 55
Aston Waikiki Beachside Hotel, 75
Atlantis submarine, 75, 211
Avalon Restaurant & Bar, 141, 242

Baci Due, 134
La Bahia, 255
Bailey House, 252
Bailey's Antique and Thrift Shop, 64, 106
Baldwin Home Museum, 241
Ba-Le, 42, 101
Bali-by-the-Sea, 74, 114
Bali Hai Helicopter Tours, 338
Bali Hai Restaurant, 328
Banana Beach Bar & Grill, 171
Banana Joe's Tropical Fruit Farm, 335
Barbara Meheula, 221
Basically Books, 198
Batik Room, 221
Bear's Coffee, 198
Bebe's Galleria, 94, 97
Bed and Breakfast Hawaii, 80, 340
Bed & Breakfast Honolulu, 80, 189
Bernard Hurtig, 98
Betty's Import and Export, 96
Big Beach, 258
The Big Island (Hawaii), 12, 138, 190, 192 (map)
Big Wind Kite Factory, 283
Bishop Museum, 45
Black Pearl Collection, 335
Bloom Cottage, 264, 278
Blue Ginger, 247
Bobby McGee's Conglomeration, 85
Bon Appetit, 119
La Bourgogne, 140, 212
Boutique Marlo, 96
La Bretagne, 142
Bubba's, 325
Bull Shed, 325
Bushido, 101

353

INDEX

Buzz's Original Steak House, 137
Byron II Steak House, 126

Café Che Pasta, 41
Café Haleiwa, 174
Café Kula, 257
Café Pesto: Hilo, 197; Kawaihae, 139, 222
Café Siam, 152
Café Sistina, 135
Café Venturi, 314
California Pizza Kitchen: Honolulu, 68; Waikiki, 122
Camp House Grill, 318
CanoeHouse, 219
Capitol District, 37, 38 (map)
Cappuccino's, 78
Captain Cook, 214
Captain Dudley Worthy, 53
Captain Nemo's Ocean Emporium, 245
Captain Zodiac Raft Expeditions, 338
Carthaginian, 241
Casa di Amici, 327
Casanova Italian Restaurant & Deli, 265
La Cascata, 146, 329
Central Valley (Maui), 238
Chain of Craters Road, 206
Challenge at Manele Golf Course, 300
Charlie's Country Store, 184
Charo's Restaurant and Cuchi Cuchi Cantina, 147, 332
Chart House: Haiku Gardens, Oahu, 167; Haleiwa, Oahu, 175; Maui, 254
Cheeseburgers in Paradise, 242
Chibo Okonomiyaki Restaurant, 123
Chicken Alice's, 55
Chinaman's Hat, 169
China Sea Tattoo Parlor, 43
Chinatown, 38 (map), 41
Chinatown Mall, 101
Chinese Cultural Plaza, 43, 102
Chiu Leong, 202
Chocolates for Breakfast, 96
Ciao Mein, 75
Cindy's Lei Shoppe, 102

C. June Shoes, 94
Cloisonné Factory, Nagai, USA, 96
Club Lanai, 245
Coasters, 36
Coconut Classics, 265
Coconut Plaza, 78
Coco Palms Resort, 323, 339
The Coffee Connection, 95
Coffee Gallery, 184
Collections: Maui, 264; Oahu, 97
Colony's Kaluakoi Hotel & Golf Club, 282, 291
Compadres: Maui, 243; Oahu, 134
Contemporary Museum, 48, 103
Cook House, 288
Coronation Pavilion, 37
Crater Rim Drive, 204
Crazy Shirts, 315
Crouching Lion Inn, 137, 170
Curtis Wilson Cost Gallery, 263

Damien Molokai Tours, 288, 291
Dave's Ice Cream, 64
David Gomes, 223
David Paul's Lahaina Grill, 244
Devastation Trail, 205
Diamond Head, 64, 67 (map)
Diamond Head Beach Park, 65
Dirty Mary's, 85
Dole Cannery Square, 44
Dole Plantation, 183
Donatoni's, 218
Doong Kong Lau Hakka, 43
Duke's Lane, 94
Dynasty (Waikiki), 123
Dynasty II (Honolulu), 54, 129

East-West Center, 49
Eddie Flotte, 267
Edelweiss, 226
Eggs 'n' Things, 88
8 Bells, 334
Elephant Walk, 98
Elsie's, 198
Experience at Koele Golf Course, 299
Eye of the Whale, 338

Fair Wind, 212
Falls of Clyde, 36
Fern Grotto Inn, 324, 339

INDEX 355

First Hawaiian Bank, 62
Fook Sau Tong, 102
Fort DeRussy, 62
Fort Street Mall, 33, 99
Foster Botanical Garden, 43
Four Seasons Resort, 255, 276
Francis H. Ii Brown Golf Course, 230
Fresco, 54
Front Street, 239
Fuku-Bonsai Center, 214

Galerie Lassen, 241
Gallery of Great Things, 225
Gallery Mikado, 101
Gamelan Gallery, 198
The Garage, 89
Garden of the Gods, 299
Garden Island Inn, 310, 339
Garden Restaurant, 221
Gateway Restaurant, 172
Gaylord's, 146, 307
Gentry Pacific Center, 45
Gerard's Restaurant, 243
Ghosts' Leap, 183
Gilligan's, 310
Golden Dragon, 74, 115
Grace's Inn, 151
Grand Champions Golf and Tennis Villas, 257, 276
Grandma's, 263
Grand Wailea Resort & Spa, 256, 276
Greek Bistro, 255
Green Garden Restaurant, 318
Green Sand Beach, 209
Greeters of Hawaii, 335
Grove Farm Homestead Museum, 308
Guava Kai Plantation, 326
Gulick Delicatessen, 151

Haena State Park, 332
Haiku Gardens, 167
Haimoff & Haimoff Creations in Gold, 98
Hajjibaba's, 135
Hakone, 74
Hala Terrace, 72, 88, 127
Halawa Valley, 286
The Hale, 228, 232

Haleakala Crater, 259
Haleakala National Park Cabins, 276
Haleiwa, 174
Haleiwa Alii Beach Park, 174
Hale Kai Bed and Breakfast, 199, 233
Hale Kea, 226
Halekulani, 72
Halemaumau, 205
Halemauu Trail, 261
Hale Paliku, 199, 233
Haliimaile General Store, 145, 266
Halona, 162
Halona Blowhole Lookout, 162
Halona Cove, 163
Hamakua Coast, 228
Hamburger Mary's Organic Grill, 85
Hamura Saimin Stand, 311
Hana, 9, 269
Hana Cultural Center, 270
Hana Highway, 268
Hana Kai-Maui Resort Condominium, 271, 276
Hanakapiai Valley, 332
Hanalei, 303, 330
Hanalei Bay Resort, 328, 339
Hanalei Colony Resort, 331, 339
Hanalei Gourmet, 330
Hanalei National Wildlife Refuge, 329
Hanalei Valley Lookout, 329
Hanapepe, 318
Hanapepe Bookstore & Espresso Bar, 318
Hana Ranch Restaurant, 271
Hanatei, 127
Hanauma Bay, 68, 161
Hang Ten! Surf Bar, 180
Hanson Art Galleries, 241
Hap's Hideaway, 311
Hapuna Beach Prince Hotel, 222, 232
Hapuna Golf Course, 230
Hard Rock Café: Maui, 242; Oahu, 86, 123
Harpo's Pizza, 64
Harriett's, 96
Harry's Bar & Café, 75
Hart, Tagami and Powell Gallery and Gardens, 168
Hartwell's at Hale Kea, 140, 226

INDEX

Hau Tree Lanai, 77, 86, 124
Hawaii (state), 2 (map)
Hawaii (The Big Island), 190, 192 (map)
Hawaiiana Hotel, 78
Hawaiian Bagel, Inc., 53
Hawaiian Collection Room, 334
Hawaiian Heirloom Jewelry, 95
Hawaii Children's Museum, 104
Hawaii Heritage Center, 42
Hawaii IMAX Theater Waikiki, 63
Hawaii Kai, 68
Hawaii Maritime Museum, 36
Hawaii Prince Golf Club, 186
Hawaii Prince Hotel Waikiki, 73
Hawaii's Best Bed & Breakfasts, 80, 233
Hawaii Theater, 89
Hawaii Tropical Botanical Garden, 199
Hawaii Visitors Bureau, 63
Hawaii Volcanoes National Park, 13, 204
Hee Hing, 63
Helani Gardens, 269
Helen's Treasures, 252
Helen and Suzanne, 98
Hermès, 96
Hickam Mamala Bay Golf Course, 187
Hikiau Heiau, 215
Hildgund, 105
Hilo, 13, 138, 197
Hilo Farmers' Market, 198
Hilo Hattie's Fashion Center: Kauai, 335; Oahu, 106
Hilton Hawaiian Village, 74
Hime Woods, 97
Holoholo Kai Restaurant, 284
Holoholoku Heiau, 323
Holualoa, 212
Holualoa Inn, 213, 233
Honokohau Harbor, 210
Honolulu, 27, 125; maps: 29 (Environs), 34 (Downtown and Central), 38 (Downtown, Chinatown, and Capitol District), 51 (Kakaako and Ala Moana), 66 (Diamond Head and Waikiki)
Honolulu Academy of Arts, 40
Honolulu Airport Mini Hotel, 79
Honolulu Comedy Club, 85, 88
Honolulu Hale, 39
Honolulu Hotel, 85
Honolulu Symphony, 90
Honolulu Zoo, 61
Honopu, 322
Honpa Hongwanji Hawaii Betsuin, 47
Hookipa, 267
Horatio's, 129
Hosmer Grove, 261
Hotel Hana-Maui, 270, 276
Hotel Lanai, 295, 300
Hotel Molokai, 284, 291
House of Seafood, 314
House Without a Key, 72, 82, 86
Hui Noeau Visual Arts Center, 265
Hula Moons, 251
Hula's Bar & Lei Stand, 85
Huleia National Wildlife Refuge, 308
Hulihee Palace, 211
Hulopoe Bay, 297
Hulopoe Beach, 297
Hyatt Regency Kauai, 313, 339
Hyatt Regency Maui, 246, 276
Hyatt Regency Waikiki, 75
Hyatt Regency Waikoloa, 217, 232
Hydrangea Cottage, 203, 233
Hy's Steak House, 119

Iao Needle, 253
Iao Theater, 251
Iao Valley State Park, 253
Ihilani Resort and Spa, 180, 189
Iida's, 108
Iliiliopae Heiau, 285
Imari, 218
International Market Place, 63, 94
Iolani Palace, 37
Ira Ono, 202
Irene's Hawaiian Gifts, 108
Irifune, 64
Iroha Jaya, 64
Ironwood Hills Golf Course, 290
Islander on the Beach, 324, 339
Itoguruma, 96
Iwilei, 44

James Hoyle Gallery, 334
Jameson's by the Sea: The Big Island, 211; Oahu, 175

INDEX 357

Jaron's of Kailua, 137
Jelly's Comics and Books, 55
JJ's, 242
John Dominis, 129
Jojo's Café, 283
Jo-Ni's, 152
Jubilation, 90

Kaaawa, 169
Kaahumanu Church, 252
Kaala Art, 174
Kaala Room, 182
Kaanapali, 143, 245
Kaanapali Alii, 246, 276
Kaanapali Beach, 247
Kaanapali Beach Resort, 245
Kacho, 77
Kaena Point State Park, 182
Kahakuloa Head, 250
Kahakuloa Village, 250
Kahala, 65
Kahala Hilton Hotel, 65, 72, 88
Kahaluu, 168
Kahana Bay, 170
Kahana Bay Beach Park, 170
Kahanu Gardens, 269
Kahili Mountain Park, 316, 339
Kahoolawe, 6
Kahuku, 173
Kahului, 254
Kailua, 137
Kailua-Kona, 13, 210
Kailua Pier, 210
Kaimuki, 64
Kainaliu, 214
Kakaako, 50, 51 (map)
Kakaako Waterfront Park, 54
Kalahaku Overlook, 261
Kalaheo, 318
Kalakaua Avenue, 62
Kalalau Beach, 333
Kalalau Lookout, 321
Kalalau Trail, 332
Kalalau Valley, 321, 333
Kalanikaula, 286
Kalaupapa, 287
Kalaupapa Overlook, 288
Kalaupapa Trail, 288
Kalawao, 289
Kalihi, 45
Kaluakoi, 282

Kaluakoi Golf Course, 289
Kaluakoi Villas, 282, 291
Kamaka Hawaii, Inc., 52
Kamakahonu, 211
Kamalo, 285
Kamehame Ridge, 163
Kamigata, 132
Kamuela, 224
Kamuela Inn, 226, 232
Kamuela Museum, 225
Kaneaki Heiau, 182
Kanemitsu Bakery and Coffee
  Shop, 147, 284
Kaneohe Klipper Golf Course, 187
Ka Ning Fong, 42
Kaopeahina, 286
Kapaa, 303, 325
Kapaau, 223
Kapahulu Avenue, 63
Kapalua, 247
Kapalua Bay Hotel and Villas, 248,
  276
Kapalua Bay Resort, 248
Kapalua Designs, 249
Kapalua Golf Club, 273
Kapalua International Championship of Golf, 248
Kapalua Kids, 249
Kapalua Logo Shop, 249
Kapalua Music Festival, 248
Kapalua Wine Symposium, 248
Kapiolani Park, 61
Kapuaiwa Coconut Grove, 283
Kau, 196, 207
Kauai, 10, 145, 301, 304 (map)
Kauai Gold, 334
Kauai Lagoons Golf and Racquet
  Club, 337
Kauai Lagoons Resort, 309
Kauai Mountain Tours, 338
Kauai Museum, 307
Kau Desert Trail, 207
Kaulu o Laka Heiau, 332
Kaumahina State Wayside Park, 269
Kaumalapau Harbor, 297
Kaunakakai, 283
Kaunolu Village, 297
Kawaiahao Church, 39
Kawaihae, 222
Kawela, 285
Kea Lani Hotel, 257, 276

Keanae Arboretum, 269
Keauhou, 212
Keauhou Beach Hotel, 212, 232
Keawaula Beach, 182
Kee Beach, 332
Kenai Helicopters Hawaii, 201
Ke Nani Kai, 282, 291
Keokea, 263
Keoki's Paradise, 314
Keomuku, 299
Keoneloa Bay, 314
Keo's Thai Cuisine, 64, 131
Kepaniwai Park and Heritage Gardens, 253
Kepuhi Beach, 282
Kewalo Basin, 53
Kiahuna Golf Club, 336
Kiahuna Plantation, 313, 339
Kihei, 254
Kihei Prime Rib and Seafood, 255
Kilauea, 326
Kilauea Iki Trail, 205
Kilauea Lodge and Restaurant, 203, 232
Kilauea Point National Wildlife Refuge, 326
Kilohana Plantation, 307
Kim Chee II, 131
Kimo's Restaurant, 242
Kincha, 144, 257
King Kamehameha Hula Competition, 90
King's Trail, 259
King's Village, 96
King Tsin, 129
Kipahulu, 273
Kipuka Nene campground, 206
K. Kida Fishing Supplies, 53
Kodak Hula Show, 61, 83
Kohala Coast, 13, 139, 216
Kokee Lodge, 321, 339
Kokee Natural History Museum, 321
Kokee State Park, 320
Koko Crater, 163
Koko Crater Botanical Garden, 163
Koko Head, 68, 161
Koloa, 302, 315
Koloa Broiler, 315
Kona Arts Center, 212
Kona Coast, 13

Kona Comedy Club, 212
Kona Country Club, 231
Kona Hotel, 213, 232
Kona Inn, 211
Kona Village Resort, 217, 232
Ko Olina Golf Club, 181, 186
Kramer and Associates, 43
Kualapuu, 288
Kualoa Regional Park, 168
Kuhio Avenue, 62
Kuhio Beach, 58
Kuhio Mall, 94
Kuilima Cove, 180
Kuilima Point, 179
Kula Bay Clothing: Maui, 247; Oahu, 97
Kula Botanical Gardens, 263
Kula Experiment Station, 263
Kula Lodge and Restaurant, 263, 276
Kyo-ya, 115

Lady Judith, 108
Lahaina, 9, 141, 239
Lahaina Hotel, 244, 277
Lahaina Printsellers, 247
Lai Fong Department Store, 103
LaMariana, 36
Lamonts Gift and Sundry Shop, 98
Lanai, 148, 293, 294 (map)
Lanai City, 296
Lanaihale, 298
Lancel, 96
Lanikai Bed & Breakfast, 80
Laniloa Hotel, 173, 189
Laniloa Peninsula, 173
Lapakahi Park, 222
Lappert's Ice Cream, 315
Leahi, 87
Leather of the Sea, 96
Lehua's Bay City Bar and Grill, 198
Leileihua Golf Course, 187
Leleiwi Overlook, 261
Lewers Lounge, 72, 86
Lihue, 302, 306
Liliuokalani Gardens, 199
Liliuokalani Protestant Church, 175
Linda's Vintage Isle, 107
Lion's Coffee, 53
Little Beach, 258
A Little Bit of Saigon, 131

Little Hawaiian Craft Shop, 95
Local Guides of Maui, 249
Local Motion, 61
Lodge at Koele, 148, 297, 300
Loewe, 96
Longhi's, 142, 243
Lumahai Beach, 331
Lyman Museum and Mission House, 198
Lyon Arboretum, 50

Maalaea Harbor, 244, 250
Madaline Michaels, 241
Maharaja, 86
Mahina Lounge, 84
Maile Lounge, 73
Maile Restaurant, 72, 127
Mai Tai Bar, 73
Makaha Beach, 181
Makaha Valley Country Club, 185
Makahiki Festival, 178
Makai Market Food Court, 54, 108, 151
Makapuu Beach Park, 163
Makapuu Point, 163
Makawao, 264
Makawao Rodeo, 265
Makawao Steak & Fish House, 265
Makena, 257
Makena Golf Club, 274
Makiki Heights, 48
Malia's Cantina, 84
Malihini Hotel, 79
Mamo Howell, Inc., 106
Mana, 225
Manago Hotel, 215, 232
Mana Kai Maui Resort, 255, 277
Mandalay, 249
Manele Bay, 297
Manele Bay Hotel, 296, 300
Manoa, 49
Manoa Falls, 50
Manoa Valley Inn, 79
Maple Garden, 130
Marina Flowers, 336
Market Café, 249
Market Place, 184
Martin Lawrence Galleries, 241
Martin & MacArthur, 101
Mary Catherine's, 108
Ma's Family, Inc., 310

Matteo's, 119
Maui, 9, 141, 234, 236 (map)
Maui Child Toys & Books, 265
Maui Crafts Guild, 267
Maui Marriott Resort, 246, 277
Maui Prince Hotel, 258, 277
Maui Tropical Plantation, 251
Mauna Kea, 228
Mauna Kea Beach Hotel, 139, 220, 232
Mauna Kea Golf Course, 229
Maunakea Marketplace, 42, 102
Mauna Lani Bay Hotel & Bungalows, 219, 232
Mauna Lani Resort, 230
Mauna Loa (The Big Island), 207
Maunaloa (Molokai), 283
Maunalua Bay, 65
Mauna Ulu, 206
McInerny Galleria, 96
Mean Cuisine, 226
Memory Lane, 251
La Mer, 72, 116
Merrie Monarch Festival, 83, 197
Merriman's, 139, 226
Meyer Sugar Mill, 288
Michel's at the Colony Surf Hotel, 117
Mission Houses Museum, 39
Mitsukoshi Department Store, 97
Miyako, 77
M. Matsumoto Grocery Store, 175
The Moana, 71
Moaula Falls, 287
Mocha Java, 54
Mokolea, 250
Mokuleia Beach, 176
Molokai, 147, 279, 280 (map)
Molokai Fish & Dive, 284
Molokai Ranch Wildlife Park Safari, 283
Molokai Shores, 284, 291
Molokai Wagon Ride, 285, 290
Monarch Room, 82
Mookini Luakini, 223
Moondoggies, 242
Mountain House, 203, 233
Mountain View Bakery, 202
Mount Kamakou, 285
Mount Tantalus, 49
Munro Trail, 298

INDEX

Murphy's Bar & Grill, 44, 136
Musashi, 75

Nakalele Point, 250
Nani Maui Gardens, 199
Naniwa-ya, 87
Na Pali Coast, 11, 303, 332
Na Pali Coast State Park, 321, 332
Napili Kai Beach Club, 247, 277
National Memorial Cemetery of the Pacific, 48
National Tropical Botanical Garden, 317
Navatek I, 87
Neal Blaisdell Center, 90
New Otani Kaimana Beach Hotel, 77
Nicholas Nickolas, 76, 120
Nick's Fishmarket, 84, 120
Niihau, 2 (map), 6, 341
Niihau Helicopters, 338
Niihau Safaris, 343
Nikko, 246
Nohea Gallery, 109
North Pit, 207
Nuage Bleu, 267
Nuuanu, 47
Nuuanu Pali Drive, 47
Nuuanu Pali Lookout, 48, 166

Oahu, 136, 153, 156 (map)
Oahu Market, 42, 101
Oar House Saloon, 311
Ocean Activities Center, 245
Oheo Gulch, 272
Old Lahaina Café, 242
Old Lahaina Luau, 242
Olomana Golf Links, 186
Ono Family Restaurant, 325
Ono Hawaiian Foods, 133
Orchids, 72, 120
O'Toole's Pub, 44
Outfitters Kauai, 338
Outpost Natural Foods, 284
Outrigger Kauai Beach Hotel, 310, 339
Outrigger Polynesian Palace, 84
Outrigger Room, 313
Oviedo's, 284

A Pacific Café, 146, 325
Pacific Grill, 144, 256

Pacific Handcrafters Guild, 104
Pacific Hawaii Bed & Breakfast, 80, 189
Pacific Quest, 338
Pacific Submarine Museum, 160
Pacific Whale Foundation, 244
Pacific Whaling Museum, 185
Paia, 266
Painted Church, 216
Pake Zane, 105
Palace Theater, 198
Palapala Hoomau Congregational Church, 272
Palawai Basin, 295
Pali Highway, 47, 165
Pali Lookout, 47, 165
Palm Boulevard, 108
Palm Café, 140
Palm Terrace, 180
Pam Barton, 202
Paniolo Hale, 282, 291
Papaakoko, 171
Papakea Resort, 247, 277
Papillon Hawaiian Helicopters, 201
Papohaku, 282
Paradise Cruise, 159
Paradise Hot Dogs, 325
Paradise Lounge, 74, 84
Paradise Park, 50
Paramount Grill, 198
Parc Café, 77, 124
Parker Ranch, 224
Parker Ranch Broiler, 225
Pat's at Punaluu, 171, 189
Patti's Chinese Kitchen, 151
Pau Hana Inn, 284, 291
Pau Hana Pizza, 327
Pearl Country Club, 185
Pearl Harbor, 155
Pegge Hopper, 44, 103
Penthouse, 99
Pescatore, 138, 198
Phillip Paolo's, 211
Picnics, 268
Piero Resta, 267
Piilanihale Heiau, 269
Pikake Café, 182
Pikake Pavilion, 178
Pink Cadillac, 84
Pioneer Inn, 241
Plantation Gallery, 283

Plantation Gardens, 313
Plantation House, 249
Plantation Inn, 243, 277
Plantation Spa, 170, 189
Poi, 97
Poi Bowl, 151
Poipu, 302, 311
Poipu Bay Resort, 336
Poipu Beach Café, 312
Poipu Beach Park, 311
Poipu Beach Resort, 11, 311
Poipu Bed & Breakfast Inn, 314, 339
Polli's Mexican Restaurant, 265
Polynesian Cultural Center, 171
Polynesian Palace, 85
Prince Court, 74, 117
Prince Lot Hula Festival, 83
Princess Kaiulani, 106
Princeville, 327
Princeville Hotel, 328, 339
Princeville Resort, 11, 327
Princeville Resort Kauai Golf Course, 336
Proud Peacock Restaurant, 177
Puako, 221
Pukalani Country Club, 275
Pukoo Vacation Rental, 286, 291
Puna, 200
Punaluu, 208
Punchbowl, 48
Purdy's Natural Macadamia Nut Farm, 288
Puu Hinahina, 319
Puuhonua o Honaunau National Historical Park, 215
Puukohola Heiau, 222
Puu Manu Cottage, 227, 233
Puu o Mahuka Heiau, 178
Puu Oo, 200
Puuopelu, 225
Puu Poa, 329, 340
Puu Ulaula Overlook, 260

Queen Emma's Summer Cottage (Kauai), 317
Queen Emma Summer Palace (Oahu), 165
Queen's Surf Beach, 59

Rabang's, 284
Rabbit Island Bar & Grill, 164
Rachel's Chateau D'Or, 98
Rainbow Bazaar, 98
Ramsay Galleries & Café, 43, 89, 103
Rella Mae, 88
Reni's Back Room, 89
Restaurant Row, 52, 108
Restaurant Suntory, 120
Rex's Black Orchid, 52, 91, 135
Reyn's: Maui, 249; Oahu, 106
R. Fujioka & Sons Ltd., 176
Ritz-Carlton-Kapalua, 249, 277
Ritz-Carlton Mauna Lani, 220, 233
Robyn Buntin Galleries, 100
Robyn Buntin's Jewelry Collection, 100
Rose City Diner, 52, 136
Rose and Crown, 96
Roussel's, 138, 198
Row Bar, 52, 91, 108
Royal Copenhagen, 108
Royal Garden Restaurant, 76
Royal Hawaiian Cruises, 160
Royal Hawaiian Hotel, 73
Royal Hawaiian Shopping Center, 94
Royal Kaanapali Resort Golf Course, 274
Royal Kitchen, 43
Royal Lahaina, 247, 277
Royal Mausoleum, 47
Royal-Moana Beach, 58
Royal Peddler, 97
Royal Waikoloan, 218, 233
Roy's, 68, 128
Roy's Kahana Bar & Grill, 247
Roy's ParkBistro, 76, 121
Rumours, 76, 91
Ryan's Parkplace Bar & Grill, 136

Saddle Road, 229
St. Raphael's Church, 316
La Salsa, 52
Salvation Army Thrift Shop, 45
Sam Choy's Restaurant, 141
Sand Island, 36
Sans Souci, 59
Seaction Surfco, 60
Sea Fortune, 42
Sea Life General Store, 184
Sea Life Park, 164

INDEX

Sea Lion Café, 164
SeaMountain at Punaluu, 208, 233
Sea Ranch Cottages, 271
Seasons Restaurant, 144, 256
The Secret, 118
Seven Pools, 272
Shaka Pizza, 255
Sheraton Kauai Beach Resort, 312, 340
Sheraton Makaha Resort and Country Club, 182, 186, 189
Sheraton Maui, 246, 277
Shipwreck Beach, 298
Shirokiya's, 108
Shop Pacifica, 46, 104
Shore Bird Beach Broiler, 86, 125
Shung Chong Yuein, 102
Siam Thai, 252
Sibu Café, 211
Silversword Golf Club, 275
Silversword Stove and Fireplace, 264
Ski Guides Hawaii, 229
Sliding Sands Trail, 261
Smith's Motor Boat Service, 324
Smith's Union Bar, 42
Le Soleil, 219
South Point, 208
Spencer Health & Fitness Center, 198
Star Beachboys, 60
Star of Honolulu, 87
State Archives, 40
State Capitol, 40
Steve Goodenow, 105
Stevenson's Library, 314
Stones at Kilohana, 334
Stouffer Poipu Beach Hotel, 312, 340
Stouffer Waiohai Beach Resort, 312, 340
Studebaker's, 91, 92
Studio 7 Gallery, 213
Sugar Bar and Restaurant, 176
Suisan fish auction, 199
Summer House, 267
Sunset Beach, 179
Sunset Grill, 52
Superwhale Boutique, 247
Surf Bar, 73
Surf Room, 73, 121

Swan Court, 143
Sweetheart's Lei Shop, 102
Swimsuit Warehouse, 95
Swiss Inn, 128

Tack 'n Things, 265
Tahitian Lanai, 86
Takanawa, 74
Tak Wah Tong Chinese Herb Shop, 43
Tamarind Restaurant, 312
Tamarind Square, 41
Tamashiro's Fish Market, 46
Tasca's, 142, 243
Tedeschi Vineyards, 262
3660 On the Rise, 126
Thomas A. Jaggar Museum, 204
Thurston Lava Tube, 205
Tiffany's, 98
Tin Can Mailman, 334
Tinny Fisher's Antique Shop, 202
Titou's Surf City, 60
T. Komoda Store & Bakery, 265
Topstitch Fiber Arts, 225
Touch the East, 52
Town and Country Surf Shop, 94
Traders of the Lost Art, 252
Tradewinds, 324
Trattoria Manzo, 52
Tree Tunnel, 316
Trilogy Excursions, 245
Tropics Surf Club, 84
Tsukenjo's, 151
Tsuruya, 152
Turtle Bay Country Club, 186
Turtle Bay Hilton Golf and Tennis Resort, 180, 189
Tusitala Bookshop, 185

Ualapue, 286
Ultimate You, 53, 107
Uncle Harry's, 269
U.S. Army Museum, 62, 104
University of Hawaii, 49
USS Arizona Memorial, 159, 184
USS Bowfin, 160

Viewpoints Gallery Maui Artists Collective, 265
Village Snack and Bake Shop, 330
Villa Paradiso, 122

INDEX

Villa Roma, 96
Volcano Art Center, 204
Volcano Bed & Breakfast, 203, 233
Volcano Golf and Country Club, 231
Volcano House, 202, 233
Volcano Village, 202

Wahaula Heiau, 206
Waialua, 176
Waianae, 181
Waianapanapa State Park, 272
Waianapanapa State Park Cabins, 277
Waikapu Valley Country Club, 274
Waikiki, 8, 27, 55, 56 (map), 66 (map), 81, 113
Waikiki Aquarium, 61
Waikiki Beach, 58
Waikiki Joy Hotel, 77
Waikiki Parc Hotel, 77
Waikiki Park Plaza, 75
Waikiki Shell, 61, 82
Waikiki Shopping Plaza, 96
Waikiki Theater, 62
Waikiki Trade Center, 94
Waikiki Trolley, 70
Waikoloa Beach Golf Club, 230
Waikoloa Kings' Golf Club, 230
Waikoloa Resort, 230
Waikoloa Village Golf Club, 230
Wailana Coffee House, 88
Wailau Peninsula, 168
Wailea, 255
Wailea Golf Club, 274
Wailea Oceanfront Hotel, 255, 277
Wailua, 303, 322
Wailua Marina Restaurant, 325
Wailua Municipal Golf Course, 337
Wailua River State Park, 324
Wailuku, 251
Wailuku Gallery, 252
Waimanalo Beach, 163
Waimea: The Big Island, 139, 196, 224; Kauai, 316, 318
Waimea Bay Beach Park, 177
Waimea Canyon, 319
Waimea Canyon Lookout, 319
Waimea Countree Bed & Breakfast, 227, 233

Waimea Falls Park, 83, 177
Waimea Gardens Cottage, 227, 233
Waimea Plantation Cottages, 318, 340
Waimoku Falls, 272
Waioli Huiia Church, 330
Waioli Mission House Museum, 330
Waipio on Horseback, 228
Waipio Hotel, 228, 233
Waipio Naalapa, 228
Waipio Treehouse, 228, 233
Waipio Valley, 227
Waipio Valley Shuttle, 228
Waipio Valley Wagon Tours, 228
Waldenbooks, 96
Ward Centre, 54, 108
Ward Warehouse, 54, 108
Washington Place, 40
Waterfront Restaurant, 143, 250
Waterfront Row, 211
Wavecrest Resort, 286, 291
Wave Rider Hawaii, 60
Wave Waikiki, 84
W. C. Peacock & Co., Ltd., 72
Wellness Center, 271
Westin Kauai, 309, 340
Westin Maui, 246, 277
West Loch Municipal Golf Course, 185
Whalers Village, 247
Whalers Village Museum, 247
White Hill, 261
The Willows, 133
Windward Marine Resort, 168, 189
Wo Fat, 42, 130
Wo Wing Temple, 241
Wyland Galleries of Hawaii: Maui, 241; Oahu, 174

Yanagi Sushi, 132
Yellowfish Trading Co., 334
Yen King, 68, 130
Yong Sing, 41
Young's Noodle Factory, 103
Yummy Korean B-B-Q, 152

Zoo Fence, 99
Zoo Gift Shop, 99

BUSINESS REPLY MAIL
FIRST CLASS MAIL   PERMIT NO 45660   CHICAGO IL

POSTAGE WILL BE PAID BY ADDRESSEE

Passport Newsletter®
350 West Hubbard Street
Suite 440
Chicago, Illinois 60610-9698

NO POSTAGE
NECESSARY
IF MAILED
IN THE
UNITED STATES

"This is the granddaddy of travel letters... *Passport* emphasizes culture, comfort, and quality...it can glow with praise, or bite with disapproval."

Condé Nast Traveler

"*The* first and unquestionably the best luxury travel newsletter."

Alan Tucker, General Editor
Berlitz Travellers Guides

Since 1965, *Passport*, the monthly letter for discriminating travelers, has revealed hard-to-find information about the world's best destinations. Return this card for a free issue or call 800-542-6670. Available worldwide!

Please send a free issue of *Passport* to:

Name _____

Address _____

City _____ State _____ Zip _____

Here's what others say...

"As a longtime reader of *Passport*, I trust it as a source of intelligence and ideas on independent travel."

Alan Deutschman
Associate Editor
Fortune Magazine

"The best little newsletter in America."
Crain's Chicago Business

"*Passport* has been appearing for more than 20 years with a brisk, colorful roundup of travel information. Substance prevails over style."
National Geographic Traveler

"In *Passport*, I consistently find the kind of information I want from a travel newsletter—sophisticated, concise and straightforward, without a lot of ego to get in the way."
Travel Editor
Town and Country Magazine